Praise for *The Suffragents*

"Among the pleasures of Kroeger's carefully developed storyline is the view of how important political figures such as Theodore Roosevelt and Woodrow Wilson came around to accepting the idea that women deserved the vote ... A vigorous, readable revisitation of the events of a century and more ago but with plenty of subtle lessons in the book for modern-day civil rights activists, too."

— *Kirkus Reviews*

"*The Suffragents* is the product of formidable research. It's a fresh contribution in which the big picture is composed of a vast mosaic of forgotten facts ... *The Suffragents* adds an original and welcome new dimension to the field of women's studies."

— *Foreword Reviews*

"Not all the suffragists who risked ridicule to march down Fifth Avenue in the big parades touting votes for women wore dresses. Brooke Kroeger meticulously documents the largely unsung role of men who publicly supported their wives, mothers, sisters, or lovers in the final dramatic decade of women's seventy-year battle for the ballot."

— Linda J. Lumsden, author of *Inez: The Life and Times of Inez Milholland* and *Rampant Women: Suffragists and the Right of Assembly*

"Women 'need' men to get the rights they deserve: after all, men had to vote to let women vote. Brooke Kroeger gives us the first history of the Men's League for Woman Suffrage, the 'Gentleman's Auxiliary' of the women's movement. Eschewing the spotlight, they supported gender equality, as we all should, because it's quite simply the right thing to do. With this gift, Kroeger gives us back a bit of our history."

— Michael S. Kimmel, coeditor of *Against the Tide: Pro-Feminist Men in the United States, 1776–1990: A Documentary History*

# The Suffragents

Previous books by Brooke Kroeger

*Nellie Bly: Daredevil, Reporter, Feminist*

*Fannie: The Talent for Success of Writer Fannie Hurst*

*Passing: When People Can't Be Who They Are*

*Undercover Reporting: The Truth about Deception*

———◀◦▶———

# The Suffragents

*How Women Used Men to Get the Vote*

Brooke Kroeger

excelsior editions

AN IMPRINT OF STATE UNIVERSITY OF NEW YORK PRESS

*On the cover*: Men's League Suffrage Parade delegation marches into Union Square, 1915 Suffrage Parade, New York City. (C. Catt Collection, Bryn Mawr College Library)

Published by State University of New York Press, Albany

Excelsior Editions is an imprint of State University of New York Press

For information, contact State University of New York Press, Albany, NY
www.sunypress.edu

Production, Dana Foote
Marketing, Katherine Dias

**Library of Congress Cataloging-in-Publication Data**

Names: Kroeger, Brooke, 1949– author.
Title: The suffragents : how women used men to get the vote / by Brooke Kroeger.
Description: Albany : State University of New York Press, Albany, 2017. | "Excelsior editions." | Includes bibliographical references and index.
Identifiers: LCCN 2016044034 (print) | LCCN 2017000548 (ebook) | ISBN 9781438466293 (hardcover : alk. paper) | ISBN 9781438466309 (pbk. : alk. paper) | ISBN 9781438466316 (e-book)
Subjects: LCSH: Men's League for Woman Suffrage (New York, N.Y.) | Women—Suffrage—New York (State)—History.
Classification: LCC JK1896 .K57 2017 (print) | LCC JK1896 (ebook) | DDC 324.6/2309747—dc23
LC record available at https://lccn.loc.gov/2016044034

10 9 8 7 6 5 4 3 2 1

# Contents

# Illustrations

# Acknowledgments

I offer my gratitude:

To the able researchers who assisted at various points in this project: My students Maggy Donaldson, Mireia Triguero-Roura, Katie Whittaker, Kat Thornton, and Jesse Coburn, and our librarian Katherine Boss; the Long Island Collection Librarians at the East Hampton Library, Gina Piastuck and Andrea Meyer; and my friend, Marilynn Abrams. Alisha Stendecker, Emily Wishingrad, and Kiara Tringali provided great help via the Schuster Institute for Investigative Reporting at Brandeis University, where I am a Senior Fellow.

To the librarians and archivists who safeguard document and photographic material at the Library of Congress, at the Schlesinger Library of the Radcliffe Institute (Lindsey Bailey) and Houghton libraries at Harvard University, and in the special collections libraries at the New York Public Library (David Rosado), Vassar, Yale, Bryn Mawr, Dartmouth, Columbia (Jocelyn K. Wilk), Princeton, New York University, Brandeis, Rochester, the Lilly Library at Indiana University, Rice University Library, University of Houston Library, the Woodrow Wilson Presidential Library, the Alice Paul Institute, at the Library of Congress, the New-York Historical Society, the Museum of the City of New York, the Newberry Library, and at the public libraries of New York City, Troy, and Buffalo, the historical societies of Geneva, Ticonderoga, Keene, Lake George, and Rockland County, and elsewhere around the state and beyond. Special acknowledgment to director Dennis Fabiszak at the East Hampton Library. Newspaper repositories from Fulton History, the Library of Congress's Chronicling America, Newspapers.com, NewspaperArchive.com, and Proquest were essential in the process.

To Patricia O'Toole, Adam Vine, Clay Smith, Gioia Diliberto, Dinitia Smith, Antonia Petrash, Amy Shore, Shelley Stamp, Todd Coleman, Philippa Brophy, and Holly Hilliard for their support, knowledge, insight, and good counsel; to Michael S. Kimmel, for affirming my earliest impression of the League's unique value, to Alison MacKeen, Christoph Irmscher, Jen Balderama McDonald, Steve

Wasserman, Clay Smith, and Adam Vine for astute responses to early drafts of the manuscript; to Ben Weinstein, Katy Dwyer, Gail Gregg, and Prianka Srinivasan for artful photographic assistance; to Geraldine Baum and Robert S. Boynton for help in articulating the scope of the project in brief.

To Heddi Siebel, James Marten, Harriet Todd, Susan Schwartz, Kenneth Florey, James Van Houten, and Nancy Cook for dipping into their personal files for historic or family photographs.

To New York University for giving me an academic home, the space, and support to pursue such projects, and the remarkable colleagues and students who have buoyed me over nearly two decades.

To Amanda Lanne-Camilli, Jessica Kirschner, Chelsea Miller, Dana Foote, Katherine Dias, and Pat Hadley-Miller at State University of New York Press; to graphic designer Amane Kaneko; and to Sue Morreale of Partners Composition for the care they took with this project.

To all the suffrage, men's history, biographers, and Woodrow Wilson scholars whose books and papers appear in the text and bibliography, or in citations in the notes of this book. All of them helped me make sense of so much of the rest of the material I gathered.

And, as always, to Alex Goren, the twenty-first-century embodiment of everything truly grand about manhood in relation to women, much in the mold of those who led the Men's League for Woman Suffrage, a subject that he and I, and so many others, had no notion of until now.

# An Introduction

On May 6, 1911, under perfect blue skies, ten thousand spectators lined both sides of Fifth Avenue "from the curb to the building line" for the second annual New York Suffrage Day parade. Somewhere between three thousand and five thousand marchers strode in a stream of purple, green, and white, from Fifty-Seventh Street to a giant rally in Union Square. Bicolored banners demarcated the groups by their worldly work as architects, typists, aviators, explorers, nurses, physicians, actresses, shirtwaist makers, cooks, painters, writers, chauffeurs, sculptors, journalists, editors, milliners, hairdressers, office holders, librarians, decorators, teachers, farmers, artists' models, "even pilots with steamboats painted on their banners." Women's work was the point. The *New York Sun* repeated the entire list at the top of its front-page story.

To draw broad attention for this spectacle, the women had help from a single troupe of men in their midst—eighty-nine in all, by most accounts—dressed not in the Scottish kilts of the bagpipers or the smartly pressed uniforms of the bands, but in suits, ties, fedoras, and the odd top hat. They marched four abreast in the footsteps of the women, under a banner of their own.

These men were not random supporters, but representatives of a momentous, yet subtly managed development in the suffrage movement's seventh decade. Eighteen months earlier, 150 titans of publishing, industry, finance, science, medicine, and academia; of the clergy, the military, of letters and of the law; men of means or influence or both, had joined together under their own charter to become what their banner proclaimed them, the Men's League for Woman Suffrage. Since the end of 1909, they had been speaking, writing, editing or publishing, planning, and lobbying New York's governor and legislators on behalf of the suffrage cause. They did so until the vote was won.

Among the League's most notable members were George Foster Peabody, Max Eastman, Oswald Garrison Villard, John Dewey, Rabbi Stephen S. Wise, Frederick Nathan, George Creel, George Harvey, James Lees Laidlaw, Norman

Men's League delegation in the New York Suffrage Day Parade, May 6, 1911. (Miller NAWSA Suffrage Scrapbooks, 1897–1911; Scrapbook 9, p. 77; Library of Congress, Rare Book and Special Collections Division)

Hapgood, and fellow travelers such as Dudley Field Malone and W.E.B. Du Bois. Many of their names resound through history as political kingmakers and promoters of such progressive causes as civil rights, child welfare, the educational advancement of black Americans, and, later, disarmament. They were leaders or members of celebrated organizations like the National Association for the Advancement of Colored People and the People's Institute, with its mission of "teaching the theory and practice of government and social philosophy to workers and recent immigrants." A number of them would be among those in Woodrow Wilson's circles. But on this day in the spring of 1911, they had gathered for the sole purpose of pressing for the right of women to vote.

American men as individuals had publicly supported the rights of women as far back as 1775, when Thomas Paine published his essay, "An Occasional Letter on the Female Sex." After the Seneca Falls Convention to support women's rights in 1848, other men wrote more specifically in support of women's enfranchisement, notably William Lloyd Garrison, Ralph Waldo Emerson, and Frederick Douglass. In England, John Stuart Mill's *The Subjection of Women*, published in 1869, echoed many of the arguments that his wife, Harriet Taylor Mill, had presented in "The Enfranchisement of Women," eighteen years earlier. And briefly, between 1874 and 1875, a Young Men's Woman Suffrage League met in New York City, fielding pro-suffrage speakers from its membership—physicians, attorneys, and professors among them—at some eighty meetings in the Plimpton Building at 30 Stuyvesant Street in what is now the East Village.

Yet to take on the cause of women's suffrage was almost always to do so at a price, especially for men. So it was on the parade line in 1911, where the men endured what, for the times, were unforgettably pernicious assaults on their masculinity. "Hold up your skirts, girls!" rowdy onlookers shouted. "You won't get any dinner unless you march all the way, Vivian!" For all two miles of the walk, a newspaper clipping recounted, the men submitted to "jeers, whistles, 'mea-a-ows,' and such cries as 'Take that handkerchief out of your cuff.'"

In the last decade-long lap of the suffrage fight, the mockery of 1911 would give way to a more muted, sometimes ironic response to the men who took up the cause. In time, male suffragists would become commonplace—and then, all but forgotten as an orchestrated movement force.

This is not so surprising. The story of the triumph of the suffrage cause has long belonged to the women, and rightly so. In the century since New York State granted women the vote in November 1917, strikingly few details about the men's efforts have thus emerged. No known source to date examines in depth the origins, mission, or growth of the Men's League for Woman Suffrage, which ultimately stretched to include thousands of adherents across thirty-five states and other parts of the developed world.

At points during the battle and after it was won, the women of the organized suffrage movement recognized the sizable contributions of their elite male allies. The official account of the period, Ida Husted Harper's *The History of the Woman Suffrage Movement*, recalls the "invaluable help" the men provided and acknowledges the "influential factor" they became during crucial votes in the

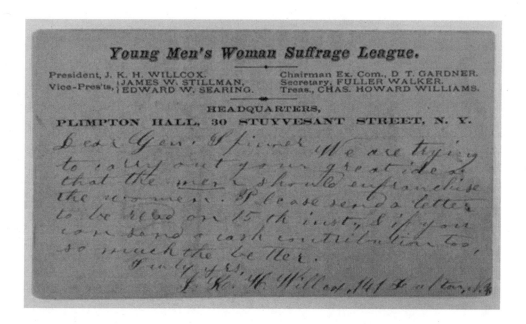

An 1874 postcard from J.K.H. Willcox, president of the short-lived Young Men's Woman Suffrage League, possibly to General Francis E. Spinner, Treasurer of the United States from 1861 to 1875. (Courtesy of Kenneth Florey, from *American Woman Suffrage Postcards* [Jefferson, NC: McFarland & Company, 2015], p. 93)

New York legislature. It acknowledges the abundant prestige they lent. Yet even in this multivolume chronicle, reference beyond these few comments is scant. We get little more than some of the men's names, along with a misdated reference to the valor the men of the New York league demonstrated during the 1911 parade.

This book seeks to retrieve a long-forgotten sliver of history—to tell the story of how, in the course of women's protracted and hard-fought battle to gain the vote in the United States, men played a consequential role that they did not aggrandize or promote, except when it served the suffrage cause for them to do so. Drawing on biographical sketches, correspondence, and a multitude of references in newspapers and magazines of the period, the book recounts efforts that years later would fail to receive even passing mention in the often prominent published obituaries of the League's key male figures.

Specifically, this book is about how the Men's League for Woman Suffrage of the State of New York came to be formed, in 1908; how hard its members worked under the direction of the extraordinary women who led the suffrage charge in that period; and why what transpired may hold some lessons worth reflecting upon, even today. It shows how in that final decade leading up to the passage of the New York State suffrage amendment in 1917, these "Mere Men," these "Suffragents," the British moniker by which they were so often disdainfully called, helped inspire a gradual but dramatic tonal shift in response to the larger suffrage movement in the way mass-circulation newspapers and magazines covered it, and in the way politicians, government officials, and both the general and male voting public responded to it.

From a contemporary standpoint, it is remarkable to consider that one hundred years ago, these prominent men—highly respected and influential, their exploits chronicled regularly in the national media—not only gave their names to the cause of women's rights or called in the odd favor, but rather invested in the fight. They created and ran an organization expressly committed to an effort that, up until the point at which they joined, had been seen as women's work for a marginal nonstarter of a cause. From the beginning of their involvement, these men willingly acted on orders from and in tandem with the women who ran the greater state and national suffrage campaigns. How many times in American history has such collaboration happened, especially with this balance of power?

This episode in the suffrage epic provides a means of observing the shift in the common perception of the suffrage movement as a whole. It also demonstrates the strategic brilliance of a decision by leaders in NAWSA, the National American

Woman Suffrage Association, the main suffrage organization in the United States, to cultivate relationships with the well-heeled and the well-connected—women as well as men. In this period, Katherine Duer Mackay, wife of Clarence Mackay, of the AT&T Mackays, and Alva Smith Vanderbilt Belmont, widow of the businessman and politician O.H.P. Belmont, formed and presided over influential prosuffrage societies. Dashing prosuffrage couples of the period were Laidlaw, the financier who was on the board of directors of what became Standard & Poor's, and his wife, Harriet Burton Laidlaw; Nathan, the wealthy scion of an important Sephardic Jewish family, and his wife, the social activist Maud Nathan, his first cousin, also born a Nathan; Narcissa Cox Vanderlip and her husband, Frank A. Vanderlip, who was the president of the National City Bank of New York. All were deeply involved, as were Vira Boarman Whitehouse and her husband, the stockbroker James Norman de Rapelye Whitehouse. In short order, the media attention they attracted brightly burnished the movement's image in the mainstream press.

Over the course of these crucial years, the staunchly antisuffrage editorial stance of such newspapers as the *New York Times* and the *New York Herald* bled a little less heavily onto their news pages. Editorialists, especially at the *Times*, took longer. As the Men's League emerged in New York, and was rapidly cloned in city and county chapters across the state and well beyond, the mocking derision and dismissiveness that initially dominated coverage of the "Mere Men" in particular, and of the suffrage movement more broadly, gave way to acceptance of an idea whose time was about to come.

The men of New York were not the first to organize. In Britain, male supporters of the women's vote formed the first known men's league in 1907. Men in Holland organized in 1908. On this side of the Atlantic, prominent men in Chicago created a league in January 1909, ten months ahead of the New York chapter's first formal meeting in November. Nonetheless, New York is hallowed ground for the women's movement in the United States. It is the geographical home of Seneca Falls, site of the landmark convention long credited with bringing the suffrage movement into being. Susan B. Anthony and Elizabeth Cady Stanton, the two most revered names in the movement's history, are daughters of the Empire State. As the country's undisputed media capital, much of the vital journalism, creative writing, speechifying, and pamphleteering for and about the movement emanated from Gotham's publishing precincts. And by 1909, thanks to new financial support from wealthy society matrons supporting the cause, NAWSA at last had the wherewithal to establish impressive headquarters in New

York City at precisely the moment the Men's League was being founded in Max Eastman's Greenwich Village apartment.

In addition, the dazzling pageantry, cleverly targeted recruitment gimmicks, and regimental campaign operations of these years were both New York–born and New York–borne creations in which the men joined as full partners. As the movement grew in strength and acceptance, its important new champions attracted beneficial press, whether they gave speeches, appeared at marches or at social gatherings, worked the halls of influence in Albany and Washington, or crafted or published buzz-worthy essays or attention-getting diatribes in the form of letters to the editor.

Beyond the arc of change in press coverage and public perception, it is worth noting other aspects of the male suffragists' lives. For one, there are the personal relationships that motivated them to take up what in 1908 was still widely viewed as a laughably unimportant cause. Standing for the rights of workers was surely a factor for reformers like Eastman. His sister, Crystal Eastman; his girlfriend for part of this period, Inez Milholland, who remained a close friend; and his first wife Ida Rauh, were all deeply involved with the labor reform movement, notably the shirtwaist workers strike of 1909–1910. Unsurprisingly, behind nearly every one of the men who put the most energy and time into the suffrage movement was an ardent movement activist (or two, or three, or four) who, as in Eastman's case, also happened to be his wife, his mother, his sister, or his love interest. Daughters could also prove persuasive, as evidenced by the involvement of John Milholland, father of Inez, and ultimately by the evolving position of President Woodrow Wilson, two of whose daughters, Margaret and Jessie, were known to be prosuffrage.

Worth appraisal, too, is the strategic decision of NAWSA President Anna Howard Shaw and her colleagues, after a long period of reluctance, to solicit or embrace the offers of support from these particular new allies. NAWSA did this assuming that participation was likely to be nominal. Shaw asked little. Yet the new male activists, like their society lady counterparts, gave of themselves far beyond what NAWSA's leaders had expected. In fact, before too long, these dignified gents showed a surprising willingness to don costumes, act, dance, and work the streets. They attended city, county, state, national, and international meetings. They joined delegations and hosted lavish banquets. They lobbied at the state and national levels and issued loud, formal, headline-producing protests when the police in New York and Washington mistreated marchers or left them unprotected against the onslaught of catcalling, brick-batting mobs. The lawyers among them stepped up to represent the women suffragists who wound up in court.

Robert Cameron Beadle, secretary of the Men's League of New York after Eastman, rode horseback from New York to Washington, DC, with a women's equestrian delegation. The Nathans and Laidlaws made statewide automobile recruitment trips. On separate occasions, the two couples went national, traveling out West to work on separate state suffrage campaigns.

As Shaw had presumed would happen, the planning minutiae and execution of the men's involvement in major events often fell to the women. That the women accepted this without apparent disappointment or rancor is unsurprising. Logistical and administrative tasks must have seemed a minor encumbrance given the potential of high-level, highly useful male participation in the cause.

Of course, in this period there were also vocal male detractors from the same professional and editorial classes. *Pearson's* and *Ladies' Home Journal* commissioned major antisuffrage investigations by the journalist Richard Barry that in turn brought a barrage of published rebuttal. Men's antisuffrage groups formed in reaction, but with not nearly the staying power, constancy, support, or impact of the male forces that supported the cause. And yet more than once, an invited male speaker—including a sitting president—stunned his hosts and audiences by speaking publicly against women's suffrage at movement-sponsored events.

With few exceptions, it is also evident from the relative paucity of references to suffrage in the biographies, autobiographies, and personal correspondence of the Men's League's influential founders—Peabody, Wise, and Villard in particular—that local, state, and national elections, affairs of state, and civil rights took clear precedence over suffrage on their agendas. This was true even at moments when suffrage was as big a front-page story.

All the same, real support was offered and real support was meant, felt, and acted upon. This was especially apparent during the two years of focused campaigning that led to the climax of the story this book tells: the New York legislative and voter victories of 1917. Who else but the prominent men among the movement's declared backers had such ready personal access to the—also male—state and federal legislators and government leaders, to publishers, or to the editorial elite? It worked to the movement's extreme advantage that so many League members and leaders were themselves publishers and the editorial elite. Twice, Eastman sparred publicly with Theodore Roosevelt. At various points, Peabody, Villard, Wise, Creel, Harvey, Hapgood, Malone, and Eastman all had Woodrow Wilson's ear. Most of them were among Wilson's earliest political backers; Eastman had his respect. Creel, in the critical period when Wilson at long last came out in favor of the federal suffrage amendment, was on "terms of intimacy" with the president, meeting with him almost daily in his capacity as chair of the Committee on Public Information after the United States entered World War I in 1917.

No doubt an accumulation of other factors, far greater than the Men's Leagues, led to the ultimate success of the women's suffrage campaign: seven long decades of effort by passionate women, the changing times and political winds, the burgeoning public support, the growing number of states where women with the vote could influence outcomes; the movingly sacrificial role women played after the United States entered World War I. Still, once the details are known, it is hard to ignore the boost that the men provided. Their involvement amounted to more than an "influential factor" or "invaluable help." Much more. Their commitment showcases the value elite individuals who act with care can bring to marginalized movements, particularly those with social justice aims. The impact of Men's League actions a century ago speaks loudly to the strategic importance of cultivating people with influence and magnetic media appeal, those who can attract positive public attention, open access to those in positions of power, and alter public perception.

It was a major departure for men of such stature to decide that it mattered for women to vote, to recognize that as a chartered prosuffrage organization, men could wield influence in ways that women could not, and to understand that to make a difference, they would be required to offer more than an early twentieth-century equivalent of a celebrity endorsement or a goodwill ambassadorship—the kinds of gestures we see most often today. The founders of the Men's League knew that to help sway the course of history, they needed a full-fledged national, then multinational organization, with all the effort and expense that implied. They needed an entity in which men of great standing would subordinate themselves to women in a women-driven enterprise devoted to a "women's cause," and would claim center stage only when called upon or needed to do so. For that is exactly what happened.

William Lloyd Garrison    Israel Zangwill    W.E.B. Du Bois    Stephen S. Wise

H.G. Wells    Thomas Hardy    Bertrand Russell    John S. Crosby

Oswald Garrison Villard    John Dewey    George Harvey    Charles Sprague Smith

Charles F. Aked    Frederick Douglass    William M. Ivins    Melville Stone

# 1

# "If Men Should Be Wanted"

## 1907–1908

Early in 1908, Oswald Garrison Villard, the progressive editor and publisher of the *Nation* and the *New York Evening Post*, replied to a letter of invitation from the president of the National American Woman Suffrage Association, known as NAWSA, the Reverend Doctor Anna Howard Shaw. She asked him to speak at a suffrage convention in Buffalo, scheduled for October 15, a date, Villard replied, that was too far in the future for him to commit. On top of that, to "prepare an elaborate address" was out of the question, he said, as he was already "taxed to the limit of my strength." But in the letter, Villard also proposed a fresh idea that had started to gain ground in Europe: the formation of a prosuffrage club composed exclusively of men.

These would be not just any men, Villard suggested, but those with the stature to rival his own as the wealthy scion of an illustrious American family of reformers and industrialists. Villard envisioned a group of at least one hundred members and many vice presidents meant to function mostly in name—those who could "impress the public and legislators." That would mean men with influence in all the important avenues of thought and power, those self-assured enough to ignore the ridicule that public support for women's suffrage was bound to draw. Such a membership, Villard said, could entice others in the same political, professional, social, and charitable circles to plunk down a dollar in annual dues and heighten their interest in the suffragists' cause or at least lessen their derision, something much of the New York press did its best to foster. Villard initially reasoned that to do no more than announce the names of influential men willing to associate themselves with the women's movement in such a direct and public way would attract good publicity and bring useful direct and subliminal support. "I have wanted to suggest this for a long while," he wrote to Shaw, "but have feared that if I did suggest it the work of organizing would be placed upon my shoulders, and I cannot undertake a single additional responsibility, not even one that requires merely the signature of letters."

In approaching Villard to address the convention, Shaw had been acting on word from Villard's mother, the suffragist Helen Frances Garrison Villard, known always as "Fanny." His mother had let it be known that her accomplished son was willing once again to stump for the cause. He had done so in his "maiden speech" in 1896 to the Massachusetts Woman Suffrage Association. Twenty-five at the time, three years after his graduation from Harvard, Villard was pursuing a master's degree and served as a teaching assistant to "The Grand Old Man" of American History, Professor Albert Bushnell Hart. Villard used the occasion of his suffrage association speech to push for getting women the vote and to urge Harvard to start admitting women as a way to prepare them for their duties as citizens.

He was by no means the first American man to publicly support women's suffrage. Frederick Douglass, the prominent abolitionist, had done so in a newspaper column as early as 1848, the week of the first Woman's Rights Convention at Seneca Falls, which he attended. His last public act the day of his death, February 20, 1895, was an appearance during a secret meeting in Washington, DC, of the Women's Council. Anna Howard Shaw and his lifelong friend, Susan B. Anthony, had both escorted him to the platform, where he was roundly applauded And William Lloyd Garrison, Villard's maternal grandfather, addressed the fourth women's suffrage convention in Cleveland in 1853. A bold handful of other prominent men had also spoken out or written over the years.

In 1902, by which point Villard had succeeded his father, Henry Villard, as publisher of both the *Post* and the *Nation*, he joined other male supporters of suffrage in "An Evening with the New Man," a Valentine's Day–themed event at that year's NAWSA national convention, in Washington, DC. Their appearance prompted some of the earliest headlines announcing men's support for the women's cause. In the *Washington Post* it was

## MEN CHAMPION CAUSE:
### WOMAN SUFFRAGISTS NOT ALONE IN THEIR BATTLE

And in the *Washington Times*:

## NEW MAN'S VIEWS ON WOMAN SUFFRAGE

Shaw's reply to Villard on February 6, 1908, made a point of reminding him of the great joy his remarks at that convention had given Anthony, who had died March 13, 1906, as had his "splendid stand for helpful reforms." Yet in his earlier letter, Villard had already told her that it was not another convention speech that he had in mind. He was offering to use his considerable influence in "an appeal to the Legislature, if men should be wanted for that purpose."

Such a proposal was not much of a reach for a man of Villard's lineage. His father was a former reporter and war correspondent who made his money in railroads and bought the *Post* and its supplement, the *Nation*, in 1881. He also played a key role in the history of the railroad and the development of electricity in the United States. As owner of the Edison Lamp Company and the Edison Machine Works, which eventually became General Electric, the elder Villard subsidized Thomas Edison's research for years. The younger Villard's "close and binding" relationship with his mother was also clearly an influence. Fanny was a valued suffrage campaigner. "It gives me joy to remember," she once said, "that not only my father, William Lloyd Garrison, but also my good German-born husband believed in equal rights for women." It was a position her son had also embraced.

At the time of the younger Villard's proposal to Shaw, the militant British suffragette Anne Cobden-Sanderson was winding up a much-publicized US speaking tour that took her to Chicago, Boston, Philadelphia, and New York City between late October of 1907 and early January of 1908. Villard's *Evening Post*, like all the major newspapers, gave her ample coverage. During those three busy months on the road, Cobden-Sanderson spent almost as much time insulting her American hosts as she did recounting her own harrowing saga of arrest and incarceration for demonstrating in front of the House of Commons a year earlier. Her conviction had put her away in the clothes of a jailbird in Holloway Prison, where for a month she scrubbed the floor of her eight-by-twelve cell and subsisted on weak tea in the morning, six ounces of bread throughout the day, and two baked potatoes with a cup of cocoa at night. She was quick to note to her American audiences that her prison record obliged her to slink over the Canadian border to enter the United States to avoid possible deportation had she been faced with the obligatory question of port officials: "Have you ever been arrested?"

Throughout her visit, in both public remarks and comments to reporters, Cobden-Sanderson scoffed at the comparatively slow pace of the US movement's progress. Britain, she said, was "years ahead of American women in our fight for equal rights." This she attributed in part to the new militancy of its women, an approach that her American counterparts had not yet embraced. American suffragists, she said, favored club life over action. Not the British. "We believe in doing real things not in talking about them," she said, adding that her American sisters behaved in a manner far "too ultra-refined" to do the hard work that eventual victory demanded.

Cobden-Sanderson reserved her harshest critique for the American society dame who "steeps herself in the degradation of luxury. She adorns her person until I often am reminded of a Turkish harem. She measures all humanity by its clothes, as her husband measures all his fellow men by their wealth and their ability to acquire more wealth." She scoffed at the poor judgment American women showed more generally, at the superficial way they evaluated leadership and thought about the world. (Months later, after her return to England, she would say that American women demonstrated "timid conventionality of thought" and the inability to grasp a profound idea.) She singled out the wealthy antisuffragist as one who "has no time to think of the vital questions of the hour, no civic pride, because she is too busy adorning her person and steeping herself in the luxury which deadens the soul to know what really is going on in the great pulsing world of the 'under dog'—the stratum of humanity beneath her own." To a reporter for the *New York Times*, she said, "I don't want to be uncomplimentary, but really, I don't believe the average American woman would know what to do with the ballot if she had it. She has had no political training whatever, and, as I have said, she doesn't care for public affairs."

Villard, however, cared greatly about such matters, and on December 3, 1907, he had concretized a commitment to suffrage among his many causes. He joined the committee formed to lead the campaign to win support from the lawmakers in Albany. "After reading your note to my mother in regard to the onerous duties of the Cooperative Legislative Committee," he wrote to its leader, Anne Fitzhugh Miller, who also headed one of the state's largest political equality clubs in upstate Geneva, "I shall be glad to become a member of it."

The major event of Cobden-Sanderson's US tour came on December 12, 1907, when some four thousand people crowded Cooper Union to hear her speak at what was billed as the inauguration of "the greatest suffragist crusade in the history of New York." The movement paragon Harriot Stanton Blatch, daughter of Elizabeth Cady Stanton, had recently returned to the United States from England, where she had been working with her British suffrage sisters. Blatch introduced her British guest as "The Cobden" and proclaimed her a "martyr to the great cause of women." In response, the *Sun* reported, "The house shook with applause." From the podium, Cobden-Sanderson said the size and enthusiasm of the gathering had restored her hope for the American crusade. This time she denounced those women who did not want the ballot as "parasites at the top" and again railed against the superficiality of their "idle luxurious lives." Press reports of the event devoted more column inches to repeating the British suffragette's already well-reported insults than to her fresher remarks. They also devoted several

Oswald Garrison Villard
No. 20 Vesey Street
New York

December 3, 1907.

Miss Nannie Miller,
    Geneva, N. Y.

My dear Miss Miller:

        After reading your note to my mother
in regard to the onerous duties of the Cooperating Legislative
Committee, I shall be glad to become a member of it.

        Yours very truly,

        Oswald Garrison Villard

Letter from Oswald Garrison Villard to Anne Fitzhugh Miller, December 3, 1907. (Miller NAWSA Suffrage Scrapbooks, 1897–1911; Scrapbook 6, 1907, p. 25; December 3, 1907; Library of Congress, Rare Book and Special Collections Division)

paragraphs to expressions of disappointment that a widely rumored attempt to deport Cobden-Sanderson from the stage had not materialized.

Two nights later, the *New York Tribune* covered her speech at a gathering of the Interurban Woman Suffrage Council at Memorial Hall in Brooklyn. The reporter chided the dozen men in attendance for their subservience, noting that two of their number had been reduced not only to walking the aisles for contributions but to strong-arming the other men present into offering up dollar bills along with the loose change in their pockets. The event's female organizer had even sent them onto the platform to collect from the seated dignitaries, including the prominent Democrat John S. Crosby, who presided. Crosby "did not deign to make a speech," the *Tribune* said, and "looked miserable indeed" after he misidentified the woman designated to second the resolutions. The headline:

## EVE BACK IN THE GARDEN:
### MERE MAN QUAILS AT INTERURBAN WOMAN SUFFRAGE MEETING.

As for Cobden-Sanderson's remarks, the newest was a comment that she had never met so many timid people so afraid of consequences.

In a letter to Shaw, Villard put a positive spin on the British guest's repeated barbs. "So far as Mrs. Sanderson is concerned," he wrote, "while we regret her tactlessness, I cannot but feel that her visit has done some good, and that a certain amount of criticism of our American workers is justifiable." More than that, something Cobden-Sanderson had emphasized throughout her speaking tour as another huge failing of the US movement seemed to have lodged itself in Villard's eardrum. She spoke several times of the failure of American women "to enlist the sympathy of the men of America." In Britain, she told the *Boston Globe*, "Nearly all of our most distinguished men are in favor of the emancipation of women."

<hr/>

Cobden-Sanderson's observations, along with the emergence of organized men's groups in Britain early in 1907, were the foreground to the grand idea Villard presented in his letter to Shaw of January 7, 1908. "This leads me to one subject that has long been on my mind," he wrote. "Why could not a Men's Equal Suffrage Club be started here?" With the right secretary to recruit the membership and then charter and publicize the organization, he felt sure that such a group could be formed with "some excellent names on it."

Soon after, a snide editorial in Villard's *New York Evening Post* described as "rather startling" Cobden-Sanderson's contention that the smug self-satisfaction of American women had complicated the work of the suffrage movement and added to its mission the need to first "create the very foundation of discontent on which all striving for reform is based."

Shaw's reply to Villard's proposal came a good month after she received his letter. The idea for a men's organization, she told him, was one the women's movement had contemplated more than once over the years but had been wont to act upon. Hesitation, she said, always came down to the "undoubted fact" that the men who could do the most good for suffrage, those whose "influence and interest would enable them to draw to such a society others whose names would be really helpful," were far too occupied with other matters to be of any real use. So many men, she explained, did not consider women's suffrage a vital issue and those who did tended not to be in good standing with the men whose own positions would make them valuable as allies. Better not to attempt such a plan, she wrote, "unless the names secured would be in themselves helpful. Any others might constantly involve us in all sorts of *isms*, and we have more of them now than we can ward off with some of our over-zealous women."

Another issue she did not mention was the ingrained opposition of serious, respected men like Woodrow Wilson, then the president of Princeton University with its all-male student body. Around this time, an interviewer paraphrased Wilson as having said that women did not really want the franchise, and it would not be an unmixed blessing for the rest of the world if they had it. The interviewer added Wilson's words in quotation marks: "It may be true that women in various parts of the world would have to fight against severe odds, but in America, at least, they are almost too much protected. Not that I would have this otherwise, because I think a woman should have all the protection that is legitimately possible." Women, as a rule, Wilson said, favor goodness over ability "and are apt to be not a little influenced by charm of manner." He also said that because women did not exercise their right to the ballot in many of the states where the franchise had been granted, he thought the cause soon might become "a dead letter."

Yet NAWSA, on the strength of Villard's proposal and its own deliberations, was ready to reconsider. Since Villard was "so occupied with business," Shaw proposed letting the women draw up plans for the league for his review. The women would work to secure the names of prospective charter members from across the country. They would also undertake all the administrative chores but "would not assume to have any control whatever over the organized group after the names were collected."

Villard replied to Shaw a week later, nudging her plan for the League closer to his own vision of it. Forming a New York State organization first would be the best course, he argued, and suggested a number of prominent men whose names would get such a group off the ground. But even before that, the League would need its own secretary. "It would be stronger than if it were organized by your National Association," Villard said. "I am sure that we can get plenty of helpful practical men here who will not be carried away with *isms*, and whose names would really carry weight."

———◄○►———

Villard began putting out feelers for a secretary. As coconspirator, he engaged Rabbi Stephen S. Wise, who later was said to have agreed to "the share the ignominy" of organizing such a League "provided someone turned up who would do the work." The rabbi had recently returned to New York from a pastorate in Portland,

Oregon, where he had developed a reputation as an outspoken reformer. He had been a prime candidate to lead Temple Emanu-el, the flagship synagogue for all of Reform Judaism, but stunningly withdrew because of the board's insistence that it preapprove all sermons as a condition of the offer, a galling stipulation to a seventh-generation rabbi in a line that stretched back two centuries to his native Hungary. Wise not only rejected the idea but he publicly condemned it. He then established his own New York congregation, the Free Synagogue.

During Wise's early childhood his father moved the family to Brooklyn, where he had accepted a pulpit. In school, at City College and then at Columbia, Wise excelled in Greek, Latin, and literature. Affairs of state and social justice engaged him as much as Jewish life and faith. Emblematic of this dual passion was an essay he wrote, at age fifteen, about Abraham Lincoln, which his brother Otto Irving Wise published in the first issue of the *Literary Review*, a publication he started in 1889. The essay compared Lincoln's role as "Great Emancipator" to the role Moses played for the Hebrews.

Wise's outspoken interest in women's rights dates back at least to 1906 in Portland, as evidenced by a letter he wrote to the suffragist and historian Eva Emery Dye, responding to her invitation to speak on the subject. So it is not surprising that in the summer of 1908, he sent Villard a clipping about a witty address that the British author and humorist Israel Zangwill had delivered at Oxford. This was more than a year after the British men's league for women's suffrage had been formed. Zangwill pointed out how "pretty girls" had taken over the leadership of the British movement, undoing in the process the long-standing and thoroughly unattractive caricature of a movement stalwart. It was an image, Zangwill said, that he and a few other "ugly, elderly, masculine and eye-glassed" men had taken upon their selves to restore. "One of these noble beings stands before you, absolutely incarnating the ancient ideal," he said, adding, "I am a suffragette." Zangwill went on to decry the notion that gender should be the criterion for shutting anyone out of the polling booth. "Why is Florence Nightingale's opinion of the candidate for her constituency less valuable than the chimney-sweeper's?" he asked. "We suffragettes demand votes for women, not because they are women, but because they are fellow citizens. The sex of a voter is no more anyone's concern," he said, "than the color of the voter's hair." He based his assertion on "the purse," on the obligations of women as taxpayers. Taxpayers ought to be able to vote. Grasp that, he said, "and you will escape tangling yourself in a whole network of fallacies."

Other left-wing intellectuals joined Zangwill in these views, among them Bertrand Russell, who stood as a Suffragist candidate in a by-election at Wimbledon in 1907. As a group, the British League was neither partisan nor militant. It grew from an initial thirty-two members to nearly ten times that size. In the kinds of movement engagement its members chose, mostly publicity and propaganda, it led the way for its American counterparts. The British men wrote and spoke at meetings and rallies, marched in parades, and acted as street-level organizers. The composition of the American and British groups also bore similarities. In Britain, the league included former government ministers, clergy members, military leaders, academics, and writers such as H.G. Wells, Thomas Hardy, and E.M. Forster, whom, along with Zangwill, the antisuffragists—the "antis"—were quick to attack in letters to the editors of the *London Times* and *Irish Times.*

Mary Augusta Ward, the British novelist who wrote under her married name as Mrs. Humphry Ward, responded in print to counter Zangwill's position. She saw no contradiction in saying both "that women have often shown a disinclination to vote when suffrage of different kinds was open to them," as had been the case in some of the American states where women had the vote, and that for both men and women to be voters "might become a political danger" in Socialist hands. Zangwill replied that Ward's problem was that as both a novelist and a woman, she knew the other members of her sex too well "and despises them for their weaknesses, their follies, and their caprices," drawing "the conclusion that her own sex cannot be trusted with a vote." Ward told Zangwill he was far too fixated on the importance of the parliamentary vote. It was only the "political machinery" that mattered, she said, and each of the sexes had its own more important role to play in its workings.

Villard thanked Wise for the clipping and replied, "I have been advocating for nearly a year past the formation of a man's society for Woman's suffrage, and

A 1908 campaign button of the British Men's League for Women's Suffrage. (LSE Collections, UK)

certainly think we should be at it next fall. Won't you keep your eyes open for a young man who would take the position of secretary? If we can find him the rest should be comparatively easy." As it turned out, Villard's appeal was not the only such recruitment invitation Wise received in this period. In early September of 1908, Harriot Stanton Blatch invited the rabbi into the "inner circle" of the Equal Franchise Society, a group then being formed by the socialite Katherine Duer Mackay, wife of Clarence Mackay, the cofounder of American Telephone & Telegraph. Blatch described this new society as "an important suffrage committee" bent on finding "the best way to push on woman's suffrage in our backward country."

Noteworthy is that the request to Wise came not from Mackay but from Blatch. This was a clear sign of how closely tied Mackay's society was to NAWSA, as was another organization then coming into being, the Political Equality League, founded by another socialite, Alva Belmont, who had become engaged with suffrage earlier in the year after the death of her second husband, Oliver Hazard Perry Belmont. It had become a movement strategy to cultivate lady members from society's higher social strata in an effort to draw favorable public attention to the suffrage cause. As Villard had pointed out to Shaw, the more these groups appeared to be separate from NAWSA, to be distinct bastions of support, acting in concert with the main body but independently, the better for the movement over all.

As to the specific purpose of Mackay's group, the *New York Times* described it in terms much blunter than Blatch's. This by-invitation-only initiative directed at men as well as women, a *Times* article noted, would "take the organized work more into the ranks of society than it has yet been." More evidence of the impact of NAWSA's nascent strategy came with the December 4 Carnegie Hall appearance of another celebrated suffragette, Ethel Snowden, the wife of the British MP Philip Snowden. A front-page headline in the *New York Times* acknowledged how the usual crowd for a suffrage event was changing:

## SOCIETY WELL REPRESENTED AT MEETING ADDRESSED BY ENGLISH SUFFRAGETTE

The article included the names of all the illustrious husbands seated with their wives in the boxes and noted that two men, Rabbi Wise and the Reverend Charles Aked of the Fifth Avenue Baptist Church, were among the featured speakers. Aked, like Wise, was an obvious choice to address the crowd. Only a month earlier, his lengthy examination of the emergence as a political force of the "remarkable" suffrage movement in England had appeared in the *North American Review.*

Although women occupied the top leadership positions in Mackay's new Equal Franchise Society, the third and fourth vice presidencies went to William M. Ivins, the president of the City Club, and Colonel George Harvey, the wealthy Democratic Party kingmaker who was editor and publisher of both the *North American Review* and *Harper's Weekly*. Other prominent men listed among the Society's founders included Wise and John Dewey, the philosopher and Columbia professor; Rollo Ogden, the *Evening Post* editorialist who, in 1919, would become chief editor of the *New York Times*, and Charles Sprague Smith, another Columbia professor and the director of the People's Institute.

In a splashier spread two months later, the *Times* found reason to reintroduce Mackay's group, this time playing down its social cachet to emphasize its seriousness of purpose. "Although organized and managed by women known for their prominence in society," the *Times* said, "it is a practical working organization with all of its members laboring for the desired end—the ballot for women on equal terms with men." As if it were not already abundantly clear, a well-placed sidebar to the piece confirmed the value to the movement of having important men in these ranks. It featured statements not from Mackay or her nearest women lieutenants, but from the professors, the rabbi, and the editor–cum–kingmaker, under a headline that affirmed the women's wise choice to include them:

## WELL-KNOWN MEN ADVOCATE IT
### GEORGE HARVEY, RABBI WISE, AND OTHERS
### CONTEND THAT WOMEN SHOULD VOTE

Each offered a succinct explanation of his prosuffrage stance. Smith dismissed the arguments against women's suffrage as "very light weight," adding that the extension of the vote to women was "as inevitable as the next sunrise, a part of the great forward social movement we are now experiencing." Harvey dismissed the antisuffragist notion that voting women would do the community ill. "How do they account for the fact that whenever and wherever equal suffrage has been established reversion to partial suffrage, as a result of the experience, has never in a single instance been decreed or even suggested?" Dewey argued that "the principle of indirect influence by charm and personality" was inherently immoral and actually one of the chief reasons for supporting women's suffrage. Wise said he wanted to help right a flagrant wrong. "As long as women are shut out from citizenship and the exercise of the ballot, which is the symbol of citizenship, ours is no democracy," he wrote, "—that is, rule of the people."

Max Eastman

Stewart Woodford

J. Howard Melish

Samuel J. Barrows

David J. Brewer

William Dean Howells

Rollo Ogden

Finley Peter Dunne

John Wesley Hill

George Foster Peabody

Charles Beard

John B. Stanchfield

Barton Aylesworth

Nathaniel Schmidt

Charles C. Burlingham

Arthur Levy (Leeds)

Julius Mayer

# 2

# "The Favor of Such Men"

## 1909

It took a full year, but by February 1909, Villard and Wise had found the perfect choice for a League secretary in Max Eastman, a charming, dashingly handsome new denizen of Greenwich Village with impressive academic and social credentials. On the first day of the month, Eastman wrote home about a project "on foot" that an unnamed editorial writer at Villard's *Evening Post* thought would interest him.

Eastman was the son of two progressive Congregational ministers in upstate Elmira, New York, a couple who counted Mark Twain and the Reverend Thomas Beecher among their close friends. He was a 1905 graduate of Williams College with a doctoral fellowship from Columbia, awarded in the spring of 1908. He was also John Dewey's protégé in the university's philosophy department. His mother, the Reverend Annis Ford Eastman, was well connected to the suffrage insiders in the upper northwestern corner of New York. And he was dating no less an emerging suffrage luminary than the recent Vassar graduate Inez Milholland. In the second decade of the twentieth century, the lovely, mercurial, blue-eyed Milholland played the glamorous role Gloria Steinem would effectively reprise in the second feminist wave a half century later.

Eastman may have come to the attention of Villard and his cohort through any number of channels. There were his mother's upstate suffrage connections. Dewey, his mentor, was already out front for the movement and was also allied with Villard and Wise among those involved with W.E.B. Du Bois and Ida B. Wells in establishing the NAACP. And Eastman, in his own right, was already receiving national notice for his published work on themes as disparate as poetry and patriotism. The *International Journal of Ethics*, the *North American Review*, and the *Atlantic Monthly* all had carried his essays, and newspapers around the country had featured his name and work in their monthly what-to-read-in-the-magazines columns.

In a 1912 essay and again in his 1948 memoir, Eastman gives a version of the League's early history that adds another dimension to the Shaw-Villard exchanges of 1907–1908. Independently of Villard, Eastman, too, had the idea for a men's league and he writes of saying as much early on to a reporter, who, he said, published his remark in the *New York Herald*. So, in Eastman's creation story, even though Villard and Wise may have thought he "merely turned up," Eastman said he was "more or less of a league before I ever saw them."

His version goes on to say that Villard gave him cards of introduction to twelve men of "civic importance" along with two dollars in League dues, a gesture that for Eastman held high symbolic value. "This was by no means the only contribution he made," Eastman recalled, "but it was the most effective. That two dollars sealed my responsibility. It weighed me down even heavier than the newspaper clipping. I was the organizer now for certain. I held the funds. There was nothing to do but go ahead and organize."

Actual recruitment appears to have begun almost as soon as Eastman was hired, given the clues he left in an essay in his hometown *Elmira Star-Gazette* published on February 20, 1909, the fifth in a series on suffrage by the town's "well-known citizens." In it, Eastman called for an end to both the poisonous atmosphere of New York State politics and the characterization of women as innocents, because, he said, women "are interested in the problems of humanity. That is why we have hopes of them." The essay does not mention the work Eastman was doing to get the League under way. This honored Villard's request to wait to announce the League until it could make a much bigger publicity boom, to keep the plans out of the press until at least one hundred prominent men could be named as members. The value of having a top newspaper publisher think up the strategy for the League's early publicity cannot be overestimated. As Villard had written to Shaw when the two of them first discussed the idea, only then should the League's existence be "worked for all it is worth by our local press agents," with members poised to appear at hearings and wherever else they might be needed. And so in the *Star-Gazette*, Eastman stopped short of revealing the plans underway, even though the news a few weeks earlier that men in Chicago had formed a league of their own provided the perfect opening for him to promote his own similar efforts.

He did, however, go so far as to say that he knew of New Yorkers who "would like to see the atmosphere of politics cleared up by someone who has moral ideals, and they would like to see women's ideals and the 'ideals of woman' drained of sentiment, and hitched up into some sort of working contact with reality. They would like to have wives who have a real and effective knowledge of their world," he wrote. "They would like to have mothers aware of the environment and the problems into which they are educating their sons." He went only so far as to name "certain persons" who had "resolved upon Woman's Suffrage." Villard and Wise were prominent on that list, of course, along with ten others, presumably all the men from Villard's list of "civic wonders." This is not to say that Eastman's early recruitment efforts were without rebuff. In his later recounts, he told the story of his first jolting reproach from an attorney he tried to recruit and how it put him off the task for at least two weeks. The man proclaimed himself far too ardent a suffragist to subscribe to anything that could put the cause in such a ridiculous light.

The day after the *Star-Gazette* piece appeared, Eastman's mother shared her excitement over "a great hearing at Albany this week" with Anna Shaw and "other splendid speakers" and a mass meeting in the Assembly Chamber to follow. "I'd love to be in it!" she wrote. "Maybe I shall vote before I die. Can't you feel that Susan B. Anthony is in all this new movement all over the world?" That Albany event, on February 24, attracted half a dozen men among more than a hundred women. One of the six was George Foster Peabody, the well-known industrialist and philanthropist. With an assist from Villard, Eastman must have "captured" Peabody for the suffrage cause between his submission of the *Star-Gazette* essay and the Albany gathering. In no time, Peabody became the League's president and main financial backer. As Eastman would later acknowledge, the League owed not only its "pecuniary life" to Peabody but also "a great part of its early standing before the public."

The spring brought more suffrage news highlighting the patronage of men. In April, *Common Cause*, the weekly house organ of the British women's movement, lavishly praised the work of Britain's Men's League and extolled "the devotion and determination of its leaders," although without offering any specifics. The writer also took the opportunity to empathize with the difficult position of the British league, as it remained deliberately neutral in the pro- versus antimilitancy debate. "The situation arose, doubtless, from a most chivalrous desire to fight the women's battle and to avoid carping at the methods they saw fit to employ. But it is a position of unstable equilibrium, and we would far rather see men doing that part of the work which women cannot do."

Doing "that part of the work," George Harvey became an exemplar of what this new male enthusiasm for suffrage could mean with his early actions in New York on behalf of promoting Katherine Duer Mackay and her new

Equal Franchise Society. First, he committed the headline-worthy act of hosting a luncheon table at the banquet at which Mackay gave her inaugural speech. The *New York Times* declared the occasion the "first time a man ever held that position in a similar gathering in this city" and noted the presence of Dewey among the few men present in a sea of five hundred women.

Two months later, Harvey went a step further. In the pages of *Harper's Weekly*, he ran a fetching full-page "new portrait" of Mackay in a head-turning *Alençon* lace-trimmed gown. Its caption applauded the "influential factor" she had become in "bringing the question of Woman Suffrage into general prominence." The accompanying article, by William Hemingway, could not have been more effusive in its appraisal of Mackay's new organization, which was not even three months old. "And of all the influences now at work in the cause, already triumphant in several Western States, none is more significant of its irresistible advance than the organization of the Equal Franchise Society," Hemingway wrote. That was just the lead. The article went on to mention charter members and officers, including Harvey as a third vice president. Hemingway marveled at Mackay's ability to attract "so many persons of prominence in the social, professional, and financial worlds." He noted how vividly this illustrated "the rapidity with which the movement for woman suffrage is spreading."

For his part, Eastman obsessed over a suffrage speech he had agreed to give on April 17 at the New York University School of Law as he sent out letters of invitation to "four or five hundred more civic gentlemen," all men he thought would be "open to reason." He invited them to join the League, which then called itself the Voters' Woman Suffrage League. From Villard's advice, along with Eastman's own sometimes disappointing exchanges with the initial twelve prospects, he formulated what he thought would be a more winning approach to this next, larger group of possible members. Eastman assured them that the League's main function would simply be to exist—no meetings!—and that its membership roster would remain secret until it contained one hundred prominent names. Yet by May 1909, a month in which the socialist leader Daniel De Leon delivered a major address on women's suffrage at Cooper Union, the League had attracted only sixteen new members despite the hundreds of circulars that had been sent all over the state. This wide dissemination of membership appeals made the secret impossible to keep. On May 23, 1909, a *New York Times* reporter broke the story on the newspaper's front page. Thankfully for Eastman, the twenty-eight names on the rolls by that point had enough civic potency to ensure "very delicate handling," even from the editorially antisuffrage *Times*.

The headline was playful. The article quoted only Eastman and credited him alone with the idea for the organization.

## MALE SUFFRAGETTES NOW IN THE FIELD
### The Deeper Notes to Join the Soprano Chorus for Women's Votes.

## BIRTH OF AN UPLIFT IDEA
### Scope of Operations Will Determine How Far Advanced This Movement Is to Be.

In addition to listing the names, the report noted the organization's "one curious feature": "The league will do no active work of any kind, at least for the present, but will simply announce itself, also its membership, and then stand pat. This fact seems at first sight to put it far below the Suffragettes, whose watchword is activity." The mockery was mild, but to Eastman, a thoroughly "sickening experience," he recalled in his memoir, his "first taste of public ridicule reinforced with a private rebuff." That rejection came from Doctor John Winters Brannan, the president of the board of Bellevue Hospital and son-in-law of Charles Dana, the editor of the *New York Sun*. Brannan's wife, Eunice, was an important suffrage figure in the state. Immediately, Brannan sent Eastman a "brief and caustic resignation." To his mother, Eastman confided, "Dr. John Brannan resigned from my league when it came out in the *Times*. Poor cuss—I wish I could." Nonetheless, Peabody allayed Eastman's concern with a comforting response. The *Times* front page would help recruitment, Peabody told him, and then fade from memory. All would be new again when the group was ready to go public.

Forty names appear on a surviving copy of the circular that made the rounds that summer of 1909 as another suffrage-related opportunity came Eastman's way. Among his papers is the handwritten copy of "what must be the ms. [manuscript] of my first speech," to a movement gathering. It was not in Ontario, New York, where his later recollection placed it, but in the Rochester suburb of Charlotte, for a Monroe County suffrage meeting. Advance publicity identified Eastman as the "secretary of the new organization of men in New York, favoring woman suffrage."

This first summons for Eastman to speak at an official suffrage event had the scent of nepotism; his mother thought it would be amusing to have him replace her as the keynote speaker. Given how stale the prosuffrage arguments had become, he urged reflection on the larger importance of the act of coming together in and of itself. He drew a comparison with the reason people go to church, which, this son of two members of the clergy said, was less to be freshly inspired than to reaffirm their faith, to symbolize their common commitment by the act of gathering week after week.

The appearance did not go well. "The speech was to last forty-five minutes and the fee was fifteen dollars," he recalled years later, "but I prepared a speech that any audience would have paid fifteen hundred dollars to get away from." Indeed, his hand-written notes sprawl wordily, digressively, over sixty-two pages of executive-size stationery. "It might, if I talked fast and left no time for rhetorical pauses, have been compressed to the size of a small college education," he later recalled. Fresh in his mind years later was the panic he felt, and how he "plunged and floundered around in that thorough preparation like a man trying to find his way out of a swamp." He never did. "I just kept talking slower and slower until finally I stopped through sheer lack of momentum." And yet "in the misery of it," Eastman said, he learned "all at once, in a lump, without hesitance or self-persuasion," how to capture and keep an audience riveted with his words. A speech, he realized, must have only one dimension. It must start at the beginning and flow to the end. It should be "rapid, clear and energetic and make but one point." It must run, he said, "like a river between high banks."

The debacle at Charlotte went unremarked upon in newspaper reports, but Eastman's presence had put the new men of suffrage in the news all the same. The address of Harriet May Mills, the state suffrage organizer, drew the attention of the *Rochester Democrat and Chronicle*, as she emphasized the new male effort in New York City and its plans to cover the state. The headline read:

## NOTHING CAN DO MORE GOOD THAN THE FAVOR OF SUCH MEN AS ARE NOW ON THE SIDE OF EQUAL FRANCHISE

However lacking Eastman's appearance may have been in oratorical fireworks or finesse, it brought an invitation from Shaw herself to speak at the forthcoming state suffrage convention in Troy.

————◄○►————

Suddenly, the new and hairier faces of suffrage were very much in the cultural conversation. *American Magazine*'s June issue had Mr. Dooley, the popular recurring character created by Finley Peter Dunne, a newspaper humorist from Chicago, reflecting satirically on the movement's heightened profile as "society queens take up the cause." He depicted his fictional ladies debating whether their favorite department stores should install polling booths, or if election days should be postponed in bad weather, or if they could have their footmen cast ballots for them, or if they might be allowed to simply telephone in their votes.

The satire's setting was a Michigan Avenue mansion but could easily have been a townhouse in Manhattan, given Katherine Mackay's announcement soon afterward of a summer lecture series she was organizing at Columbia University, sponsored by her Equal Franchise Society. She had enlisted Dewey as the inaugural speaker. He was an obvious choice, not only because he was one of the Society's charter signatories and had been an esteemed member of the university's faculty since 1904, but also because he had so often argued against subjugation of any kind on the basis of race, ethnicity, or gender. In addition, Dewey's wife, Alice, soon became a district leader for the suffrage movement.

For the lecture, the audience crowded Columbia's Hamilton Hall "to the doors," a *Boston Globe* article noted, but its reporter was more taken with Mackay than with Dewey, and how the society matron's presence demonstrated the seriousness of her commitment, given that so many women of her class had fled the city to escape its summer heat. Her attire got a paragraph: "A picturesque frock of cream lace with a high girdle of black satin" and "a new shaped French toque with a big bunch of aigrettes ticking perkily up in the back."

The New York press focused instead on Dewey's remarks. The *Times* carried his statement that "there might be some justice in denying to woman the privilege of franchise, if she were not permitted to own real estate or were not required to pay taxes on her holdings." He added that the proper definition of a good husband would be the "man who had confidence and faith enough in his wife's ability to turn his pay envelope over to her every Saturday night, after having made small deductions for tobacco and other personal expenses." The *Herald* drove home Dewey's belief that the country's educational system would benefit from the enfranchisement of women, and the *Tribune* elaborated on the professor's opposition to the theory of Stanley Hall, the distinguished president of Clark University and an authority on child culture, that female teachers feminized boys. In the *Christian Science Monitor*, Dewey was quoted as saying that the jump from municipal to national politics was a long one, but that women were no less interested in national affairs than were men. "Now, take the tariff," he said. "The women are certainly the ultimate consumers, and, if it can be said that the men regulate the production, women may certainly claim the distinction of regulating the consumption."

By July 1909, Eastman had enlisted his mother to help dash off letters to potential Men's League recruits or their wives or mothers. She also double-checked her son's notes, suggested additional names, and pressed her contacts upstate to add others. By mid-August, the *Woman's Journal*, the weekly suffrage periodical, was calling on women across the country to help organize their men for suffrage, to "appeal personally and individually to the men of their respective districts to make the affirmative vote a majority," especially in states with active proposed suffrage amendments pending in their legislatures.

The article laid out a plan: preparation needed to be "systematic and per-sistent," with state organizers put in place to create county organizations that in turn would appoint precinct committees of voters. "The women of each precinct," the article said, "should be everywhere a power behind the throne, inspiring and animating their fathers, brothers, lovers, husbands and sons. Every man in each of these three States should be personally asked to join the league by some woman whom he respects and esteems." It asked women to assure support to those can-didates who favored the amendment and to "quietly but earnestly" oppose those who did not. "Press, pulpit, Grange, labor union, church, school, college, factory, railroads and business concerns should be conciliated and enlisted." For too long, the *Journal* said, women's suffrage had been seen exclusively as a women's question. Men had not considered the cause to be their own. The notice added that an appeal to men "made without bluster in a quiet, winning, womanly way, without threats or manifestations of personal ill-will to opponents, will prove invaluable."

## STATE WOMAN SUFFRAGE ASSOCIATION WILL MEET NEXT WEEK AT TROY—TO BE THE LARGEST EVER HELD

In this way, Villard's *Evening Post* blared the coming state suffrage conven-tion of October 1909 a week before it started, making a point of noting that both Eastman and Peabody would be featured. Eastman described the women who gathered in Troy as "the jolliest bunch of reformers that ever got together." Coverage of the event omits mention of Peabody but reports that Eastman put his crisp new delivery to work to revisit his "stale arguments" theme from Charlotte. He was by no means the first person to highlight suffrage's rhetorical failing. As far back as 1879, *Harper's Weekly* had said that both sides of the suffrage debate

Dear Sir:

We write to ask you to become a member of our Voters' Woman Suffrage League. The league is to consist of men only, and we hope to have among its members from two to five prominent citizens in each senatorial district of the state. We have already over fifty such men in New York City.

We feel that an organization of men supporting the enfranchisement of women will have a peculiarly strong influence both upon those who regard the cause as trivial, and upon those who are moved only by opinions that are reinforced by ballots. In this position we have the support of the leading women advocates of the cause.

The league will not hold meetings, nor for the present do active work. It will simply make its existence and membership known, and be represented at important meetings and legislative hearings by such prominent members as are willing to appear.

There will be nominal dues of $1.00 a year for membership. Beyond this we ask nothing of you but your name and influence.

We enclose a copy of our "Constitution," and if the cause and our method of supporting it appeal to you, we ask that you sign it and return it to the Secretary as soon as possible.

The following have already joined the league.

William M. Ivins
George Foster Peabody
William Dean Howells
Charles C. Burlingham
John Mitchell
Edward T. Devine
William Jay Schieffelin
George Harvey
Oswald Garrison Villard
Hamilton Holt
Dr. Simon Flexner
Dr. Julius Rudisch
Prof. John Dewey
Prof. Vladimir Simkhovitch
Prof. Dickinson S. Miller
Prof. James H. Robinson
Prof. W. P. Trent
Prof. James Shotwell
Prof. W. P. Montague
Prof. Charles Beard
Rev. Thomas C. Hall

Rev. J. Howard Melish
Rev. Leighton Williams
Rev. John P. Peters
Rabbi Stephen S. Wise
Charles H. Strong
Nelson Spencer
Louis R. Ehrich
William Adams Delano
Charles B. Reed
John E. Milholland
Charles Rann Kennedy
Edwin Markham
Edmond Kelley
George F. Kunz
John Mead Howells
Henry S. Marlor
Robert H. Elder
William H. Ingersoll
Charles Sprague Smith
Josiah Strong

Very truly yours,

VOTERS' WOMAN SUFFRAGE LEAGUE,

Address:
   Max Eastman,
      118 E. Chemung Pl.
         Elmira, N. Y.

by

Secretary.

Men's League circular, ca. summer 1909 (Max Eastman Collection I, Lilly Library, Indiana University) were too full of "familiar assertions." What was needed, Eastman said, was a new way to express arguments, with a shift in emphasis that connected more readily with current popular thought. He dismissed two of the longest-held notions—that to grant women the vote was a matter of justice and that doing so would purify politics. But he remained keen on a third one: that democracy demanded this rectification. As the *Troy Times* quoted him as saying, more important than the role women might play in improving politics was the way politics would further the development of women. "The most excellent achievement of the industrial era is the physical, moral, social and intellectual liberation of women," Eastman said, "and no other act will so hasten and certify this next step in the history of life as to give it a political expression and guarantee."

He added a fourth measure, one that would do the most to persuade US lawmakers to support the suffrage amendment and one at the heart of this new male initiative: "Induce men to present it." "That is the way we get things in America," he went on, "and when the thing you are trying to get is a chance to vote, you are in an extreme predicament. The end which you are trying to attain is the very means by which you might attain it." With that, he provided a sneak preview of the forthcoming Men's League of New York State and explained how the status of its members as voters—the very thing the women of New York lacked—would help the women's cause.

The address at Troy brought accolades to Eastman, who attracted "the largest audience of the convention," along with offers for future speaking engagements. To his mother, he forwarded one "lovely letter" of appreciation and promised to share with her in person ("I would blush to write it down") the praise from the other male speaker at Troy, the Reverend John Wesley Hill, pastor of New York City's Metropolitan Temple. Hill also invited Eastman to address his congregants. "I've had two other invitations already," Eastman went on, "—one from Emma Yard Ivins to speak in New York, and one from Buffalo to speak with Mrs. Snowden!"

Ivins was the wife of William Ivins, the leader of the Republican Party and at the time, in Eastman's later estimation, "the most eminent asset the movement then had in New York City." Mrs. Snowden was, of course, Ethel Snowden, whom he described as the "beautiful and femininely eloquent blue-eyed wife of the British MP, subsequently Chancellor of the Exchequer and Viscount Snowden," and as "the sensation of the year in lecture circles."

For Eastman, coming off what he considered a disaster in Charlotte, his appearance at the Troy convention was a personal triumph. "I had it in my head and on my tongue to the last dot and letter," he wrote in his memoir, happily recalling how the newfound revenue source from speaking engagements secured the money-making side of his "three-cornered life scheme": earn a living, contribute to the lives of neighbors and the progress of the commonweal, and if time remains, express oneself.

Troy certainly mattered in the New York suffrage organizational scheme, but the most important event of October 1909 came a few days later. Emmeline Pankhurst, the English suffragette, filled all three thousand seats and all the available standing room at Carnegie Hall for her appearance on October 25. The *New York Times* reported that even after more than three hundred people had been turned away, "there was still a line of persistent ones extending up the street and around the corner."

The newspapers said the number of men in the crowd were too few to warrant notice, although Eastman and Dewey appear to have been among them. ("Sitting as a distinguished guest on the Carnegie Hall platform is very poor sport," Eastman told his mother soon after the event. "It means you sit in an audience of four or five hundred, to whom the speaker turns his back while endeavoring unsuccessfully to make himself heard to an audience of four or five thousand in exactly the opposite direction.") All the same, his letter to her rhapsodized over what he had witnessed. "I think Mrs. Pankhurst is one of the greatest persons I shall ever see," he wrote. "I think of her when I wake up and when I am going to sleep. She is a great political leader, besides being a complete and triumphant soul, and I hope she will succeed soon enough to lead another movement on the *inside*—just born to be great and show a slow-minded generation what women can be and do." Dewey, he added, was equally in her thrall. He had told his own daughter that Pankhurst would be "spoken of with Washington and Lincoln!"

◄○►

And then, just in time to dampen the suffrage spirit ahead of the state convention at Buffalo, came a crafty waffle from President William Howard Taft, one that nonetheless set off a wider public conversation on the rights of and opportunities for women. "I am not a rabid suffragist," Taft told a group of students—"800 as pretty girls as could be found in all the south," the *Atlanta Constitution* noted. They had gathered in Columbia, Mississippi, on November 2 to hear Taft speak at the State Institute and College. "The truth is I am not in favor of suffrage for women," he began, "until I can be convinced that all the women desire it; and when they desire it I am in favor of giving it to them, and when they desire it they will get it too." He did acknowledge that one great advantage of women's having the vote would be that it could "open the avenues of self-support to them" in new ways. "The great principle of popular government," he went on, "is that every class in the community, assuming that it has intelligence enough to know its own interest, can be better trusted to know its own interest, can be better trusted to look after that interest than any other class, however altruistic that class."

On November 5, the *Washington Post* followed up on the Taft speech, pointing out that the Capitol's social leaders supported the president's "liberal views," including his call to widen the self-support options open to women so that marriage could become more choice than necessity. But the article did not mention his disappointing comment on suffrage. In the *New York Times*, however, an "anti" did bring up Taft's suffrage remark in a letter to the editor. It read: "Mr. Taft is pretty safe in saying, 'I am not in favor of suffrage for women until I can be convinced that all the women desire it.' For when did all women desire the same thing, and if suffrage for women depended upon that, we 'anti's would have nothing to fear." The letter was signed only with the initials C.R.R.P.

At around the same time, the *Washington Post* carried an item that quoted Frederick Shipley, a New Yorker staying in a DC hotel, saying how struck he was that his city's mayor, George B. McClellan, was adding three women to the Board of Education. True, before Brooklyn became a borough, there had been a woman on its school board, but this was the first such move in the history of Greater New York. Shipley ascribed great portent to the decision, saying it signaled "the change in public sentiment regarding woman suffrage." He quickly added that he himself had "no decided opinions" about whether to give women the vote, "but I am sure I can detect a more favorable attitude toward the woman's suffrage movement on the part of the general public and many of the newspapers than existed a few years ago," he said. "It cannot be denied that the women of this campaign have made decided headway."

The *New York Times* seemed to concur with Shipley. It splashed across the top half of a page in its Sunday paper of November 7 all the "vigor and energy" the Votes for Women movement had suddenly begun to display. Its second page carried large photographs of the two beautiful new headquarters offices recently established, one financed by Katherine Mackay for the Equal Franchise Society and the other by Alva Belmont to provide the state and national organizations with a suitable New York City beachhead. The *Times* attributed this "infusion of power into the movement that had been dragging along for half a century" to "a factor that has never before entered the fight—the organization of the contest by women of wealth and social position who within the last year have enlisted actively in it and have given it the sinews of war." Soon enough, there would be men of fine standing to add to that winning formula.

———◄○►———

November of 1909 brought Eastman to Buffalo's Central Presbyterian Church for the evening event with Ethel Snowden under the auspices of the city's Political Equality League. He got star billing alongside the visiting British celebrity. The place was packed. "Mr. Max Eastman has but lately taken to the platform, but his success, as stated, has become very marked," said the *Elmira Star-Gazette*, so proud of its native son for sharing both stage and topic with Snowden, "that fiery and eloquent apostle of woman suffrage." Decades later, Eastman recalled the appearance. "We spoke at Buffalo to an audience of five thousand. Leonora O'Reilly spoke there, too, representing the woman worker. We were all young and all gaily rather than somberly idealistic. It was a big event in the liveliest social movement of the time, and I was off to a flying start on another rather accidental career. I should certainly not have chosen to get my first taste of fame as a suffrage orator. But so it fell out."

The *Buffalo Courier* emphasized Eastman's appeal to attract new League members, urging the men present to send their dollar in dues and the women to persuade their husbands, sons, brothers, and beaus to do the same. "It is one thing to believe in a movement," he said, "and another thing to lick a stamp to advance it." He was back on his "reinvigorate those stale old arguments" theme from Charlotte and Troy, again favoring the idea that granting suffrage was a matter of practical expediency over the more time-honored themes of justice and equality. Government needed the peculiarly womanly qualities of mind and emotion, he said, along with feminine idealism. "Men throw a sop up to God in the shape of the purity and virtues of their women at home and then go out and about the devil's business," he said, adding that what the country was in want of were not "beautiful, cloistered saints" but human beings out in the world, acting on their convictions.

As an example, he mentioned the strike then underway in New York City, a months-long protest that would ultimately involve some twenty-thousand women in the city's shirtwaist factories before the conflict was settled in February 1910. Eastman told the crowd that these women workers were being subjected to harassment, beatings, and arrests for exercising their right to strike. He dismissed the oft-repeated notion that women would purify politics, saying again that politics would further the development of women.

During the appearance, Snowden told the crowd she wasn't as convinced as Eastman that the old arguments had outlived their usefulness because they remained important in debating the antis, who, she scoffed, must have forged most of their positions in the Garden of Eden. In later remarks on her lecture tour, she disappointed suffragists in Washington, DC, by saying that unlike in England, where women far outnumbered men, the fact of a US population with two million more men than women meant that the women were being too well treated to appreciate the extent of their political slavery.

The Buffalo press praised the "most excellent impression" Eastman had made. He was not at all the "long-haired individual" the columnist had expected to be "exhaling the impression that he was so busy looking after ideals that he couldn't get together enough money to keep well fed and well clothed." Instead, the audience encountered "a tall, broad-shouldered, wholesome youth with a keen mind, a winning personality, and the gift of speech," a "twentieth century knight championing the cause of womanhood, not as picturesque as practical, a figure suited to these modern days, however, and the modern style of chivalry."

◄◦►

For the new men of suffrage, November 1909 was all about preparation for the League's official launch, even though membership dues arrived in slow drips. NAWSA's third mass meeting in the month of November not only filled Carnegie Hall, the *New York Times* reported, but included "many men who came out for woman suffrage," including the professors, clergy, and editors who had been announced as guests on stage. "They may not all have been present," the newspaper said, "but the platform was filled to capacity."

Peabody was a featured speaker. He titled his remarks "The Man's Part of the Work" and used the occasion to define "true chivalry" as being "based on the woman ideal, 'the everlasting woman,' to use Goethe's often misapplied phrase. It is the part of men to see to it in short order that women inspect our political institutions, criticize, examine, question and help us with their voices and their votes to set things right."

Newspaper readers were familiar with Peabody's generosity and advocacy efforts. He had long supported the advancement of African Americans and had a prominent role in national Democratic Party politics—he served as the party's treasurer in 1904–1905. But as a feminist, the forty-seven-year-old philanthropist was just coming to be known. In a letter to her son, Annis Eastman was moved to express some curiosity about Peabody's wife. "I don't think Mrs. Peabody is rich—I sort of think she is dead," her son replied, "but I'm not sure. Indeed I'm not sure there ever was any Mrs. Peabody." In fact, there wasn't a wife, at least not until years later, when Peabody married Katrina Trask, a late-blooming suffrage sympathizer and childhood friend, who by then was the widow of Peabody's late business partner and close friend, Spencer Trask. Bachelors were well represented among the league's early members. The *Brooklyn Eagle* took snide notes of these surprising new feminists, these new men of suffrage. "Men's Leagues for Woman's Suffrage are chiefly favored by bachelors," it read. "That confidence is in inverse ratio with knowledge is an inevitable reflection."

On November 19, Eastman had compiled the League's complete member-ship list to date—it came to 103 names—and sent it to Anne Fitzhugh Miller in Geneva. "I hope it will 'work,'" he wrote in an accompanying note. "We hold our meeting to elect officers, etc., in the City Club the 29th."

———◦———

The publicity campaign began. On November 24, the *New York Times* and *New York Sun* reported that another New York men's league had been "perpetrated at the much-clubbed Columbia University" as a "boom to woman suffrage." This was for a college-based chapter of the League, which perhaps confusingly made East-man its president in addition to his duties as executive secretary of the statewide organization. Three days later, the *Lowell Sun* in Massachusetts, for some reason, preemptively reported that Peabody, "banker, director in many corporations, and trustee of Hampton Institute and of several colleges," had accepted the presidency of the new Men's League for Woman Suffrage of New York City.

Peabody's earlier prediction was about to be proved right. There was no adverse impact from the *New York Times'* premature scoop back in April. All the city newspapers and other outlets across the state and beyond carried the first press release of the newly formed New York State organization on their inside pages. They reported on its first—closed—meeting, as if it were not already old news. The League announced its new name, shared its actual charter and its Con-stitution and, after that November 29 meeting at the City Club, the names of its A-list of elected officers, including the formidable number of first and second

A unique meeting was held at the City Club in New York last night.[#1]  It was a meeting of men who favor equal franchise, and they came together for the purpose of establishing a "Voters' League for Woman Suffrage". This It is a New York State league, and has already upon its roll many of the best known men of the State in politics, commerce, education, and law, as well as in reform circles.  This appears from the list of honorary and executive officers elected at last night's meeting.  Mr. George Foster Peabody, financier and philanthropist, is the president of the league.  The vice-presidents are:  William Dean Howells, William M. Ivins, Congressman Herbert Parsons, George F. Kunz of Tiffany's, President Langdon C. Stewardson of Hobart College, Prof. Nathaniel Schmidt of Cornell, Congressman William S. Bennett, Rev. John P. Peters, Rabbi Stephen S. Wise, William J. Schieffelin, Chairman of the Citizens' Union, John Mitchell, vice-president of the American Federation of Labor, and Z. R. Brockway, ex-mayor of Elmira.

The executive committee consists of Prof. John Dewey and Prof. Vladimir Simkhovitch of Columbia University, Dr. Simon Flexner, director of the Rockefeller Institute, Oswald Garrison Villard, Charles C. Burlingham, Charles H. Strong, the president of the City Club, and Max Eastman, the secretary of the league.

An advisory committee was also elected, in which the following names appear:        Carlton Sprague, of Buffalo, Hamilton Holt, Prof. Henry R. Seager, Louis Ehrich, William A. Delano, Prof. W. P. Trent, Edward Lauterbach, Prof. James H. Robinson, Rev. W. C. Gannett of Rochester, Richard Welling, Thomas W. Hotchkiss, Walston H. Brown, G. E. Francis of Syracuse, Alexander D. Jenney of Syracuse, Edward T. Devine, John E. Milholland, Nelson S. Spencer, Lee DeForest, Rev. J. Howard Melish, George Harvey, Edwin Markham, James S. Clarkson, Thos. F. Fennell of Elmira, Prof. Herbert E. Mills, of Poughkeepsie, Theodore Williams.

The headquarters of the Voters' League will be in New York City, at 118 Waverly Place, but it is understood that its work will extend throughout the state.  Just what that work is to be in detail will depend upon the exigencies that arise as the movement for equal suffrage advances, but it may be assumed from the names of the men who compose it, that this league will have no small influence and play no small part in hastening the reform that it advocates.  The constitution adopted at the meeting last

------------------------------------------------------------------------

#1   Monday, Nov. 29.

First press release of the newly formed Men's League for Woman Suffrage, November 29, 1909 (Miller NAWSA Suffrage Scrapbooks, 1897–1911; Scrapbook 8, p. 119; Library of Congress, Rare Book and Special Collections Division)

vice-presidents that Villard had urged be designated. The membership roster by then contained one hundred and fifty dazzlingly important men. Town and city papers across the state highlighted the names of their favorite sons.

Most newspapers barely edited the press release for publication, but not so Pennsylvania's *Williamsport Gazette-Bulletin*. It produced a biting front-page headline under a frightfully austere photograph of Alva Belmont in a large hat of spikey aigrette feathers, which, the article said, had been obtained by capturing the old birds alive and leaving their young to starve to death in the nest. "It may be upon this 'meat' that this our militant suffragette has fed that she has become so great an advocate of the use of dog whips on mere men." The headline?

## STRENUOUS SUFFRAGETTE APPROVES OF HORSEWHIPPING MEN SOMETIMES

Under that came subheads and the only known report of the League's founding that included some original reporting:

## MEN FOR SUFFRAGE IN SPITE OF WHIPS

### ORGANIZATION OF GENTLEMEN SUFFRAGETTES PERFECTED AND WILL MOVE ON THE NEW YORK LEGISLATURE WITH A DEMAND THAT IT SURRENDER OR DIE—STATE TO BE AROUSED.

The article included a quote from Villard: "We expect to move on the legislature this winter, and hope to do all we can to arouse public sentiment to the justice of the equal suffrage movement. The names of the men who have attached themselves to the movement are a sufficient guarantee of the character of our organization. Mr. Peabody, the president, is extremely enthusiastic and he said at the meeting yesterday afternoon that he had never seen a more representative list of names than the roster of our membership contains. We are going to get to work at once."

In 1912, Eastman's delightful version of the backstory of the League's launch managed to misdate the founding to 1910, when its charter and founding membership list were first published in booklet form. He framed his essay as a guide to how to organize such a group, saying that barring the press was one of the League's most effective publicity launch tactics, since reporters were never to know how many "of those dignitaries elected to office were actually present to participate in their own election," nor was he going to tell. "Suffice it to say," he wrote, "that some fifty of the biggest and best men of New York appear to have met at the City Club and organized themselves into a league for woman suffrage, the newspapers of New York City and State were full of their pictures, interviews with them, statements that they meant business and that many thousands of dollars were behind the movement. Well, they were—a glance at the names would prove that—and if they have stayed behind, it has not been the fault of the executive committee."

———◇———

Indeed, the League did not, in the *Times*'s phrase, "stand pat." On November 30, the day after the launch meeting, Dewey presided as platform chairman for the Pankhurst appearance at Cooper Union. As if to underscore this new support from unexpected quarters, the December issue of *Ladies' World* carried Supreme Court Justice David J. Brewer's case for women's suffrage, in which he deflected the most common arguments of the antis, as he had signaled a year and a half earlier in an unusually profeminist July 4 speech in Ulster County. Not more than two days later, on December 2, the League staged "the first public meeting in the interests of woman's fight for franchise in which all the speakers were men," as the *Sun* put it. Three men spoke, including William Ivins and East-man, who repeated his "familiar arguments" theme. Eastman also reoffered his contention that it would take the involvement of men for women to have any effect in arguing their case before the legislature. Men were far more likely to respond to arguments if other men presented them, he said, catching some flak from a clergyman in the crowd for comparing the repetition of tried-and-true old suffrage arguments to rereading the Bible. The minister shot back, "It would have been a good thing for you, young man, if you had kept up the practice." "Well," Eastman replied, "I don't think it did me very much good. At any rate, the public needs to be rejuvenated on some of those suffrage arguments. They must be adapted to present conditions."

To his mother, whose help had been indispensable, Eastman wrote in grati-tude of the "great wave of love" that came over him as he sat "surrounded by our secretarial debris, and thank God you helped me with this! It never would have got done if you hadn't. I love you devotedly—even if I can't keep your pace when you first get up and it has been a beautiful time, your being here." And yet, he confided, "I fear I am losing my poetic soul for I don't seem to care much as the day's action unrolls, about those newspapers. Once you get up on your horse, I guess, you ride right over those things."

The male push on Albany then began, a mere three weeks after the League's initial meeting. The newspapers noted that Villard and Peabody had joined a suffrage delegation dispatched to the capital to meet with New York Governor Charles Evans Hughes. Elsewhere in the country, Ethel Snowden, by then off lecturing in other cities, noted that men would approach her practically everywhere she went, asking how to get in touch with the League in New York to find out how to form their own local chapters. As for Eastman, he was already geared up for the role he was about to accept as one of the movement's most effective if somewhat reluctant orators, a designation that continued well after he stepped down as League secretary about a year later.

By his own count, Eastman's personal archive contains twenty-six suffrage speeches, many published between 1910 and 1913 by NAWSA, the *North American Review*, the Equal Franchise Society, or the Men's League itself. In private correspondence and in passages from his memoir, Eastman freely acknowledges how much his suffrage speeches "intersect and inter-ramify in various complicated ways, one biting a slice out of another to save labor in writing and memorizing, so that on the whole the job was one of repetition." His method was to select the elements he planned to use and then spend twenty minutes on the train refreshing his memory before the presentation. The rest of the trip, he said, "I would read philosophy, or write poetry, or dream of things as remote as possible from this evangel job, which so happily united martyrdom with money earning!"

Recruiting for the League continued. Thanking his mother for a loaf of nut bread she had sent ("my teeth rattle with anticipation of its meaty resistance"), he boasted to her on December 6 about the "latest acquisition of my league," the former New York Attorney General Julius Mayer. And he mentioned that its executive committee would convene that very day—never mind that the Men's League had promised to hold no meetings. "The world moves," he told her in anticipation of a Christmas visit home. "I'll give it a final push the next two weeks and then I'll retire into Aunt Mary's room and speculate about it until January."

Edwin Markham

John Punnett Peters

Ben B. Lindsey

William Gordon
VerPlanck

Robert Owen

Clarence Mackay

Raymond Robins

Samuel Untermyer

Hamilton Holt

Robert H. Elder

John Hyde Braly

Charles L. Guy

William E. Borah

John E. Milholland

Herbert Parsons

Jesse Lynch Williams

3

# "What Can We Do to Persuade You?"

## 1910

It was not long before the Mere Men of Suffrage established their multipronged approach to championing the cause. The best speakers spoke, the best writers wrote. Well-positioned editors and publishers assigned and placed stories that cast the movement in an attractive light alongside all the other favorable notice the new bursts of support from socially prominent men and women had generated. Others helped grow the League's membership across the state and enabled new chapters elsewhere to proliferate. The most politically connected League members worked their important contacts.

Early in January, George Foster Peabody, Alva Belmont, and Katherine Mackay became half of a reinvigorated state suffrage committee charged with succeeding in a mission that had repeatedly failed. Their mandate was to get a bill introduced in the New York legislature to eliminate the word *male* from the state constitution's suffrage clause. The presence of a man in such a cadre was so unexpected that at least one out-of-state newspaper added a "Mrs." before Peabody's name. There was no Mrs. Peabody at the time.

Other Men's Leaguers—Villard, Rabbi Wise, and William Ivins of the City Club, among them—also served on the suffrage committee for the 1910 legislative session, along with the Reverend Doctor Charles Aked, whose name does not appear on the initial 1910 League charter. Yet Aked had been a strong and faithful voice for women's suffrage from as early as 1908, once going so far as to rank the importance of votes for women with the birth of Christ.

On January 21, Eastman wrote to his mother that he, too, had gone to Albany to work on the renewed legislative initiative, but it was the bigger guns—Peabody and Villard as well as Villard's mother, Fanny—who met with Governor Hughes the following day. Their task was to urge him to recommend that the amendment be submitted for debate. Yet although Hughes was reported to

Pages of the constitution, charter, and first membership roster of the New York Men's League for Woman Suffrage, 1910. (Miller NAWSA Suffrage Scrapbooks, 1897–1911; Scrapbook 9, p. 82; Library of Congress, Rare Book and Special Collections Division)

have "seemed much impressed by the statements made," he remained unmoved. From Albany, Eastman traveled to Ontario, New York, less than a hundred miles north of Elmira—"as my father's and mother's son for 25 dollars an hour. They know what is worth paying for, and I pray God I may not turn out the empty sepulchre of their sainted rhetoric." His preacher parents were well known and respected throughout the area as they had served other local congregations and had a family cottage in Glenora.

Much on Eastman's mind in the early part of the year was the New York shirtwaist workers strike. The walkout had been raging since the Monday before Thanksgiving 1909, and Eastman's sister, Crystal, and his girlfriend, Inez Milholland, were both deeply involved in working with the strikers. So was their friend, Ida Rauh, whom Eastman would later marry. On January 21, Eastman wrote home to say how hard he was finding it to "combine being in love, and earning my living, and taking a Ph.D., and running a reform society with the fulfillment of the desires of filial love . . . especially when your lady love is spending part of the time in jail." Milholland's efforts on behalf of the strikers had more than once led to her arrest.

For Eastman, the line from what would become an enduring chapter in the history of workers' rights to the matter of women's equality was short and taut. The plight of the strikers became the centerpiece of a new prosuffrage argument he began to make, especially to audiences of men. To be for or against women's suffrage, he would say, had come down to nothing more than a matter of tastes. "You dislike women's voting and we like it, and that [is] all the argument there is between us. What can we do to persuade you?"

He went on to assert there was common ground to be found in reaction to the strike. "One of the things that everyone dislikes is an unfair fight," he said, "and such a fight has been waging in New York City for the last three months. It is one of the old fights of the people against oppression. It is being waged by poor women, and it is being waged not only against the competing capitalists who employ them, but against those capitalists backed up by illegal assistance from a government in which women have no position."

The law recognized the rights of union members and their employers during a strike or a lockout, and supposedly ensured fair play with a series of established rules and precedents. Fair play included the rights of strikers to picket and to persuade other workers not to take their jobs, and it prohibited strikers from using threats, violence, or intimidation of any kind. "Their power, at the most, is limited to persuasion and the social opprobrium attaching to the word 'scab,'"

Eastman said. "And the usual function of police and magistrates at a male strike is to prevent the strikers from assaulting or intimidating the scabs."

Yet in this instance, the opposite was happening. The police and magistrates had joined forces with employers to intimidate the striking women, "so that they should be afraid to exercise their right to picket, afraid to patrol the vicinity of the factory, afraid even to sneak up beside a scab and whisper—'Say—did you know there was a strike on?'" The strikers, he said, had been "abused with vile language." They had been "attacked and injured by thugs hired by their employers." Arrests, "high-handed sentencing," and fines had been used to intimidate them. They had been sentenced "not only upon trumped-up charges, but in some cases without even a charge which would make them criminally liable."

Members of the Women's Trade Union League, who were of a generally higher social class and who sympathized with the strikers, had been subject to the same abuse. Eastman took this as evidence "that the official discrimination here is not predominantly against workers but against women." In a footnote, he added that there were exceptions among the police and magistrates and that the "partiality of the courts abated somewhat after the indignation of the public was aroused—a fact which shows that the magistrates have a regard for certain members of the community that they have not for the working women themselves."

"It is a state of affairs that every just man will heartily detest," he concluded. "It is a state of affairs to which he will wish to apply a remedy. And if he happens to be a democrat, as well as a just man, he will not experiment with others until he has applied the remedy which history declares to be a prerequisite to the cure of all oppression, the bestowal of a portion of sovereignty upon the oppressed."

———◦———

Even this early into Eastman's tenure as a sought-after movement spokesman, he had begun to feel discomfort—"disgrace" was the word he used—over the quasi-mercenary nature of his lucrative new mission. Yet the esteem in which he held the suffragists tempered his unease. In a letter to his mother, he anointed the suffragists "the finest in the land." The anterooms where they congregated before meetings were full of good humor. "They're different from mere reformers," he wrote, "they're the people that want to live—which gives me the joyful thought that maybe the prophets of democracy itself were not the one-eyed jackasses that reformers seem to have to be today."

He also reported on his "sort of success in Poughkeepsie" on January 16, sharing the stage with the British suffragette Edith Arnold and the writer Richard F. Connell. "It was a big dingy dim-lighted opera house with a wedge-shaped audience—wedgier than the shape of the room, I mean—and that is enough to destroy all hope of anything brilliant from me." The organizer, he said, was grateful Eastman had "saved the day" after Connell stunned everyone by speaking in favor of confining women to their traditional roles. Eastman said the audience wasn't "handsome—and by a handsome audience I mean an audience that uses its hands—but they giggled with some discrimination."

The *Poughkeepsie Daily Eagle* carried more details, saying Arnold had "slightly bored her audience" by droning on too long about the history of the British movement but Eastman had been "well-received." At the hotel afterward, so many people besieged him that he couldn't finish a sentence. "I felt like one of those agitated mechanical toys you see drawing the crowds on 42nd Street," he wrote home. "I wish I could draw the same kind of crowd."

Not all of Eastman's venues were large auditoriums. In Mrs. Herbert Carpenter's drawing room in New York City, an appearance on January 21 provided fodder for an amusing newspaper item. The wildlife author E. Thompson Seton parted the curtains to join those assembled, but at the sight of all the frilly frocks and feathery hats, he fled. As he reached the front door, he heard Eastman's "despairing wail" and his cry of, "Don't go; please don't."

From this appearance, the press picked up on another fresh riff Eastman had added to his standard remarks. The next generation of mothers, he told his audience, "ought to be something more than a lot of grown-up babies. They ought to know enough about the actual affairs of life to enable them to give their sons some little idea of what they will have to encounter when they go out into the world." To his own mother, he sent the newspaper clippings about the appearance, adding embarrassedly that he had been "dragged into this particular event by accident" and had no intention of "making speeches to ladies' afternoon societies as a regular business."

More helpful publicity appeared in the press in this period. Men from the states and territories that had already given women the vote were especially articulate in expressing their support. Judge Ben B. Lindsey of Colorado weighed in on suffrage in comments carried by the *New York Evening World* and reprinted in other newspapers. Women voters were fifty times as likely as men to be honest and would always support a moral issue and "fight harder than men for their children and their homes," he said, adding, "And that is the greatest countrywide problem we have to solve." He went on to say, "The home is the place where 'the beast's blows strike deepest.' I believe that the surest and swiftest way of overcoming him would be to enfranchise all women. In fact I doubt if we can ever overcome him till women are permitted to help."

Prosuffrage attitudes were becoming common enough among people of note that the usually hostile *New York Sun* gave an entire page of its last Sunday paper in January to evidence of this widening support.

## SUFFRAGISTS IN ALL RANKS.
### THE CRY 'VOTES FOR WOMEN' HEARD ON ALL SIDES

Under the headline came paragraph after paragraph of quotations from artists, singers, actors, scholars, clergy members, and educators who by then had begun counting themselves as movement supporters.

Rabbi Wise, too, did his part for the cause in this period, making suffrage the topic of his sermon on February 5, which rated notice in the *New York Tribune*. But capturing far more media attention that day—"Dogs of war were unloosed," the *New York Herald* reported—was a confrontation at the regular Saturday luncheon of Ivins's City Club. Villard presided over the discussion, which lasted three hours. Eastman and Anna Howard Shaw spoke in favor of the ballot for women. Against were two New York City ministers who, the *Herald* said, "minced no words in their bitter denunciation of the suffragettes and the cause which they represent."

Both the *Tribune* and *Herald* said the first speaker used a neutral start to lull the prosuffrage audience into an accepting mood but then decried the movement as "the gravest social and political peril of the age." The tirade went on long enough for Villard to tap the minister "gently on the arm" and whisper, "Your time is up." The remarks so visibly soured Shaw's mood that as soon as she finished speaking, she walked straight off the platform and out of the building. The speaker who followed Shaw was even more vitriolic than the first. He read an attack on the voting suffragists of Colorado, written by an antisuffragist whom he identified only as a woman. In her diatribe, she described her nemeses as "unfeminine souls in the drabbled finery of their sex" and went on:

They call each other by their last names, without prefix. They congregate in cafes and discuss the situation over glasses, just as men do. They go into the lowest quarters of the city and penetrate the vilest dives to dig up voters and influence these apologies for men by distinctly feminine wiles. They unload a group of besotted male voters from an automobile at a polling booth with all the bravado of a Tammany brave who has been securing a Bowery lodging house. And at rounding up 'repeaters' they have been proved unequalled . . .

Women in the room called out, demanding to know the name of the person who had written the screed. Villard promptly called the luncheon to a close.

The vocal male opponents of suffrage had clearly begun to mount their own offensive. *Pearson's* promoted a fifteen-page article on suffrage in its February 1910 number under the byline of Richard Barry, a journalist described by the editors as "a distinguished war correspondent and trained observer." In a round of interviews, he asked three questions of several major suffrage leaders: Why do women want the ballot? What will they do with the ballot if they get it? And what methods are they using and proposing to use in their attempt to get it? A published explanation for the piece from the magazine's editors said their purpose in publishing it was to explain "why the equal suffrage movement is now so prominent—reasons that are really surprising though they may seem obvious."

Barry cited a poll that Harriot Blatch had conducted in the New York Senate to "secure an expression of opinion on woman suffrage. The result showed sixteen in favor, eight opposed, six non-committal and twenty-one unrecorded." Of these results, Blatch was quoted as telling Barry, "If ever figures could lie, those which poll men's opinions of woman suffrage are the ones. I am too old a bird at this game to believe any American man when he tells me he is in favor of woman suffrage. That is the distressing part of our work."

Barry's piece concluded with five reasons women's suffrage had become so topical: the increased number of women entering industrial fields; the emergence of suffrage militancy in Britain; the need for frothy new topics for political debate; "the fact that nearly every newspaper in the country has at least one woman reporter, that nearly every woman reporter is a suffragist"; and, most significantly, the newly active entrance into the suffrage ranks of the women of "saffron society," Alva Belmont and Katherine Mackay in particular. Although it was clearly not his intention, Barry's summation effectively affirmed the wisdom of the suffrage movement's new outreach strategy, not to mention the still relevant case for promoting diversity in media hiring. He was not the only reporter at the time to point out the significance of suffrage's new publicity-generating adherents. A column item in the *National Tribune* told of how exhausted Belmont had become from working for the cause, a fatigue so acute that her doctor had ordered her to Europe for rest. She had most recently made news by erasing the "color line," as the *San Francisco Call* declared in a headline, by expressly inviting black women to join her Political Equality League and prompting forty new black members to join during a meeting in early February. "I feel that unless this cause means freedom and equal rights to all women of every race, of every creed, rich or poor," she said, "its doctrines are worthless and it must fail." The *National Tribune* counted up her financial contributions to the movement, which by March of 1910, totaled $32,000—what it cost at the time to build a 298-seat theater in Midtown Manhattan.

Cue the requisite catfight. That same item reported that the movement's embrace of socially prominent women and the welcome publicity they were attracting had created some dissension in the ranks, including from the suffrage leader Carrie Chapman Catt, who "had things pretty much her own way" until Belmont came along. "Catt is evidently one of those women who likes to 'run things' and Mrs. Belmont, one of those who objects to being 'run.'" Not only that, the item said, but the movement as a whole had been so receptive to Belmont's energy and generosity that she was getting serious consideration as a candidate for NAWSA's presidency, the job firmly held by Anna Howard Shaw.

The gossip came and went without further mention in the press, but Barry's article so infuriated movement leaders who found it "critical to the cause" that they responded in force. An editorial in the *Woman's Journal* found the piece too loose with the facts. Barry had referred to the married Matilda Joslyn Gage as a "determined spinster," when she was not; said that Blatch had put both her daughters through Cornell, when one of them had died in early childhood; and reported that Belmont—she of the "saffron society"—had been named honorary president of the New York organization, when no such office existed. Such "flagrant errors," the editorial said, cast the rest of Barry's reporting in doubt. "It is no wonder that, in purporting to give interviews with women for whose opinions he has so little sympathy, he should report them as saying many things which their friends know they never could or would have said."

◄◦►

A double bill of Belmont and Eastman during February 1910 commanded crowds across the state. They previewed their performance at a meeting of Belmont's group in Harlem on the first day of the month, then made appearances over the next two weeks in Binghamton, despite its antisuffrage reputation; in Eastman's hometown, Elmira, where a raging blizzard did not deter a crowd from gathering; in Geneva and Ithaca, and on to the great suffrage stronghold Buffalo, the upstate city with the largest concentration of Men's League members. The *Elmira Star-Gazette* could barely contain its pride as it quoted from the praise other newspapers were heaping on its hometown boy, not only for the quality of his oratory and his enviable good looks but for the charm and skill he had demonstrated in organizing the Men's League. The newspaper also mentioned that all this activity had obliged him to take a leave from the philosophy department at Columbia. The headline:

## YOUNG ELMIRAN CREATES A STIR
### MAX EASTMAN HAS ATTRACTED MUCH ATTENTION BY HIS UNIQUE SPEECHES IN FAVOR OF WOMAN'S SUFFRAGE.

Eastman's mother wrote to him to express her delight. "It is idle to tell you all the praises I had for you yesterday at Mrs. Billings' party," she said. "Some were worthwhile especially Dr. Moore, who said you were a revelation to hear." And yet Eastman's success had caused her to wax wistful about the lack of American female orators who could do as well, "that there is no woman to stand on your level—no Mrs. Pankhurst or Mrs. Snowden—logical, fair, and yet a woman."

———◄○►———

All these appearances took place ahead of a heavily promoted mass meeting in Albany that Mackay had taken the lead in organizing for February 16. Even at this early stage of men's involvement, the inverted dynamic that would be their steadfast response to the female suffrage leadership was well forged. Eastman, for example, felt free enough to propose that Mackay limit the speakers to men only: so many legislators had been invited, and so many still needed persuading. His rationale in making the suggestion was a clear outgrowth of his oft-repeated belief that it would take men to convince men. Shaw, Belmont, and Harper thought otherwise, and their opinion prevailed. At the event, Eastman appeared on what was otherwise an all-female bill. Peabody, as the Men's League's president, had honored seating in the front row but made no known remarks.

More than two thousand people crowded Hermanus Bleecker Hall, including workers and socialists who had done their best to get out the word. Mackay had her own box, draped with the blue banner of her Equal Franchise Society. Reporters also spotted the state attorney general in another box and the Republican leader of Albany County, but not the chairman of the Republican State Committee, an absence the *New York Times* pointed out. On the auditorium floor were "several members of the Legislature and not a few State officers." The head of the state suffrage organization remarked on how much the recent formation of the New York Men's League had buoyed the movement.

Eastman spoke first. For this packed audience of New Yorkers from the city and upstate, he drew both on his current status as a resident of Greenwich Village—his apartment was slightly west of Washington Square, at 118 Waverly Place—and on his deep upstate roots. "If you had lived near the scene of the shirtwaist strike in New York for three months as I have," he said, "you would not say anything against the sovereignty of women. . . . When the whole system for three months is working against the rights of the people, you question our democracy." Summoning Elmira, which he still considered home, he said: "When we hear there that a politician from up our way is disgraced at Albany, we say, 'Well, he was good to his family.' What we want to do is make all politicians good to their families and then take their families into the conduct of the government. They will help to keep our institutions free from corruption and graft."

No little thanks to Eastman's highly quotable remarks, the meeting attracted what the women's movement most desired from its investment in new affiliations: significant favorable coverage in all the New York newspapers that would grow its popular appeal with the electorate and with more women. In fact, only the *Brooklyn Eagle* seemed unimpressed by the number of noteworthy men this heavily women-dominated gathering managed to attract. The *Sun* gave the event the most prominent coverage, under a headline on its second page. The article featured Eastman's sharp denunciation of how Mayor William Jay Gaynor, the police, and the courts had handled the shirtwaist strike. The *Sun* was also alone in reporting that Belmont and Mackay had shared the expense of promoting and staging the event, which cost between $2,000 and $3,000—a sum that would be more than $50,000 now—and were said to be "glad of it." Eastman found

# FACTS

## AS TO

# WOMAN SUFFRAGE

## IN THE

## STATE OF NEW YORK

In 1894 *300,000* persons signed the petition in favor of giving women the vote in New York State. Since then there has been an enormous growth of public opinion favorable to woman suffrage.

One indication of this growth is the number of new suffrage organizations, some twenty in number totalling several thousand members, which have been formed within the last few years.

Among these are:

The Equal Franchise Society with *500* members.

The Collegiate Equal Suffrage League—*600* members.

The Men's League for Woman Suffrage—*200* members.

The New York State Woman Suffrage Association, founded in 1869, has organized under it over one hundred and fifty local clubs numbering in active and enrolled members *70,000*.

Of this number *25,000* were added by the Equality League of Self-Supporting Women which was formed three years ago, in January, 1907.

The Letter Carriers Union numbering *2400* has declared in favor of Woman Suffrage.

The New York State Grange numbering over *90,000* members has passed resolutions in favor of Woman Suffrage.

The New York State Women's Christian Temperance Union numbering *30,000* has passed resolutions in favor of Woman Suffrage.

The Western Federation of New York State Women's Clubs numbering *35,000* has voted in favor of Woman Suffrage.

The Working Men's Federation of the State of New York numbering *400,000* has declared for Woman Suffrage.

This record of growth in public opinion favorable to Woman Suffrage surely raises the question to one worthy of careful consideration by the representatives of the State of New York.

THE EQUAL FRANCHISE SOCIETY,

Headquarters: The Ten Eyck,

Albany, N. Y.

"Facts as to Woman Suffrage," ca. February 1910, campaign flyer of the Equal Franchise Society. (Miller NAWSA Suffrage Scrapbooks, 1897–1911; Scrapbook 9, p. 50; pp. 48 and 49 blank; Library of Congress, Rare Book and Special Collections Division) the Albany event to be a "terrible ordeal" and told his mother he thought his speech had been an "utter failure," even though "Mr. Peabody loved it and wants to pay for having it delivered just as often as it can be between now and April!"

Not to be outdone, the antisuffragist forces staged a parallel meeting at which they read out a telegram from Theodore Roosevelt. In it, he declared himself tepid on the subject of suffrage. "Those who know Mr. Roosevelt," scoffed the *Times*, "know he is not tepid about anything."

———◄○►———

In the space of eight weeks, in January and February alone, Eastman made speeches for suffrage at least eleven times. His activism, however, was still cut through with ambivalence. As he left his apartment to speak in Mount Vernon in late February, more on his mind was concern for Milholland, who had fallen ill. He worried when her parents insisted on faith healers rather than surgery, although she ultimately had her appendix removed in March of 1910. A slow recovery put her back in the hospital two months later. ("I won't venture to describe my state of mind," Eastman wrote his mother.) He was also growing weary of the speaking-circuit grind. "I can't make these old speeches over many more times," he groaned in writing. "I'm getting sick to death of 'em." Yet money was unquestionably a strong incentive. In his missives home, he noted that his February earnings from speaker fees totaled $225 on top of the $40 a month he earned from his teaching post at Columbia. That made him the richest member of his family, he later recalled, "to the considerable amazement of all."

With hindsight more than thirty years in the making, Eastman, in his memoir, expounds further on how stumping for suffrage made him feel. At the time, he never quite admitted how much he would rather have stayed home. "There was nothing harder for a man with my mamma's-boy complex to do than stand up and be counted as a 'male suffragette,'" he wrote. "It meant not only that I had asserted my manhood, but that I had passed beyond the need of asserting it. I am not such a sissy that I dare not champion the rights of women: that extreme demand upon myself was, I think, a part of my motive in accepting the role of suffrage orator." He then acknowledged the practical explanation for his perseverance. "It solved magically my second chief problem: how to earn a living with a part-time job that did not consist of writing."

In a development mostly but not entirely unrelated, Villard and his wife traveled by steamer to Bermuda on February 18 and met up—Villard's memoir says by chance—with Woodrow Wilson, who at his wife's insistence was on the island seeking respite from his battles as university president with Princeton's combative board. Villard recalled that on the return steamer, as he and Wilson walked the deck, he broached the subject of Wilson's running for governor of New Jersey. Should he do so, Villard said, both he and the *Post* would prove fervent backers. Wilson vacillated until the last minute and only announced that he would be a candidate five months later, on July 12. That summer, Villard wrote to express his eagerness to meet with the candidate. "We want to exert a greater influence in New Jersey than ever before, in your behalf," Villard said, adding, "Believe me, nothing has so inspired and invigorated us here in the office for a long time as the prospect that we may have the pleasure and satisfaction of battling for you for the Governorship of New Jersey."

Other key members of the Men's League shared this view, including George Harvey, who at the Lotos Club as far back as 1906 had surprised a room full of college presidents and much of the New York press by persuasively proclaiming Wilson the next Democratic nominee for president of the United States, effectively launching Wilson's political career. Villard would later say, "I was the second influential newspaper man to put myself behind the Wilson boom. The first was George Harvey."

Back in Albany, the suffragists planned a second mass gathering for March 9, in the Assembly Chamber, when the judiciary committee of the Assembly was scheduled to meet. The hearing attracted trainloads of women from across the state, representing both the pro and anti forces. On the pro side, the *New York Sun* said, "Some of them seemed to think that there was special significance in the fact that Peabody and Samuel Untermyer added their oratory to that of the women advocates of the cause." Untermyer was a wealthy lawyer and civic leader whose remarks made all the newspapers. "In every great controversy for freedom the law has always been in the wrong. It represents the ultra conservatism of the nation," he said, adding that this was "particularly true of the present movement. Women are eligible with men for the electric chair, the prison, and the tax roll. It seems intolerable that they should be ineligible for the ballot, the jury box, and to have their part in framing the laws under which they are required to live."

The State Senate was not in session, so no members of its judiciary committee were officially present at the hearing, although a couple of them briefly looked in. In the end, the women themselves urged that no referendum be held, given the costs, since there was no guarantee the legislature would act on the advice such a referendum would produce from the electorate.

And so despite all the expense, passion, and effort, the Albany campaign of 1910 ended, as it had so many times before, without enough support to guarantee success. Yet, as the *New York Tribune* pointed out, women on both sides of the question had managed to deliver a "bewildering quantity of argument," adding, "At the last report from the members they had completely survived, though with some suffering. The bill advocated by the suffragists suffered most, and there is small hope of its recovery."

◄○►

All the same, in 1910, even without any game-changing inroads into the legislature, more men of importance publicly proclaimed their prosuffrage stances. The author and socialist Franklin H. Wentworth gave an address at Carnegie Hall, titled "The Woman's Portion," at an event under the auspices of the Woman of the Socialist Party. Another author, Frederic Arnold Kummer, published a short story in the March 1910 issue of *Smart Set*, poking fun at the adverse effect all this meeting attendance was having on the institution of marriage. Although his send-up wasn't exactly prosuffrage, it highlighted a big issue of the day: the impact on couples of women's support for the cause. "Mrs. Hathaway has given up her political work," is the way the story ends, "having taken up a new hobby—her husband. Also she is learning to cook."

The Brooklyn papers dubbed Eastman the "hero of the evening" to "the wealth and aristocracy of Flushing" for an address "sparked with wit" that he gave on March 16 in Queens in an appearance with Carrie Chapman Catt. By this point, Eastman never missed an opportunity to cite the "wonderful work" the Men's League was doing in "assisting the women in getting the ballot." Provocatively, he declared, "I am not a suffragist and I don't believe that any woman in America is. What I want, and I believe there are a great many other men in this country of the same opinion, is to get equal rights for women."

———◄●►———

In April came big news surrounding the NAWSA national convention in Washington, DC. Taft had agreed to become the first US president to address such a gathering along with

## OTHER DISTINGUISHED MEN.

That was how the *Washington Herald* headlined the expected appearances of Eastman, Senator Robert L. Owen of Oklahoma, and the Chicago labor activist Raymond Robins, who appeared with his wife, Margaret Robins of the National Women's Trade Union League. In all, by the *Chicago Tribune*'s count, a thousand women attended the convention along with twenty-five men.

Given Taft's dodge on the suffrage question in his Mississippi speech in November of 1909, it might have occurred to NAWSA's leaders that inviting him to address their convention involved some risk, albeit outweighed by the fact of his presence on a NAWSA stage. This no doubt became clearer as his remarks unfolded. "I am not entirely certain that I ought to have come here tonight, but your committee which invited me assured me that I should be welcome even if I did not support all the views which are to be advanced in this convention," Taft began. "But I consider that this movement represents a sufficient part of the intelligence of the community to justify my coming here and welcoming you to Washington."

The president recalled how, as a sixteen-year-old in Cincinnati, he had chosen for his graduation subject women's suffrage, which he strongly advocated at the time, as did his father. Yet since then, he said, his views had changed. Then he used a truly unfortunate allusion to emphasize a typical anti-argument: how the indifference or opposition to the suffrage cause of so many intelligent, patriotic women made granting all women the vote an untenable prospect. His words:

> The theory that Hottentots or any uneducated and altogether unintel-
> ligent class is fitted for self-government is a theory that I wholly dissent
> from, but this qualification is not applicable to the question here. The

other qualification to which I call attention is that the class should as a whole care enough to look after its interests, to take part as a whole in the exercises of political power if it is conferred. Now, if it does not care enough for this then it seems to me that the danger is, if the power is conferred, that it may be exercised by that part of the class least desirable as political constituents and may be neglected by many of those who are intelligent and patriotic and would be most desirable as members of the electorate.

After that, as the *New York Times*' front-page headline blared the next day,

## SUFFRAGETTES HISS TAFT, THEIR GUEST

It was a reaction Taft later said had not offended him in the least, although the *Washington Post*'s front-page headline included the line:

## PRESIDENT COLORS, BUT REMAINS CALM UNDER INSULT

The newspapers described the hissing as sustained and said it emanated from several parts of the hall. As it died down, the president offered a quick and condescending rejoinder. "Now my dear ladies," he said, "you must show yourselves equal to self-government by exercising in listening to opposing arguments that degree of restraint without which successful self-government is impossible." The outbursts stopped and when Taft finished speaking, applause was loud. The well-wishing that followed struck reporters as sincere.

NAWSA's reflection on this episode consumes six pages of apologia in the movement's official history. Its account adds context, including previously unreported details from the suffragists' perspective, and copies of letters and other documents to explain what happened before, during, and after the outbursts. The leadership clearly considered the episode an embarrassment. "A most unwise and ungracious act," Shaw is quoted as saying to the full assemblage the morning after it occurred. "We feel the keenest possible regret over it." NAWSA's version reported only a "slight hissing in the back part of the room," followed by Shaw's springing to her feet with an exclamation of "Oh, my children!" after which the audience became quiet and respectful.

On the third day of the convention, Eastman delivered his own speech, titled "Woman and Democracy," in which he countered Taft's assertion that to grant women the vote before all American women expressed the desire for it would mean that only the "least desirable" among them would be brought into the political process. Eastman acknowledged that the first women to vote might well strengthen "the forces of Tammany for a time, but then a better class of women in New York would come to the polls against it." The *Washington Times* praised Eastman as among the week's most notable speakers, but declared not Eastman but John Braly of Los Angeles "the most ardent suffragist of them all."

Braly's involvement with the movement began in 1910 with his founding of the California Political Equality League. Beyond his family, he considered his work for the passage of the state suffrage amendment in California, which his parents had settled as early pioneers, the proudest accomplishment of his life. "I saw that the men must be awakened," he wrote in his autobiography, self-published in 1912. "Prominent men must be fully aroused to this vital question, men whose names would carry weight with not only the influential women, but with all high-minded thinking people." Like the New York league, the California organization began with one hundred prominent members, but unlike New York's all-male group, its West Coast counterpart included women, too. After the Washington convention, Braly and his wife remained on the East Coast for another two months, to get closer to those at the movement's epicenter as they prepared for the westernmost campaign.

———◦———

For spring, the attention within the suffragist ranks turned to May 21, the date of the first of what would be five New York Suffrage Day parades between 1910 and 1913. The Men's League did not float a delegation of marchers the first year, as Harper's history of the movement mistakenly records, but gaining more favor with more men had been one of the movement's strategic objectives in deciding to mount such a grand and costly spectacle. Harper explained this at length in an essay for the *New York Sun*.

Thousands of men who would never attend a meeting gladly "stood for three hours in Union Square," she wrote, and listened to prosuffrage arguments under continuous heavy showers. The *New York Times* estimated the number of men and women who watched the parade at ten thousand, calling it "the biggest suffrage demonstration ever held in the United States." The event started at Fifty-Ninth Street and gathered more women by the time the procession reached Seventeenth Street and flowed into Union Square. As flags waved and banners swung, the crowd, Harper wrote, "realized for the first time that women's suffrage was a vital tangible question and began to think about it. Scores of women inspired by the sight fell into line and thus identified themselves with the movement." Politicians saw the parade or read "the fifty columns devoted to it by the New York papers," allowing them to understand "as never before that the women meant business and that woman suffrage was henceforth to be a political issue." Among the dozens of speakers in Union Square was one man, a charter member of the Men's League, Robert H. Elder, the assistant district attorney.

Harper also noted the immediate impact of the spectacle. Five days later, the State Senate at Albany called the suffrage bill out of committee, "after this had been persistently refused all winter." The "sixty-three automobiles" that had rolled down Fifth Avenue, carrying the movement's many female leaders, "emphasized as words could not do that every member from New York would face a political organization of women on his return home to whom he must account for his vote on this bill."

—◦—

In the months ahead, more prominent men wrote prosuffrage essays. In the *Outlook*, the labor and civil rights activist Paul Kennaday published "Where Women Vote," a report about the women of Australia and New Zealand. "'How does it feel to be an enfranchised woman?' I asked a New Zealand woman one day shortly after my arrival in her daring little land of successful big experiments. 'And how does it feel to be an enfranchised man?' was the wise and complete answer to my rather silly joke." The women's magazine the *Delineator* included an article by Senator William E. Borah of Idaho, who reminded readers how early in its statehood Idaho had given the vote to women, and explained why he personally supported women's suffrage. He echoed Judge Lindsey of Colorado in saying, "when a moral question is up for consideration, the majority vote of the women has been a power upon the right side."

The Quaint Club and the Twilight Club joined forces for a dinner at the National Arts Club in New York City on May 24 that featured guests from the Men's League. John E. Milholland, father of Inez, was tapped as the toastmaster. In the course of the evening, a charged debate erupted over the importance of the English writer and philosopher Mary Wollstonecraft. Editors at the *New York Times* were so amused, they published this headline:

## THE SUFFRAGE CAUSE INVADES THE MEN'S CLUBS

Stories about the cause also stormed the magazines. The *Chautauquan* devoted the whole of its June 1910 issue to women's organizations, including fifteen pages of prosuffrage material cobbled together from information provided by NAWSA and several other suffrage groups. The magazine also published five pages of antisuffrage material under the byline of Mrs. Barclay Hazard.

Summer was quiet, but the fall brought renewed energy to the movement with the opening of enlarged suffrage headquarters in New York City and a flurry of new initiatives designed, as the headline in the *New York Tribune* told its readers,

### TO CONVERT MERE MAN
#### Great Suffrage Demonstration
#### Planned for October 29.

That was the original plan, starting with a huge parade and pageant. But organizers soon rescheduled the event until the spring because of the work and expense involved. The *New York Times* reported that thirty-five of the forty artists asked to assist with designs for banners had responded positively and that Peabody, Harvey, Herbert Parsons of J.P. Morgan, and the painter William Glackens were among those who had contributed to defray the costs.

The League also covered Eastman's expenses to attend both of the New York State political party conventions of 1910, so he could consort with the Republicans in Saratoga on September 27 and 28 and the Democrats in Rochester the following two days. Eastman made his by now usual complement of suffrage speeches that month. In October, he spoke at the Boston funeral of the beloved suffragist Julia Ward Howe—a clear tribute to Eastman's prowess and the Men's League itself as suffrage's newest organized ally. Eastman put a new top on his standard address and described Howe in unvarnished but glowing terms as "one of those people who have a genius for life itself and who give a joyful flavor not to books but to the actual onward experience of the world they live in."

Although Eastman had been announced as a speaker for the Woman Suffrage Political Convention at Carnegie Hall on October 28, he did not appear. He was summoned home on October 21, the day after his eulogy for Howe. His beloved mother had worked in the morning and then unexpectedly suffered a stroke by afternoon, complications from which caused her death two days later.

Earlier in the month, Annis Eastman's last letters to her son seemed to presage her end. She worried over having mislaid Eastman's dissertation before having had a chance to read it, as if sensing that the opportunity had been forever lost. For Eastman, the death of his mother was a profound event and deeply felt, to be sure, but, "In a pattern of behavior that would repeat itself again and again when people close to him died," Eastman's biographer, Christoph Irmscher, writes, "Max had absolutely nothing to say about it." He was not among the eulogists at her memorial service on October 30 in Elmira, at the Park Church, which she and her husband had served. The Reverend Doctor William C. Gannett of the Unitarian Church in Rochester, the late Susan B. Anthony's congregation, offered one. He was a charter member of the Men's League. Of Annis Eastman, he said, "She was the type of woman to come, who shall move with power, not in the home alone, but in that larger home of the community." The wish she had expressed to be able to vote in her lifetime, which had seemed so nearly within her grasp a year earlier, would remain just that.

At the Carnegie Hall event, Snowden was the convention's main attraction, coupled with her distinguished parliamentarian husband, or, as the *Tribune* called him, the "Man Suffragette." The *New York Tribune* captured the "gloriously political" mood of the day in its story's lead paragraph, even as it acknowledged that a political convention without the right to vote might have seemed "like *Hamlet* without the melancholy Dane."

Author Jesse Lynch Williams got attention in the press for his essay in the December issue of McClure's *Ladies' World*—"one of the best issues of that admirable publication that we have seen," a reviewer reported, adding that Williams had "calmly, logically and without bias" responded one by one to the "ordinary arguments against granting women the vote"—"It would destroy the home," "Women cannot go to war." "It's unwomanly." "My husband says it's absurd."

For the Men's League, the most important event of the season was its hosting of "the largest suffrage dinner ever given" in New York, at the Aldine Club on December 13, an occasion the *New York Times* found "notable for the many men present." Peabody gave a rousing speech to the six hundred attendees, noting with pleasure how many men had responded to the cards placed on each table inviting them to sign up for League membership on the spot. "I do not think there are many men antis," he said.

Not long before the Aldine Club dinner, the journalist Richard Barry—him again—had caused a firestorm with his latest article on the Votes for Women movement. *Ladies' Home Journal* assigned him to investigate, as the title of the

*Will you suggest some men (+ women) to invite?*
*M.E.*

# THE MEN'S LEAGUE FOR WOMAN SUFFRAGE

REQUESTS THE HONOR OF YOUR PRESENCE AT A

## DINNER

TO BE HELD AT THE

ALDINE CLUB, 200 FIFTH AVENUE

TUESDAY EVENING, DECEMBER THIRTEENTH

AT SEVEN-THIRTY O'CLOCK

GUEST OF HONOR

### MRS. PHILIP SNOWDEN

SPEAKERS

GEORGE FOSTER PEABODY, PRESIDING

JOHN MITCHELL
VICE-PRESIDENT NATIONAL CIVIC FEDERATION

HON. HENRY GEORGE, JR.
CONGRESSMAN-ELECT

HAMILTON HOLT
EDITOR THE INDEPENDENT

MRS. CARRIE CHAPMAN CATT
CHAIRMAN WOMAN SUFFRAGE PARTY

REV. J. HOWARD MELISH
RECTOR CHURCH OF THE HOLY TRINITY

HON. CHARLES L. GUY
JUDGE OF THE SUPREME COURT

COMMITTEE

| CHARLES C. BURLINGHAM | DR. SIMON FLEXNER |
| PROF. JOHN DEWEY | PROF. VLADIMIR SIMKHOVITCH |
| OSWALD GARRISON VILLARD | CHARLES H. STRONG |
| MAX EASTMAN | |

DINNER CARDS, TWO DOLLARS

Men's League Dinner Invitation, December 13, 1910, with hand notation by Max Eastman. (Miller NAWSA Suffrage Scrapbooks, 1897–1911; Scrapbook 9, p. 83; Library of Congress, Rare Book and Special Collections Division) piece proclaimed, "What Women Have Actually Done Where They Vote: A Personal Investigation into the Laws, Records and Results of the Four Equal-Suffrage States of America: Colorado, Idaho, Utah, and Wyoming."

In a precede, the magazine's editor, Edward Bok, said that although from a policy standpoint *Ladies' Home Journal* opposed women's suffrage,

> it stood prepared and ready impartially to print the results of Mr. Barry's investigation no matter which side the investigation favoured. What *Ladies Home Journal* wanted was to get at the actual truth from the actual authoritative records of the States. And these, it believes, are presented in Mr. Barry's article.

Bok listed the reasons for granting women the vote in those states as the positive impact it would have on women's wages and working conditions, on reforms in child labor, on marriage laws, and on the regulation of "the social evil." Barry's findings made that impact look soft at best. For instance, Oklahoma, which was considered to have the best child labor laws in the United States, built its model on the laws of New York, Illinois, Massachusetts, Ohio, Wisconsin, and Nebraska—not one of which had yet amended its constitution in favor of women voters.

As to women's working conditions, Barry asserted that laws limiting the number of hours a woman could work had been passed in twenty states, but not in any of the four with suffrage for women. He quoted Carrie Chapman Catt as saying, that when women will have the vote, prostitution would end. And yet in Denver, he found illegitimate births among young girls increasing at as alarming a rate as they were in Utah. "Idaho and Wyoming, being rural communities, can show a better record," he wrote, "but still no better than similar communities elsewhere."

*Twentieth Century Magazine* carried Ethel C. Macomber's challenge to what she considered to be Barry's unscrupulous handling of statistics. His table on divorce in Colorado, for example, showed a marked increase in filings since the granting of the vote but failed to note how much the population had grown in the same period.

NAWSA responded in pamphlet form with a paragraph-by-paragraph refutation of Barry's investigation, titled "The Truth Versus Richard Barry." "Certain utterly frivolous charges," it advised, "are ignored." The *Literary Digest* summed up the anger Barry's article had caused by quoting the protestations of Colorado's *Denver News*. In a caustic response, the *News* objected to Barry's contention that wherever suffrage had been enacted, it had perpetrated only evil. The newspaper described Barry's reporting as a pile of "petty slanders of the Barry-Bok type." "If one might believe the wild wailings of Dicky Barry and Great Aunt Bok," the item said, "woman suffrage is the Beast of Revelation, the source of all evil, the organ of all the woes of four States, and now to become the fountain of misrule for a fifth [Washington]. Luckily, no one believes such slanders save the author and the publisher of the same."

The *New York Times* covered Barry's report as if its findings were hard science. The suffragists were so exercised over what he had written that they stormed an anti event at which Barry was the featured speaker. The ensuing debate in letters to the *Times* kept going from mid-November 1910, when the *Ladies' Home Journal* piece first appeared as its December number, until early February 1911. This was no doubt encouraged by the article's January 1911 reprint in the British women's magazine, *Lady's Realm*. Major pro and anti leaders called out flaws in Barry's presentation of facts, firing off rebuttals, and then answering the slings that came back. Barry, for instance, claimed that he had quoted Catt correctly in his *Pearson's* article back in February 1910, even though he had omitted her name, and that if she really had objected to what was published, she would have said so at the time. Alice Stone Blackwell responded quickly, reminding Barry and the *Times* that indeed her *Woman's Journal* had promptly taken issue with the accuracy of the *Pearson's* article as soon as it appeared.

Another anti involved in the letter-writing barrage was Annie Nathan Meyer, a founder of Barnard College. In an interesting twist of internecine social engagement, Meyer was the sister of Maud Nathan, the suffragist leader and president of the Consumer's League of New York, as well as the sister-in-law and first cousin of Frederick Nathan, Maud's husband (and first cousin, too). In 1911, Frederick Nathan would emerge locally, nationally, and internationally in Men's League affairs, as would two other new key figures: Peabody's close associate and aide de camp, Robert Cameron Beadle, and James Lees Laidlaw, a scion of Old New York. Laidlaw could trace his Colonial American heritage back through fifty different lines. His wife, Harriet Burton Laidlaw, was the Manhattan borough leader for suffrage at the time and would quickly rise through the state suffrage ranks.

———◄◦►———

Theodore Roosevelt liked to say he had been advocating for women's rights as far back as 1880, when he chose the subject as his senior thesis at Harvard. He equivocated, however, on giving suffrage any place whatsoever during his two terms as president, a stance he foreshadowed in an 1898 letter he wrote to the suffragist Lillie Devereux Blake on stationery from the New York Republican State Committee of New York:

> I believe in Woman's Suffrage, as you know, but I believe a good deal more in equal pay for equal work for women. I do not know whether we could get Women's Suffrage. I do not think it would accomplish nearly as much as you believe, and I would much rather provide for something we could get, and which would certainly do good.

While he was in office, he infuriated the suffrage supporters of New York City in December 1908 when he went on record in favor of suffrage in a letter that just as quickly added that he was "not an enthusiastic advocate of it, because I do not regard it as a very important matter." At the time, Roosevelt said he could not see that any benefit had accrued to women in states that had adopted suffrage when compared with adjoining jurisdictions that had not. The anti forces found the letter useful enough to read out at a meeting in New York City the same month.

Six months after Roosevelt left office, his position on suffrage had not much changed, as evidenced by his appearance at the Duchess County Fair in Poughkeepsie on September 29, 1910. His wide-ranging remarks gave Eastman grist for one of his own major addresses, which the *North American Review* published a few months later under the title, "Is Woman Suffrage Important?" What caught Eastman's attention was the "high tribute" Roosevelt paid "to the mother who does her duty," quickly adding that "the man who doesn't help her is the meanest creature in God's created universe." It was a setup for a stinging comment on women's place. "As to that," Roosevelt said, "decent men should be thinking about women's rights all the time, and while the men are doing that—the women should be attending to their duties."

Eastman saw Roosevelt's phrasing as a way to supplant "a political issue with a moral platitude." Eastman led his next essay with those very words. He went on from there to explain more fully why so many men had moved with such conviction to involve themselves in women's suffrage, and to point out Roosevelt's flawed framing of the issue. He said it revealed that Roosevelt still saw the movement as "a clamor for rights," which was not a motivator for even "one fiftieth" of the women involved in the cause and for none of the men. "The heart of their enthusiasm is not an acknowledgment that equal suffrage is abstractly right or just," Eastman wrote, "but a conviction that it is important. In my opinion, it has an importance too far-reaching for the grasp of persons immersed in politics or business."

Robert Cameron Beadle

James Lees Laidlaw

Simon Flexner

Frederick Nathan

George Creel

Harvey Washington Wiley

James Brady

Peter J. Brady

George Middleton

Witter Bynner

Vladimir Simkhovitch

Harold Spielberg

Richard Le Gallienne

Upton Sinclair

Arthur Brisbane

Norman Hapgood

4

# "Jeers and Abuse"

## 1911

In February of 1911, as activists again pressed for passage of a suffrage amendment to the New York constitution, they staged a "Suffrage Week" in Albany and Manhattan, laying on "every conceivable scheme calculated to bring the question before the public." Eastman traveled upstate to represent what the *New York Tribune* described as "between four and five hundred Republicans and Democrats of the state who had joined together in a league for the purpose of securing suffrage for women." Two Coloradans were featured speakers, Judge Ben B. Lindsey and the suffrage state's former governor, Charles S. Thomas.

Eastman told a gathering at the Hotel Ten Eyck that extending the rights of citizenship to American women had become a necessity, especially given how many of them had joined the workforce year after year, many laboring under conditions that endangered health and motherhood. By 1900, he said, one fifth of the entire female population of the United States had been counted as employed outside the home.

In New York City, the Hotel Astor became the site of a Susan B. Anthony Suffrage Bazaar, featuring a committee composed of Villard's mother, Fanny, and *Mesdames* Robert Elder, James Lees Laidlaw, Frederick Nathan, Samuel Untermyer, Simon Flexner, and Stephen Wise, all women whose husbands were among the League's most visible leaders. Such a list points out how many of the League's mainstays engaged in the movement as husbands who offered valuable direct and indirect financial contributions to the campaign alongside the often-sacrificial volunteerism of their wives and their own considerable actions as movement men.

Objects for sale at the bazaar were as diverse as the supporters the suffragists hoped to attract: a child's bathrobe, pickled tomatoes and various homemade jams, a photograph of Anthony, two autographed novels, a copper kettle, a suffrage

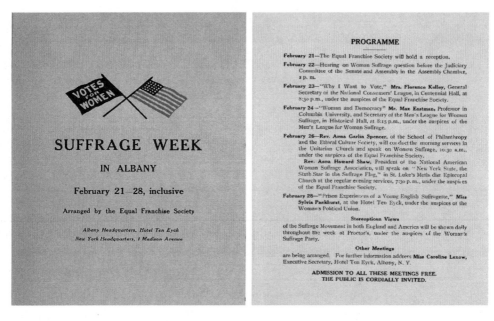

PROGRAMME

**February 21**—The Equal Franchise Society will hold a reception.

**February 22**—Hearing on Woman Suffrage question before the Judiciary Committee of the Senate and Assembly in the Assembly Chamber, 2 p. m.

**February 23**—"Why I Want to Vote," **Mrs. Florence Kelley,** General Secretary of the National Consumers' League, in Centennial Hall, at 8:30 p.m., under the auspices of the Equal Franchise Society.

**February 24**—"Woman and Democracy," **Mr. Max Eastman,** Professor in Columbia University, and Secretary of the Men's League for Woman Suffrage, in Historical Hall, at 8:15 p.m., under the auspices of the Men's League for Woman Suffrage.

**February 26**—**Rev. Anna Garlin Spencer,** of the School of Philanthropy and the Ethical Culture Society, will conduct the morning services in the Unitarian Church and speak on Woman Suffrage, 10:30 a.m., under the auspices of the Equal Franchise Society.

**Rev. Anna Howard Shaw,** President of the National American Woman Suffrage Association, will speak on "New York State, the Sixth Star in the Suffrage Flag," in St. Luke's Methodist Episcopal Church at the regular evening services, 7:30 p.m., under the auspices of the Equal Franchise Society.

**February 28**—"Prison Experiences of a Young English Suffragette," **Miss Sylvia Pankhurst,** at the Hotel Ten Eyck, under the auspices of the Woman's Political Union.

**Stereopticon Views**

of the Suffrage Movement in both England and America will be shown daily throughout the week at Proctor's, under the auspices of the Woman's Suffrage Party.

**Other Meetings**

are being arranged. For further information address **Miss Caroline Lexow,** Executive Secretary, Hotel Ten Eyck, Albany, N. Y.

**ADMISSION TO ALL THESE MEETINGS FREE.**
**THE PUBLIC IS CORDIALLY INVITED.**

SUFFRAGE WEEK

IN ALBANY

February 21–28, inclusive

Arranged by the Equal Franchise Society

*Albany Headquarters, Hotel Ten Eyck*
*New York Headquarters, 1 Madison Avenue*

Suffrage Week program, Albany, February 21–28, 1911. (Miller NAWSA Suffrage Scrapbooks, 1911, Library of Congress, Rare Book and Special Collections Division)

sash in the movement's signature purple and yellow, and a yellow pin cushion. The actress Grace Filkins took on the role of an anti and harangued audiences packed into a "Chamber of Horrors." "This dreadful hysteria among a certain class of my sex makes me shudder," she said. "Why, one can't pick up a daily newspaper without finding some stuff about why these creatures want to vote, and often it's in the middle of the fashion column. Only this morning I was reading a most practical article on how to get ink stains out of rugs when my eye caught an unpleasant reference to child labor and what women want to do about it. I have always told my children not to associate with any one whose parents are in trade." Inez Milholland read palms amid elaborate tableaux, one of which depicted the "ideal woman," a waxen figure in a stylish frock who, when turned around, revealed she had a hollow head. Another portrayed a group of women lawyers, doctors, teachers, and factory workers as they implored Uncle Sam to give them the vote.

Back in Albany, there were street signs, newspaper ads, films about the suffrage cause, and indoor and open air mass meetings. Days of speakers on platforms culminated at week's end with the appearance of Britain's Sylvia Pankhurst, daughter of Emmeline, who titled her remarks the "Prison Experience of a Young

Suffragette." A crowd of women as large, if not larger than 1910's, again converged on the capital to advocate for legislative passage of the suffrage amendment. Just as many antis showed up to press against it.

Judge Lindsey enchanted the prosuffrage gathering with his views on the relative purity of women in politics. The *New York Tribune* said he instantly became a hero in the eyes of the thousand women assembled as he "quickly put to flight the arguments of that doubting magazine writer, Richard Barry, who so sacrilegiously attacked the way women were governing Colorado." Anger over Barry's piece was still simmering, months after its publication. Barry appeared in Albany on behalf of the antis.

Eastman spoke about the wave of militancy overtaking the British movement. Such a tactic, he said wryly, would never work on this side of the Atlantic, because American women had so little to militate against. For instance, when an American woman would call out from the gallery of Congress to know how a representative stood on suffrage for women, the congressman would smile gallantly and then reassure her that this had been his position since before she was born. Eastman, along with Wise, Charles Beard, and George Creel, another increasingly active male suffragist, would come to hold more nuanced views of the British movement's aggressive tactics. However, under Peabody's leadership, the US Men's League as a body did not even attempt the neutrality that its British cousins had adopted. It would consistently oppose militancy of any kind.

At the end of February, John and Alice Dewey endured an infuriating episode. A newspaper reported they would be holding a suffrage meeting at their apartment in Harlem to which "Negroes" had been invited. The building they lived in, the St. Cecilia, was on St. Nicholas Terrace, alongside St. Nicholas Park at 130th Street. Its leasing company at the time took steps to obtain an injunction to prevent the gathering. The *New York Times* reported that with no more evidence than a newspaper item to support its claim, the effort failed. The Deweys, when asked, simply declined to confirm or deny. *The Anti-Suffragist* newsletter reported with some glee that the meeting had to be called off. It quoted the *Baltimore Sun* saying, "If the woman suffragists wish to gain converts for their cause in the States lying south of the Mason and Dixon line, they have gone about it in a queer way."

————◆————

As Woodrow Wilson prepared to take office as New Jersey's governor—he had won decisively in November—the president and secretary of the New Jersey Woman Suffrage Association were among the first to write to him. A letter from Clara Schlee Laddey and Mary Loring Colvin arrived a full two weeks before his inauguration. "In the press of present issues the cause this Association represents may not seem big or vital," their letter said, "but we assure you, when we think of the noble army of women who for the past sixty years have given their strength and their lives that the cause might triumph, we, who are endeavoring to carry on the work do feel it to be both big and vital." Wilson's papers include no reply.

Virginia Tyler Hudson, a reporter for the *Globe and Commercial Advertiser* of New York, won an interview with the new governor and, among other questions, asked: How about suffrage for women? The governor's eyes lit up, she wrote. "'Ah, there is my wife,' he exclaimed. 'I must speak to her a moment. Thank you so much for your interest and for not detaining me long.'"

Villard had been making his own unrelated appeal to Wilson since the November election. He wanted the governor to appoint as his secretary one of the *New York Evening Post*'s subeditors, a former reporter for the *New York Sun* named Charles Albert Selden, who conveniently happened to live in New Jersey. Wilson did not respond to Villard about the idea for some weeks. Finally Wilson explained that "the plot thickens around me here," for the New Jersey machine forces of Senator James Smith Jr. had begun mounting against him. The machine had turned itself inside out to undermine Wilson because Wilson had turned his back on Smith and his cronies, who had gone to great lengths to help get him elected. He was going to need a secretary with knowledge of New Jersey politics in the extreme, experience that Selden lacked. Wilson said he hoped Selden would not be too disappointed. Villard replied that indeed Selden wished he had been asked to serve "for he is as keen as the rest of us for your great fight" to combat corruption and machine politics in the state, but that he, like all the top editors at the *Post*, also understood and supported Wilson's decision to choose a political lieutenant for the job. Villard added that the *Post* planned to send another reporter to New Jersey, which Wilson said he would welcome. "Certainly nothing has done greater service," Wilson wrote, than "the splendid support of the *Evening Post* in our fight on this side of the river." Rabbi Wise was a Republican but made a point in this period of cultivating a relationship with Wilson, too.

———◦———

George Creel was one of Wilson's earliest and most loyal supporters. It was an enchantment that started when Creel was a young reporter in Kansas City and Wilson, then president of Princeton, came to town to speak to a group of high school students. The admiration—"devotion" was Creel's word—only grew. He and Judge Lindsey had a major piece in the February number of the *Delineator* that found its way into the middle of the Richard Barry imbroglio. The article documented how well women's suffrage was working out in Colorado, where Lindsey was based, and where Creel had been an editor of the *Rocky Mountain News* and Denver's chief of police.

Soon after the *Delineator* hit the newsstands in mid-January, Annie Nathan Meyer dismissed the article in a letter to the *New York Times*, saying it offered no response to any of Barry's points. Caroline I. Reilly, NAWSA's press chairman, shot back on behalf of the suffragists. Meyer, she wrote, was "laboring under a misapprehension." Although the *Delineator* article appeared in mid-January, it had been assigned many months earlier. The writers had turned it in well before the publication date of Barry's latest piece. Reilly said that Creel and Lindsay never meant it as a response to Barry, whom she described with scorn as "the gentleman who spent a short time in Denver, where he claims to have gleaned facts from 'an old Senator,' 'a prominent woman,' 'one of the highest officials,' 'a political manager,' and so on up and down the line." Even after Creel had read the Barry article, Reilly wrote, he had not considered responding because Barry's work rang so false that "no intelligent person would take it seriously."

Creel shared both Lindsey's Colorado roots and his enthusiasm for suffrage, which, in Creel's case, he liked to say, sprung directly from "the deep conviction that my mother outweighed any man when it came to brains and character." This was even though both Creel's mother and his wife, the actress Blanche Bates, were professed antis. He said his years in Colorado, where women had been voting since 1893, gave him special "value as an eyewitness," and he spent a good deal of time with Carrie Chapman Catt and Anna Howard Shaw "supporting their arguments with a personal report."

Catt, as president of the International Women's Suffrage Association in 1911, had its Stockholm convention to prepare for in April. Surviving reports describe this sixth gathering as a triumph for the world body. "Even the small and weak associations have caught the note and changed from discouragement to hope," wrote Mary Gray Peck, a conference attendee and Catt's eventual biographer. Since the London convention in 1909, the group's membership had grown from seven to twenty-seven national delegations, and in that time, women in fifteen of those countries had won what Peck described as "full political and industrial victories."

The writer enumerated five aspects of the 1911 assembly that distinguished it from the previous ones: the gracious hospitality of the Swedes; the "sculptural stateliness" of Catt's address; the strong denunciation of women's "economic serfdom" and a new emphasis on women in industry; the presence of the first delegation from the General Federation of Women's Clubs of the United States; and finally, a development the Scandinavian press seized upon: the appearance of "courageous gentlemen from six devoted lands," who came to form the International Men's League. Their photo appeared in all the newspapers, Peck said. "The men's leagues have come in for more laughter than anything else, hitherto," she wrote, "but when the brethren get up spunk enough to attend congresses with the sistren, and call themselves together to form a world organization, it has got beyond being a laughing matter." Frederick Nathan, the businessman husband of Maud, and Robert Elder, the prominent criminal lawyer and former prosecutor, represented the New York League as NAWSA's first "fraternal delegates." Eight other men came from England, Holland, Germany, Hungary, and France. Together their presence prompted a group of Swedish "writers, preachers, journalists and other progressive specimens" to form a national league of their own, with the prominent parliamentarian Ernst Beckman as president.

Wilson was one of two keynote speakers at the fourth anniversary celebration of Wise's Free Synagogue at the Hotel Astor, in April. The other was Senator William Borah, the progressive Democrat from the suffrage state of Idaho, who said humbly that he had come only to pay tribute to his friend, Doctor Wise, and for the first time to hear Wilson speak. The New Jersey governor's address was prescient and presidential. "We are in the presence of a great body of changing opinions," he said,

> and with that will come a change of atmospheric conditions, a general readjustment of our economic and political relations with each other. There is no reason for being afraid of the prospect, however, for if there will be a revolution it will be a revolution carrying sympathy with it, and that which breeds sympathy makes for reform. . . . A nation can gain distinction only by the use of its moral powers. That nation is not only great but is truly noble which uses its powers in the direction of right.

---

The growing interest in the male view of suffrage prompted a published symposium in the May pages of the *International* magazine, a New York–based monthly. It featured a number of well-known male supporters and antagonists along with

First International Men's League for Woman Suffrage gathering in Stockholm, June 14, 1911. Standing: (*left to right*) Frederick Nathan, New York; Dr. Charles V. Drysdale, London; Franz Lohnhoff, Bremen; W.A.E. Mansfelt, Utrecht. Sitting: (*left to right*) Alexander Pataj, Budapest; F.F.W. Vehrer, Holland; J. Dubreuil de St. Germain, Paris; Dr. F.A. Bather, England. (From Maud Nathan's memoir, *Once Upon a Time and Today* [New York: G.P. Putnam's Sons, 1933])

women who represented both sides of the issue. Four questions were posed: What are the most powerful arguments for and against women's suffrage? Would you favor an educational or property qualification? Do you favor militancy? Should a woman's moral standing be a factor in her eligibility to vote? League responses came from Peabody, Dewey, Upton Sinclair, the editor and author Hamilton Holt, and the East Aurora writer Elbert Hubbard, along with three other men. The symposium represented one of the few times Dewey laid out his views on the subject in writing: Argument pro? (Democracy needs it to be complete.) Against? (No response.) Militancy? (Experience hasn't shown it to work in the United States but "it is a familiar habit of English political life to make no changes except under great pressure. This being the case, the women certainly needed some way of demonstrating that they were in earnest.") What about a property or educational qualification requirement? (No. "It is the masses—the poor—that most need the protection of the ballot.") Should a woman's moral standing affect her right to vote? (No. "There is enough of a double standard of morality now.

When a man's 'moral standing affects' his right to vote, it should also affect a woman's—not till then.")

The May Suffrage Day Parade was the movement's spring focus in New York City. In preparation, the Men's League organized a mass "Winning the Vote" meeting that filled the auditorium at Cooper Union on May 2, four days before the parade on May 6. The League summoned an array of marquee names to speak, listing them all on a poster to drive home the point that winning would require strong support from influential men. James Brady, the former governor of Idaho, was one of the speakers, as was Peter J. Brady, no known relation, of the Allied Printing Trades. Eastman, of course, was listed, along with the New York legislator Harold Spielberg. From the editorial world, Arthur Brisbane, editor of the *New York Evening Journal*, was on the bill, along with Norman Hapgood, then editor of *Collier's Weekly*.

———◇———

Neither Hapgood's nor Brisbane's name appears in the surviving League membership booklets of 1910 or 1912, but both were known suffrage advocates. As early as January of 1909, while the League's formation was still under wraps, Brisbane expressed his support for the cause. To an audience of five hundred people at the Boston City Club, he predicted imminent victory for the women. Men had reached a point in their evolution where mercy and charity could prevail, he said, and it was time for the better half of the human race—women—to take part in government.

For the Cooper Union event, the illness of his brother forced Brisbane to cancel his appearance, but he sent a letter that Hapgood read to the crowd. In it, Brisbane dismissed the common contention of suffrage opponents that bad women voters would use their ballots in support of bad men. In Brisbane's view, even the most wretched woman would vote for good men, because she knew all about bad men only too well. As for Eastman, his speech dismissed the notion that women would do better to organize in trade unions rather than as expectant voters. What good would unionism have done for men, he asked, if they had not already had the franchise? As it happened, on May 4, between the meeting at Cooper Union and the parade, Eastman eloped to Patterson, New Jersey, with the multitalented Ida Rauh—lawyer, suffragist, activist, sculptor, poet, actor—and left on a honeymoon in Europe the following day. There was no formal announcement of the nuptials, not even to Eastman's father. At the Cooper Union meeting, organizers had announced their expectation of a delegation two hundred strong—safety in numbers—so no man should feel hesitant about joining them.

## BIG CROWDS CHEER SUFFRAGIST PARADE

Under that headline, on May 7, the *New York Tribune* reported on the first suffrage procession in New York movement history to include a male delegation. The actual number of men who lined up to march that morning was fewer than half of the earlier prediction, varying from the eighty-plus to the ninety-plus in press reports and the much later recollections of the men who participated. A year later, the League itself would put the number at one hundred. Along with the women, the men walked the forty blocks of Fifth Avenue from Fifty-Seventh Street to Seventeenth Street. The *Tribune* reporter focused heavily on a single marcher, identified as J.S. Terwilliger, who said he was "a militant suffragist and wanted to march with the women to show his colors plainly." Terwilliger bore the banner of the Brooklyn delegation and marched with the Twenty-Third Assembly District instead of with the League. In doing so, he whetted the crowd's appetite for the League delegation yet to come. As the *Tribune* reported, "Even a heavy mustache could not conceal the mutterings of revolt, and there was no attempt to hide a deep scowl."

Nathan, Laidlaw, and Dewey led the League's men. As they came into view, the crowd "let loose with everything it had," hurling abuse and insults. Among the numerous barbs and epithets, the *Tribune* said, "'Lizzie' was the kindest."

The *Chicago Tribune* also captured the crowd's hostile reaction to the presence of these marching men, reporting heavily on the taunts they attracted. The newspaper singled out Upton Sinclair—the by-then world-famous author who in *The Jungle* had chronicled the revolting conditions of Chicago's meatpacking industry—noting that Sinclair had "for some reason" walked only a few blocks before dropping out of formation. Nonetheless, as the parade pushed farther south, "more men with pennants joined the original brave band of eighty-nine men and swelled the trousered company to more than 100."

> At Forty-Seventh Street a young man walked right out to the head of the column of men marchers, and placing his widespread finger tips lightly against his chest, his big arm at strained akimbo, addressed the men column in an artificial soprano.
>
> "I dee-fy you!" he cried.
>
> The men marchers looked straight ahead solemnly, while the crowd laughed as a grinning policeman swirled the young man off the asphalt and on toward outer darkness.

"Hold up your skirts, girls," was shouted from the curb toward the eighty-nine braves.

"You won't get any dinner unless you march all the way, Vivian," hooted another.

"Wait till I get my wrapper and I'll join the ranks, too," cooed someone else from the sidelines.

As for the *New York Tribune*, it expressed how impressed it was by the number of male converts that the parade had brought to the suffrage cause and extolled the ovation the suffragists had given their brave male counterparts as the Men's League delegation reached Union Square. "There was a mad rush of women from all points to meet them," the newspaper said, "and feminine attempts at hurrahs rent the air." A two-page spread in *Harper's Weekly* referred to the Men's League delegation as the "husband's section" and noted how the crowds "hooted from one end of the avenue to the other" at Dewey, Nathan, and Laidlaw. It quoted Harriot Blatch saying, "The real martyrs to-day were the men." The published history of the movement would later make the point more dramatically: "No act of men during the whole history of woman suffrage required more courage than that of the eighty-seven who marched up Fifth Avenue on that occasion, jeered by the crowds that lined the sidewalks." Of those who bore parade line assaults and recalled them years later, Wise would describe the jeering as "what now sounds like rather amusing jabs that questioned our masculinity."

Hamilton Holt, the publisher of the *Independent*, was most struck by the rash of "verbal bouquets and brickbats." Charles Strong, two decades later, still stung by the "jeers and abuse" the men had endured in line, would recall Laidlaw's "courage and calm indifference." "It meant much for him to do this," Strong would say, "for he was in the very forefront and faced the derision of the men in his own clubs, as they sat in their windows and watched us go by. It was not only in parade but in quiet council that he led." George Middleton, the playwright, devoted several pages of his memoir to a recollection of the day. Villard and Eastman marched along with Dewey and Laidlaw, he remembered. For Middleton, the poets Richard Le Gallienne and Witter Bynner also stood out in memory, as did the men's arrival in Union Square and how the women greeted them with wild cheers and spring flowers. Middleton had kept an aged clipping from the day, the text of which he included verbatim:

They displayed a hardihood and dauntlessness beyond even that of the women, to whom public parading was a terror; for while the women

# HARPER'S WEEKLY
## A JOURNAL OF CIVILIZATION

VOL. LV.      New York, May 20, 1911      No. 2839

Copyright, 1911, by Harper & Brothers. All rights reserved

## MARCHING ON TO SUFFRAGE

Three thousand women, headed by pipers, marched down Fifth Avenue, New York, from Fifty-seventh Street to Union Square, on Saturday, May 6th, in demonstration of their desire for the suffrage. Banners and allegorical floats lent a spectacular element to the procession, which was heartily cheered by crowds along the route

A view of the Suffrage Day Parade, May 6, 1911. (*Harper's Weekly: A Journal of Civilization*, Vol. LV, No. 2839, May 20, 1911, p. 3)

were gazed upon with respect and frequent applause, the men every step of the two-mile walk had to submit to jeers, whistles, "mea-a-ows," and such cries as "Take that handkerchief out of your cuff," "Oh, you gay deceiver," "you forgot to shave this morning," etc., etc. Not one of them deserted the ranks.

Villard's memories of the episode, too, were clear. The delegation got into formation under the windows of the University Club at Fifty-Fourth Street and Fifth Avenue, he would later write. Looking up, Villard said he could discern through the glass "the faces of scoffing friends, who were doubtless much outraged at this latest proof of the insanity of that crank Villard." He could still hear the boos, hisses, and ridicule that continued throughout the parade "without a moment's cessation." It was the crowd's general assumption that none was marching of his own free will "and reflections upon the masculinity of our wives and our low estate in our own homes were common," Villard said. Among the milder queries were "Did she make you come?" and "Who's doing the cooking while you're out?" In Union Square, Villard spoke from his automobile, featured alongside his mother and Anna Shaw. The entire experience was exhilarating, he recalled, putting in words how the experience had galvanized what turned out to be a commonly felt resolve. "I feel like beginning work now for the next year's parade and I am determined to have at least 500 men in line at that time, and instead of 3,000 women there ought to be 20,000. I do not know when I have enjoyed a day more and wish I could do it over again tomorrow."

In Albany nine days later, the bill for the constitutional amendment made its way out of the Judiciary Committee for the first time. The vote was six in favor, two opposed. On July 12, the Senate voted. The final count was a loss: fourteen in favor, seventeen against.

———◄○►———

In June, Woodrow Wilson was back in Trenton from a Western swing, billed not-a-campaign, where, with Californians preparing to vote on the suffrage question in the fall, he again had to dodge a request that he state his views. "Suffrage is not a national issue so far," he was quoted as saying. The poet Witter Bynner asked Wilson by letter to express his position point blank. This was Wilson's unequivocal reply:

I must say very frankly that my personal judgment is strongly against it. I believe that the social changes it would involve would not justify the gains that would be accomplished by it. In the midst of my busy days it is impossible for me to argue the matter as I should like to in a casual letter, but I owe it to you to give to you this very frank statement of my views.

———◇———

New chapters of the Men's League were proliferating. In early fall, one listing fifty vice presidents launched in Orange County, California and Brooklyn's Kings County opened, too. In the same period, Anna Shaw took a sharp jab from W.E.B. Du Bois in the October issue of the NAACP's *Crisis* magazine over her "barefaced falsehood" that all black people opposed women's suffrage. In the same editorial, Du Bois denounced a prevailing attitude in the movement to "not touch the Negro problem" because of its potential to offend supporters and potential supporters in the South, as the *Baltimore Sun*'s reaction to the incident at the Dewey apartment had pointed up. "Such contradiction hurts the Woman's Suffrage movement far more than it hurts black folk," Du Bois wrote. "No wonder Europe sneers at American democracy." Du Bois's name does not appear on any surviving Men's League roster or letterhead, but over the coming nine years, he would argue persuasively to ambivalent or downright hostile members of the black community for its voters to support the women's cause. The magazine carried numerous editorials on the subject and published major suffrage symposia twice at critical campaign junctures.

The California suffrage campaign proved victorious, making the state the sixth to grant the vote to women, and the suffragists of New York celebrated at Cooper Union as if the win had been their own. The surprise speaker was none other than Britain's Emmeline Pankhurst, who said the whole women's suffrage world rejoiced in the victory.

———◇———

Eastman, with his new wife, was back in Elmira on November 23 to lecture not on suffrage but on the greatest need of the public schools, a subject he admitted as he started that he did not know all that much about. He suggested that the teaching of history could be made more attractive if it were taught in general periods rather than as a series "of kings and the dates of their births and deaths," and he thought the emphasis on Greek and Latin was exaggerated, and regretted the time he spent studying them. The Triangle Shirtwaist fire of March 25 was still much on his mind. "We cannot blame the schools so much for teaching unimportant facts but we can blame them for not teaching important facts," he said. "We can blame them for filling children's heads full of dead roots and old fashioned ghost stories and strange looking tubes and triangles of all kinds and then not giving them even a hint of those life and earth parts of the earth, which are of supreme importance to every creature that tries to live and grow upon it." To Eastman this was "the most important fact in the world, that there are men and women starving and freezing and contracting the diseases of poverty when they are willing to work."

He traveled on to Syracuse where Rauh made a suffrage address and he spoke to the local Chamber of Commerce, whose director called his remarks "one of the best talks ever given us." But the visit also brought a rash of gossipy upstate chatter when Eastman and Rauh explained their radical views on marriage and why they had decided she should retain her surname. The "Mrs.," the couple asserted, was nothing more than a "a badge of slavery." Their attitudes generated local controversy, prompting the *Elmira Star-Gazette*'s pseudonymous columnist, The Growler, to say how lamentable it was for "so many men of ordinarily calm and conservative demeanor to get in bad on a recent topic of public comment."

———◄◦►———

Anna Shaw wrote to Rabbi Wise in early December, asking if he would speak for suffrage in Portland. She told him how glad she was to hear he was preparing an address titled "Is Woman a Parasite?" "I think we have flattered women too much," she gamely responded, "and it would be a good thing for us all to know more of the truth about ourselves. The same, of course, is equally true of men."

Peabody and Villard suddenly piped up at full volume, too. In a letter to the *Harvard Crimson* on December 4, Villard vehemently protested his alma mater's decision to bar Pankhurst from speaking on campus and urged "all the undergraduates who can to hear her speak for the double purpose of thus making amends for the university's lamentable blunder and of hearing one of the ablest orators of the day." Bynner, another Harvard graduate, sent his protest to the college's alumni bulletin, calling the decision "discourteous, ill advised and unfair," an action meant only to "justify, in this particular, Harvard's name as a closed shop." Peabody was even more emphatic in his first suffrage foray into print. NAWSA's 1911 national convention had been held in Louisville from October 19 to 23, and the editor of the *Louisville Courier Journal*, Colonel Henry Watterson, had used the occasion to accuse the city's guests of pitting a "transcendant [*sic*] influence for good against a dangerous influence for evil." "We are afraid," he warned ominously, "she will find when it is too late that she has been playing with fire." One of Peabody's visits to Athens, Georgia, as a benefactor of the University of Georgia, happened to coincide with the local newspaper's reprint of Watterson's column. Peabody wrote a letter to the editor of the *Athens Banner*, taking strong exception to Watterson's dismissal of women's suffrage as an "untried project," to his assertion that the suffragists were "putting the ballot against the home," and to his prediction that women's influence would "degenerate in proportion to her political activities." "The truth is," Peabody wrote, "humanity's vital need is that men and women should in all things work together—man should never be in a place or position where women should not go. The excuse that politics is 'pitch' is in itself the completest argument for woman's full entrance into its every department, for man, being without her, has made the conditions as they are, and thus confesses he cannot reform them alone."

The *Atlanta Constitution*, in turn, republished Peabody's response under the heading "Letter from a Distinguished Georgian," describing Peabody as a native son who had moved up East. A precede the *Constitution* supplied reflected on how much Peabody embodied the fervency of the men who supported women's suffrage, men who had "come forward and unhesitatingly proclaimed their views," not as politicians or courters of public opinion but as men "who seem impelled by the duty they feel of a just cause."

The cheers of Georgia's suffrage sisters resounded all the way to Boston, where the *Woman's Journal* carried Peabody's letter in full and praised him for protesting the nose-holding welcome Watterson had given the conventioneers. "The officers and members of the Men's League for Woman Suffrage," the *Journal* noted, "are taking a more and more active part in the work, with both voice and pen."

The convention's keynote speaker had been Dr. Harvey Washington Wiley, the nation's chief chemist. He, too, could not have more emphatically disagreed with Watterson. Wiley was the "Father of the Pure Food and Drug Act" after it became law in 1906. He was a staunch opponent of adulterated foods and cola drinks and had been a supporter of women's suffrage, he declared to the conventioneers, for at least twenty-five years. In his view, a country's greatness could be measured by how much soap it used per head, how much sugar its people consumed, and how it treated its women. Solving America's big problems, he went on, required the efforts of women as well as men. "Women," he said, "are a tower of strength to every public man who is trying to do his duty. I don't know why she has been kept from the polls. Surely not because of lack of intellect."

Dudley Field Malone     Edwin Mead     Lincoln Steffens     Louis D. Brandeis

Frederick S. Greene     Winter Russell     Frederic C. Howe     Joel Elias Spingarn

Gardner Hale     A.S.G. Taylor     Swinburne Hale     Algernon Crapsey

Will Irwin     Joseph Fels     William Sulzer     Theodore Roosevelt

# 5

# "The Change in Public Sentiment Is Remarkable"

## 1912

By 1912, the men of the American women's suffrage movement had become even more visible, their efforts fully chronicled in the press. The number of names on the New York Men's League's roster had nearly tripled from its original list of one hundred and fifty members in 1909–1910. The organization's sharpened political intent appeared pointedly in the formatting of the new edition of its charter, membership, and constitution. The booklet lists sixty-one officers and advisory and executive committee members along with a statewide membership of 436 men, grouped, as if to emphasize their political force and intent, by the New York State county or assembly district of their home or business addresses. Listed under each category are anywhere from one to a score of impressive names. The booklet also enumerates all of the League's major activities in its first two years, including its legislative action in Albany, it representation at important gatherings, the speaking engagements of its members, the two pamphlets published under its own imprint, the banquet it hosted for six hundred guests, the two smaller events it organized, and the help its members lent to the formation of League chapters in other states.

Among the year's numerous highlights was the appearance of League-member bylines over articles in prestige publications, several of which became League-published pamphlets. The Columbia historian Charles Beard reminded any man who opposed granting the vote to women how recently it was that priests and nobles had regarded people of his own common class "exactly as he regards woman to-day." And New York's immigration commissioner, Frederic C. Howe, wrote an article that appeared first in *Collier's* under the headline, "Why I Want Woman Suffrage: What the Ballot Will Do for Women and for Men."

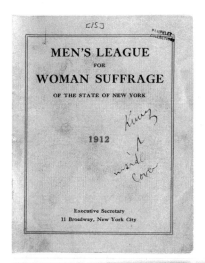

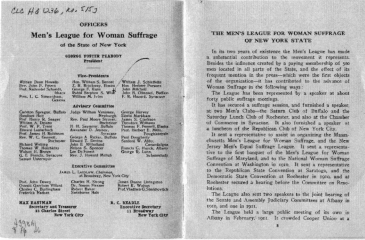

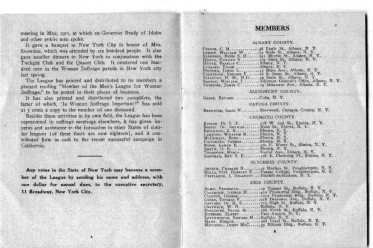

The 1912 constitution, charter, and membership roster of the Men's League for Woman Suffrage of the State of New York. (Rare Books and Manuscripts, Library of Congress) *(continues on next two pages)*

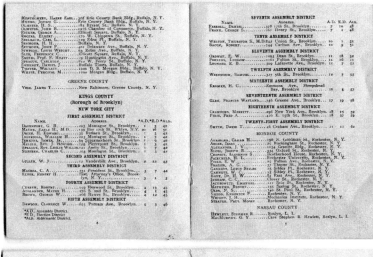

| Name | Address |
|---|---|
| Montgomery, Harry Earl | 3rd Erie County Bank Bldg., Buffalo, N. Y. |
| Munro, Josiah G. | Erie County Bank Bldg., Buffalo, N. Y. |
| Olmsted, H. S. | 183 Bryant St., Buffalo. N. Y. |
| Olmsted, John B. | 1216 Chamber of Commerce, Buffalo, N. Y. |
| Ricker, George A. | Ellicott Square, Buffalo, N. Y. |
| Rogers, Elbert | 170 W. Chippewa St., Buffalo, N. Y. |
| Seelbach, Carl L. | 129 Edna Pl., Buffalo, N. Y. |
| Seymour, H. H. | Buffalo, N. Y. |
| Seymour, John P. | 401 Delaware Ave., Buffalo, N. Y. |
| Simpson, Louis Wright | 63 Robie Ave., Buffalo, N. Y. |
| Slee, Frederick C. | Ellicott Square, Buffalo, N. Y. |
| Smith, Prof. F. Hyatt | 29 Huntingtin Ave., Buffalo, N. Y. |
| Sprague, Carleton | 810 W. Ferry St., Buffalo, N. Y. |
| Sweeney, Daniel J. | Buffalo Times, Buffalo, N. Y. |
| Thayer, Wallace | 1000 D. S. Morgan Bldg., Buffalo, N. Y. |
| White, Percival M. | 1200 Morgan Bldg., Buffalo, N. Y. |

## GREENE COUNTY

| Name | Address |
|---|---|
| Vose, James T. | New Baltimore, Greene County, N. Y. |

## KINGS COUNTY
## (Borough of Brooklyn)
## NEW YORK CITY

### FIRST ASSEMBLY DISTRICT

| Name. | Address. | *A.D. | *E.D. | *Ald. |
|---|---|---|---|---|
| Davenport, G. B. | 203 Montague St., Brooklyn | 1 | 3 | 42 |
| Mayne, Earle H., M.D. | 139 Bay 17th St., B'klyn, N.Y. | 20 | 16 | 57 |
| Drier, H. Edward | 35 Remsen St., Brooklyn | 1 | 5 | 42 |
| Ingersoll, William H. | 203 Montague St., Brooklyn | 1 | 3 | 42 |
| Jenkins, James, Jr. | 69 Schermerhorn St., Brooklyn | 1 | 9 | 40 |
| Melish, Rev. J. Howard | 129 Pierrepont St., Brooklyn | 1 | 3 | 42 |
| Sprague, Rev. Leslie Willis | 121 Amity St., Brooklyn | 1 | 7 | 42 |
| Suffern, Charles C. | 203 Montague St., Brooklyn | 1 | 3 | 42 |

### SECOND ASSEMBLY DISTRICT

| Name. | Address. | *A.D. | *E.D. | *Ald. |
|---|---|---|---|---|
| Gillen, W. J. | 12 Vanderbilt Ave., Brooklyn | 2 | 22 | 43 |

### THIRD ASSEMBLY DISTRICT

| Name. | Address. | *A.D. | *E.D. | *Ald. |
|---|---|---|---|---|
| Macrea, C. A. | 231 President St., Brooklyn | 3 | 7 | 44 |
| Elder, Robert H. | Dist. Attorney's Office, Brooklyn, N. Y. | 3 | 1 | 3 |

### FOURTH ASSEMBLY DISTRICT

| Name. | Address. | *A.D. | *E.D. | *Ald. |
|---|---|---|---|---|
| Curren, Robert | 159 Heywood St., Brooklyn | 4 | 13 | 45 |
| Auslander, Meyer H. | 276 S. 2nd St., Brooklyn | 4 | 1 | 45 |
| Brown, George W. | 266 Hewes St., Brooklyn | 4 | 12 | 45 |

### FIFTH ASSEMBLY DISTRICT

| Name. | Address. | *A.D. | *E.D. | *Ald. |
|---|---|---|---|---|
| Dawson, Clarence W. | 655 Putnam Ave., Brooklyn | 5 | 3 | 46 |

*A.D., Assembly District.
*E.D., Election District
*Ald., Aldermanic District.



### SEVENTH ASSEMBLY DISTRICT

| Name. | Address. | A.D. | E.D. | Ald. |
|---|---|---|---|---|
| Farrell, Daniel | 378 17th St., Brooklyn | 7 | 10 | 48 |
| Frank, George S. | 261 Henry St., Brooklyn | 7 | 1 | 48 |

### TENTH ASSEMBLY DISTRICT

| Name. | Address. | A.D. | E.D. | Ald. |
|---|---|---|---|---|
| Welton, Thurston S., M.D. | 842 Union St., Brooklyn | 10 | 1 | 51 |
| Bacon, Robert | 544 Carlton Ave., Brooklyn | 10 | 9 | 51 |

### ELEVENTH ASSEMBLY DISTRICT

| Name. | Address. | A.D. | E.D. | Ald. |
|---|---|---|---|---|
| Ordway, E. W. | 1093 Dean St., Brooklyn | 11 | 18 | 52 |
| Perkins, Ludlow | 1161 Fulton St., Brooklyn | 11 | 16 | 11 |
| Leonard, R. B. | 309 Lafayette Ave., Brooklyn | 11 | 7 | 52 |

### TWELFTH ASSEMBLY DISTRICT

| Name. | Address. | A.D. | E.D. | Ald. |
|---|---|---|---|---|
| Weinstein, Samuel | 327 5th St., Brooklyn | 12 | 7 | 53 |

### SIXTEENTH ASSEMBLY DISTRICT

| Name. | Address. | A.D. | E.D. | Ald. |
|---|---|---|---|---|
| Kromke, H. C. | Emmons Ave., Sheepshead Bay, Brooklyn | 16 | 5 | 57 |

### SEVENTEENTH ASSEMBLY DISTRICT

| Name. | Address. | A.D. | E.D. | Ald. |
|---|---|---|---|---|
| Glen, Francis Wayland | 736 Greene Ave., Brooklyn | 17 | 19 | 58 |

### EIGHTEENTH ASSEMBLY DISTRICT

| Name. | Address. | A.D. | E.D. | Ald. |
|---|---|---|---|---|
| Crawford, Merritt | 296 New York Ave., Brooklyn | 18 | 15 | 59 |
| Pirie, Fred A. | 426 E. 15th St., Brooklyn | 18 | 37 | 59 |

### TWENTY-FIRST ASSEMBLY DISTRICT

| Name. | Address. | A.D. | E.D. | Ald. |
|---|---|---|---|---|
| Smith, David T. | 46 Graham Ave., Brooklyn | 21 | 11 | 62 |

## MONROE COUNTY

| Name | Address |
|---|---|
| Aurrakian, Cahan H. | 198 N. Goodman St., Rochester, N. Y. |
| Adler, Isaac | 25 Buckingham St., Rochester, N. Y. |
| Alexander, J. V. | 1134 Granite Bldg., Rochester, N. Y. |
| Bloss, Joseph B. | 334 Oxford St., Rochester, N. Y. |
| Chapsey, Algernon S. | Brotherhood House, Rochester, N. Y. |
| Fairchild, H. L. | Rochester University, Rochester, N. Y. |
| Fiske, E. W. | 25 Fulton Ave., Rochester, N. Y. |
| Frazier, A. G. | 37 Thayer St., Rochester, N. Y. |
| Gannett, Louis Stiles | 15 Sibley Pl., Rochester, N. Y. |
| Gannett, W. C. | 15 Sibley Pl., Rochester, N. Y. |
| Hoyt, Dr. H. W. | 84 East Ave., Rochester, N. Y. |
| Inshaw, C. C. | Clover St., Rochester, N. Y. |
| Jacubowitz, Emanuel | 111 Scio St., Rochester, N. Y. |
| Mathews, Robert | 135 Spring St., Rochester, N. Y. |
| Olds, N. S. | 140 St. Paul St., Rochester, N. Y. |
| Shedd, Kendrick P. | Rochester, N. Y. |
| Wright, J. H. | Mechanics Institute, Rochester, N. Y. |
| Strayer, Paul Moore | Rochester, N. Y. |

## NASSAU COUNTY

| Name | Address |
|---|---|
| Hewlett, Stephen R. | Roslyn, L. I. |
| MacMurphy, G. Y. | Care Stephen R. Hewlett, Roslyn, L. I. |



## NEW YORK COUNTY
## (Boroughs of Manhattan and the Bronx)
## NEW YORK CITY

### FIRST ASSEMBLY DISTRICT

| Name. | Address. | *A.D. | E.D. | Ald. |
|---|---|---|---|---|
| Barkley, Chas. B. | 149 Broadway, N.Y.C. | 1 | 3 | 1 |
| Bell, Robert P. | 299 Broadway, N.Y.C. | 1 | 5 | 1 |
| Benedict, Wm. L. | 56 Wall St., N.Y.C. | 1 | 2 | 2 |
| Bennett, Hon. Wm. S. | 60 Wall St., N.Y.C. | 1 | 2 | 2 |
| Bigelow, Richard | 18 Broadway, N.Y.C. | 1 | 1 | 1 |
| Blumberg, Alexander J. | 82 Wall St., N.Y.C. | 1 | 2 | 2 |
| Burlingham, James C. | 27 William St., N.Y.C. | 1 | 1 | 1 |
| Byrne, Andrew | 302 Broadway, N.Y.C. | 1 | 5 | 1 |
| Carpenter, Herbert S. | 71 Broadway, N.Y.C. | 1 | 1 | 1 |
| Clark, Walter L. | 111 Broadway, N.Y.C. | 1 | 2 | 1 |
| Clarkson, James S. | New York City | 1 | 1 | 1 |
| Cooper, G. S. | 49 Wall St., N.Y.C. | 1 | 1 | 2 |
| Corbin, Floyd S. | 10 Wall St., N.Y.C. | 1 | 2 | 1 |
| Cox, Edwin M. | 15 Broad St., N.Y.C. | 1 | 1 | 1 |
| Cox, Wilmot T. | 34 Pine St., N.Y.C. | 1 | 2 | 1 |
| Crawford, G. H. | 32 Liberty St., N.Y.C. | 1 | 2 | 1 |
| Gibson, H. S. | 59 William St., N.Y.C. | 1 | 2 | 1 |
| Greeley, Harold Dudley | 2 Rector St., N.Y.C. | 1 | 2 | 1 |
| Ingersoll, Raymond V. | 261 Broadway, N.Y.C. | 1 | 5 | 1 |
| Ivins, Wm. M. | 27 William St., N.Y.C. | 1 | 1 | 1 |
| Judson, William H. | 6 Broadway, N.Y.C. | 1 | 1 | 1 |
| Kotzen, A. A. | 309 Broadway, N.Y.C. | 1 | 5 | 1 |
| Laidlaw, James L. | 26 Broadway, N.Y.C. | 1 | 1 | 1 |
| Leight, Morris | 309 Broadway, N.Y.C. | 1 | 5 | 1 |
| Leubuscher, Frederic Cyrus | 258 Broadway, N.Y.C. | 1 | 3 | 1 |
| Levy, Jefferson | 27 Pine St., N.Y.C. | 1 | 2 | 1 |
| Major, A. | 161 Pearl St., N.Y.C. | 1 | 4 | .. |
| Mannes, David | 327 Amsterdam Ave., N.Y.C. | 1 | 4 | .. |
| Martin, Newell | 1 Nassau St., N.Y.C. | 1 | 2 | 1 |
| Middleton, Larry | 313 Broadway, N.Y.C. | 1 | 5 | 1 |
| Morton, Benjamin A. | 80 Broadway, N.Y.C. | 1 | 1 | 1 |
| Morton, James F., Jr. | Room 1115, 309 B'way, N.Y.C. | 1 | 5 | 1 |
| Newborg, Sidney | 2 Rector St., N.Y.C. | 1 | 2 | 1 |
| Noch, John H. | 131 Cedar St., N.Y.C. | 1 | 2 | 1 |
| Oliver, James | 220 Broadway, N.Y.C. | 1 | 3 | 1 |
| Parsons, Herbert | 52 William St., N.Y.C. | 1 | 2 | 1 |
| Post, Charles M. | 41 Wall St., N.Y.C. | 1 | 1 | 1 |
| Post, Henry Morgan | 41 Wall St., N.Y.C. | 1 | 1 | 1 |
| Powell, Andrew | 156 Broadway, N.Y.C. | 1 | 2 | 1 |
| Roe, Gilbert E. | 95 Broadway, N.Y.C. | 1 | 2 | 1 |
| Sackman, Joe | 501 Broadway, N.Y.C. | 1 | 14 | 1 |
| Skeel, Roswell, Jr. | 220 Broadway, N.Y.C. | 1 | 3 | 1 |
| Strong, Charles H. | 27 William St., N.Y.C. | 1 | 1 | 1 |
| Thurman, I. N. | 25 Broad St., N.Y.C. | 1 | 1 | 1 |
| Ver Planck, Wm. Gordon | 140 Broadway, N.Y.C. | 1 | 3 | 1 |
| Villard, Oswald G. | 20 Vesey St., N.Y.C. | 1 | 3 | 1 |
| Walling, J. H. | 239 Broadway, N.Y.C. | 1 | 3 | 1 |
| Walton, Robert K. | 34 Nassau St., N.Y.C. | 1 | 2 | 1 |

*See note bottom page 6.



| Name. | Address. | A.D. | E.D. | Ald. |
|---|---|---|---|---|
| Welling, Richard | 2 Wall St., N.Y.C. | 1 | 2 | 1 |
| Wood, William | 458 Broadway, N.Y.C. | 1 | 14 | 1 |
| Young, G. W. | 59 Cedar St., N.Y.C. | 1 | 2 | 1 |
| Dawson, Miles N. | 141 Broadway, N.Y.C. | 1 | 1 | 1 |
| Gray, C. P. | 130 Fulton St., N.Y.C. | 1 | 2 | 1 |
| Hawkins, William H. | 38 Park Row, N.Y.C. | 1 | 3 | 1 |
| Holt, Hamilton | 130 Fulton St., N.Y.C. | 1 | 2 | 1 |
| Slosson, Edwin E. | 130 Fulton St., N.Y.C. | 1 | 2 | 1 |
| Warner, Edward | 161 Bleecker St., N.Y.C. | 1 | 20 | 1 |
| Wetche, Dr. C.F. | 123 West 80th St., N.Y.C. | 1 | 18 | 1 |
| Whitney, Travis H. | Public Service Commission, Tribune Bldg., N.Y.C. | 1 | 3 | 1 |
| Marsh, Benjamin C. | Room 222, 320 B'way, N.Y.C. | 1 | 5 | 1 |
| Waters, John R. | 90 West St. | 1 | 2 | 1 |

### SECOND ASSEMBLY DISTRICT

| Name. | Address. | A.D. | E.D. | Ald. |
|---|---|---|---|---|
| Brown, Walston H. | 45 Wall St., N.Y.C. | 2 | 2 | 2 |
| Butler, James B. | 76 William St., N.Y.C. | 2 | 2 | 2 |
| Daly, Joseph F. | 54 Wall St., N.Y.C. | 2 | 2 | 2 |
| Day, Jr., Clarence S. | 45 Wall St., N.Y.C. | 2 | 1 | 2 |
| Hale, Swinburne | 49 Wall St., N.Y.C. | 2 | 1 | 2 |
| Hays, Arthur Garfield | 60 Wall St., N.Y.C. | 2 | 2 | 2 |
| Howells, John Meade | 100 William St., N.Y.C. | 2 | 2 | 2 |
| Lauterbach, Edward | 22 William St., N.Y.C. | 2 | 1 | 2 |
| Loines, Russell H. | 49 Wall St., N.Y.C. | 2 | 1 | 2 |
| Shainwald, Ralph L. | 100 William St., N.Y.C. | 2 | 2 | 2 |
| Untermyer, Samuel | 37 Wall St., N.Y.C. | 2 | 1 | 2 |
| Willcox, William G. | 3 S. William St., N.Y.C. | 2 | 1 | 2 |
| Child, Edward S. | 209 Clinton St., N.Y.C. | 2 | 17 | 2 |
| Untermyer, Samuel | 37 Wall St., N.Y.C. | 2 | 1 | 2 |
| Payne, C. Q. | 82 Beaver St., N.Y.C. | 2 | 1 | 2 |
| Harvey, George | Franklin Square, N.Y.C. | 2 | 4 | 2 |
| Tunick, Dr. I. S. | 258 Henry St., N.Y.C. | 2 | 19 | 2 |

### THIRD ASSEMBLY DISTRICT

| Name. | Address. | A.D. | E.D. | Ald. |
|---|---|---|---|---|
| Guy, Justice Charles L. | Court House, N.Y.C. | 3 | 1 | 3 |
| Lenz, Rudolph | Bible House, Astor Pl., N.Y.C. | 3 | 22 | 3 |
| Lourens, Marinus M. | 202 E. 12th St., N.Y.C. | 3 | 20 | 3 |
| Strong, Josiah | Bible House, N.Y.C. | 3 | 22 | 3 |
| Fagan, Louis | 346 Broadway, N.Y.C. | 3 | 1 | 3 |

### FIFTH ASSEMBLY DISTRICT

| Name. | Address. | A.D. | E.D. | Ald. |
|---|---|---|---|---|
| Barnard, Seymour | 26 Jones St., N.Y.C. | 5 | 4 | 5 |
| Gleason, A. H. | 416 W. 13th St., N.Y.C. | 5 | 16 | 5 |
| Goan, Orrin S. | 11th St. and 9th Ave., N.Y.C. | 5 | 18 | 5 |
| Lewis, Read | 26 Jones St., N.Y.C. | 5 | 4 | 5 |
| McAfee, James R. | 71 8th Ave., N.Y.C. | 5 | 14 | 5 |
| O'Brien, Joseph | 210 W. 4th St., N.Y.C. | 5 | 5 | 5 |
| Simkhovitch, Prof. V. G. | 26 Jones St., N.Y.C. | 5 | 4 | 5 |
| Styles, G. W. | Grove & Bleecker Sts., N.Y.C. | 5 | 5 | 5 |

### SIXTH ASSEMBLY DISTRICT

| Name. | Address. | A.D. | E.D. | Ald. |
|---|---|---|---|---|
| Golden, Alexander | 346 E. 10th St., N.Y.C. | 6 | 15 | 6 |

### EIGHTH ASSEMBLY DISTRICT

| Name. | Address. | A.D. | E.D. | Ald. |
|---|---|---|---|---|
| Knowlton, Willard, M.D. | University Settlement, Rivington St., N.Y.C. | 8 | 15 | 8 |



### TENTH ASSEMBLY DISTRICT

| Name. | Address. | A.D. | E.D. | Ald. |
|---|---|---|---|---|
| Cohen, Joseph | 200 Orchard St., N.Y.C. | 10 | 2 | 10 |
| Rauch, William | 42 2nd Ave., N.Y.C. | 10 | 4 | 10 |

### TWELFTH ASSEMBLY DISTRICT

| Name. | Address. | A.D. | E.D. | Ald. |
|---|---|---|---|---|
| Mackenzie, J. D. | 220 W. 17th St., N.Y.C. | 12 | 9 | 12 |
| Stone, C. D. | 450 E. 16th St., N.Y.C. | 12 | 6 | 12 |
| MacKenzie, J. D. | 220 E. 17th St., N.Y.C. | 12 | 9 | 12 |

### THIRTEENTH ASSEMBLY DISTRICT

| Name. | Address. | A.D. | E.D. | Ald. |
|---|---|---|---|---|
| Williams, Rev. Leighton | 312 W. 54th St., N.Y.C. | 13 | 5 | 13 |

### FOURTEENTH ASSEMBLY DISTRICT

| Name. | Address. | A.D. | E.D. | Ald. |
|---|---|---|---|---|
| Aldrich, Chester H. | 142 E. 33rd St., N.Y.C. | 14 | 12 | 14 |

### FIFTEENTH ASSEMBLY DISTRICT

| Name. | Address. | A.D. | E.D. | Ald. |
|---|---|---|---|---|
| Brenon, A. St. John | 235 W. 76th St., N.Y.C. | 15 | 13 | 15 |
| Butler, Henry P. | 116 W. 88th St., N.Y.C. | 15 | 25 | 15 |
| Corvin, Cecil S. | 223 W. 83rd St., N.Y.C. | 15 | 21 | 15 |
| Crosby, John Sherwin | 125 W. 82nd St., N.Y.C. | 15 | 20 | 15 |
| Crowell, Frank | Bretton Hall, Broadway and 85th St., N.Y.C. | 15 | 23 | 15 |
| Devine, Edward T. | 105 E. 22nd St., N.Y.C. | 15 | 26 | 15 |
| Dickerman, Hudson | 221 W. 83rd St., N.Y.C. | 15 | 21 | 15 |
| Dougherty, Paul | 23 W. 67th St., N.Y.C. | 15 | 2 | 15 |
| Duryea, Oscar | 200 W. 72nd St., N.Y.C. | 15 | 8 | 15 |
| Engel, Max Robert | 272 W. 89th St., N.Y.C. | 15 | 26 | 15 |
| Field, Lowell T. | 60 W. 75th St., N.Y.C. | 15 | 11 | 15 |
| Frank, Henry | 132 W. 70th St., N.Y.C. | 15 | 17 | 15 |
| Goldmark, James | 331 W. 83rd St., N.Y.C. | 15 | 24 | 15 |
| Goodman, Edward | 106 W. 86th St., N.Y.C. | 15 | 24 | 15 |
| Henry Charles Seton, 2nd | 2 W. 95th St., N.Y.C. | 15 | 5 | 15 |
| Horne, Ralph W. | 181 W. 87th St., N.Y.C. | 15 | 25 | 15 |
| Hoy, Charles T. | 173 W. 79th St., N.Y.C. | 15 | 17 | 15 |
| Kennedy, Charles Rann | 257 W. 86th St., N.Y.C. | 15 | 26 | 15 |
| Kramer, Dr. G. | 233 W. 83rd St., N.Y.C. | 15 | 21 | 15 |
| Levy, Arthur S., Jr. | 110 Central Park W., N.Y.C. | 15 | 7 | 15 |
| Mendelson, Dr. Walter | 159 W. 74th St., N.Y.C. | 15 | 11 | 15 |
| Mender, Rev. H. Perierra | 99 Central Park West, N.Y.C. | 15 | 6 | 15 |
| Nathan, Frederick | 162 W. 86th St., N.Y.C. | 15 | 24 | 15 |
| Parsmon, Charles | 26 W. 83rd St., N.Y.C. | 15 | 19 | 15 |
| Pease, Dr. Charles Griffin | 101 W. 72nd St., N.Y.C. | 15 | 8 | 15 |
| Peters, Rev. John P. | 225 W. 99th St., N.Y.C. | 15 | 15 | 15 |
| Phillips, N. Taylor | 250 W. 75th St., N.Y.C. | 15 | 9 | 15 |
| Rawitser, S. | 20 W. 72nd St., N.Y.C. | 15 | 7 | 15 |
| Spingarn, Prof. J. E. | 9 W. 73rd St., N.Y.C. | 15 | 7 | 15 |
| King, J. B. | Ansonia Hotel, N.Y.C. | 15 | 9 | 15 |
| King, J. B. | 73rd St. and Broadway (The Ansonia), N.Y.C. | 15 | 9 | 15 |

### SEVENTEENTH ASSEMBLY DISTRICT

| Name. | Address. | A.D. | E.D. | Ald. |
|---|---|---|---|---|
| Andrews, Dr. Charles L. | 39 W. 105th St., N.Y.C. | 17 | 26 | 17 |
| Brainerd, Charles C. | 319 W. 95th St., N.Y.C. | 17 | 8 | 17 |
| Brown, Ray | 294 W. 92nd St., N.Y.C. | 17 | 7 | 17 |
| Mosenthal, Walter J. | 16 W. 85th St., N.Y.C. | 17 | 1 | 17 |
| Saunders, Sidney A. | 3 W. 92nd St., N.Y.C. | 17 | 4 | 17 |



| Name. | Address. | A.D. | E.D. | Ald. |
|---|---|---|---|---|
| Smith, G. W. | 50 W. 93rd St., N.Y.C. | 17 | 4 | 17 |
| Welch, D. C. | 309 W. 93rd St., N.Y.C. | 17 | 7 | 17 |
| Wise, Rabbi Stephen S. | 23 W. 90th St., N.Y.C. | 17 | 3 | 17 |

### EIGHTEENTH ASSEMBLY DISTRICT

| Name. | Address. | A.D. | E.D. | Ald. |
|---|---|---|---|---|
| Clark, Dr. Paul | Rockefeller Institute, N.Y.C. | 18 | 9 | 18 |
| Strunsky, Albert | 440 E. 58th St., N.Y.C. | 18 | 3 | 18 |
| Strunsky, Hyman | 440 E. 58th St., N.Y.C. | 18 | 3 | 18 |
| Taylor, O. E. | 318 W. 37th St., N.Y.C. | 18 | 2 | 18 |
| Opdycke, Leonard E. | 117 E. 69th St., N.Y.C. | 18 | 13 | 18 |

### NINETEENTH ASSEMBLY DISTRICT

| Name. | Address. | A.D. | E.D. | Ald. |
|---|---|---|---|---|
| Beard, Prof. Charles | Columbia University, N.Y.C. | 19 | 24 | 19 |
| Brett, George M. | 1120 Amsterdam Ave., N.Y.C. | 19 | 24 | 19 |
| Dow, Arthur W. | 501 W. 120th St., N.Y.C. | 19 | 26 | 19 |
| Dreiser, Theodore | 608 Riverside Drive, N.Y.C. | 19 | 35 | 19 |
| Fagnani, Prof. Charles P. | Columbia University, N.Y.C. | 19 | 24 | 19 |
| Humphrey, E. F. | Livingston Hall, Columbia University, N.Y.C. | 19 | 4 | 19 |
| Lord, Prof. Herbert | Columbia University, N.Y.C. | 19 | 24 | 19 |
| Miller, Prof. Dickinson | Columbia University, N.Y.C. | 19 | 24 | 19 |
| Montague, Prof. W. P. | Columbia University, N.Y.C. | 19 | 24 | 19 |
| Owen, W. G. | 514 W. 122nd St., N.Y.C. | 19 | 26 | 19 |
| Pitkin, Dr. W. B. | Columbia University, N.Y.C. | 19 | 24 | 19 |
| Rathbun, Frank H. | 540 W. 122nd St., N.Y.C. | 19 | 26 | 19 |
| Richard, Prof. Ernst | Columbia University, N.Y.C. | 19 | 24 | 19 |
| Robinson, Prof. James H. | 567 W. 113th St., N.Y.C. | 19 | 24 | 19 |
| Sait, Edward M. | Columbia University, N.Y.C. | 19 | 24 | 19 |
| Seager, Henry R. | Columbia University, N.Y.C. | 19 | 24 | 19 |
| Shotwell, Prof. James | Columbia University, N.Y.C. | 19 | 24 | 19 |
| Trent, Prof. W. P. | Columbia University, N.Y.C. | 19 | 24 | 19 |
| Whitin, E. Stagg | 501 W. 113th St., N.Y.C. | 19 | 7 | 19 |
| Woarms, Edwin H. | 245 W. 101st St., N.Y.C. | 19 | 1 | 19 |
| Woodbridge, F. J. E. | Columbia University, N.Y.C. | 19 | 24 | 19 |
| Woolston, H. B. | 131 W. 121st St., N.Y.C. | 19 | 28 | 19 |
| White, Gaylord S. | 235-242 E. 104th St., N.Y.C. | 19 | 3 | 19 |
| Dewey, Prof. John | 2880 Broadway, N.Y.C. | 19 | 8 | 19 |
| Brounoff, Platon | 1829 7th Ave., N.Y.C. | 19 | 13 | 19 |

### TWENTY-FIRST ASSEMBLY DISTRICT

| Name. | Address. | A.D. | E.D. | Ald. |
|---|---|---|---|---|
| Baldwin, Samuel A. | 611 W. 137th St., N.Y.C. | 21 | 31 | 21 |
| George, Henry, Jr. | 57 Hamilton Pl., N.Y.C. | 21 | 32 | 21 |
| Moody, Prof. Herbert R. | College of City of N. Y. | 21 | 26 | 21 |
| Overstreet, H. A. | College of City of N. Y. | 21 | 26 | 21 |
| Plumpton, Albert | 640 W. 139th St., N.Y.C. | 21 | 33 | 21 |
| Schapiro, Prof. J. S. | City College, N.Y.C. | 21 | 26 | 21 |
| Sondheim, Leopold | 587 Riverside Drive, N.Y.C. | 21 | 30 | 21 |
| Tucker, J. F. | 520 W. 134th St., N.Y.C. | 21 | 28 | 21 |

### TWENTY-THIRD ASSEMBLY DISTRICT

| Name. | Address. | A.D. | E.D. | Ald. |
|---|---|---|---|---|
| Carsall, Charles | 555 W. 182nd St., N.Y.C. | 23 | 51 | 23 |
| Kendrick, Leon V. | 471 W. 145th St., N.Y.C. | 23 | 20 | 24 |
| Lockhead, Joseph Wm. | 2469 7th Ave., N.Y.C. | 23 | 5 | 23 |

### TWENTY-FOURTH ASSEMBLY DISTRICT

| Name. | Address. | A.D. | E.D. | Ald. |
|---|---|---|---|---|
| Cohen, Samuel A. | 105 E. 104th St., N.Y.C. | 24 | 24 | 25 |

## TWENTY-FIFTH ASSEMBLY DISTRICT

| Name | Address | A.D. | E.D. | A.D. |
|---|---|---|---|---|
| Abspacher, L. Kaufman | 145 E. 18th St., N.Y.C. | 25 | 19 | 26 |
| Baldwin, Evelyn Briggs | 10 W. 24th St., N.Y.C. | 25 | 23 | 26 |
| Brannan, John W., M.D. | 11 W. 12th St., N.Y.C. | 25 | 13 | 26 |
| Buchanan, Thompson | 158 Waverly Pl., N.Y.C. | 25 | 8 | 26 |
| Dukker, Witter | 10 Gramercy Park, N.Y.C. | 25 | 18 | 26 |
| Eastman, Max | 11 Charles St., N.Y.C. | 25 | 5 | 26 |
| Farrel, C. P. | 117 E. 21st St., N.Y.C. | 25 | 26 | 26 |
| Hall, J. | 88 4th Ave., N.Y.C. | 25 | 11 | 26 |
| Ibbett, Edwin S. | 120 E. 22nd St., N.Y.C. | 25 | 18 | 26 |
| Kellogg, Paul U. | 105 E. 22nd St., N.Y.C. | 25 | 26 | 26 |
| Mann, Rev. Baldwin | 10 Waverly Place, N.Y.C. | 25 | 9 | 26 |
| Mann, Roy | 5 Washington Sq., S., N.Y.C. | 25 | 7 | 26 |
| Miller, Jefferson D. | 8 W. 13th St., N.Y.C. | 25 | 1 | 26 |
| Mitchell, John | 100900 Metrop'n Bldg., N.Y.C. | 25 | 15 | 26 |
| Mitchell, William W. | 50 W. 10th St., N.Y.C. | 25 | 12 | 26 |
| Mobey, A. | 125 W. 23rd St., N.Y.C. | 25 | 22 | 26 |
| Nash, Arthur C. | 7 E. 22nd St., N.Y.C. | 25 | 25 | 26 |
| Poole, Ernest | 130 W. 11th St., N.Y.C. | 25 | 6 | 26 |
| Ruff, Theodore F. | 10 W. 10th St., N.Y.C. | 25 | 12 | 26 |
| Sawyer, Philip | 118 9th Ave., N.Y.C. | 25 | 17 | 26 |
| Segwick, H. | 120 E. 22nd St., N.Y.C. | 25 | 26 | 26 |
| Stebbins, E. Vail | 53 W. 9th St., N.Y.C. | 25 | 12 | 26 |
| Stowe, Lyman Beecher | 152 Washington Square, N.Y.C. | 25 | 9 | 26 |
| Tokati, Beza | 42 6th Ave., N.Y.C. | 25 | 24 | 26 |
| Townsend, A. | 30 W. 12th St., N.Y.C. | 25 | 12 | 26 |
| Tuesug, J. W., M.D. | 27 E. 11th St., N.Y.C. | 25 | 12 | 26 |
| Underhill, Morris | 102 E. 31st St., N.Y.C. | 25 | 27 | 26 |
| Wanless, Dr. Richard | 125 E. 15th St., N.Y.C. | 25 | 18 | 26 |
| Weyl, Walter | 29 W. 11th St., N.Y.C. | 25 | 13 | 26 |
| Williams, Theodore | 26th St. and Bway, N.Y.C. | 25 | 24 | 26 |
| Wohltjear, Frederick L. | 10 W. 12th St., N.Y.C. | 25 | 13 | 26 |
| Irving, Alexander | 14 Gramercy Park, N.Y.C. | 25 | 18 | 26 |
| Wilson, Paul C. | 80 Washington Sq., E., N.Y.C. | 25 | 9 | 26 |
| Foote, Dr. E. B. | 120 Lexington Ave., N.Y.C. | 25 | 27 | 26 |

## TWENTY-SEVENTH ASSEMBLY DISTRICT

| Name | Address | A.D. | E.D. | A.D. |
|---|---|---|---|---|
| Barclay, Charles B. | Hotel Ritz Carlton, N.Y.C. | 27 | 19 | 28 |
| Brotman, A. M. | 10 W. 39th St., N.Y.C. | 27 | 12 | 28 |
| Bigelham, Herbert D. | 240 Lexington Ave., N.Y.C. | 27 | 13 | 28 |
| Burritt, Wm. Nield | 13 E. 72nd St., N.Y.C. | 27 | 15 | 28 |
| Chatfield, Morton Thomas | 103 5th Ave., N.Y.C. | 27 | 13 | 28 |
| Cochran, J. O. M. | 51 E. 30th St., N.Y.C. | 27 | 15 | 28 |
| DeForest, Lee | 101 Park Ave., N.Y.C. | 27 | 19 | 28 |
| Delano, Wm. Adams | 4 35th St., N.Y.C. | 27 | 12 | 28 |
| Rev. Robert Freeling | 18 W. 44th St., N.Y.C. | 27 | 17 | 28 |
| Greve, Frederick S. | 150 E. 72th St., N.Y.C. | 27 | 19 | 28 |
| Goldsaker, Carl F. | 5 E. 87th St., N.Y.C. | 27 | 12 | 28 |
| Gunn, John D. | 2117 Woodcrest Ave., N.Y.C. | 27 | 19 | 28 |
| Hackstaff, J. Frank | Broadway & 126th St., N.Y.C. | 27 | 15 | 28 |
| Hertz, B. Russell | 45 E. 42nd St., N.Y.C. | 27 | 12 | 28 |
| Hopkins, Henry, Jr. | 85 W. 85th St., N.Y.C. | 27 | 11 | 28 |
| Kunz, George F. | 401 5th Ave., N.Y.C. | 27 | 16 | 28 |
| McIver, Francis | 19 W. 44th St., N.Y.C. | 27 | 12 | 28 |

## TWENTY-EIGHTH ASSEMBLY DISTRICT

| Name | Address | A.D. | E.D. | A.D. |
|---|---|---|---|---|
| Mielziner, Leo | 58 W. 37th St., N.Y.C. | 27 | 24 | 28 |
| Reamer, J. M. | 283 7th Ave., N.Y.C. | 27 | 7 | 28 |
| Schieffelin, W. Jay | 5 E. 66th St., N.Y.C. | 27 | 16 | 28 |
| Smith, Nelson | 10 W. 48th St., N.Y.C. | 27 | 10 | 28 |
| Townsend, James D. | 61 E. 42nd St., N.Y.C. | 27 | 19 | 28 |
| Van Ingen, W. B. | 58 W. 57th St., N.Y.C. | 27 | 12 | 28 |
| Walling, Wm. English | 18 W. 38th St., N.Y.C. | 27 | 12 | 28 |
| Goldberg, Samuel W. | 58 8th Ave., N.Y.C. | 27 | 10 | 28 |
| Milholland, John E. | Hotel Manhattan, N.Y.C. | 27 | 19 | 28 |
| Fuchman, David | 35 W. 46th St., N.Y.C. | 27 | 21 | 28 |
| Kidder, E. J. | 178 W. 44th St., N.Y.C. | 27 | 11 | 28 |

## TWENTY-EIGHTH ASSEMBLY DISTRICT

| Name | Address | A.D. | E.D. | A.D. |
|---|---|---|---|---|
| Cameron, Emile | 15 W. 43rd St. (Dwight Sch'l) | 28 | 20 | 27 |
| Gazzolo, Alexander | 2204 2nd Ave., N.Y.C. | 28 | 9 | 29 |

## TWENTY-NINTH ASSEMBLY DISTRICT

| Name | Address | A.D. | E.D. | A.D. |
|---|---|---|---|---|
| Austin, Dr. Eugene | 616 Madison Ave., N.Y.C. | 29 | 19 | 30 |
| Batcheller, Adams | 128 E. 65th St., N.Y.C. | 29 | 30 | 30 |
| Bush, Prof. Wendell T. | 11 W. 69th St., N.Y.C. | 29 | 2 | 29 |
| Fletcher, Dr. Simon | 160 E. 61st St., N.Y.C. | 29 | 9 | 30 |
| Hall, Bolton | 33 E. 61st St., N.Y.C. | 29 | 19 | 30 |
| Hotchkiss, Thomas W. | 609 Madison Ave., N.Y.C. | 29 | 10 | 30 |
| Howells, William Dean | 130 W. 59th St., N.Y.C. | 29 | 5 | 30 |
| Jaeger, Dr. Charles H. | 475 Park Ave., N.Y.C. | 29 | 7 | 30 |
| Marcus, Henry S. | 18 W. 76th St., N.Y.C. | 29 | 17 | 30 |
| Rudolph, Dr. Julius | 39 E. 63rd St., N.Y.C. | 29 | 10 | 30 |
| Schwyzer, Fritz, M.D. | 52 E. 78th St., N.Y.C. | 29 | 7 | 29 |
| Spencer, Nelson S. | 130 W. 59th St., N.Y.C. | 29 | 4 | 30 |
| Thaw, A. Blair | 125 E. 66th St., N.Y.C. | 29 | 11 | 30 |
| Hall, Rev. Thomas C. | 700 Park Ave., N.Y.C. | 29 | 12 | 30 |
| Martin, Alfred | 595 Madison Ave., N.Y.C. | 29 | 16 | 30 |

## THIRTY-FIRST ASSEMBLY DISTRICT

| Name | Address | A.D. | E.D. | A.D. |
|---|---|---|---|---|
| Andrews, Harvey T. | 25 Mt. Morris Place, W. | 31 | 22 | 33 |
| Berkeley, Max | 25 Mt. Morris Park, W.N.Y.C. | 31 | 22 | 33 |
| Elia, D. E. | 11 E. 124th St., N.Y.C. | 31 | 29 | 33 |
| Friedman, Robert | 132 W. 117th St., N.Y.C. | 31 | 5 | 33 |
| Mayer, Dr. George | 153 W. Morris Ave., N.Y.C. | 31 | 25 | 33 |
| Magaw, Ernest | 40 W. 119th St., N.Y.C. | 31 | 1 | 33 |

## THIRTY-SECOND ASSEMBLY DISTRICT

| Name | Address | A.D. | E.D. | A.D. |
|---|---|---|---|---|
| Bjorkman, Edwin | 941 Simpson St., N.Y.C. | 32 | 31 | 34 |
| Blick, Samuel D. | 1040 Simpson St., N.Y.C. | 32 | 31 | 34 |

## THIRTY-FIFTH ASSEMBLY DISTRICT

| Name | Address | A.D. | E.D. | A.D. |
|---|---|---|---|---|
| Corbin, Floyd S. | 1733 Oxford St., N.Y. | 35 | 40 | 41 |
| Raffin, Edward | 1110 Mt. Hope Pl., N.Y.C. | 35 | 20 | 39 |
| Frankfurter, Felix | 1045 Clay Ave., N.Y.C. | 35 | 5 | 29 |

## ONONDAGA COUNTY

Francis, G. E. .... Syracuse, N.Y.
Jenney, Alexander D. .... Syracuse, N.Y.
Marlow, Dr. F. W. .... 200 Highland St., Syracuse, N.Y.

---

Coolidge, Robert .... 1908 W. Genesee St., Syracuse, N.Y.
Clarence .... 100 W. Belden St., Syracuse, N.Y.
Illman, Paul .... 331 S. Warren St., Syracuse, N.Y.
Dorr, Rev. John Francis .... 411 James St., Syracuse, N.Y.
Hazard, F. R. .... P. O. Box 2, Syracuse, N.Y.
Hazard, J. G. .... Solvay Process Co., Syracuse, N.Y.
Ring, G. M. .... Dewitt St., Syracuse, N.Y.
Caster, Charles H. .... 274 Comstock Ave., Syracuse, N.Y.

## ONTARIO COUNTY

Abbey, Sanford W. .... Canandaigua, N.Y.
Lewis, Alfred G. .... Waldo Springs Farm, Geneva, N.Y.
Nash, Francis Philip .... Geneva, N.Y.

## ORANGE COUNTY

Batter, Henry E. .... P. O. B. 153, Newburgh, N.Y.
Howard, Harold Shafter .... 73 Grand St., Newburgh, N.Y.
Vanamee, Judge William .... 64 2nd St., Newburgh, N.Y.

## QUEENS COUNTY

Clarke, Christopher .... 242 Sanford Ave., Flushing, N.Y.
Eton, Rev. James H. .... Flushing, L.I.
Koon, Rodney G. .... Flushing, L.I.
Lennville, Henry E. .... Jamaica High School, Jamaica, N.Y.
Nelson, Alfred .... 702 Amity St., Flushing, N.Y.
Nelson, Norman P. .... 702 Amity St., Flushing, N.Y.
Yore, E. D. .... Flushing, L.I.

## RENSSELAER COUNTY

Brown, W. A. .... 2424 Broadway, Rensselaer, N.Y.
Joseph, Rabbi Theodore F. .... Troy, N.Y.
Keach, Calvin T. .... Hall Bldg., Troy, N.Y.
Mayer, George E. .... 3504 6th Ave., Troy, N.Y.
Murdock, Prof. J. C. .... 1827 7th Ave., Troy, N.Y.
Warenorg, M. .... 226 4th St., Troy, N.Y.
Winn, Rev. Arthur R. ....

## RICHMOND COUNTY

Clark, Hon. Lester W. .... New Brighton, S.I., N.Y.C.
Markham, Edwin .... Westerleigh, S.I., N.Y.C.

## SARATOGA COUNTY

Humphrey, J. F. .... Saratoga Springs, N.Y.
Janes, R. L. .... 184 Philadelphia St., Saratoga, N.Y.
Lester, Willard .... Saratoga Springs, N.Y.
Steenborgh, D. D. .... Waterford, N.Y.

## SCHENECTADY COUNTY

Fulton, George W. .... 345 State St., Schenectady, N.Y.
Lunn, George R. .... 230 Union St., Schenectady, N.Y.

---

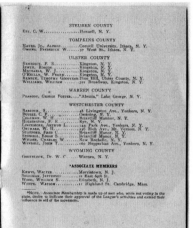

## STEUBEN COUNTY

Ett, C. W. .... Hornell, N.Y.

## TOMPKINS COUNTY

Hayes, Jr., Alfred .... Cornell University, Ithaca, N.Y.
Owens, Frederick W. .... 37 West St., Ithaca, N.Y.

## ULSTER COUNTY

Benedict, F. S. .... Kingston, N.Y.
Irwin, Roscoe .... Kingston, N.Y.
Michaels, W. J. .... Kingston, N.Y.
O'Reilly, W. Frank .... Kingston, N.Y.
Remick, Timothy Goodyear .... Pine Hill, Ulster County, N.Y.
Williams, William .... 301 Broadway, Kingston, N.Y.

## WARREN COUNTY

Peabody, George Foster .... "Abenia," Lake George, N.Y.

## WESTCHESTER COUNTY

Babcock, S. .... 48 Livingston Ave., Yonkers, N.Y.
Bourle, C. P. .... Ossining, N.Y.
Coleman, W. H. .... Briarcliff Manor, N.Y.
Hollbertson, F. R. .... Rye, N.Y.
Linfeimore, Arthur L. .... 144 Park Ave., Yonkers, N.Y.
Orchard, W. .... 236 Rich Ave., Mt. Vernon, N.Y.
Stafford, Fred C. .... Briarcliff Manor, N.Y.
Stowers, Edgar S. .... Briarcliff Manor, N.Y.
Warren, Charles W. .... New Rochelle, N.Y.
Winbel, John T. .... 160 Nepperhan Ave., Yonkers, N.Y.

## WYOMING COUNTY

Goshlock, Dr. W. C. .... Warsaw, N.Y.

## *ASSOCIATE MEMBERS

Kenvy, Walter .... Morristown, N.J.
Salvidian, Jefferson .... 12 East 64th St.
Wood, William S. .... Elizabeth, N.J.
White, Watson .... 11 Highland St., Cambridge, Mass.

*Note.—Associate Membership is made up of men who, while not voting in the state, desire to indicate their approval of the League's activities and extend their influence in aid of the movement.

---

# CONSTITUTION
### OF THE
## Men's League for Woman Suffrage
### OF THE
### State of New York

### I.

The name of this organization shall be the Men's League for Woman Suffrage of the State of New York.

### II.

The purpose of this League shall be to express approval of the movement of women to attain the full suffrage in this country, and to aid them in their efforts toward that end by public appearances in behalf of the cause, by the circulation of literature, the holding of meetings, and in such other ways as may from time to time seem desirable.

### III.

The officers of the League shall be a President, five or more Vice-Presidents, a Secretary, and a Treasurer. The offices of Secretary and Treasurer may be held by the same person.

### IV.

Any voter in the State of New York may become a member of this League.

### V.

The annual dues for membership shall be one dollar.

Howe was the husband of the widely admired suffragist Marie Jenney Howe. In a 1923 memoir, he confessed to his onetime ambivalence about the cause, and observed how the entrenched attitudes of his upbringing—"my mind simply held fast to the assumptions of my boyhood, which social prejudices seemed to justify"—had led him to stand in the way of his wife's professional advancement, especially during the couple's years in Cleveland before their move to New York City, in 1914. "I see again the resistance of the mind to facts that involve sacrifice or personal discomfort, that involve disapproval by one's class or the society in which one lives," he wrote. "As to women, I followed the changing mores. I spoke for women's suffrage without much wanting it. And I urged freedom for women without liking it. My mind gave way, but not my instincts." He wondered if this was not also true of many of the men who spoke for and worked for women's equality. "My own unwillingness to abdicate masculine power," he wrote, "made me better understand men's unwillingness to abdicate economic power."

For the magazine the *Housekeeper*, Judge Lindsey imagined that if he were a woman in 1912, he would think about politics as "nothing more nor less than public housekeeping—the mere expression of the common will in matters that pertain to the common good." And Edwin Mead, the peace movement activist, gave the lie to the "silly contention" of some male opponents that only if women were to become arms-bearing soldiers or policemen could they qualify for the franchise.

———◁▷———

In Villard's much later recollection, the greatest disaster of 1912 proved to be not only one of the worst in history, but also a profound reminder of how much the act of journalism meant to him, above and beyond his absorption in the management of the *Post* and the *Nation*, and his involvement "in politics, the Negro," and his other causes, which included suffrage and efforts to establish the New York State Police. There were also the many Wednesdays he had spent writing his well-received book, *John Brown: Fifty Years After*, published in 1910.

"I suppose most veterans of my time will agree with me that the greatest of peace time 'stories' was the sinking of the *Titanic*," his 1939 memoir recounts of the events of April 14 and 15, 1912, and the more than 2,200 passengers and crew who perished. The disaster had within it, he said, "every element of stark, overpowering human tragedy—pathos, superb courage, heroic resignation in the face of death. Gross incompetency and criminal mismanagement there were, too, and some cases of cowardice. Still it was, all in all, a triumph for the human spirit. No one who had a hand in getting out the issues which bore such tidings can ever forget those hours or be free from the desire to be a part again of such journalistic emergencies."

Women reacting publicly to the *Titanic* news deplored the impact of the then extant "women and children first" rule of the sea. It had meant a wildly disproportionate number of deaths among men—1,680 among the passengers and crew alongside 434 women and 112 children. The survival rate for women and children was 75 percent and 50 percent, respectively, compared with only 19 percent for the men. The anarchist Emma Goldman, an antagonist of the women's suffrage movement, published an essay in the *Denver Post* objecting to the privileging of women's lives over those of men. "I fear very much that the ladies who have so readily accepted the dictations of the men, who stood by when the men were beaten back from the lifeboats," she wrote, "have demonstrated their utter unfitness and inferiority, not merely to the title of man's equal, but to her traditional fame of goodness, love and self-sacrifice." Suffrage leaders were also quick to decry the practice. Harriot Stanton Blatch described it as an outmoded remnant of "barbarous times"; Inez Milholland suggested "children first" would be a better idea, with women helping the men. And to an audience in Boston, Anna Shaw warmly praised the sacrifice of the men who had "acted from the loftiest motives," but quickly added that she did not believe there should be "different standings of loyalty, courage and devotion." Women, she said, do not "want a standard that sets them apart."

◄○►

In its March issue, the *Crisis* carried commentary by the white suffragist Martha Gruening, director of the Frederick Douglass Center, in which she extolled with specifics the late black leader's unwavering support for the women's cause and took issue, as Du Bois had done the year before, with Anna Shaw's contention that black voters did not support women's suffrage. To this Du Bois subjoined without comment a proposed resolution that Gruening had submitted at the convention in Louisville the preceding November. It called on "the women who are trying to lift themselves out of the class of the disfranchised, the class of the insane and criminal," to "express their sympathy with the black men and women who are fighting the same battle." The resolution did not get out of committee. By June of 1912, Du Bois reported in the magazine that Shaw had written to the *Crisis* to declare that NAWSA did not discriminate against people of color, that "we know no distinction of race," and that if "they do not belong to us it is merely because they have not organized and have not made application for membership." Du Bois offered more reporting about what had happened surrounding the abortive Louisville resolution and quoted from a letter Shaw had signed, in which she gave her reason for opposing the measure: "I do not feel that we should go into a Southern State to hold our national convention and then introduce any subject which we know beforehand will do nothing but create discord and inharmony in the convention." Shaw went on:

> I am in favor of colored people voting, but white women have no enemy in the world who does more to defeat our amendments, when submitted, than colored men, and until women are recognized and permitted to vote, I am opposed to introducing into our woman suffrage convention a resolution in behalf of men who, if our resolution were carried, would go straight to the polls and defeat us every time.

By August, however, Du Bois reminded the forty thousand to fifty thousand black voters of Ohio that if they supported the enfranchisement of women in their state in the coming referendum, they would be doubling the state's black vote. "If woman suffrage wins in Ohio, it will sweep the Middle West and East in less than a generation," Du Bois predicted. "As Negroes have a larger proportion of women than the whites our relative voting importance in the North will be increased." Beyond that, he said, black women of all classes needed to stand as "high in counsel" in America as they had in the African fatherland. His editorial the following month led off the *Crisis*'s "Woman's Suffrage Number," with its eight-page symposium on the suffrage question, led by Fanny Garrison Villard's disquisition on the support her father had given to agitation against slavery and to women's rights. Du Bois cited "three cogent reasons" why black voters should care about women's suffrage: because it was a "great human question," because "any agitation, discussion or reopening of the problem of voting must inevitably be a discussion of the right of black folk to vote in America and Africa," and because "votes for women mean votes for black women."

The *Independent* featured an article by Edward J. Ward, the husband of the English painter Henrietta Ward, under a facetious headline: "Women Should Mind Their Own Business." What was that business? Just about everything, Ward suggested, except waging war or, when there was no war to fight, strutting around with a marching band. "This, it seems to me," Ward deadpanned, "they should not do." George Middleton so often tagged along when his wife and muse, Fola La Follette, stumped for suffrage that he found himself "absorbing material in which to dip my pen." He put his talent to work for the movement in one-act plays that featured La Follette, who happened to be the daughter of the progressive Republican senator from Wisconsin, Robert "Fighting Bob" La Follette.

——◇——

Villard, meanwhile, put focus on Wilson's presidential aspirations. In a letter, he assured Wilson that he was having weekly conferences with Wilson's other political advisers, which prompted Wilson to respond by return letter, "Indeed I do know that you are keeping in close touch with me, and it gives me a feeling of reassurance and strength." The national press quoted Villard as saying that Wilson was the only Democratic presidential hopeful not fettered to big business. The publisher's ties to Wilson would hold for some years, but not Wilson's with George Harvey, the *Harper's Weekly* editor, a member of the League's advisory committee who would later be promoted to the rank of vice president. A chill had descended on their relationship as Wilson got closer to the nomination and began to distance himself from the more conservative forces within the Democratic Party. The relationship didn't completely fall apart until Wilson's dinner at the Manhattan Club in late January with Harvey and Watterson of the *Louisville Courier Journal*, another conservative power player. The governor responded bluntly to an awkward but direct question Harvey put to him: Was the lavish support Harvey was laying on in *Harper's* doing Wilson more political harm than good? Wilson had to concede the former, given Harvey's known close ties to J.P. Morgan. Such a connection didn't reflect well on the candidate—the scent of big business was too pungent for a social reformer.

Word of their exchange got out and cast Wilson as a terrible ingrate, given all that Harvey had done to get him launched politically. Polite apologies went back and forth in private letters that Villard, in hopes of playing peacemaker and repairing the damage to Wilson, obtained permission to reprint in full on the front page of the *Post*. But neither the private nor the public effort mended the rift. Although Harvey did not withdraw his personal support, he did stop publishing Wilson ballyhoo.

At the end of January, Wilson received a letter from Edith M. Whitmore, the chairwoman of the Woman Suffrage Party of Staten Island. She reminded him about the suffrage sash that had been draped over his shoulder during his campaign stop in the borough for the Richmond County Fair back in September, and then asked: "As many thousands of women are going to vote for you in the West, may I ask for publication in our New York papers if those votes are not legal according to our Federal Constitution? If so why are they not legal if cast in New York? I have voted in Colorado; am I constitutionally disfranchised in New York? Also I wish to ask if you favor woman suffrage and if elected will you openly do so?"

Wilson's response was among the first of many attempts to avoid being pinned down on the suffrage question. Whitmore's letter had put a "very difficult question" to him, he wrote in reply. "I can only say that my own mind is in the midst of the debate which it involves. I do not feel that I am ready to utter any confident judgment as yet about it. I am honestly trying to work my way toward a just conclusion."

———◁○▷———

In February, Theodore Roosevelt managed to rile Eastman again, publishing a five-page essay in the *Outlook* that articulated a position on suffrage that equivocated at every turn. It included such lines as

> I believe in woman's rights. I believe even more earnestly in the performance of duty by both men and women; for unless the average man and the average woman live lives of duty, not only our democracy but civilization itself will perish,

and

> I believe in suffrage wherever the women want it. Where they do not want it, the suffrage should not be forced upon them.

Eastman called the essay "the most versatile and gymnastic piece of work I have ever seen." He slammed the former president as a "chameleon" and even compared him to the anarchist Emma Goldman. The only difference, Eastman said, was that "Emma Goldman goes just one step further." Roosevelt, he said, "dismisses the importance of citizenship. He admits that women are suffering from evils, but he does not think the right to vote would help them to get better things. . . . The fact that the greatest politician of today thinks that suffrage is not important is interesting and illuminating."

Eastman also took issue with Roosevelt's point that only a tenth of women wanted the vote. "Give it to those who don't know enough to know they want it. It will serve as a stimulus to them. They will learn to use it and the world will be better for it. Democracy as I understand it means a free and equal opportunity to get along. If this is true, I think women ought to have this opportunity as well as men."

Wise was the only man to speak at a mass meeting in Carnegie Hall on March 29, when Katherine Mackay ("in a low-necked tunic gown of black velvet over white lace spangled with silver, with tuberoses at her breast") and Anna Howard Shaw ("her white hair and square-set face showing above a plain dark dress") sparred reasonably politely but very publicly over how well American men treated American women. Mackay emphatically condemned "the shocking exhibition the women of London have recently made in their warfare"—and warfare was the right word for the British militants, she declared, adding that American men had always treated their women "with all the reverence they deserved."

Shaw, in her speech, shot back. "Well treated?" she asked. "When year after year we have been ridiculed and reviled by our legislators, who have addressed the women who went to plead for the ballot in terms which would have been unfit for the commonest of women. . . . They have belittled everything we women have done." Shaw's harshness might well have sprung from the bad news from Albany that day. The Assembly had voted seventy-eight to fifty-seven in favor of the suffrage amendment but then an opponent among the assemblymen "moved to reconsider the vote and lay the motion on the table." That motion passed by a vote of sixty-nine to sixty-seven, which stopped the bill from going on to the Senate.

Later in the year, the *Masses*—the magazine of socialist politics—appointed Eastman as its new editor, in part thanks to his engaging essay in the *Woman Voter* of October 1912, about the founding of the Men's League. At the time, the *Masses* was in financial trouble so deep that the month of September had passed without publication of a new issue. Eastman had impressed the magazine's regular cartoonist, Art Young, when they met at a dinner with Jack London. Young shared the Men's League article with his colleagues "to show how Max could handle words and ideas," which brought Eastman's candidacy for the editorship to the fore. "All the others acquiesced in the nomination," Young would later recall, "and we all signed a letter to Max, which said: 'You are elected editor of the Masses, no pay.'"

Robert Cameron Beadle, Peabody's close associate, stepped into Eastman's administrative role in the League, and although Peabody retained the honorific of president, Laidlaw, as head of the executive committee, became the "active head of the organization." In April, Laidlaw spoke at a dinner in the League's honor, hosted by the Equal Suffrage League of New York. On the same program were the attorney Winter Russell, who gave witness as to why he had become a suffragist, and the Democratic party leader John Crosby, an ally from the start, who titled his speech, "The Right of the Ballot."

———◇———

Peabody, in this period, had been reaching out to Wilson more actively about his prospective nomination as the Democrats' candidate for the presidency. Twice in March he wrote to the governor to express his confidence in him and to invite him to visit him at his home in upstate New York. The philanthropist had long been active in Democratic politics before he decided to step aside to devote more time to social causes.

Eastman tells a good story in his memoir about forging his own "friendly relation" with Wilson in 1912 and how he seized the opportunity to educate the then Democratic presidential hopeful on the suffrage question. The two men shared the dais at the annual banquet of the Syracuse Chamber of Commerce on April 7, as the governor campaigned for the nomination. For a welcome change, Eastman had been invited to address the crowd of more than three hundred dinner guests as a noted "humorist" rather than as a suffragist. The organizers challenged him to keep Wilson laughing by offering an extra dollar for every minute he managed to do so. Eastman took home an additional forty dollars over his regular fee.

The story goes that Wilson asked Eastman to give him a short course on the suffrage question and the two men ended up conversing on the subject for several hours. Wilson gave Eastman the impression that the women of suffrage, in the governor's view, were more fervent about avoiding their duties at home than in demanding their rights. "I like to think I did some important teaching during those hours," Eastman later recalled. "I never taught with a more subtly stimulated personal elation."

Eastman found Wilson to be a man with manner too smooth and thoughts not concrete enough for great oratory, but someone who in private conversation had the ability to inspire with "a heady mixture of self-esteem and admiration.

He was scrupulously attentive to your thought and meticulously candid in stating his own." How, Eastman wondered, could this man in high office who aspired to even higher office "be so candid without giving anything away. The topic of sex relations leads into many an intimate speculation, and by the time we rose for our speeches, Wilson and I were in a smilingly friendly mood."

His assessment of Wilson's personal views on suffrage dovetails with what two journalists would write in books published not long after Wilson's death in 1924. James Kerney, the editor of the *Trenton Times*, was among Wilson's most trusted New Jersey advisers, and David Lawrence covered Wilson continuously from 1906 until he died. In Kerney's view, Wilson believed deeply that women belonged in the home and abhorred the "foolishness of those who engaged in politics and actively agitated for the vote." Lawrence offered more detail: Wilson's attitude toward women was one of "chivalrous admiration." Conversations with brilliant women stimulated him, and he "never seemed wittier than in their company." In private, he almost always used the word "lady" or "ladies" to refer to women, and in his mind, "a woman was something finer than man, finer than politics, finer than life as men lived it. She was a creature to be exalted, put on a pedestal, worshiped, cared for and protected."

For Wilson, the idea of a woman in politics, business, or a profession was anathema, "offensive to his sensibilities," Lawrence wrote. Both journalists noted Wilson's aversion to what Kerney said he privately called those "masculinized women." Lawrence agreed, saying Wilson's prejudices against the suffragists stemmed partly from a belief that they were of the "aggressive, masculine-like, harsh-voiced type"—everything his Southern womanly ideal was not. "He actually encountered such types in the early suffrage campaigns," Lawrence wrote, "and disliked them."

Yet with the presidential campaign looming, these were views Wilson would not be featuring. Evasion continued to be his choice of response. On his visit to Pittsburgh only two days after Eastman's congenial efforts at persuasion, a suffragist walked straight up to him to ask that he declare his position on suffrage. His response resembled what he had told the Richmond County chair. "It is a big question and I am only about half way through it," he said. "My mind works somewhat slowly and on this subject I really have not come to any conclusion."

———◦———

In the *New York American* on April 14, a headline read:

## POLITICAL PARTY TO AID SUFFRAGETTES
### MEN'S LEAGUE TO ORGANIZE ON SAME LINES AS OTHER PARTIES FOR CAMPAIGN.

### IN ALL ELECTION DISTRICTS
#### NEARLY 500 MEN PLEDGE THEMSELVES TO MARCH IN PARADE HERE ON MAY 4

The *New York Tribune* put Harriot Blatch at the top of its front page to explain why the suffrage movement was investing so heavily in spectacle. "Logic and sermons never convince," she wrote, borrowing Walt Whitman's phrase. Emotions do. So do music and marching groups of people, far more than the most careful argument. Parades demonstrate strength in numbers, organizing ability and "that we have sense of form and color." Parades also have news value, which "feeds the enthusiasm of our army" and generates great publicity. "Look at our daily press," she wrote, "note the space it is giving to the May 4 demonstration, and surely the question is answered why we have a parade."

In fact, for days before and after the 1912 extravaganza, the newspapers abounded with pages of full-scale photographs and sidebars. Directly under Blatch's essay the day before the parade, the *Tribune* gave front-page notice of the

### HOST OF MEN TO MARCH
### IN BIG SUFFRAGE PARADE

and asked:

> Who said that the only man who believed woman should vote was the husbandette of a suffragette? 'Tis a base slander, as all may know who see "the most important section" of the great parade to-morrow—namely, the Men's League—for the largest division of that most important section will be college youths, who were never known to take their opinions from anybody, much less a petticoat.

The *Sun* also singled out the men for featured coverage, impressed by the projected number of marchers:

## MEN WILL MARCH
### Over 1,600 Have Promised to Take
### Part in Votes for Women Parade.

The League expected nearly twenty times the number of men who marched in 1911. Frederick Nathan, the US Men's League's international representative, announced the figure at a meeting the New York Equal Suffrage League held to honor the Men's League. He said his estimate did not even include the boy's brigade, which the ten-year-old son of Wise, James Wise, would lead. Delegations were expected from the men's leagues of Harvard, Yale, Princeton, and the very active New Jersey, Massachusetts, and Connecticut Men's League chapters.

Would they smoke, a reporter asked Beadle. "Why of course we shall smoke," he replied. "All of us who have acquired the habit: why shouldn't we?" But another prospective marcher, Charles Alexander Montgomery, who described himself to the reporter as a suffragist for the past twenty-seven years, opposed the idea. He was marching in a separate male delegation of prohibitionists who opposed riotous behavior. "Smoke—our delegation?" He seemed shocked at the suggestion. "Do you not realize this is a parade for a principle?"

Beadle pointed out how many outsiders would be in the Men's Leagues corps, especially compared with the previous year's courageous band, almost all of them League members. "The change in public sentiment is remarkable," Beadle said. "If there is a corresponding increase in favor of suffrage by next year there won't be anybody to see the parade; they'll be marching."

The *New York Evening World* fixated on the thirty-seven-cent straw bonnets that twenty thousand women marchers had arranged to wear, along with, as the front-page headline announced:

### 20,000 WOMEN,
### All Hats Alike,
### in Suffrage Parade

A *New York Times* editorial was uncharacteristically full of praise for the ardor and valor of these men, predicting the head count would be eight hundred in all, and noting that the marchers would represent "every trade and profession except the clergy," an oversight, the *Times* scolded, that surely needed to be rectified. The tone, however, was still snide. "This is important news and not to be trifled with," it said. "The men who have professed to believe in woman suffrage have always been numerous. But these men are going to do more than profess, they are going to march before the eyes of the more or less unsympathetic multitude."

The writer went on to acknowledge what a choice it must be for a man to make the leap from sitting passively on a platform to being willing to get up and march "behind a gaudy banner to the inspiration of the squeaking fife," closely watched by the crowd as "boy onlookers" pelt him with "endearing names." "There must be strong inducement to make men march in a woman's parade," the editorial said. "Some may be looking for customers. We suspect the waist-makers and the dentists, for instance. But the majority must firmly believe in the righteousness of the cause, and also in the value to it of their public appearance in line. They are courageous fellows. The march of the 800 may be renowned." To all of them, the newspaper extended "our sympathy and admiration."

THE TYPE HAS CHANGED.

Cartoon by Boardman Robinson. (*New York Tribune*, February 24, 1911, p. 7)

Parade Day arrived and the amid the twenty thousand bonneted women came a veritable "Who's Who," of New York men, "jeered from the sidewalks" as they marched four abreast, the *Times* reported, "but unabashed in their convictions." As the *New York Times* reported, "Men of every sort, and their number, grown tremendously from the scanty and much-derided eighty of last year, was close to a thousand. Some said that there were more than two thousand, but these estimates were much too large." The college delegation stepped into formation right behind the League and Wise's son, James, indeed, led a charming brigade of boys. Frederick S. Greene, president of the Waterproofing Company, was the Men's League's grand marshal. Efforts to recruit Theodore Roosevelt for that role had failed, along with an invitation from Beadle for him to join the New York League. Roosevelt's secretary declined the second invitation on his behalf.

All in all, the Men's League's efforts had paid off. The change in public perception of male involvement from the suffrage parade of 1911 to the parade of 1912 was downright stunning, as the headline over the *New York Tribune's* parade story acknowledged:

## HOST OF PROUD MEN MARCH FOR WOMEN
### NEARLY A THOUSAND PROMINENT
### CITIZENS, EACH WITH A GOOD
### REASON FOR BEING THERE.

### NONE ACTUATED BY FEAR
### GREETED BY CHEERS ALL ALONG THE LINE,
### INSTEAD OF HISSES AND MISSILES WHICH
### ASSAILED THEM LAST YEAR.

Greene told the *Tribune* reporter that it was clear from the response to the day's demonstration that "the question of equal suffrage is no longer regarded as a joke." The report included answers from a handful of Men's Leaguers to the question: Why did you march? Laidlaw said, to "give political support to the women and moral support to the men." From Wise it was, "I should be ashamed, believing as I do in equal suffrage, not to march." Bynner, the poet, was epigrammatic: "I march because I have two parents."

Middleton included those quotes in a May 18 "Snap Shots" column he wrote for his father-in-law's *La Follette's*. He described how vastly different his experiences were as a "Charter Parader" in 1911, driven to march by the force of his feet alone, and then as a marcher in 1912, propelled by a sense of absolute exhilaration. The distinguished but paltry band of 1911, he said, seemed "dangerously like the varieties of certain brands of well-advertised pickles." He noted how he and his fellow male marchers had been derided as "Lizzies" with "brow-beating wives" and "petulantly insisting sweethearts." In contrast, the thousand who marched in 1912 actually felt somewhat disappointed that they had not been able to "inspire better jests." "If it hadn't been for my pedal palpitude," Middleton wrote, "I wouldn't have been able to know how greatly the woman suffrage movement had advanced toward complete realization. I learned by contrast."

The parade also gave rise to new and further uses for these male colleagues, more evidence of the movement functions for which they remained particularly well suited, such as added political heft. Men's Leaguers joined the delegation that met with Commissioner Rhinelander Waldo to protest the parade's startling lack of police protection.

The day came to a close with a rally that stuffed Carnegie Hall with supporters from "pit to gallery." Outside, so great was the crush of people on Fifty-Seventh Street that only a narrow gulley of passageway down the center of the road remained. Six cars spent four hours that night overtaking Broadway from Fifty-Ninth Street to Thirtieth Street, then toured Manhattan and the Bronx, stopping on street corners for the passengers to stump for the cause. Swinburne Hale and his brother, Gardner Hale, both took turns at street corners, producing alongside their female companions the necessary "oratorical fire," some of which Swinburne reserved for a letter to editor of the *New York Times*, published May 19. "Is there any magic in our form of adult male republic that compels us to persevere in eternal reverence for it?" he began. "As a lawyer, I fail to see it."

---

Around this time, in the spring of 1912, Laidlaw made headlines with a mission statement for the many Men's League chapters then being formed across the country. He explained in a simple sentence the twofold purpose of these unique organizations, which, under his leadership, had broadened beyond Villard's more elitist conception to include any and all male recruits—read voters—who supported the suffrage cause. Laidlaw reiterated that the Leagues had come into being "to give moral support to men and to give political support to women." The rest of his words provide the best contemporaneous articulation on record about why the Men's Leagues kept forming and growing throughout this period:

There are many men who inwardly feel the justice of equal suffrage, but who are not ready to acknowledge it publicly, unless backed by numbers. There are other men who are not even ready to give the subject consideration until they see that a large number of men are willing to be counted in favor of it. The man who is so prejudice that he will not consider it at all will pass away with this generation if not sooner.

The usefulness of the Men's Leagues politically to women constitutes one of the unanswerable arguments for woman suffrage. Legislators are mainly responsible to voters, and voters only. In the majority of States in this country, earnest, determined women are besieging the Legislatures, endeavoring to bring about the submission of a woman suffrage amendment to the people. How long and burdensome is this effort on the part of non-voters, everyone knows. If a well-organized minority of men voters demand equal suffrage legislation from the Legislatures they will get it. After that, it is only a question of propaganda, and the Men's Leagues come in again on the first proposition of moral support.

The great educational work in the woman's movement has been done by women, th[r]ough a vast expenditure of energy and against great odds. There is still work to be done and hard work. We men can make it easier and happier work if we join in it, and no longer stand aside, as too many men have done, leaving the women to toil and struggle, making up in vital energy what they lack in political power.

<hr>

## FEUDS AND FACTIONS THAT REND THE SUFFRAGETES

The huge success of the parade had the newspaper, the *New York Press*, trying to ferret out how a movement with so many disparate ideas and enmities among so many influential leaders could manage to come together and to execute so remarkable a feat. In a piece under the "Feuds and Factors" headline, it examined the divisiveness among the leaders in New York City and across the state. It called attention to "an atmosphere deeply polar in temperature" in the interactions of the various suffrage organizations and their leaders. It gave special attention to the "coolness" between Carrie Chapman Catt of the International Suffrage Alliance ("a feminine Lochinvar come out of the West") and NAWSA's Anna Howard Shaw, the designated heir to the movement's leadership of Susan B. Anthony herself. Blatch was said to have skirmished with Catt over Catt's love of organization and Blatch's support for the militant Pankhurst. And yet the newspapers, the *Press* went on, seemed far more obsessed with Mackay's diminishing involvement than with anything else. The story said that at this point, she was no more than a member of the Equal Franchise League, which she had founded and funded. "She formed no attractions in a democratic leadership," the *Press* said, "and after a year or two dropped out of active work. She made, however, one real contribution to the movement. She removed the taboo from suffrage in that section of society which is spelled with a capital 'S.' She made it perfectly good form for

Black-lettered yellow Men's League for Woman Suffrage campaign ribbon. (Photograph courtesy of Kenneth Florey and his suffrage memorabilia collection)

the grandest dame to be a suffragist if she wanted to." Alva Belmont, by contrast, was more popular within the ranks than Mackay, the *Press* said. "Her ascension to the movement received so much newspaper attention over the country that large numbers of people supposed it was the first appearance of the suffrage movement in America and that Mrs. Belmont had introduced and was conducting it."

Of the Men's League, the *Press* made no mention. And yet its distinguished members were serving the movement in much the same way, even though they lacked the journalistic enticement of fetching fashion photographs of themselves, adorned in feathers and French lace.

Leadership issues were swirling rapidly enough in June of 1912 for unfounded talk of Eastman assuming high office within the Woman's Suffrage Party to circulate. This brought on a burst of hilarity among his unnamed friends. One typed, unsigned note that included a newspaper item read:

> Sir: The Men's League members of the neighborhood are wondering
> if all these brothers hadn't happened to read the enclosed treat?

And another:

> When running for the vice presidency of the Women's Party, to
> which we read you have been unanimously elected, may we suggest
> the enclosed for a platform, called "a Square Deal for the Youngsters?"

Later that month, the Men's League announced it would stage a major nighttime march—by torchlight—and with great fanfare took credit for this initiative as its representative made an event of signing the application for a city parade permit. November 9 was to be the date, right after the general elections. The *New York Times* wanted to know the Men's League's "impelling motives" for organizing an event of such magnitude and sought an explanation from Eastman, who was by then making waves as editor of the *Masses*. To this he replied in a letter that the *Times* chose to headline

### A SOCIALIST-SUFFRAGIST PARADE.

Eastman enclosed one of his pamphlets with his letter of response. "Is Woman Suffrage Important?" was considered an organizing document for the League, he said, and had already sold about twelve thousand copies. The *Times* explicated the essay in an editorial and told its readers that the League was not expecting women to purify or morally elevate the electorate, nor did it deny that women have "a body of passionate interests that men only partially share." However, the *Times* went on to equate the interests Eastman delineated with the interests of socialism, which the *Times*, and by extension, many of its affluent readers, opposed. "It is not just now necessary for us to oppose the 'real reasons' for the agitation by the Men's League," the editorial said. "We are content with stating them from its official pamphlet."

———◦———

Promotional stunts to publicize and popularize the movement got even more inventive as the years progressed. "Suffragettes in moving pictures!" began one story about three suffrage-themed silent films. "Well, say, pretty soon they'll be breaking into baseball against the Giants and then we won't be able to get away from 'em anywhere."

One of the films featured Jane Addams, Shaw, and an unnamed actor playing New York's US Senator James A. O'Gorman, along with Eastman, Beadle, Laidlaw, and Greene. The title of the third film was *Suffrage and the Men*. "The plays are real ones," the *Tribune* added, "with lots of love interest and pathos. The suffrage doctrine, in fact, is a very small pill with a great deal of pink coating."

During the summer of 1912, the Nathans set off on a transcontinental trip in a "high power touring car, decorated with suffrage colors and placarded conspicuously with 'Votes for Women.'" Stops included Ohio, Wisconsin, and Texas, where the suffrage question was before the legislatures. In Chicago, Frederick Nathan was reported to have been at the Republican National Convention "lobbying for a woman suffrage plank" while his wife, as president of the New York Consumers League, was "boosting the pure food propaganda." By June 22, the couple wound up in San Francisco so that Maud Nathan could represent New York as a delegate to the biennial convention of the General Federation for Women's Clubs.

———◦———

Peabody in this period was putting his political prowess to use not for suffrage, directly, but for Wilson. The governor's prospective candidacy for the Democratic nomination for president had fallen into jeopardy just before the party's national convention in Baltimore. Like Villard, Peabody was an early and important backer of Wilson's, and he sent a letter expressing continued faith.

Wilson responded tardily, blaming a cold, though he said Peabody's letter had come to him as "water upon a parched land." Wilson told Peabody that support for his presidential bid, which had seemed assured only a few weeks earlier, was evaporating to the point that "there seems small chance of service on a large scale. . . . The powers have shunted me. I do not repine; but I do feel like a man in leash—and such confidence in me as you express was needed." Peabody then got busy drumming up support and asked to have a "fairly full conference" with the governor soon. Wilson responded immediately with an invitation to visit him at Sea Girt, his New Jersey retreat. That response came June 23, two days before the start of the 1912 Democratic National Convention in Baltimore, where Wilson became the party's presidential nominee.

There is a July 1912 entry in Rabbi Wise's diary in which he, a longtime Republican, reflects on his growing interest in a Wilson candidacy. By this point he had written to Peabody to consult about Wilson and Peabody had expressed his "unlimited confidence" in the man, who he felt sure could be trusted. Wise then wrote as much to Wilson, saying that even though he didn't care "a halfpenny for the Democratic Party," he believed that Wilson's election might mean the "ending of both parties in their old estate."

Wise then wrote to Peabody, proposing that several Wilson supporters get together to draw up some "unofficial planks for the Wilson platform." Many pages in Peabody's studied calligraphy came back to explain why such a move would hurt more than help. Wise agreed with Peabody by return letter but still hoped for assurance that Wilson would commit to a "program of social democracy with all that term implies." Wise was distrustful of many of the party bosses in Wilson's camp and the influence they might yet wield. Peabody wrote back that he did not see this as a risk.

———◦———

A new issue brewed for Wilson at the Progressive, or Bull Moose, Party convention, held in Chicago that August. Roosevelt—who had formed the party after a break with the Republicans—ended his equivocation and pulled a bold publicity-generating move: Jane Addams became the first woman ever to nominate or second a presidential nomination at a national convention, as Roosevelt became the party's candidate.

The *New York Times* called Addams "the great figure" of the day's session and said her actions were "appreciated to the full by everyone of the thousand delegates and the eight thousand spectators," especially as she "descended from the platform waving a great banner inscribed with 'Votes for Women,' the whole convention burst out spontaneously and frantically into 'Mine eyes have seen the glory of the coming of the Lord.'"

Ida Harper, the suffrage historian, was dubious. The *New York Times* published at length a letter from her, raising questions with Addams for her convention display and asking if Roosevelt had "set a trap" into which the suffragists had fallen. Despite impressions to the contrary in the press, almost none of the women who attended the convention did so as representatives of the suffrage movement, Harper said. "So much for the capture of the suffragists by the Progressive Party!" She further explained that with the big crowd that met "the conquering hero" at the railroad station and the parade of hundreds of women who had marched into the convention hall, the women of Chicago had created a false impression. Harper asked rhetorically, what did Addams secure from the Progressives that "would not have been given if she had maintained a non-partisan attitude?" NAWSA's standing policy was not to take partisan sides.

In Harper's view, the women's suffrage and other humanitarian policies of the Progressives were "foreordained and predestined before the party was born, and she lost her contest for the rights of the negro," because Roosevelt had decided to exclude African Americans from his platform—including them would have lost him more votes in the South than he could win in the North. "There in a sentence is expressed the political character of the man. Women were included in the program because a million and a half already can vote, and the number is pretty sure to be at least doubled this Fall."

How well the Progressives would keep their pledges was yet to be proved, Harper concluded. "With the rapid advance in public sentiment toward woman suffrage it is now the highest wisdom for its advocates to remain strictly non-partisan and seek for support from the most advanced men in all parties."

Not a week after the Progressives had ended their meeting in Chicago, Villard asked to meet Wilson to get his views on four matters: the political situation in New York, the Navy, the Negro, and women's suffrage, especially in light of Roosevelt's latest grandstand play. Wilson said he favored a big Navy, which Villard opposed, but the editor liked the governor's response on the Negro question—his willingness to give assurance in writing of equal treatment under the law and equal opportunity in political appointments. Villard, like Wise and

Dewey, were still involved with the NAACP and all continued to serve as its strong advocates. They also, like Peabody, lent support to a number of institutions devoted to African American education.

Villard warned Wilson that Roosevelt was bound to make headway with this about-face on suffrage, especially in the states in which women could already vote. Villard presented Wilson with a letter he had just received from Susan Walker Fitzgerald, NAWSA's recording secretary, "begging a statement" from Wilson on the suffrage question. She said Roosevelt's sudden advocacy would cost Wilson thousands of votes in Massachusetts.

"I have no doubt it is true," was Wilson's reply, Villard reported, adding that he knew that Roosevelt would gain enormous advantage in the women's suffrage states. And yet Villard took away from the meeting the sense that Wilson would rather lose the election than come out for a measure in which he did not believe. And he did not believe. "I cannot do anything," Wilson told Villard. Villard expressed understanding. "You certainly cannot change now unless you are converted, without putting yourself in Roosevelt's class," he said. That was exactly it, Wilson replied.

The governor of Massachusetts, Eugene Noble Foss, wrote privately to Wilson around the same time to ask if he planned to speak out on the suffrage question. The suffragists in his state were pressuring him heavily to find out where Wilson stood on the matter. Foss said he favored submitting the question to a popular state vote, and Wilson agreed. He said "very frankly" that he did not think bringing the suffrage question into the national campaign was a good idea; that it was a state and not a national issue. "My own judgment in the matter is in an uncertain balance," he said, "I mean my judgment as a voting citizen."

------◄○►------

On August 21, the *Times* prominently featured on its front page a denunciation of Addams's endorsement of Roosevelt in the form of a brief but potent interview with the president emeritus of Harvard, Charles W. Eliot. "Women have no proper share in a political convention," Eliot said, as he accused Addams of showing "very bad taste" and Roosevelt of the same for acknowledging Addams so graciously from the podium. Eliot went on: "And I was surprised that he should so unreservedly play the cards of the women's movement in his convention. I think he will repent doing so. . . . We need women to bear children and attend to their homes. The men ought to be able to regulate their own politics to meet all needs without direct assistance of the women."

Roosevelt detailed the Bull Moose Party platform in a speech delivered at St. Johnsbury, Vermont, on August 30. Again he came out strongly for suffrage. "We recognize that there cannot be identity of function," he said, using a phrase repurposed from earlier remarks, "but that there should be equality of right, between men and women, and we are therefore for equal suffrage for men and women." He also defended Addams and assailed Eliot for criticizing her and the *Times* for publishing his reaction. "I do not believe that there is identity of function between men and women," he said once again, "but I do believe that there should be equality of right. I see no reason why voting should interfere with women's home life any more than it interferes with the every day work of the man which enables him to support the home."

◀◦▶

All throughout the summer, the suffrage movement had been staging mass meetings across Long Island, two hundred of them, including one at which Eastman spoke in East Hampton, rating coverage in the *Brooklyn Eagle*. "The audience was large and enthusiastic," the *Eagle* reported, "many of the summer colony attending."

In September, without props or makeup, Eastman, Beadle, Laidlaw, and other Men's Leaguers performed at Hammerstein's Ballroom in a fairly disastrous attempt at a vaudeville sketch. This was the Men's League's contribution to Votes-for-Women week in New York City. The skit concluded with Eastman giving a twenty-minute discourse on suffrage that sent more than a few audience members heading for the doors. His argument was a good one, the suffragists who were present offered in defense. "But," the *New York Tribune* allowed, "it wasn't what that vaudeville audience had paid their money to hear and see." The *Tribune's* headline said it all:

## NONE BRAVER THAN THESE
### SIX MEN FACE VAUDEVILLE AUDIENCE FOR SUFFRAGETTES

◀◦▶

October brought the State Democratic Party Convention at Syracuse and a flurry of telegrams, first from Beadle to the erstwhile Republican Wise, imploring him to show up and commit for Wilson, and then from Peabody himself. Ida Husted Harper covered the convention for the *New York Tribune*, noting that the state's women were agitating for a suffrage plank in the party's 1912 campaign platform.

"From the time Woodrow Wilson started out to be elected Governor of New Jersey he put his own particular brand on the slogan, 'The People Must Rule,' and it is still working overtime. Does he mean it literally," she asked, "or is he using it in the 'academic' sense?" The Prohibitionists, Socialists, and Progressives all had declared for suffrage and the Republicans were demanding a referendum. "Whereabouts in the procession," she asked, "do the Democrats propose to take their place?"

Wilson made two New York campaign appearances after the state convention, one stormed by cheering crowds at Carnegie Hall, the *New York Times* reported, and the other at the Brooklyn Academy of Music. That appearance was marred by a suffrage militant named Maud Malone, who for ten long minutes cut in half his speech about the insidious power of lobbyists and the private influence of big business on the political process. She insisted on getting an answer to a question she asked loudly from her seat in the first balcony: "How about votes for women?"

A yell came in response: "Put her out." Wilson held up his hand in a gesture for order and "in his softest voice asked: What is it, Madame?"

"Mr. Wilson," Malone stood erect in her suffrage purple dress and replied, "You just said you were trying to destroy a monopoly, and I ask you what about woman suffrage? The men have a monopoly." This, according to the *Times*, brought laughter and restored the crowd's good humor.

Wilson replied, "Woman suffrage, madame, is not a question that is dealt with by the National Government at all. I am here only as the representative of the national party."

The crowd again cheered amid calls for her removal from the auditorium, but Malone persisted. "I am speaking to you as an American, Mr. Wilson."

Wilson: "I hope you will not consider it a discourtesy if I decline to answer on this occasion."

More jeers came from the crowd but Malone did not relent. The event chairman admonished her to stop and so did an usher, who took hold of her arm. Wilson moved about the stage, trying to restore order. "I am sure the lady will not insist," Wilson then said, "when I positively decline to discuss the question now."

Malone: "Why do you decline?"

A judge, Otto Kempner, walked up to Malone and warned her that she was risking arrest. In the end, a police captain, a lieutenant, and a patrolman seized her and escorted her to the nearest exit. They arrested her for creating a public disturbance and Wilson continued with his prepared remarks.

At about this time, in late October of 1912, suffrage temporarily lost another bastion of surefire editorial good will. Support for Wilson in the pages of *Collier's* cost the Men's League's Norman Hapgood his editorship. The magazine's publisher, Robert Joseph Collier, was Theodore Roosevelt's close friend and supporter.

A diary entry of Wise's during this time reports that Peabody telephoned him to express his concern that if elected, Wilson might surround himself with people who would try to circumvent him in the matters such as the lowering of tariff rates. Wilson ran into Wise at a meeting in New York and asked him to come up to his hotel room. Wise, making note of Wilson's room number, 607, parsed the figure with some mystical numerology as Wilson's lucky number, six plus seven equals thirteen. "I said to him as we entered the room—Governor, I have saved you the trouble of thinking about your foreign policies. Mr. Peabody and I have settled that trifle for you." About the suffrage question, however, all the Men's Leaguers among Wilson's strong supporters continued to pedal softly.

---

## "AN APPEAL TO MEN"

As president of the National Men's League, Laidlaw signed an item under a big headline that appeared in the *Woman's Journal* the week before the November general election. It urged help for the movement from men of sound reason— "the wage earners and businessmen who have it in our power to raise money, to circulate literature, to make speeches, and to campaign actively for one of the greatest issues now facing the American people." Form Men's League chapters in your hometowns, the note went on, adding, "It ought to hurt any man's pride to let it be said that the women of American have to beg and implore and campaign and make so many sacrifices to gain a thing that belongs to them as a matter of right." Another item in the same issue provided the program for an International Men's League Congress in London that had been called to plan the next big international meeting in Budapest the following June. Both Frederick Nathan and Rabbi Wise represented the US league.

On November 5, Wilson won the election to become the nation's twenty-eighth President. Blatch wasted no time before she wrote to Wise, reminding the rabbi that he had "expressed assurances" that it would not be long before Governor Wilson "declared himself in regard to suffrage." "Now," she wrote, "has that auspicious moment not arrived? ... Is not this the moment, I might say the solemn moment when he stands facing the Duties of the chief executive of our land, to declare himself in regard to the greatest movement of our times?"

Shaw was quoted in the *New York Times* expressing the hope that Wilson "will favor the cause of suffrage" and saying that Roosevelt, as president, had refused the women's request, saying the time was not ripe for it. This was especially disappointing because he had voted for women's suffrage as a member of the New York Legislature and had recommended it once in a speech while he was New York's governor. "When he went to the White House, however," she said, "he would not make any recommendation to Congress on the subject. That was one of the reasons why the women in five of the six States in which they have the right of suffrage voted against him at the election on Tuesday." She said they put "absolutely no faith" in the declarations he made at the Progressive Party Convention in Chicago, adding, "He would not help them when he could and they did not trust him or any of his promises made in the stress of a desperate political campaign."

Election Day wins gave the vote to the women of Michigan, Kansas, Oregon, and Arizona but not Wisconsin, where the electorate defeated that state's suffrage amendment proposal. Shaw was quoted as saying that if the southern states had approved suffrage before the general election, Wilson might have come around to supporting the change in the federal Constitution.

The election also brought a win to William Sulzer, who resigned his long-held seat in the US House of Representatives to become New York's thirty-ninth governor, one who, at least before his election, never lost an opportunity to assure the suffragists of his loyal and unbending support. Blatch, Stanton's daughter, was quick to remember that Sulzer learned his suffrage lessons directly from her mother—their admiration was mutual—and he offered to introduce a suffrage plank at the state Democratic convention in Syracuse.

———◄◦►———

So stood the political situation as the suffragists ramped up for the November torchlight parade. "Unfortunately, the suffragists cannot show their numbers by their votes," the *New York Tribune* explained pityingly to its readers before the upcoming November pageant, "and so they must do it as far as possible by their paraders."

The procession was staged as planned by nightfall and again summoned some twenty thousand women, many in Grecian robes, some in chariots, all carrying twenty-five-cent torches—the *New York Times* described them as "big yellow pumpkin-shaped lanterns." The *Times* estimated that four hundred thousand cheering onlookers watched the "long river of fire." The *New York Sun's* front page said the procession included as great an array of old and young, rich and poor, as there had been in May.

## MEN'S BRIGADE UNAFFECTED BY JEERS— GAY ROBES AND SASHES WORN.

The *Sun* had more explanation in a section after the jump. Despite a few sneers and a moment of commotion, its reporter wrote, "If any had come to scoff they kept their peace."

Laidlaw served as the Men's League's marshal and Beadle as his second in command, but Frederick Greene, on behalf of the League's role in the event, was accorded the honor of opening the entire procession alongside the parade's Grand Marshal, Mrs. Beatrice Forbes-Robertson Hale. As the League's delegation came into view, crowds applauded the men "for their zeal and courage," the *Sun* said. But "after all it was woman's night, and the women had acquitted themselves gloriously from start to finish, so the crowd told them noisily."

Governor-elect Sulzer had been expected to march but he bowed out at the last minute with no explanation offered except a vague one about other pressing business. In place of the torches the women carried, the men all attached miners' lamps to their hats, ignoring the likely damage the lights might cause. "A big boom in the hat business probably will be the result," the *Sun* quipped, "but what's the cost of a new topper when it's for the cause?"

The *New York Times* gave the parade front-page coverage with two pages of jumps. It reported "LITTLE JEERING" and some "Good-Natured Chaff from the Sidelines," and said that in addition to the five hundred men in the League's division there were "many men marching with their wives and sisters under the banners of the different women's organizations." "Each of them had carried either the yellow flag of suffrage that was another emblem of the night or a torch." For special notice among the League marchers, the *Times* singled out two of the writers, Will Irwin and Bayard Veiller, the author of *Within the Law*. The police, all the newspapers said, were far better prepared this round and the marchers had no complaints about the level of security.

The night was an all-around triumph for which credit accrued where it was due. The Men's League may have announced itself as chief organizer and

James Lees Laidlaw as a marshal in the Torchlight Parade of 1912. (Courtesy of Schlesinger Library, Radcliffe Institute, Harvard University, from the memorial book, *James Lees Laidlaw* [Privately printed, 1932])

applied for the permit, and Beadle and Laidlaw were surely as involved as they were reported to have been in the planning. But in the end, credit in the press went to the actual prime orchestrator, Laidlaw's wife, Harriet. Nonetheless, to the *New York Morning Telegraph*, Carrie Chapman Catt would soon describe the League—"the thinking men of our country—the brains of our colleges, of commerce and literature"—as what it had become to the movement in two short years. Put simply, she said, "a blessing to us."

———◦———

More performances rounded out the year. Beadle dressed up as Uncle Sam in a stovepipe hat and a suit of Old Glories to welcome Catt home in a mass meeting at Carnegie Hall on November 19. Peabody represented the League on a stage that had "most of the nations of the earth processing across the platform and laying their flats at Mrs. Catt's feet."

The fourth annual NAWSA convention, held in Philadelphia, was the first in which the suffragists devoted an entire evening's program to speeches from prominent members of the National Men's League, with Laidlaw presiding. The banker not surprisingly focused his remarks again on the preposterous economics of the situation. Women had property rights but no say in the laws that govern the control and disposition of that property. They had the right to enter into businesses or trades but none—not as owners, not as workers—to control the conditions that surrounded those enterprises. Training to become better mothers and housekeepers was available to women, but they had no right to say which laws should protect homes and children. And women had the right to compete against men in the workplace, as teachers, lawyers, doctors and scientists, but without any right of political expression.

Some $2,000 was raised unexpectedly on the prompt of Joseph Fels, the millionaire Pennsylvania soap manufacturer and proponent of the Single Tax, who was one of the speakers along with Frederic C. Howe; the architect Alfredo Samuel Guido Taylor of the Connecticut League, Bynner of the Harvard College League, and the writer Jesse Lynch Williams. The *Woman's Journal* described them all as "courageous and justice-loving men" who were among those who had proved themselves to be "invaluable allies" of the movement from its very beginning. Yet this moment was unique. Only now had men "old and young, men of the most diverse professions, parties and creeds" come together "in such large numbers actually organized to work for the cause."

Under Harper's byline again, the *New York Tribune* gave the male suffragists their due. "The men are holding the boards tonight, and the women are in their natural position of adoring the superior sex," she wrote. "This Men's League for Woman Suffrage is a pretty nice organization, however—the only one which is standing by the women without intending to exploit them. They deserve all of the bouquets they can get if they have use for bouquets." She ended by scoffing at the request of Edward Bok, the suffrage-hating editor of *Ladies' Home Journal*, for a seat on the platform at the last day's mass meeting. "He'll get it all right," Harper wrote. "An armchair in the middle of the platform, with the spotlight turned on full."

Men's night, Harper said, brought enthusiasm to its highest pitch. The speakers "representing the highest and best in their various kinds of business and profession, made their splendid pleas for the political equality of women and told of their organization, already numbering over twenty-thousand." Laidlaw, as president of the national men's league, offered some specifics to buttress his economics argument. He noted the number of women working in mills and factories and that in New York City's commercial high schools, eighty-five percent of pupils pursuing a business education were girls. Why give women the right to enter business or trades, he asked, "without the right to control the conditions surrounding their business or trades?" Why say to them, "'Now you have assumed new responsibilities, go out in the world and compete with men,' and then handicap them by depriving them of political expression?"

Two huge issues dominated the convention: a move by Western delegates to get NAWSA's headquarters moved out of New York, and a debate over whether suffragists should engage in partisan politics during the election campaign or remain above the fray. New York remained the headquarters but the suffragists upheld Addams's position in favor of partisanship in a vote of 371 to 38. Belmont threatened to resign over the defeat, but in the end simply expressed "sorrow more than anger" and did not desert the cause.

In Blatch's postelection note to Wise, she suggested that Wilson appear at a rally in Carnegie Hall the following week—for citizenship, not suffrage—no purple or yellow banners—and repeat his nomination speech, one she thought contained "the noblest exposition on democracy" she had ever heard. Laidlaw and Beadle were prominent on stage that night but the telegrams Blatch sent inviting Wilson and Sulzer to appear, came to naught.

For Sulzer, the *Washington Post* had a preinaugural taunt on its editorial page in late December:

All the tact and diplomacy of William Sulzer will be called into play shortly after his inauguration as governor of New York, when the suffragettes demand that he commit himself to the cause of equal rights for women. New York is to be the Gettysburg of the woman's suffrage movement in the United States. Battles have been fought and won elsewhere, but upon the result in New York will depend the success of the suffrage movement in the East. Let the women win New York and the war is over. Let them lose and they will be set back ten years.

On December 21, at the Waldorf Astoria, the Woman's Democratic Club of New York staged a reception and "breakfast"—at three o'clock in the afternoon—to honor President Wilson's wife and daughters. The first to speak was the young attorney Dudley Field Malone, an early and fervent Wilson campaigner in New Jersey when Wilson ran for governor. Malone was quick to point out that he was not related to the now infamous Wilson interrupter, the suffragist Maud Malone.

His name does not show up on the New York Men's League membership roster of 1912 or at any point thereafter, but he was very much a suffragist from this point on. He had been married for five years to the daughter of Senator James O'Gorman, Patricia O'Gorman Malone, but she does not appear to have been the force behind his growing interest in the cause. In November of 1913, at the end of Malone's brief tenure as Wilson's Third Assistant Secretary of State, the *Boston Globe* interviewed his wife, shortly before the couple moved back to their home town for him to accept his next plum patronage position from Wilson, as Collector of the Port of New York. The profile quoted Patricia Malone as saying that she had not formed an opinion on suffrage or any other modern women's avocation since she had been far too busy "decking out her house." She also offered that Malone had persuaded her to leave Barnard before completing her degree. Since her only vocational aspiration was matrimony, he had argued, it made no sense for another year of school to delay their union. Her comments may have been little more than a contrived bit of press posturing in support of the Wilson administration's position, but they argue nonetheless against Patricia Malone as the likely source of her husband's growing suffrage fervor.

At the Waldorf, Malone told the crush of women in attendance that he wanted to talk about suffrage. As he was uncertain of where Mrs. Wilson or her daughters stood on the topic, however, he was reluctant to raise it. Instead, he took a diplomatic out and said only that since it was unclear who among those in the room wanted the vote and who did not, he would steer clear of what the *New York Tribune* described as "his favorite subject." He would go on to play a much more decisive and public role in the suffrage drama.

Charles Edward Russell

Charles S. Thomas

William A. De Ford

Gilson Gardner

Ward Melville

William F. "Buffalo Bill"
Cody

James Tanner

Herbert Warbasse

Donald MacKenzie
MacFadyen

George E. Green

Samuel Merwin

Martin Glynn

W.S. Moore

Gifford Pinchot

William A. Delacey

Selden Allen Day

6

# "Gettes and Gists"

## 1913

The male suffragists went on a tear throughout the whole of 1913, putting their influence to use behind the scenes and on very public stages—political and theatrical. They planned and executed yet another major pageant on Fifth Avenue. They fielded a delegation for the first suffrage parade in Washington, DC. They wrote suffrage propaganda plays and prosuffrage essays and speeches, and made their disparate opinions known on the militancy of the British suffragettes.

"Tradition," the first of the one-acts Middleton wrote for his wife, Fola La Follette, premiered in January among four "suffrage playlets" at New York's Berkeley Theater. His told the story of one man's views about the appropriate career choices of his son and daughter—and of the daughter's desire, in the playwright's words, "not to be economically dominated by her father." Over the coming year, Middleton redeveloped the idea into a full-dress three-act play titled "Nowadays," which was never produced professionally in his lifetime but had some renewed life in later years.

In early February, the Men's League joined forces with the Woman Suffrage Party at the Hotel Astor to host a "brilliant success" of a dinner for six hundred "brave and enthusiastic adherents of the cause of 'votes for women.'" The honoree was "Suffragist Sulzer," as the *New York Times* dubbed the new governor, whose inauguration had taken place the month before. Peabody introduced Sulzer at the dinner as a man who "believed in woman suffrage, still believes in it, and will help the women to win their fight in 1915."

Both Peabody and Justice Charles L. Guy of the New York Supreme Court were speakers, along with the former governor of Colorado, Charles S. Thomas, and Assistant District Attorney William A. De Ford, who publicly professed for the first time his support for the suffragists' cause. At the same time, De Ford admonished the women to receive the ballot "humbly and prayerfully," once it was won. "You are not equal to settling the great commercial and industrial problems of the day," he said. "A great proportion of the men are unfit, and the women will be until they have long exercised the power."

President Wilson offered Peabody the position of Secretary of the Treasury, but he promptly declined, explaining in a letter that he was "led by your forceful words to wonder whether there had been a lack of loyalty to you as Leader in my prompt declination, even though it was in obedience to a life-long conviction that I could render my largest quota of Public service outside of the constraints of office." The position went to William Gibbs MacAdoo. Later in the year, when the Federal Reserve Act went into effect, Peabody would become active in the new Federal Reserve Bank, working hard to encourage trust in the new system and serving on its board of directors from 1914 to 1922.

◄○►

Parade planning for May was already under way in the early winter. There was talk of asking Buffalo Bill, a reputed suffragist, to give up one of his afternoon shows at Madison Square Garden so the parade-goers and marchers could gather there for the movement to solicit funds. The plan was also to exclude for the first time the Socialist, trade unionist, and progressive delegations. Their participation had brought criticism in the past for their seeming to have agendas of their own to promote. At a meeting in New York to determine the order of the suffrage organization marchers, leaders were asked to draw lots. Laidlaw, the usual representative for the Men's League, could not be present, so Harriot Blatch drew on his behalf and happened to pick the parade's lead position for the men. "Mercy," she gasped, the *New York Tribune* reported, "that will never do." She told Laidlaw what had happened. Instantly, he offered to have the League bring up the rear. Blatch expressed great relief for "the noble generosity for which the American men are famous."

At the same time, planning for a major Inauguration Day suffrage parade in Washington had begun, prompting this column from Gilson Gardner, a reporter with good suffrage connections:

## SUFFRAGET PARADE AT WASHINGTON WILL MAKE INAUGURATION LOOK LIKE A SIDESHOW

The headline appeared over Gardner's syndicated column, datelined Washington, DC. He elaborated on the women's plans to overshadow the Wilson parade, which, he wrote, would be "nothing more than a military escort to accompany the president up the avenue." In enumerating the suffrage plans, he made special note of the "section of mere men, who are to be permitted to show their devotion to the cause of women's enfranchisement." Gardner's wife, as it happened, was Matilda Hall Gardner, the daughter of Frederick Hall, editor of the *Chicago Tribune*. She was closely allied with Alice Paul in the suffrage movement's most aggressive wing.

The Washington spectacle and its five thousand marchers surpassed all expectations, with a "wonderful allegory" representing the history of women throughout the ages. But unruly mobs descended on the marchers. They became so hostile and disruptive that Villard followed up by presenting a resolution to demand that Congress investigate why the police had allowed such chaos to erupt. He announced that President Wilson would be presented with a copy of the document as soon as possible after he took office. The League also sent

Suffrage hikers arriving in Washington, DC, for the 1913 Suffrage Parade. (George Grantham Bain Collection, Library of Congress, Prints and Photographs Division)

letters of protest to US Senator James O'Gorman of New York and Representative Richmond P. Hobson of Alabama, urging them to press the matter in their respective houses. Other Men's League chapters passed condemnatory resolutions.

There was more. Men "prominent in public affairs" gathered at the Columbia Theater in DC a week later to denounce the police department for its failure to control the crowd. "The proconsul of police is generous enough to give all the blame to his men in an effort to clear himself," the popular commentator Charles Edward Russell told the assemblage. "What, an American policeman doesn't know his business? There was something lacking in the police force besides numbers. When the police want a parade to be a success, it is a success." Starting March 6, over the course of a week, nearly one hundred witnesses testified before a US Senate subcommittee charged with investigating police conduct during the parade.

Wise sent a telegram of support to Corporal James Tanner, who chaired the meeting at the Columbia. It read: "Heartily join in the protest of meeting under your chairmanship against unworthy treatment of the women in the Suffrage

Crowd breaking up at Ninth Street, Washington, DC, Suffrage Parade, March 3, 1913. (Photo by Taylor, Washington, DC, Library of Congress, Prints and Photographs Division)

RESOLUTION PASSED APRIL 14th, 1913.

Resolved, that the Men's League for Woman
Suffrage of King's County calls upon the Congressmen from
this County to use every proper endeavor to secure a report
from the Congressional Committee appointed to investigate
the facts and causes of the insufficient police protection
afforded to the women who took part in the suffrage parade
in Washington on March 3rd. These women, many of whom were
among the finest intellectual leaders of their sex were, as
is thoroughly well known, subjected to insult, ribaldry,
and personal abuse. Evidence has been freely published that
these things were done without the opposition, and even with
the encouragement of the police, and we consider that it
would be most shameful to permit the matter to go by default.

Resolution of the Men's League for Woman Suffrage of King's County, New York, calling on Congress to investigate police inaction during the Woman Suffrage Parade of April 14, 1913. (HR 63A-H4.4; Records of the US House of Representatives, National Archives) parade. The Capital of the nation owes courtesy and chivalry to women visitors. The whole of the nation owes citizenship to its women equally with its men."

Du Bois, for his part, lashed out in his own way through the pages of the April issue of the *Crisis* against the way the shameful attacks on the women marchers had upheld the "glorious traditions of Anglo-Saxon manhood." "Again the chivalry of American white men has been magnificently vindicated," he wrote. "Down on your knees, black men, and hear the tale with awestruck faces. Learn from the Superior Race." And what was the message of these "magnificently vindicated" white men? "'Beat them back, keep them down; flatter them, call them 'visions of loveliness' and tell them that the place for woman is in the home, even if she hasn't got a home'? Hail, Columbia, Happy Land."

The clashes in Washington also prompted a new offensive from the antis, this time with help from Everett P. Wheeler, a prominent New York attorney and husband of an anti. Wheeler had been defeated in a run for New York governor in 1894. A week after the Inauguration Day parade, in a letter to the *New York Times*, he expressed perfunctory regret that there had been violence during the procession, but said there were lessons for the suffragists in the street battles:

> The teachings of many of the suffragists are abhorrent to the great majority of the American people. Inez Milholland, for example, declares that suffrage is but a small part of the purpose of the suffragists; that they intend nothing else than a social revolution. . . . What, then, did we have in Washington? A parade of women, some of them decently clad, but some of them, if we may believe the accounts, clad in a way in which no good father or mother would wish his daughter to appear in public, exposing themselves to the gaze of the crowd. . . . The spectacle to them was disgusting in the main.

Wheeler added that what the suffragists wanted would "break down the protecting barriers which courtesy and chivalry have thrown around women." To the American people, suffragism, he said, was as odious as Mormonism.

However hard Wise had been on the performance of the Capitol police, he had no known comment against the enemies of the marchers. His careful response harkened to the right-to-protest attitude he took toward militancy in the British suffrage movement, much like the one the assistant district attorney, William A. De Ford, had expressed at the Sulzer banquet in February. "I realize," De Ford said of the British suffragettes, "that they have a right to fight with hot wax if they want to." The remark, the *New York Times* reported, triggered a divided response from those assembled in the ballroom, with half of them erupting in "expressive sibilant hisses."

Wise, for his part, both privately and publicly, had gone even further. He expressed some empathy with the aggressive tactics of the British militants, especially after the authorities sentenced Sylvia Pankhurst and Zelie Emerson, who was an American, to two months of hard labor for breaking windows. Alice Lewisohn, an actress and the cofounder of New York's Neighborhood Playhouse, wrote to Wise to ask that he organize a meeting of prominent Men's League members with the apparent intention of making a formal protest to the British government. Wise canvassed his colleagues in the League for reaction. His papers include an exchange of telegrams he initiated with Peabody about the possibility of the League's issuing a statement in support of the militants. "Some friends think time has come for protest through mass meeting against British treatment of suffragettes," he cabled. "Would you favor such a plan? Have we the right to protest? Would it be wise and helpful?" Peabody's cabled reply on March 21, 1913, was unequivocal:

NO I HAVE NO CONFIDENCE IN OR RESPECT FOR MRS PANKHURST AND HER LAW BREAKING ASSOCIATES I AM AGAINST ALL WAR I DON'T THINK WE SHOULD INTERFERE WITH AFFAIRS OF ENGLAND THEIR INSANE PERFORMANCES HAVE IN MY OPINION GREATLY INJURED OUR CAUSE HERE.

Four days later, Wise replied to Lewisohn by letter and, without mentioning Peabody or his hostile reaction, told her he had "talked to enough men and women during the past few days definitely to have reached the conclusion that it would not be possible to bring together any strong and widely representative meeting for the purposes we have in mind." He noted that Americans were generally opposed to lawlessness and did not, "as I see it, understand that the militant suffragettes are engaged in what they conceive to be a stiff war, in which, however, they forbear to take life but merely make raids upon property."

The next day, Wise wrote to Lewisohn again, suggesting she get in touch with four of his Men's League colleagues—not Peabody or Villard, but Eastman, Howells, Ivins, and former US Representative Herbert Parsons—"probably the most valuable people for our purpose."

Eastman did his part to distinguish the British and American suffrage movements via the April issue of the *Masses*, comparing them under a headline of their different suffixes to the word *suffrage*.

## GETTES AND GISTS

He noted how while London suffragettes had been known to collect as much as $40,000 from one crowd, "Over here it is about all you can do to collect forty cents toward a polite series of parlor meetings." American women, he said, were more hung up on respectability than their British counterparts and lacked the "maternal instinct" to be mothers of a new revolution rather than daughters of a previous one. That, he said, was one reason for the lack of militancy in the US movement, but another was the "radical difference in the average male on this side of the ocean," where men constituted half the population. Unlike in Britain, where women had a two-million-strong majority, the American male "lacks the social sanction for so high a quantity of contemptuous superiority as the British male allows himself," Eastman wrote, and he appears to have "more facility of spirit" and "a little less pig-headedness" than the "pure Anglo-Saxon. By the grace of God, we are mongrels."

He saw no need to justify the militancy in Britain, because "it needs no justification. Only I would like to point out to some of our horrified sisters and brothers that we were fairly well united on militant tactics ourselves the last time we were up against a British cabinet." He asked, "Are you burning up with indignation that such things as window-smashing and stone-throwing and the distribution of the mail can happen at the hands of civilized women? Then direct the flames of your passion against those smug and respectable tyrants of political power who have driven women to these acts in a fight for what belongs to them, both now and eternally."

In a May editorial in the *Crisis*, Du Bois expressed satisfaction over a different move, some recent steps taken by NAWSA to give "a severe and, let us hope, final setback" to "the attempt to draw the color line in the woman's suffrage movement." That meant, he said, that a "great and good cause can go forward with unbedraggled skirts. Let every black man and woman fight for the new democracy which knows no race or sex." And Eastman, who had been scheduled to give a lecture at the Opera House in the Oneida County village of Clinton, said in advance to the local newspaper, the *Clinton Courier*, that he would be answering three questions: Why was the suffrage movement so rapidly enlisting men as well as women all over the country; what was the significance of the thousands of men taking part in the annual suffrage parades; and what interest should men have in the women's fight? "Equal suffrage is a practical issue in the political field," he told the newspaper, and "the Men's League is in the fight for it there." The League, he said, would "not lie down until it has abolished that political privilege which made its own separate existence necessary."

In fact, Eastman's Clinton visit had to be rescheduled for Halloween night. But in a May editorial published in anticipation of his appearance, the Clinton newspaper praised the young man's many achievements, and especially, his role in the creation of the League, which was nearing its fourth anniversary. "The fact that this reads like ancient history now marks the speed with which the Suffrage movement has travelled," the newspaper said, noting that the state's roster had climbed to nearly three thousand men and that national league membership had reached ten thousand. "The day of big headlines and heroics for the men who believe in Suffrage," Eastman told the Clinton editor, "is past."

As if on cue that May, Wheeler stepped up his offensive by announcing the founding of a men's anti-suffrage group that would be "in sympathy" with the Women's Anti-Suffrage Association but, borrowing a strategy from the proforces, "entirely independent of it." He called it the New York State Association Opposed to the Political Suffrage for Women, later changed to the simpler Man Suffrage Association. He said the first name he had seriously considered was the "Society for the Prevention of Cruelty to Women."

Across the Atlantic Ocean, in mid-June, distinguished members of the International Men's League for Woman Suffrage took their most visible role yet at the Seventh Conference of the International Woman Suffrage Alliance in Budapest, Hungary. Britain's Dr. Charles V. Drysdale, a prominent engineer, led a session he titled, "What Can Men Do to Help the Movement for Woman Suffrage?" Rabbi Wise was back in the land of his birth for the congress, but as a US delegate alongside Frederick Nathan. On the last day, Wise joined two professors, Emanuel Beke of Hungary and Dr. Emil von Hoffmansthal of Austria, for a rousing session called, "Woman Suffrage and Men's Economic, Ethical and Political Interest." British, German, and Hungarian luminaries offered more "vigorous" speeches in support of the movement. Coupled with the fervor supplied by the enthusiasm of the Hungarian Men's League and its intellectually impressive leadership, the US suffrage movement's official history reported, "it seemed almost as if the men had taken possession of the congress."

Charles V. Drysdale of Britain and a group of men lead a panel of the International Men's League at the Seventh Conference of the International Woman Suffrage Alliance in Budapest, June 15–21, 1913. (Manuscripts and Archives Division, the New York Public Library, Astor, Lenox and Tilden Foundations)

Villard, in this period, as chairman of the board of the NAACP, took on the protests of his fellow leaders and the organization's membership against the segregationist policies of the Wilson administration, both in appointments that would put a black person in charge of whites and in the racial separation of government facilities for civil service employees. He urged Wilson, as the country's first Southern-born president, to "win the confidence and interest of these people who ask nothing [but] fair play,—nothing but what they are entitled to under the Constitution." Wilson replied that the discontentment distressed him, as the segregation was in their interest. Three weeks later, Villard joined the NAACP's president, Moorfield Storey, and Du Bois, as its publicity director, to raise the alarm more loudly. "Men and women alike have the badge of inferiority pressed upon them by Government decree," they wrote to Wilson. "For the lowly of all classes you have lifted up your voice and not in vain. Shall ten millions of our citizens say that their civic liberties and rights are not safe in your hands?" Wilson replied to Villard that he was in a delicate and difficult position, "blocked by the sentiment of the Senators."

Villard did not relent. He wrote the president again, both thanking him and expressing disappointment that Wilson had decided not to appoint a Race Commission. "You will surely not let the Senators manoeuvre you into such a position that the colored people and their friends" could say that Wilson had not lived up to his campaign promises. Wilson said on this score that their differences were only practical—that his own concern was with the potential efficiency of such a commission.

The back and forth over Wilson's hesitancy on segregation and the discrimination he had introduced within the civil service kept up until well into November. Villard remained unconvinced by Wilson's argument that the matter called for extremely delicate handling, because of the opposition from the senators from the South, among other reasons. For Villard, it was a disappointing response, not only considering all that he personally had done to get the black vote behind Wilson, but also, as in the matter of suffrage, because promoting these initiatives was a simple matter of right versus wrong.

———◆◇◆———

In early July, the *Brooklyn Eagle* published an antisuffrage essay by a local clubwoman named Florence Shumway, who enumerated ten reasons women did not need the ballot. She argued, among other points, that not having the vote kept women away from temptation, and that women were too busy at home for public service. Her words ignited such a "storm of protest from suffrage quarters" that the *Eagle* sent a reporter to elicit reaction from three Brooklynites, all prominent men and all members of the New York Men's League. The response of Herbert Warbasse, the assistant district attorney for Kings' County, raised a practical point: with Brooklyn tax rates sky high, "is it not time Brooklyn women taxpayers had the right to use some other power than 'indirect influence?'" (Two years earlier, Warbasse had won the heart of Bertha Bradley, his future wife, on the strength of a rousing Fourth of July prosuffrage speech he had made while visiting his brother's summer home in Woods Hole, Massachusetts. The *Eagle* had announced their engagement under the headline "Suffrage Romance: Warbasse to Wed.")

Warbasse's colleague in the DA's office, Robert Elder, another well-known lawyer and League member, acknowledged how natural it was for men to want to subordinate women. "He has even debauched her," he said, "and is doing so yet. Possessing no efficient political power, she has been compelled to remain in an endurable position." The next day, Ward Melville, a philanthropist and business-man, chimed in, explaining that supporters of the vote did not believe suffrage would be a "universal panacea," that it would end the evils of government, nor would women who voted be less susceptible to evil inclination than men. "We feel the vote is a right," Melville said, "that no man has a right to set himself upon a pinnacle. . . . Who has said to him that he is by nature the superior and the governor of his mate?"

Four days later, the newspaper gave Shumway space to advance her argu-ments. The ballot alone would not correct "Sex Evil," she said. Women had greater influence without the vote. They would not be able to combat machine politics and they were not ready for universal suffrage. In general, she said, each sex has duties "Peculiar to Itself."

——◦——

## MEN'S LEAGUE TO RIDE
### WILL JOIN SUFFRAGISTS IN "ON TO WASHINGTON" CAMPAIGN.

## PLAYLETS ALONG ROUTE
### LEISURELY ADVANCE ON SENATE WILL GATHER SENTIMENT FOR CAUSE.

In July, the League launched an inventive summer promotion, one that became even cleverer with an assist from the plans of Alice Paul and Lucy Burns of NAWSA's Congressional Committee. Robert Cameron Beadle had announced in mid-June that Men's League members would start from New York on a horseback pilgrimage and spend a month getting themselves to Washington, DC, in time for an "On to the Senate" demonstration on August 1 that Paul and Burns had already begun planning. There, they would meet with "suffragists from all over the country" who intended to "rise up and move on the Senate," demanding that it bring the federal suffrage bill to a vote. Only a few men signed on as horsemen, among them, Beadle, Melville, and Donald MacKenzie MacFadyen, a Princeton University football star in his recent college days who planned to ride the horse he had won for sixty-seven cents in a lottery. The group planned stops at church suppers and country clubs, and the presentation of three "thrilling and convincing suffragette playlets."

President Wilson's wife, Ellen, known as "Nell," wrote to her husband on July 23 from their home in Windsor, Vermont, to say she had "escaped" a visit from a group of suffragists on their way to Washington who had not paid her the courtesy of writing ahead to say they would be stopping by. "They simply *came*," she wrote, "and called up on the telephone to know if I would see them." She had them told she was leaving the house for an important meeting, a literal truth, even though her plans were for the afternoon. They told her that they did not expect her to put herself on the record for them but that simply receiving them would be a big help to their cause. "Doubtless it *would*," she wrote, "for it would be considered putting myself on record!"

The *Washington Post* reported that delegations of men and women from all over the country had arrived in DC as planned and "bombarded senators with petitions bearing thousands of signatures urging consideration of a woman suffrage constitutional amendment." The Senate "siege" of July 31, as the next day's *Post's* headline called it, followed a demonstration and parade that started in Hyattsville, Maryland, and extended all the way down Pennsylvania Avenue to the Capitol grounds. Eleven senators spoke in favor of the amendment, presented by the Oklahoma Democrat, Senator Robert L. Owen, who had spoken at the 1910 NAWSA convention in Washington, the one the Taft hissing incident had marred. Laidlaw, as president of the National Men's League, announced at the evening banquet that the organization's men were "busily at work" getting every county in New York State organized for the suffrage fight before the legislature in 1915.

Governor Sulzer signed the suffrage petition that circulated in Washington but soon found himself in a political quagmire, under fire from Tammany operatives who wanted to force him out of office. A Joint New York Legislative Investigating Committee accused him of "making false statements of campaign contributions, diverting funds to purchase stock, speculating in stocks while pressing for anti-exchange legislation and using his office to gain support for favorite measures." Action was urged. Peabody, Villard, and later Wise exchanged letters about the governor, all agreeing his time was up. Villard called Sulzer a fraud, and Peabody said he had lost the ability to lead. Both immediately began thinking about whom to push as possible successors.

<>

The state suffrage convention was held in Binghamton that year, from October 14 to 17. If the Men's League fielded a delegation from New York headquarters, it is not apparent from the press coverage, which seemed more concerned with the refusal of a local hardware store to sell a hammer to the British "jailbird" Elizabeth Freeman, the first woman in Binghamton to have thrown a stone at a shop window. Twenty men marched with six hundred women in the town's first suffrage parade, watched by five thousand locals. George E. Green, a former New York State senator, became the "hero of the occasion" by organizing a local Men's League chapter on the spot and addressing the crowd alongside the mayor's wife and Carrie Chapman Catt. Laidlaw did him one better by pledging with his wife to help the 1915 amendment campaign with the sum of $2,500, to be given in increments of $100 a month for twenty-five months. Pledges to the cause that day totaled $8,593.

That same month, with Emmeline Pankhurst set to travel to the United States, concerns about violence rose. When she arrived in New York on October 18, the Immigration Board of Special Inquiry detained her. It took the intervention of Wilson himself to allow her entry into the country since there were no concerns about her "moral turpitude" and it was further understood that she had not come to agitate for militancy.

The suffragette appeared at Madison Square Garden, where she, Freeman, Lucy Burns, and Mary Keeghan, all of whom had been jailed in Britain, took the stage in prison garb. Pankhurst also appeared at a Woman's Political Union event at the Aldine Club, attended by three hundred people. Members of the audience hissed as Pankhurst came to the podium and the reception was tepid, the *New York Times* reported. Pankhurst spoke of the British movement and got tears in her eyes when she told of the imprisonment and force-feeding of her daughter, Sylvia. One reason for militancy, she told the crowd, was that women had determined not to wait for evolution.

━━━◄○►━━━

By November, Sulzer, not even a year into his tenure as governor, had been impeached. Another Democrat, Martin H. Glynn, succeeded him to serve out the term, but was defeated in the next election by Charles S. Whitman. Glynn was the former publisher and editor of the *Albany Times Union*, and known to be prosuffrage, a position complicated by his wife's opposition to the cause. Wise, for one, however, was no fan of Glynn, whom he considered a clumsy user of patronage with a "mania for economizing at the expense of the poor." He did support Whitman, however, a friend from earlier political skirmishes.

That month, the magazine *The Trend* published Beadle's version of the Men's League's early history. He repeated much of the information in Eastman's earlier essay but offered a more historical take. He traced the League's origins and purpose back to the first women's suffrage organization, founded May 13, 1869, as the Brooklyn Equal Rights Association. The Reverend Celia Burleigh was its first leader, and three preachers and a professor, all men, served as vice-presidents.

Although the movement had grown steadily since then, Beadle wrote, the greatest surge in momentum had been recent, thanks to "women of superb ability" who had managed to rivet the attention of the public to the movement's progress. The League stance was always to put the women first, but he did mention the men who had been "awakened to the importance of woman's viewpoint in politics."

Founding credit for the League Beadle attributed not to Villard but to Eastman alone, quoting at length from Eastman's 1912 account as it appeared in the *Woman Voter*. Beadle praised his predecessor—Eastman at that point had become the League's first vice president—as "a keen student of human needs and human nature, a professor of Psychology [*sic*] in one of the great universities, a man of winning personality and vigorous logic both on and off the platform." It was a return of the compliment Eastman had paid Beadle in his earlier origins essay. "One of my best services as secretary," Eastman wrote, was his passing of the Men's League baton to Beadle. As to Villard, Beadle wrote that as a member of the League's "front rank," he was "never too busy to give serious and faithful thought" to the organization's welfare. Beadle also mentioned, as Eastman had done, the symbolic importance of the first dollar in dues Villard had handed over to get the organization going, back in 1909.

Beadle also wrote of how the League's mission had evolved from its earliest days, when its intent had been to do little more than present an impressive list of prominent names. Instead, it had evolved into an active campaigning force, ready to engage at the state, national, and international levels. The "pressure or need" to enlarge the mission, he said, had caused the policy to change "gradually, almost imperceptibly." The League began to seek "quantity as well as quality of names." In the space of not quite four years, membership numbers across the country and the world had reached into the many thousands.

He extolled the leadership Peabody, his employer, had provided in the early period, saying that it had stemmed from the "high regard which he always had for his mother's ability and keenness, as well as his broad understanding of problems of education and civic reform generally." He added that Peabody's contribution extended far beyond the monetary, carrying the League with his "breadth of vision and inspiring ideals." Of Laidlaw, as Peabody's successor, Beadle said, "Probably no man in the State is better fitted to hold this important office." He pointed out that one of Laidlaw's most admired qualities was his ability to let bad ideas die in the arguments of others without pointing out to them the error of their ways. "It is this quality," Beadle said, "that has won for him the sobriquet of the 'Sphinx.'"

Since the League's founding in New York City, Beadle noted, it had spawned chapters in twenty-three other states—twenty-four if you counted Illinois, which predated New York by several months. "What do you think of a movement," he wrote, "that spreads from New York to California, from Maryland to Minnesota in less than three years?" Under Laidlaw's leadership, he said, the national men's league had already mounted a convention in Philadelphia and was planning a second one in Washington, DC, for December of 1913.

Beadle ended his essay with an appeal. The Men's League, he said, intended "with tremendous effort to bear its full share of burdens of the campaign" and wanted "every man in the State who believes in the cause for which it is fighting to join its ranks."

———◄◦►———

In November, Wise spoke before the School Voters League in Boston, urging the state to subsidize the homes of the poor rather than permitting children to earn wages before they were ready. Child labor was one of his pet causes, but he also used the occasion to touch on suffrage with elements of his promised "parasite" speech, saying he was ashamed of the antis "who fly from one bridge table to another, and at the same time say that a woman who goes out into the world and takes part in making humanity better destroys family life. I say that a woman who does this brings back to her home much more than she takes away from it."

Laidlaw and Charles Beard ended the year by representing the Men's League at the forty-fifth annual suffrage convention in Washington, which started in a boot-splattering deluge. The *New York Tribune*'s Washington bureau wondered if the rain was a bad omen and found the entire scene highly amusing. The writer noted Anna Shaw's "shimmering gray silk" gown and Harriet Laidlaw's "gorgeous pale purple velvet" before repeating a conversation overheard during the opening dinner at the New Willard Hotel:

HE—Want to vote, these women, do they? Well, they'd better learn how to dress.

SHE—Yes! How can a woman help being a frump when she's bothering about the vote?

And just then Mrs. Laidlaw appeared, a radiant refutation of that criticism.

The article went on to report that the night before the convention, one hundred "faithful men of Washington" met at the Public Library to form a local men's league with a membership of judges, generals, and ministers of high standing to "work for the federal amendment, backing up the women's Congressional committee." Among them was Commodore W.S. Moore, who had testified in March before the Senate subcommittee hearings on police inaction during the Washington suffrage parade.

Nevertheless, with so much exhilarating momentum and so many suffragists in town, there was deep disappointment when President Wilson neglected to mention the women's vote in his State of the Union address on December 2. Anna Shaw expressed her sense of letdown to the delegates, especially because Wilson's speech had so specifically urged a change in US policy toward four of the country's territories: full independence for the Philippines, an expansion of rights for Hawaii and Puerto Rico, and a full territorial form of government for Alaska, which had been incorporated in August of 1912. For the rights of American women, the president offered not a word. "We feel that President Wilson has fallen short of the greatest opportunity which has come to him or ever will come to him," Shaw said. "No other President has had such an opportunity." She went on, citing what had happened at the most recent international suffrage convention. "I feel that I must make this statement as broad as it is for the reason that we at Budapest last year realized that womankind throughout the world looked to the United States to blaze the way for the extension of universal suffrage in every quarter of the globe. President Wilson has missed the one thing that might have made it possible for him never to have been forgotten." She brought the session to a close by calling for a vote on a resolution noting the president's failure, introduced by Dr. J. William Funk of Baltimore. It passed.

While the suffrage convention was in session, both Laidlaw and Beard were among those who gave statements to members of the Committee on Rules of the House of Representatives during hearings on December 3, 4, and 5, in favor of a resolution to establish a Committee on Woman Suffrage. For Congress, it was the first debate over the enfranchisement of women in twenty-six years. Laidlaw expressed his personal dismay at the outdated attitudes of suffrage's opponents. Democracy, he said, means the right of the individual to join in the government, with rights to protect him or herself under law. Beard, the historian, argued in his statement that women's rising economic independence would bring them the vote, which in turn would "sharpen her intellect, force upon her an interest in the social and economic conditions which are determining her own destiny in so great a measure, and finally give her that self-respect and self-sufficiency which prevent her from being content with the alternate adoration and contempt of the opposite sex."

Everett Wheeler addressed the committee on behalf of his anti group, the Man Suffrage Society, holding up a photograph of Shaw. "When I saw this person here shake her clenched fist and declare 'We demand our rights,' I said to myself, 'clenched fists mean fight,'" he said. "The manhood of this nation has been trained to respect and revere womanhood, and I claim that for American manhood today, but if we are challenged to fight this movement there will be blows to give as well as take."

On December 9, Wilson met in the Oval Office with a delegation of fifty-five women led by Shaw. She put a request forward in three tiers: First, that the president urge Congress to submit a suffrage amendment to the states. If that was not possible, that he urge that the vote be given to the male citizens of Hawaii and Alaska. And if that was not possible, then that he encourage the House Rules Committee to follow the Senate's lead and appoint a women's suffrage committee of its own, as League members had advocated before the House—men to men—a few days earlier.

Wilson replied that he was not a free man, that he was not at liberty to "urge upon Congress in messages policies which have not had the organic consideration of those for whom I am spokesman." He said he would never present to any legislature his private views on any subject because he, as a government official, was no longer a spokesman for himself. That meant he could not be in the position of "starting anything." He did conceded that when a member of the

Rules Committee had asked him what he thought about the House instituting a committee, as the Senate had done, his personal response had been that he thought it would be a proper thing to do. "I wanted to tell you that to show you that I am strictly living up to my principles," he told the delegation. "When my private opinion is asked by those who are cooperating with me, I am most glad to give it; but I am not at liberty until I speak for somebody besides myself to urge legislation upon the Congress."

Adolph Lewisohn     Floyd Dell     Theodore Dreiser     Gilbert E. Roe

William H. Howell     Frederick Peterson     Walter Lionel George     Franklin P. Mall

Frederick Davenport     Edwin Björkman     Theodore Douglas Robinson     Carl Lincoln Schurz

# 7

# "This Whole Feminist Front"

## 1914

By 1914, there was little the Men's League was not ready to try in service to the cause. Its fifth year in action began with a prosuffrage literary gathering at Cooper Union on January 12. Among the male notables were W.E.B. Du Bois, Theodore Dreiser, and Lincoln Steffens, who told the women present that if they really wanted the vote they should "go out and get it," the way the women of England were doing. "Destroy buildings or anything else you want to. If you haven't power of any other sort you must use force," he said. "If a thing is necessary, it is right." As the *New York Tribune* observed, "For a feminine victory feast it was a most astonishingly masculine assemblage."

Three days later, a "Voters Dance" at the Masonic Temple in Brooklyn generated amused coverage before the event. The *New York Times* explained the need for two ballrooms: one for old dances and another for the tango or the turkey trot. A week later, another suffrage dance at the Hotel Astor involved enough husbands and Men's League members for the *New York World* to quip in a headline:

AT LEAST THEY'LL ATTEND EN BLOC AND PROVE THEY HAVE NOT BEEN DISRUPTED BY "VOTES FOR WOMEN."

Wise joined Colorado's first female state senator, Helen Ring Robinson, to spar with antisuffrage speakers at a meeting of the Economic Club. For his remarks, the rabbi repurposed his line about feminism being the deadly foe of what he called "hareminism." He also put in a word of support for the militant British suffragettes, much to the dismay of the antis in the room.

American suffragists had not thrown any bombs, bricks, or stones, nor would they, but at Carnegie Hall the following week, they hurled "hisses, hoots and catcalls" at opposition speakers in a debate sponsored by the Civic Forum, billed as "What Men Think of Woman Suffrage." The factions faced off on either side of the first balcony. The Men's League, the Women's Political Union, and the Equal Franchise Society took the right side and antis comprised of the New York State Men's Association Opposed to Political Suffrage for Women and its female counterparts took the left. The outbursts from both camps were so disruptive that the evening's chairman had to demand out loud that the unruly conduct cease. The fracas put the event on the front page of the *Times*.

At a Men's League meeting that winter, the attorney Gilbert E. Roe laid out all the ways New York law discriminated against women, a presentation the League turned into a pamphlet because of the "wide interest" his disquisition generated. For a reason no known documentation helps to explain, Beadle included a note with the published text to tell readers that the League was a "cooperating organization" in the Empire State Campaign Committee. Had the men of suffrage begun to get too much publicity? "While it is apparent that most of the campaigning will have to be done by the women," Beadle's note read, "still the interest and support of men, if only to the extent of a large membership list for the Men's League, is of immense value." Roe cited more than fifteen ways the law worked against women. He started with income and property, and the

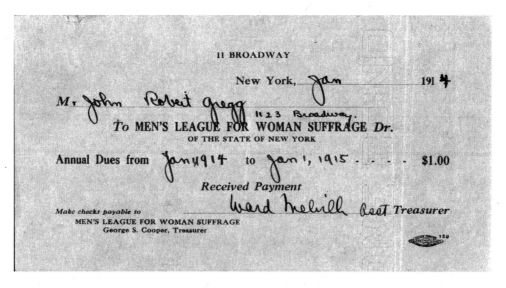

Men's League for Woman Suffrage membership fee receipt, January 1, 1914, signed by Ward Melville. (John Robert Gregg Papers, Box 127, Folder 9, Rare Books and Manuscripts Division, New York Public Library)

often-made point that the government taxed women as it did men even though women had no vote in determining either the tax rates or how tax revenue might be spent. He also mentioned inheritance rights; under the law, when husband and wife had joint earnings, women got a much worse deal.

———◦———

A twelve-page essay in the December 1913 issue of the *Atlantic Monthly* offered what turned out to be an incendiary view of feminism. It was the work of the British writer Walter Lionel George, an avowed feminist and the author of a new book that year, *Woman of Tomorrow*. He also pointed out the clear distinction between feminists and suffragists. George had become a prominent spokesman for the feminist movement in England—the "storm center" of the struggle for suffrage, as the editors of the *Atlantic* noted. They had asked him to "state quite clearly the terms upon which leaders of his party" would be "willing to negotiate a lasting peace."

It was important, George said, not to confound the suffragist struggle with feminist propaganda, which "rests upon a revolutionary biological principle," he said. That is, that there are no differences between men and women; there are only sexual majorities. The male principle, he said, may be found in women and the female principle in men. The feminists, he said, are "promoters of a sex war and should not hesitate to declare it." Suffrage, on the other hand, is "but part of the greater propaganda; while Suffragism desires to remove an inequality, Feminism purports to alter radically the mental attitudes of men and women."

Suffragists, he said, were content to attain immediate ends; feminists aimed at ultimate ones. Suffragists sought to alter the law; feminists wanted not only to undo convention but to diminish it to the point of erasing the differences between the sexes. "To put the matter less obscurely," he wrote, feminists recognize "no masculine or feminine '*spheres*.'" Feminists accept women's inferiority, he said, but see it as transitory, a condition that would end once the handicaps imposed on women were removed. George's piece also examined the condition of women with respect to work, wages, law, and marriage. It generated enough attention for the *New York Times Sunday* magazine to republish it later in the month.

Soon after, in an article in the news pages of the *New York Times*, a prominent biologist at the Massachusetts Institute of Technology, William T. Sedgwick, dismissed George's articulation of feminism as "biological bosh." The report quoted Sedgwick as saying that although the human embryo may not manifest sex characteristics in its earliest stages, it does soon enough, "and thence forward differentiation is continuous on the birth, and from this to puberty, and death from old age." From there Sedgwick went on to discuss what he termed nature's "mistakes"—"departures from the normal, developments where the sex characteristics are not as sharply defined as they should be. Hence we have masculine women and feminine men. It is not surprising that it seems to be these very masculine women, these mistakes of nature, aided and abetted by their counterparts, the feminine men, who are largely responsible for the feminist movement."

The rest of Sedgwick's statements could not have been more hostile. The *Times* ran an editorial the following day, noting that American suffragists rejected George's theories as much as the *Times* itself discounted Sedgwick's "masculinized" depiction of the women who comprised the suffrage movement's base. However, the editorial did accuse "these gentlewomen," these suffragists, of acting as "advance agents of the whole feminist movement,"and thus setting the nation on a dangerous course. "If suffragism succeeds," the editorial predicted, "the success of similar movements will inevitably follow, and as woman claims her new and perilous privileges, man will develop into a dominating brute."

Up rose the prosuffrage biologists with responses of their own. Within three weeks, by February 15, the *Times* had assembled a slew of indignant male feminists, most of whom were scientists straight off the Men's League's membership roster. They accused Sedgwick of being, as the headline pointed out,

## MEDIAEVAL, INSULTING AND INTOLERANT.

Doctor Simon Flexner, director of the Rockefeller Institute for Medical Research, led off by acknowledging that "no one with any knowledge of anatomy or physiology would today contend that men and women are precisely the same." However, that did not mean he shared Sedgwick's view that these anatomical differences had any bearing on the brain or on intelligence.

NAWSA reproduced in pamphlet form the statement offered to the *Times* by Doctor Frederick Peterson, a professor in Columbia University's Department of Nervous and Mental Diseases. It was titled, "Normal Women Not Neurotic." Peterson said he felt sure that if George's vision of the feminism ideal were to prevail, the "race would rise up to protect itself" from Sedgwick's dire forecast of a "total destruction of wifehood and the home, a total destruction of all the tender relations and associations that home involves." However, Peterson also said, at this time, "our only concern need be with the question of enfranchisement for women, already granted in many States and on the eve of affirmation in others."

William H. Howell of Johns Hopkins, a professor of physiology, found George's interpretation of feminism as abhorrent as he found Sedgwick's predictions for the future dissolution of the family. "When, however, the argument from physiology is used against the granting of suffrage to woman or against her privilege of preparing adequately to make an independent living," he wrote, "it must be recognized that the few facts of physiology which can be supposed to have a bearing on these questions are not in themselves significant or determinative." Franklin P. Mall, also of Hopkins, a professor of anatomy, added that in twenty years of teaching both male and female students, he had yet to discern any gender-related differences between them.

Only days after the debate in the pages of the *Times*, twelve speakers took the stage at Cooper Union to provide their definitions of feminism. More than half the speakers were men, and all of these men were associated with the League: Middleton, Eastman, and Eastman's colleague from the *Masses*, Floyd Dell; Creel, Jesse Lynch Williams, Will Irwin, and Edwin Björkman, the literary critic, journalist, and author. Each took pains to define the term, but it was Middleton who captured the most attention with his arresting opening line: "Feminism means trouble," he said, "trouble means agitation; agitation means movement; movement means life; life means adjustment and readjustment—so does feminism." Middleton's best quip that day—"Marriage is a link, not a handcuff"—made the newspapers two years later, although it was attributed to Max Eastman's sister, Crystal Eastman, who repeated the line as she refused alimony in her divorce from Wallace J. Benedict.

Years later, Middleton would ponder in print why at the beginning of 1914 "this whole feminist front should have aroused such intense feeling." Pages of his memoir recounted the event at Cooper Union and explained why so many of the plays he wrote in this period had a feminist theme, what he described as the "shifting standards of man and woman in relation to each other."

Irwin's remarks also captured attention. He assailed the false chivalry that had turned the nineteenth-century woman into "nothing but an animated clothes horse," a diminished role that had evolved from the loss of function. Home in the seventeenth century, he said, was "to some extent a factory and a school." That role changed over the next two hundred years with the rise of industrialization and the rightful entrusting of education to "more expert hands."

Middleton also examined this theme, saying that men needed to be freed from the burden of parasitic wives and grown children. The Socialist daily the *New York Evening Call* focused, not surprisingly, on Eastman, who, as editor of the *Masses*, was under indictment at the time, charged with libeling the Associated Press by indicating the news agency had favored employers in its reporting on a strike in West Virginia. Roe, as Eastman's attorney, got the suit dismissed. At the feminism meeting, Eastman "roused the audience to a high pitch" with "sarcastic shafts" directed at prominent feminist leaders who seemed more interested in talking about feminism than in doing anything about it.

Toward the end of January, the Laidlaws traveled to Montana to help in the suffrage campaign for that state and went on to California and Nevada for more suffrage work. Villard's *New York Evening Post* made much of the Laidlaw pilgrimage, reprinted Eastman's feminism speech from the Cooper Union meeting, and splayed over two pages an account of how amazingly well the movement was doing:

## VICTORY IN NEW YORK IN 1915
### REPORTS OF THE WINNING FIGHT FOR SUFFRAGE FROM EVERY NOOK AND CORNER OF THE EMPIRE STATE.

Beside the article was an attention-getting photograph, a full-length vertical portrait with a biographical sketch of another socially prominent woman the movement had recently attracted, the president of the Collegiate Equal Suffrage League of New York, Mrs. Charles Tiffany.

◄○►

That winter, there were calls in the House and the Senate to consider a suffrage amendment to the federal Constitution. Four hundred wage-earning women from East Coast states set out at noon from the Public Library in the center of the capital's Mount Vernon Square for a 12:45 p.m. audience at the White House to implore President Wilson for his support. Police officers, Secret Service agents, and "an army of moving picture men" stopped the women at the entrance to the Executive Offices. From there a smaller delegation, escorted by three members of the Secret Service, marched into the president's office. They asked Wilson to urge the Democratic Party to favor the change in federal law. Wilson stuck to his principle—not to recommend anything to Congress that his party had not pledged to support during its most recent convention. At the head of the delegation was Elizabeth Glendower Evans, a prominent New York social reformer. She reminded Wilson that when she visited him before his election in 1912, he had "given her hope" that as president, he would urge this change.

Wilson replied as he had done before, that at the time, he was speaking as an individual, not as a representative of his party. "Of course," she snapped back. "You were gunning for votes then." The president let the rude retort pass and held out his hand to shake each visitor's as she prepared to leave. Only about half the women were willing. As the *New York World* summarized the encounter, "They came, they saw and they went away angry."

In early March, Wilson did support the wish of federal employees who wanted to join "in the agitation for woman suffrage." He told the Civil Service Commissioner, John Avery McIlhenny, that he had no objection to this, so long as the women conformed to department regulations. "I am sure that you will pardon the candor with which I speak upon this matter of importance," Wilson wrote McIlhenny, "and that you will understand the liberty I am taking in making this recommendation." The following month, he reported to Colonel Edward Mandell House, his close adviser, that a woman had written him to say that the women in her state—a state where women already had the vote—would oppose him in the next election "unless he did certain things."

An even larger delegation of women came calling at the White House on June 30, this time, five hundred organized clubwomen from every state in the union. In advance of the visit, Senator John Randolph Thornton, a Democrat from Louisiana, wrote to Wilson chummily, wishing the president well before the "onslaught," with the hope he would "emerge sound in both body and mind." Again Wilson told the women that he was obliged to follow his party's platform and that suffrage was a matter for the states.

"Granted it is a state matter," asked the journalist Rheta Childe Dorr, a suffragist and one of the delegation's leaders, but "would it not give this great movement a mighty impetus if the resolution now pending before Congress were passed?"

Wilson replied that the resolution was for an amendment to the Constitution.

"The states would have to pass upon it before it became an amendment," Dorr said. "Would it not be a state matter then?"

Yes, Wilson conceded, although he added, "by a very different process, for by that process it would be forced upon the minority; they would have to accept it."

"Mr. President," Dorr replied, "don't you think that when the Constitution was made it was agreed that when three fourths of the states wanted a reform that the other fourth would receive it also?"

"I cannot say what was agreed upon," he replied. "I can only say that I have tried to answer your question, and I do not think it is quite proper that I submit myself to cross examination."

To Senator Thornton, Wilson reported the next day that he had "come through the ordeal yesterday intact, I believe."

Four days later, Wilson received a thank you letter on behalf of the National Association Opposed to Woman Suffrage from Josephine Jewell Dodge, the organization's president and a leader in the children's day nursery movement. She praised the president's "judicial attitude" toward the prosuffrage delegation and "our regret that any body of women should have so presumed on your courtesy in receiving them as to subject you to personal questions."

——◦►——

Creel was back in the news in the March issue of *Century* magazine, with a piece titled "What Have Women Done with the Vote?" It included charts and graphs documenting the effectiveness of women's suffrage in the states where it had already been won. This article, too, became a movement pamphlet. Because of it, Alice Hill Chittenden, the president of the New York State Association Opposed to Woman Suffrage, took Creel on in a letter to the *Times*. She singled out his choice of example: how women voters in Seattle had helped oust the "open city" mayor, Hiram Gill, who had advocated for tolerance of sin industries, such as gambling and prostitution. She pointed out that Gill had just been reelected. Creel responded via the *Times* that Gill had publicly repented in a manner so believable that "decent, privilege-fighting men and women of the community" had gotten behind him once again.

Over the coming years, Creel would repeatedly display his skill at crafting letters to the editor that provoked meaningful debate from leading thinkers on both sides of the suffrage question. On April 18, the *Times* published another of his letters, this one attacking something said at an antisuffrage gathering. The night of the event, the antis had managed to collect $40,000 on the strength of declarations from most of the evening's speakers that to give women the vote would mean the "disintegration of the home."

"Whose home? What home?" Creel asked. "Surely they cannot mean the dark, squalid holes in the 13,000 licensed tenements in New York City alone, where whole families and adult boarders sleep, eat, and work in a single room, toiling incredible hours for incredible pittances?" Or, he asked, did they mean the dog houses and barracks of the cannery workers of the Gulf States, or the homes of the 150 girls locked into the Triangle Shirtwaist Factory who perished when it caught fire in March of 1911 or "the tattered tents of striking miners in the mountain sides of Colorado and West Virginia? Or the sickening hovels in the Pennsylvania coal region?" Facetiously he asked the antis to clarify which homes they were talking about so that the actual danger could be assessed.

Marie Collins Rooney, president of an organization of antis known as the Guidon Club, replied on behalf of the anti constituency. The American home, no matter how humble, she wrote to the *Times*, "is not the vile place of mere existence depicted by the writer of this letter . . . but it is nevertheless the abode of a loving husband and wife and of children who are the joy of their parents and the glory and hope of the Republic."

In May, Creel and Upton Sinclair financed Judge Lindsey's trip to Washington to see the president and ask him to intervene on behalf of the striking miners of Ludlow, Colorado. At the hands of the camp guards of the Colorado Fuel & Iron Company and the Colorado National Guard, the miners had suffered a gruesome attack that left two dozen of them dead. Also that month, Creel spoke on suffrage in Kansas City, accompanied by his actor wife, Blanche Bates, who did not hesitate to tell interviewers that she did not believe in the suffrage cause. Creel could do no more than shrug. "I made her take all that clinging vine stuff back once," he said, "and thought she had seen the light." The reporter saw through to the value of this "entirely amicable" rift in their relationship, noting how well Bates understood the publicity game. Yet even well after the suffrage battles were over, in 1923, she was expressing the same antisuffragist views.

———◦———

In March 1914, the Men's League had announced it would sponsor its own pageant in April, created and choreographed by the doyenne of designer-choreographers, Hazel MacKaye. Incorporating elaborate tableaux, barefoot dancers, and music composed by Bertha Remick and arranged by James E. Beggs, MacKaye conceived the pageant around representations of five historical periods of women in history, followed by a regiment drill. The *New York Sun* reported playfully that the League was "having a fit" trying to find men with legs shapely enough for the silk stockings required for colonial garb, adding that the attorney Swinburne Hale had at least qualified. It further reported that all the booths for the event run by various organizations had sold their requisite six hundred tickets, so the pageant's financial success was guaranteed.

As the *New York Tribune* pointed out, with or without intended irony, "This is the first large affair the Men's League has undertaken, and many women are working to make it a success." The Equal Franchise League had become a partner. Next-day newspapers could not have been more effusive about the pageant's several hundred performers, its five thousand viewers, and the story of women

```
        THE   PURITANS

         EPISODE II

            M E N


         -------my fair lady."

      (As the children start the third refrain of "Long Bridge"
       a faint sound of voices is heard in the distance)

      (Outside)
   The witch!  The witch!  Where is she!
      (A crowd of men comes running in, headed by Mistress
       Crawford)

   The witch!  The witch!  Burn her!  Hang her!  Burn her!

         -----I'll show her to ye!

      (Behind Mistress Crawford - pointing at Mistress Allen)

         ----There she is!

      (Moving toward Mistress Allen in anger)
   Burn her!  Hang her!  She hath killed the babe!

         ------standing at her side.

      (Withdrawing slightly, also)
   Beware!  Beware!  She is a witch!
```

Page from Hazel Mackaye's choreography and script for the Men's League Pageant of May 1914 at the Armory in New York City. (Rauner Special Collections Library Archive, Dartmouth College)

through time it told in allegory form. The pageant started with Native American men hunting and fishing as women trailed along carrying bundles. Next came a Puritan village where a jury of hostile men tried a woman for witchcraft.

In the Colonial scene, men turned women away from the doors of a town meeting. To depict the Civil War, neighbors hooted and jeered Susan B. Anthony for seeking the same rights for women that were being sought for African Americans. To represent the present day, men and women walked side-by-side carrying law books and surgeon's kits, only to be barred from entry at the doors to Justice Hall. "The last scene," the *New York Tribune* reported, "showed the happy future when the vote is won," followed by forty-one barefoot "yellow winged goddesses of victory" in a "dance of triumph."

And yet, as Karen Blair points out in her 1994 book, *The Torchbearers*, the pageant became controversial for the way it parodied town histories and emphasized the economic, political, and social oppression of American women. In tone and content, Blair said, the pageant was "grim" and "its message was depressing, if not paralyzing,"—not to mention downright insulting to those in the audience it was intended to convert. It was never performed again.

The big get for the Men's League membership roster in 1914 was Adolph Lewisohn, the mining magnate, investment banker, philanthropist, and obvious recruit of his wife, who had corresponded with Wise in 1913 over the possibility of Men's League support for the British militants. The *Times* saw fit to cover his maiden speech for suffrage, given at a private home in April. Lewisohn said he agreed with Creel that if suffrage were to break up some miserable homes, so be it. He had given the suffrage matter thorough consideration, he said, "and I have come to the conclusion that no harm and only good can result from it. It is justice and only injustice is harmful."

For the first time in four years, there was no parade for Suffrage Day in May. No specific reason was given. The *New York Times* speculated derisively that the "exceedingly hobbled skirts" fashionable that spring would have made a parade on Fifth Avenue "a low and tedious toddle." Nevertheless, Mayor John Purroy Mitchel was enlisted on Suffrage Day to offer keys to the city, but not to speak until the following day at a large gathering in Carnegie Hall. That speech—the *New York Tribune* labeled him "Mayor Mere Man"—could not have been more disappointing. Mitchel said that he did not believe women needed the vote to enter public life and that when enough women wanted suffrage, and wanted it enough, they would get it. Organizers complained to reporters that he sounded as if he were reading something written a century ago.

In the *Masses*, under the headline "Feminism for Men," Floyd Dell added his offbeat views to the meaning-of-feminism controversy that had erupted earlier in the year. "Irresistible economic forces are taking more and more women every year out of the economic shelter of the home, into the great world," he wrote, "making them workers and earners with men." That, in turn, would free men to quit their jobs if they wanted to without making them "a hero and a scoundrel at the same time." Feminism, he said, would at least make men free.

————◁◇▷————

Du Bois, in his editorial in the August 1914 issue of the *Crisis*, pressed the case for suffrage to the likely voters in upcoming referenda among a total black population of more than half a million in North and South Dakota, Montana, Nevada, Missouri, and Nebraska, and possibly Ohio and Oklahoma. ("Assuming that the black voters of Oklahoma will be largely disfranchised," he wrote, "it is, nevertheless, probable that 80,000 Negro voters will be asked to vote for or against the extension of the right of suffrage to women.") He responded to a reader who had wondered whether white women with the vote would be responsive to issues of importance to black people—lynching and unjust marriage laws, for instance—when they had shown no such inclination thus far. "It is the awful penalty of injustice and oppression to breed in the oppressed the desire to oppress others," Du Bois replied. He went on to build an argument that culminated in the contention that even though white women would be "as unfair in race rights as the man," in the short run, "there would be in the long run a better chance to appeal to a group that knows the disadvantage and injustice of disfranchisement by experience, than to one arrogant and careless with power. And in all cases the broader the basis of democracy the surer is the universal appeal for justice to win ultimate hearing and sympathy."

————◁◇▷————

The suffragists devised ever more brilliant ways to bring attention to their cause. In October, they organized three divisions of automobiles, driven by women, to travel to the annual New York suffrage convention at Rochester from designated cities throughout the state. One flank, stopped in Nyack, managed to get a new Men's League chapter formed before the group had even finished dinner. They honored a nonagenarian identified as John Calvin (doubtless John Calvin Blauvelt), the original Rockland County suffragist as he called himself, by promptly enrolling him as a charter member.

Neither flat tires nor "the blowing up of an automobile and the consequent arrival of the fire company" deterred any of the delegates as they proceeded to Albany and then on to Syracuse and Rochester. But there were casualties. The Laidlaws' car broke down early on, and they had to call the Red Cross for assistance. A Goshen couple, the Sewards, rescued them and then campaigned with them for three days. "Mrs. Marshall Bacon had to call in medical help at Utica," the *Sun* said, "and was ordered to take a rest. Mrs. H.A. Grant kept her car there to give any assistance needed." The suffragist known as "General Rosalie Jones," for all the suffrage hikes and pilgrimages she had led over the years, "woke her party early and ordered a stolen march on Syracuse." Apparently, the *Sun* said, she "finds chauffeuring more intricate than hiking."

Bruised and battered but triumphant, the caravan arrived in time for the convention, on October 11. Among its trophies were yellow Men's League membership slips signed by the Republican and Progressive Party politicians Frederick Davenport and Theodore Douglas Robinson. Another one bore the signature of Theodore Roosevelt, who had been scheduled to speak at Utica but failed to arrive. Five hundred men gathered to greet June Olcott's car in Cortland and "filled her hands with the signed yellow slips."

There was even more show-stopping news that month: the widow of the publisher Frank Leslie had left a million-dollar bequest to the movement, to be administered by Carrie Chapman Catt.

———◇———

Although the outbreak of war in Europe loomed over all other concerns in the fall of 1914, Villard, on November 17, wrote the White House to urge that the president see both a November 13 editorial in the *Evening Post* and another in the *New York World*. Both contained critical reactions to a recent exchange between Wilson and William Monroe Trotter, the black newspaper editor and civil rights activist. Trotter had complained bitterly about the demeaning segregation of black federal employees who had worked with their office mates for fifty years without racial friction. As Trotter told Wilson, "Mr. President, we are sorely disappointed that you take the position that the separation itself is not wrong, is not injurious, is not rightly offensive to you." At another point Trotter had said, "Only two years ago, you were heralded as perhaps the second Lincoln, and now the Afro-American leaders who supported you are hounded as false leaders and traitors to their race." The *Post*'s editorial acknowledged Trotter's bad manners in the way he addressed the President, but slammed the administration for "drawing a color line where it had not previously existed," and Wilson for being unable to put himself in the other fellow's place.

Wilson complained it was "political blackmail" to threaten, as Trotter and his delegation had done, that blacks would vote Republican in the future, but the *Post* contended this was the time-honored means voters had to show their disapproval. Wilson, it said, seemed unable to appreciate what it meant to be a victim of prejudice and injustice, "to be wronged without the power to remedy the wrong." The editorial went on:

> That Mr. Wilson is unable to visualize this is, we repeat, the more disappointing because there are so many injured persons with whom he does sympathize so understandingly. His unusual vision and imagination leave him, however, when it comes to the disenfranchisement of women and to permitting his subordinates to inflict indignities upon American citizens in the immediate vicinity of the White House.

Only a day later, Wilson replied to a letter from a female clerk in the Forest Service of the Agriculture Department, who had raised the question of women's suffrage. He expressed his admiration for the movement but reiterated his belief that it was a matter for the states to decide. On the question of a federal amendment, he added, to attempt a "sweeping change in the fundamental law of the nation itself" would mean, "running too far and too fast ahead of the general public opinion of the country."

———◦———

Moving at full force alongside the federal initiative was the suffrage amendment campaign for New York State. In December, a newly organized Men's Campaign Committee for Suffrage, under the larger Empire State group umbrella, scheduled its first meeting at the Lotos Club, aiming to "persuade the Legislature to submit a constitutional amendment for suffrage to the people without waiting for constitutional convention action," as the *New York Times* explained. Among those gathered were Roe, Laidlaw, Wise, and Charles Strong. But there was a truly awkward hitch. The Lotos Club barred women, including reporters. The men moved the meeting to the Manhattan Club, but it, too, turned out to have a men-only policy. This meant no press coverage of the action they took, save an amusing piece in the *Tribune* about their embarrassment. The newspaper dummied up a classified ad for its lead:

> WANTED—A refuge for men suffragists where women may be admitted to meetings; apply at once. Gilbert E. Roe, 65 Liberty St.

It wasn't long until Laidlaw, among the most generous of contributors to the suffrage cause, offered meeting space on the ground floor and cafeteria of his family's banking firm, Laidlaw & Company.

Calvin Tomkins

Anthony Fiala

Isaac Marcosson

Walter Lippmann

Charles Burnham

Charles H. Strong

Frank Crowninshield

Thomas E. Rush

Irving Burdick

Charles Frederick Adams

George W. Kirchwey

Leo M. Klein

Ray Stannard Baker

William Harman Black

William H. Wadhams

Irvin S. Cobb

8

# "Should Women Vote in New York?"

## 1915

The suffragists, in retrospect, declared their campaign in New York State among the greatest chapters in the entire national movement saga. True, advances came slowly for many years, but in 1915 and 1917, Ida Husted Harper's history records, New York rose "to a height never attained elsewhere and culminated in two campaigns that in number of adherents and comprehensive work were never equaled."

In January 1915, as the US Congress debated the resolution proposing a suffrage amendment to the federal Constitution, both houses of the legislature in New York State voted to submit the women's suffrage question to voters come November 2.

At the Women's Political Union in New York City, suffrage supporters gave "matinee talks" every day during that first week of the month, directed by Charles Beard and his wife, Mary Ritter Beard. After the Assembly and Senate votes in Albany, thousands among both the pro- and antisuffrage forces converged on the capital in celebration. For the suffragists, the vote meant that after nearly seventy years, the measure would be put to the state's electorate. For the antis, it effectively ensured that the all-male voters would be able to put the measure down.

The Congressional Union, which the *Tribune* had begun to characterize as "the most warlike of 'votes for women' organizations," turned the beauty parlor in Alva Belmont's suffrage offices (!) into a New York satellite headquarters; its main operation was in Washington. Belmont had become active in this wing of the movement. Doris Stevens, an Oberlin graduate from Omaha, Nebraska, was put in charge.

Anna Shaw of NAWSA had no enthusiasm for these developments. To the *New York Tribune*, she said: "If the union begins to harry the Democrats in New York" as it had done with non-supporters of suffrage in other states, "we might as well give up the ghost."

# THE RED BEHIND THE YELLOW
## SOCIALISTS WORKING FOR SUFFRAGE

Every Socialist leader admits that the extension of the franchise to women is ESSENTIAL TO THE SUCCESS OF SOCIALISM. The practical alliance between woman suffrage and the extremer forms of Socialism is a subject upon which prudent suffragists preserve a discreet silence; but the Socialists gladly advertise the fact. The New York CALL, the official organ of the Eastern English-speaking Socialists, says:

> The fight for woman suffrage is bound to be an exceptionally hard one, but it is a fight that must be won, and on none does the responsibility for success fall more heavily than upon the Socialists. And the time for Socialists to begin this great campaign, to which they are morally bound, is NOW. Socialists, Remember, that the Mobilizing for the Woman Suffrage Fight Takes Place Today.

THE AMERICAN SOCIALIST, the official organ of the party, just after the election last November, said:

> The North Dakota Association Opposed to Woman Suffrage has issued a detailed statement, declaring that an analysis of the vote on woman suffrage in this State last November showed that the Socialists voted solidly in favor of it. WE ADMIT IT.

The Socialist State Committee met in Albany in April and passed resolutions urging every member to work for the woman suffrage amendment. Following this Socialist speakers were delegated by the Socialist State Committee to speak for woman suffrage. A special woman suffrage edition of the New York CALL, published without date, says, among other things:

> Every man who is a member of the Socialist party will vote "yes" on the woman suffrage amendment. This is one of the things his party demands of him.
>
> LET US DO YOUR WORK.

The same edition also published this cartoon:

The New York State Men's League for Woman Suffrage had as one of its organizers and first secretary, Max Eastman, editor of The MASSES, an extreme Socialist publication, which printed the blasphemous poem "God's Blunder."

Some suffrage organizations deny they are working with the Socialists, but no suffrage organization has ever repudiated Socialism, and no suffrage leader of any prominence has ever written or spoken against the Socialist propaganda. On the contrary, some of the most prominent suffrage advocates are among the most extreme Socialists.

A Vote for Woman Suffrage Will Help Socialism.

## VOTE NO ON WOMAN SUFFRAGE NOVEMBER 2, 1915.
### New York State Association Opposed to Woman Suffrage.
37 West 39th Street, New York City.

Referendum propaganda from the suffrage antis against the 1915 amendment. (Max Eastman Collection I, the Lilly Library, Indiana University)

The headline over a February 6 editorial against the amendment in the *New York Times* was as hostile as ever:

## IT MUST BE DEFEATED

As for the federal initiative, President Wilson was still declining to support it, once again asserting that only the states had the right to decide if women could vote. He was gracious on January 6 to a delegation of one hundred female prosuffrage Democrats, expressing admiration for their cause as he reiterated his contention that the matter was one for the states to decide. He mentioned the meeting to his friend, Nancy Saunders Toy, who recorded his private comments in her diary. "Suffrage for women will make absolutely no change in politics—it is the home that will be disastrously affected," she quoted him as saying. "Somebody has to make the home and who is going to do it if the women don't?" On January 12, the House defeated the amendment by a vote of 204 to 174, prompting Alice Paul to vow to redouble her Congressional Union's lobbying efforts in the Senate, so that a strong affirmative vote would bring the measure back to the House with renewed strength.

In New York City, at the opening of the new Congressional Union office on January 11, Creel urged supporters to "get after" the New York congressmen who had opposed suffrage in the vote in Washington. Thirty-one of forty of them had voted against the measure. Creel's fighting words—"I'd like to see them burned alive"—made headlines. As to the work of the Congressional Union itself, he said he liked the organization's "aggressive," in his phrase "not too card indexy" approach. Index cards in various colors—yellow for prosuffrage, naturally—with profiles of the various city, state, county, and national legislatures—were a NAWSA staple.

"I used to have a prejudice against it," Creel said of Alice Paul's group, "just as I had a prejudice against the militants before I went to England and saw how just their fight was. I tell you that when you're fighting for life nothing matters but that fight. The Congressional Union can't go too far to please me."

That same month, a national men's campaign committee took shape alongside the men's statewide effort. Its executive committee included the perennials: Peabody and Wise, Nathan, Strong, Greene, and Creel, who took charge of publicity with the aid of Walter Lippmann, who in 1914 had helped found the *New Republic*. Among those on the new group's constitutional amendment committee was another longtime League activist, Samuel Untermyer, and the finance committee included many new names. As a group, the men committed to raising $20,000 for the federal initiative.

The state fight heated up. A second *New York Times* editorial on February 7 incited widespread rage. "Every man of voting age must meet the issue courageously, intelligently, with clear vision," the writer intoned. "The answer of New York State to this long pending query should be forcible and definite." The newspaper called on voters to defeat the state amendment by a majority decisive enough to vanquish once and for all this plan aimed at "deranging the state's political and social structure." The editorial went on: "The grant of suffrage to women is repugnant to instincts that strike their roots deep in the order of nature. It runs counter to human reason" and "flouts the teachings of experience and the admonitions of common sense."

The *New York Tribune* seized the opportunity to pound on its rival from the opposing point of view, responding first with the suggestion that if the *Times* had substituted the words *freedom* and *Negro* for *suffrage* and *women*, the editorial could easily have appeared in an antiabolition newspaper in the 1860s. The *Times*, the *Tribune* said, showed "no more perception than a mediaeval monk." One by one, the *Tribune* picked apart the *Times*'s every outdated argument.

Three days later, the *Tribune* ran a column and a half of appreciative responses to its prosuffrage editorial stance. These included a message from Laidlaw, who congratulated the writer for "masterful editorial handling." The *Times* fired back on Valentine's Day with six full pages of balanced pro and anti pages of commentary, under the same banner headline on every page:

## SHOULD WOMEN VOTE IN NEW YORK?

Among the dozens of letters the *Times* printed—these included reprints of commentary from the other newspapers in town—came one from Laidlaw, who said he was writing at the request of a number of his friends and members of the Men's League. "I hesitate to do this," he wrote, "because it seems to me that the editorial in question has been perhaps taken too seriously by many people. From the tone of the article it appeared to me that, in all probability, the writer intended it as a parody on the plaints of the anti-suffragists."

The humor magazine *Puck* joined the charge, devoting almost the entirety of its February 20 issue to the subject of suffrage. The magazine ceded editorial direction for that month to the state's major suffrage organizations, including the Men's League, as prominently noted in the upper right-hand corner of its cover next to a sumptuous full-color illustration, titled "The Mascot." The image depicted a young woman and a girl toddler, each draped in bright yellow "Votes for Women" sashes. A juggernaut of an editorial board came together to oversee the issue, dominated by Men's League stalwarts: Villard of the *Evening Post*; Dunne aka "Mr. Dooley"; Arthur Brisbane of the *New York Journal*; Norman Hapgood, by then running *Harper's Weekly*; Erman J. Ridgway of *Everybody's*; William Dean Howells; S.S. McClure; Ogden Mills Reid of the *New York Tribune*; Irvin S. Cobb; John O'Hara Cosgrave of the *New York World*; and Frank Munsey of Munsey

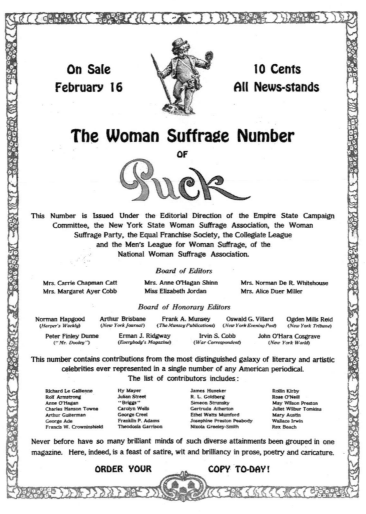

Pre-publication promotion for *Puck*'s suffrage issue, noting the Men's League members that comprised its editorial board, published February 13, 1915. (Hathi Trust via the University of Michigan, digitized by Google)

Cover image by Rolf Armstrong for the suffrage issue of *Puck*, February 20, 1915, with Men's League sponsorship and editorial direction noted in the upper right-hand corner, from several of its members from the editorial ranks. (Rolf Armstrong, *Puck* magazine, Vol. 77, No. 1981, February 20, 1915, Hathi Trust via the University of Michigan, digitized by Google)

Publications. Cartoons, aphorisms, editorials, magnificent four-color illustrations, plenty of satire, and sufficient ridicule of the antis filled the issue. A note from the editor promised that *Puck* would keep hammering away at the subject week after week, "from now until the battle for woman suffrage is won."

In February, the women of suffrage festooned Grand Central Palace with green, purple, and white for a suffrage ball attended by some seven thousand people. Among the men on the floor wearing the Women's Political Union insignia were Bynner and Swinburne Hale, along with some newer names: Carl Lincoln Schurz, the attorney and son of the better-known Carl Schurz; the state assemblyman Sidney Borg; the author A. Montgomery Handy; and the banker Hegeman Foster. They all also "acted as ticket choppers to see that everything went smoothly."

The next month, George Middleton's new book of one-act plays about contemporary women brought him favorable attention. "No one else is doing this kind of work," the *New York Times Book Review* concluded, "and his books should not be missed by readers looking for a striking presentation of the stuff that life is made of." Other sympathetic writers, organized by Creel as the Men's League publicity chairman, rode herd over various publications, divining occasions to get onto the table of contents or editorial pages. The battle plan for the newspapers of New York City appears scrawled over two pages among the Harriet Laidlaw holdings at the Schlesinger Library at Harvard. The papers also include numerous letters from Laidlaw seeking both church and African American support for the amendment.

The March 1915 *Pictorial Review* includes a lengthy Creel essay under the headline, "Chivalry versus Justice: Why the Women of the Nation Demand the Right to Vote." "There is the bland theory of vine clad cottages and dense walls of fragrant honeysuckle, behind which every right thinking woman sits in security surrounded by her babes," Creel wrote, expanding on the arguments he had advanced in the press the year before. "What of the squalid holes in 13,000 licensed tenements in New York alone?" In the *Times*, Creel assailed the antis for ignoring the poor. "Is it not significant," he asked rhetorically, "that the list of men and women primarily responsible for the Mothers' Pension law does not contain a single one of those names so prominent in the anti–equal-suffrage campaign?" The poetry editor Alice Hunt Bartlett shot back with a list of seventeen New York women in the anti camp who had achieved "the greatest reforms along civic, philanthropic, humanitarian, and charitable lines." The few she mentioned, she said, should be sufficient to refute Creel's statements "and may also lead him to follow social legislative movements a little more closely in the future."

From April on came more clever suffrage fundraisers along with highly inventive, finely targeted efforts to persuade men of all social classes to support the cause: tea dances, bridge parties, luncheons, benefits, balls, performances, a

"The Awakening," by Henry Mayer, from *Puck*, map of women's suffrage in the United States as of February 1915. (Henry Mayer, *Puck* magazine, Vol. 77, No. 1981, February 20, 1915, Library of Congress, Prints and Photographs Division)

baseball game between the Giants and the Cubs that Creel organized, and a gold- and silver-melting party. Dudley Field Malone was coming to the fore, called upon to address a suffrage meeting in Greenwich Village. W.E.B. Du Bois did his part once again in the pages of the *Crisis*, pointing out that among the more than five million people in the combined electorates of New York, New Jersey, and Pennsylvania, it was safe to say that nearly two hundred thousand of them were African Americans who "may easily hold a balance of power and certainly would be a valuable asset." He acknowledged that among black voters there was "a good deal of indifference and lack of knowledge" about woman suffrage. "We tend to oppose the principle because we do not like the reactionary attitude of most white women toward our problems." Nonetheless, he wrote, "We must remember, however, that we are facing a great question of right in which personal hatreds have no place. Every argument for Negro suffrage is an argument for woman suffrage; every argument for woman suffrage is an argument for Negro

A newspaper battle plan, Men's League, 1915. Note the well-known names listed along the left-hand side as members of the publicity committee. (Harriet Burton Laidlaw Papers, Schlesinger Library, Radcliffe Institute, Harvard University) suffrage; both are great movements in democracy. . . . The man of Negro blood who hesitates to do them justice is false to his race, his ideals and his country."

An automobile parade in New York on Suffrage Day, May 2, coincided with a Socialist parade. Together they attracted some fifty thousand spectators. Subway diggers got special attention from the suffragists, as did the longshoremen, the firemen, and the barbers. All these initiatives generated amusing but not disparaging publicity in the press.

The criminal justice reformer Judge William H. Wadhams gave a "strong suffrage speech" to the Equal Franchise Society, the *New York Times* reported. Women were now prominent in all the learned professions, he said, and others were going to work in "veritable rivers" alongside the country's men. "Have we so soon forgotten the Boston Tea Party?" he asked. "They must obey the law and pay the penalties of the law. Those who have the penalties imposed should have the privileges of citizenship." New York State, he said, had become a "bachelor barracks" that needed women to "come in to make the State what they have made the home, beautiful and lovely."

Sarah Addington, a reporter for the *New York Tribune*, shadowed the suffrage campaigners around the city to eavesdrop on responses to their pitches as they stood up in decorated automobiles or tapped the shoulders of men on street corners. Addington reported reactions ranging from animosity to indifference to full support. "And so the woman with the gentlemanly husband must remember," Addington concluded, "that other husbands are pugnacious on the subject, and the woman with the anti life-mate must console herself by thinking of such men as James L. Laidlaw."

That same month, Gertrude Foster Brown, as president of the Empire State Campaign Committee, was busy directing rehearsals for a production of Middleton's *Back of the Ballot*, a farce about suffragists recruiting a burglar to the movement. An item in the press indicated that a Broadway production was imminent, but it appears not to have happened. "I never saw it acted," Middleton said in his 1947 memoir, "but I was told it went well enough." Of his *oeuvre*, he wrote that his main interest was in the "particular personal problems feminism created. Of course I was called a propagandist, as is any author who dips into such controversies. Artistic detachment is difficult, because the mere selection of a theme or subject betrays a predisposition. . . . The unbiased detachment I then sought largely explains why some of my plays were seldom professionally produced. I knew the penalties; but I was then concerned more with interpretation than with persuasion."

July 29 was "TellaSuff Day," when "suffragists throughout the state sum-moned Mere Man to the telephone that he might declare himself," the *Tribune* reported. Women were said to have placed about a half a million calls to male voters. "When he evidenced a desire to be cautious, or non-committal, or per-verse, all the arts and wiles of feminine voice culture were brought to bear upon him that he might vote affirmatively next fall, no matter how he thought now."

The *Crisis* devoted much of its August issue to a wide-ranging symposium on the suffrage campaign, which Du Bois declared "one of the strongest cumulative attacks on sex and race discrimination in politics ever written." The Reverend Francis J. Grimke offered "The Logic of Woman Suffrage"; Alderman Oscar De Priest wrote about women's suffrage experiences in Chicago; Benjamin Brawley, the dean of Morehouse College in Atlanta, titled his entry, "Politics and Womanli-ness"; Bishop John Hurst of the African Methodist-Episcopal Church wrote about Christianity and women; and the Honorable J.W. Johnson, a former US consul to Nicaragua, titled his piece "About Aunties," arguing that the most annoying thing about the suffrage debate was the absurdity of the arguments against it. Washington, DC, District Court Justice Robert H. Terrrell described "Our Debt to Suffragists," and a professor of ancient languages at Clark University in Atlanta, W.Y. Crogman, elucidated on "Woman in the Ancient State." The author Charles W. Chestnutt tackled women's rights; the Honorable John R. Lynch wrote on states' rights and suffrage; and L.M. Hershaw on the disenfranchisement of the District of Columbia. Numerous other contributions to the symposium came from prominent African American women, including Coralie Franklin Cook, a member of the DC Board of Education, and Mary B. Talbert and Dr. Mary Fitzbutler Waring, both of the National Association of Colored Women.

The big suffrage event in August was a "Council Fire Night," kicked off with the call of a girl's trumpet, issued from a high ledge to "announce woman's readiness to hold political power." Laidlaw and Judge Charles D. Appleton were among the speakers and in the recruiting tent was an amateur soothsayer enlisted to "tell the political fortunes of suffrage leaders and predict the results at the polls on November 2."

Before the November vote in New York came a ballot on the suffrage amendment in New Jersey on October 19—"the first big test of suffrage strength" since the victory in Illinois in 1913 and the first of four upcoming contests in the East. New York, Pennsylvania, and Massachusetts came next. The *Washington Post* zeroed in on the larger stakes. The results in New Jersey, an editorialist wrote,

*The Crisis* magazine cover for its Votes for Women issue, August 1915, depicting Sojourner Truth with President Abraham Lincoln. (Composite photograph by Hinton Gilmore, *The Crisis*, August 1915, via the Modernist Journals Project [searchable database], Brown and Tulsa Universities, ongoing; http://www.modjourn.org)

will come close to settling the fate of the suffrage movement in the East. The result doubtless will influence the elections in the three nearby States in November. Each side hopes to get a definite expression from President Wilson, not merely because of the effect it will have in his own State, but because of the use that can be made of it in the elections in Massachusetts, Pennsylvania, and New York.

Should these four Eastern States vote for woman's suffrage, the fight of the suffragists will have been won. The other States soon will fall into line. Should they lose, it will mean a long wait before national suffrage becomes a reality.

By late September, the Men's League solicited campaign ammunition by seeking responses from public officials in states where women already had the ballot, responses that would counter the opposition's most common arguments, from claims that voting women would destroy the sanctity of the home to fears that the wrong kind of women would be flooding the polls. Twenty-seven men responded with emphatic counters to these mistaken impressions, including the governors of Alaska, Montana, Nevada, Colorado, Illinois, and Wyoming, various secretaries of state and attorneys general, and other high state office holders.

Wilson's own statement of intent came in a press release issued October 6, just shy of two weeks before the vote in what remained his home state: "I intend to vote for woman suffrage in New Jersey because I believe that the time has come to extend that privilege and responsibility to the women of the state," he said, "but I shall vote, not as the leader of my party in the nation, but only upon my private conviction as a citizen of New Jersey called upon by the legislature of the state to express his conviction at the polls." He went on to repeat his contention that women's suffrage should remain a state matter and that it should "in no circumstances" be made a "party question." He concluded, "My view has grown stronger at every turn of the agitation." (Wilson struck out a line from an earlier draft saying that he thought New Jersey would benefit greatly from the change, and that his "opinion in the matter has been very much strengthened by the character of the opposition to the measure.")

A few days earlier, the president's private secretary, Joseph Patrick Tumulty, had told Villard in confidence about the impending Wilson conversion. Villard just didn't buy it, however, and the revelation from Tumulty left him feeling more downcast than jubilant. Villard saw the change in Wilson's position more as an effort by Tumulty to blunt unhappiness among Wilson's supporters over his recent engagement to Edith Bolling Galt, so soon after the death of his first wife, Ellen Axon Wilson, who had succumbed to a kidney disease in the fall of 1914. While Wilson was en route to Princeton to cast his ballot, Galt had let it be known in Washington that although she was not active or vitally interested in the subject of suffrage, she opposed women's having the vote.

In Villard's 1939 memoir, he recalled saying to Tumulty about Wilson, "Naturally, I am glad to have him out for suffrage, but where does it leave him? Is he going to change his mind on everything? Don't you see that everybody will attribute this not to conviction but to the fact that he wants re-election, must win the suffrage states, and cannot allow Theodore Roosevelt to have a monopoly of the suffrage support?"

In Villard's view, Wilson's only reason to "flop" on suffrage was the politics of reelection, a move he most certainly would not have considered without Roosevelt's announced wholehearted support for it at the 1912 Progressive Party convention in Chicago. Of Wilson, Villard wrote, "He was no more convinced than before that woman suffrage was the right thing. Yet here he was, three years later, finding himself quite convinced. I could never believe it. He liked, as any proper man should, pretty women and their company but never had respect for their intellectual accomplishments or believed them else than quite inferior to men. Women no more than blacks figured in his vision of a really democratic society."

Villard's viewpoint is one that many scholars subscribe to but that others have seriously questioned. Among other factors, given that Roosevelt's support of suffrage in 1912 won him only one of the six suffrage states, they see Wilson's conversion as a reflection of an evolution in his thinking, even if it appeared to be—and was—politically expedient in the moment. In other words, his shift was not a reluctant, belated conversion solely for political ends, but one that he found as palatable as it was necessary.

Either way, the suffragists of New Jersey, buoyed by Wilson's sudden affirmation, were confident of victory, fearful only of "the bosses," the *New York Herald* said. The chairman of the New Jersey Men's League, George M. Lamonte, who was also the state's commissioner of banking and insurance, told the *New York Times* he believed that the visit of a recent delegation of the working women of New Jersey had influenced the president to vote in favor. "They implored him not to speak for his party but to speak to his party."

In the *Tribune*, Laidlaw noted how strongly the current had swung in favor of suffrage, as the Men's League helped prepare for a New York parade on October 23, a week before the New York vote. Greene, who was among those "courageous enough to march in the parade of 1911," would again serve as chief Men's League marshal, aided by a "veteran captain" to lead each of the forty companies in the men's division. The *Tribune* added: "George Middleton, playwright and author, who has a torn coat and much battered hat to prove his right to the honor, will head Division A."

———◄○►———

The district tally in Wilson's home borough of Princeton was 64 votes in favor of the suffrage amendment to 160 opposed. Statewide, the defeat was just as decisive. Every county in New Jersey except one voted against the constitutional amendment. As the *Trenton Evening Times* explained the next day, for the suffragists, the "greased political machines of the Republican and Democratic parties and their allied interests" had proved to be too much. New Jersey suffragists responded immediately by renewing their commitment to battle anew backed by their New York sisters—and brothers.

The next day's newspapers also carried stories about the suffrage forces of New York as they busily prepared for their parade. Laidlaw told the *New York Times* that he had already enrolled five thousand men as marchers and expected twice as many to show up at the designated meeting point by the start time.

The night before the parade, the male presence was strong at Carnegie Hall, where Mayor Mitchel, Senator Borah of Idaho, and Malone joined Carrie Chapman Catt and Anna Shaw on the platform. Recall that late in 1913, Malone had ascended to a sought-after patronage position as Wilson's appointee as Collector of the Port of New York, after serving for several months as the State Department's effective chief of diplomats. To rally the preparade crowd, he reviewed conditions for women in the region. Eight million New York women were compelled to work outside the home to help support their families, he reported, just as were one third of all voting-age women in New Jersey; forty percent in Massachusetts, and thirty percent of all women in Pennsylvania.

"Because my ancestor landed not at Plymouth Rock but at Castle Garden," Malone said, "I have always had a profound belief that men of all origins and all blood-relationships should be admitted to citizenship after remaining a given period under the influence of our institutions. But it is also desirable to place in the electorate every mature individual, male or female, of brains, character, intelligence, and love of country in order to perpetuate the American traditions and the American idea of democracy. If the men of New York will give the women the vote, they will contribute a mighty element of moral force to sustain our great President in his unparalleled effort to keep America at peace and actively ready to be a compelling service to all mankind."

On parade day, press estimates for the total number of marchers ranged from twenty-three thousand to sixty thousand people. The *Times* went so far as to hire a "comptometer" to verify its count and tallied 25,340 marchers. For the previous parade, May 3, 1913, the *Times* had counted 9,600 people in line. "Anyway, it was undoubtedly the biggest and best suffrage parade and, undoubtedly it made a big impression on the crowd," the *Times* reported. Mayor Mitchel watched from the parade stand, leaving Malone and the president of the city's board of alderman, George McAneny, to represent the city administration on the avenue. But it was the New Jersey marchers, thoroughly undaunted, who the spectators most admired. And, as always, the Men's League received special attention under its own subhead.

## MEN MARCHERS WERE BRAVE
### STOOD IN COLD FOUR HOURS—
### THEN TRAFFIC BROKE THEIR RANKS

Laidlaw mounted a horse to give the order that brought the marchers from East Thirteenth Street onto Fifth Avenue, but by the time the men got going it was nearly six o'clock. Streetlights illuminated the boulevard. The twenty-five hundred men who had actually assembled—not the ten thousand the Men's League president had predicted, but a vast increase over the paltry band of several score four years earlier—had been standing around since two o'clock in the afternoon, waiting for the signal to start. To kill the time, the men sang a parody of "John Brown's Body," sometimes drowned out, sometimes "swelled out with vigor" with the words

> *We will vote for Suffrage*
> *We will vote for Suffrage*
> *On next Election Day.*

Reporters spotted Villard, Creel, Middleton, and Greene among the many prominent New Yorkers in the men's formation. "There was more respect shown for the men marchers as well as for the women by those on the sidewalks than at previous parades," the *Times* reporter wrote, noting what a far cry the reception was from 1911, when the crowds saluted the men as "Lizzie." "There were many—mostly very young working girls and men, also very young—who glibly saluted the men and mildly jeered as they went along," the reporter wrote, "but compared to the other days this was of small account."

To round out the New York campaign, the suffragists staged twenty-four-hour marathon meetings on October 29, culminating in a "Monster Victory Rally" at Carnegie Hall that featured Wise among the speakers. Organizers sold one thousand tickets for a Grand Ballroom luncheon at the Hotel Astor. And in Tompkins Square Park, Creel rallied the crowd, along with the local Socialist politician Meyer London and the president of the Civil Service Commission,

Drawn by M. A. Kempf.

Atlas, Mere Man: "This thing is getting to d—d hot and heavy and slippery for me to handle alone, I need help!"

Cartoon from *The Masses* suffrage issue, October–November 1915, by M.A. Kempf. (Via the Modernist Journals Project [searchable database], Brown and Tulsa Universities, ongoing; http://www.modjourn.org)

Henry Moskowitz. As the November 2 vote drew near, NAWSA was reported to be in a state of "complete preparedness."

The *Masses* devoted its October–November issue to suffrage and included an Eastman piece, "Who's Afraid? Confessions of a Suffrage Orator." In it, he explained that his job all along was not to make people "believe in the benefits of women's freedom, it was a question of making them *like the idea*." Floyd Dell offered an article of his own, "Adventures in Anti-Land," reporting on his undercover march into antisuffrage headquarters to pick up a number of pamphlets, which he then duly studied. "Apparently," he said facetiously, "they have persuaded me of too much, these pamphlets. They show not merely that woman isn't fit to vote, they give good reasons for believing that she isn't fit to live."

In the *Crisis* magazine, Du Bois also offered a suffrage editorial just before the balloting. He implored every one of the two hundred thousand black voters being called upon to support women's suffrage in their states to vote yes. "Intelligence in voting is the only real support of democracy," Du Bois wrote. In the same editorial, he introduced an essay by the mathematician Kelly Miller, the dean of the College of Arts and Science at Howard University, who was wholly against women's suffrage. "We trust that our readers will give it careful attention and that they will compare it with that marvelous symposium which we had the pleasure to publish in our August number," Du Bois wrote. He then summarized Miller's arguments as follows: that the work of bearing and rearing children made it impossible for women to take a large role in industrial and public affairs; that women were weaker than men and had adequate protection under the suffrage that men enjoyed; that where women had suffrage, no adequate results had appeared; and that office-holding women were "risky." "Meantime," Du Bois wrote, "Dean Miller will pardon us for a word in answer to his argument." Du Bois then proceeded to eviscerate the scholar's every point.

On the night before the election, a score of Men's Leaguers provided late-night relief as sidewalk campaigners on both the east and west sides of town, to allow their female counterparts to get at least one good night's rest after weeks upon weeks of working until midnight. At the balloting spots the next day, some five thousand women served as poll watchers to help ensure against fraud.

And then came the vote, and after that, the thundering disappointment of the New York count. Women carried only five counties in New York and none in Massachusetts. Pennsylvania voters defeated their amendment, too. In New York, at twenty minutes past midnight, Middleton and Will Irwin, on behalf of the Empire State Campaign Committee, "left Room 310 of the *Tribune* Building where they had been receiving returns and had a mass meeting in front of the Franklin statue," a *Tribune* reporter wrote. Their charge was not to bemoan the defeat, but to kick off yet another new campaign.

Alice Paul's Congressional Union moved swiftly to shift concentration to the push for an amendment to the federal Constitution. The organization scheduled a meeting for the next day with Creel and Beard among the speakers. Creel told the Union's membership he felt not like arguing or pleading with the opponents of suffrage but like "mutilating" them. Beard mentioned Wilson's reversal on suffrage, with his New Jersey vote, but attributed it to his gearing up for the next presidential election cycle. "This President saw a great light on the road to Damascus in 1916," Beard said, "and I am reliably told that before that he would not even let his daughter mention the subject in his house."

This time there were plenty of expressions of disappointment in political leaders, like Wilson, who had publicly offered only personal support for the measure, but not in the names of their respective organizations or constituencies. "Try a little politics," Beard advised, "and cut out the angel business for there has been altogether too much of that. I tell you 10,000 voters will have more effect upon a Congressman than all the angels."

The Empire State Committee's effectiveness over the previous two years encouraged a major consolidation. At the state convention at the Hotel Astor only ten days after the defeat, a sense of renewed energy and invigorated commitment reigned. The Men's League joined forces with three other leading suffrage groups, namely the Woman Suffrage Party of New York City, the New York State Woman's Suffrage Association, and the Equal Franchise League. NAWSA realigned the established state suffrage districts to match those of the state's congressional map.

Gertrude Brown, New York's suffrage president and wife of the newspaperman Raymond Brown, explained the reason to the *New York Times*: "The different organizations have been proud of their own identity but we are convinced that maintaining these lines of demarcation is foolish and wasteful, and each organization is now anxious to see the combination and centralization of forces made permanent."

At a state meeting on December 1, Brown said the fight would continue at the state and federal levels. "It seems preposterous to give up the State work for the Federal," she said. "The only chance we have with the Federal amendment is because we have won States and we must win more. What we do in New York will have great influence upon the nation."

"Do we look like a defeated army?" she asked the crowd the next day, when a thousand people filled the grand ballroom of the Hotel Astor to honor Carrie

Chapman Catt. "We have more enthusiasm, more workers, more money in sight and coming in, and last month we learned something of practical politics. While the men said they did not want us in politics, we were there and they liked it."

And with that the state campaign for 1917 began. The newly consolidated New York State Woman Suffrage Party, to which the Men's League was a full partner, elected its officers, none of whom was a man.

———◦———

New York geared up for the 1917 round only days before President Wilson made his annual message to Congress on December 7. That morning's *New York Tribune* carried a full report from the day before, about a Congressional Union delegation of one thousand women, an "honor guard" herded into place and kept in check by "twelve shepherdesses with crooks," who staged a grand spectacle on the White House lawn. They presented the president with a petition, 18,000 feet long, which the suffragist Sara Bard Field had brought across the continent in a "grimy little automobile laden with suitcases" from her home base in Oregon, a suffrage state. The petition contained the signatures of four million female voters, along with their prayers for suffrage "and a threat," the *Tribune* said. They urged Wilson to include their wish in his address.

Wilson received the women cordially and said that "nothing could be more impressive than the presentation of such a request in such numbers and backed by such influences as undoubtedly stand back of you." Yet he declined their request. "Unhappily," he said, "it is too late for me to consider what is to go into my message." First, because his staff had sent the text of his remarks to the newspapers a week earlier, so it was too late to make changes. And second— perhaps reflecting his longstanding "habit of the teacher"—because he wanted to focus his remarks on only one subject. That year, the priority had to be his push for sustained neutrality in the ongoing conflict in Europe, backed by a "full programme" of military preparedness.

Nonetheless, he said, he considered the women's visit "a delightful compliment, but also as a very impressive thing, which undoubtedly will make it necessary for all of us to consider very carefully what it is right for us to do."

Field, as spokeswoman for the group, harkened to Wilson's long-standing opposition to the federal amendment by offering wryly that even the greatest of men sometimes changed their minds. Wilson seemed to like the comment and replied: "I hope it is true that I am not a man set stiffly beyond the possibility of learning. I hope that I shall continue to be a learner as long as I live." At another point, he added, cracking open the door a little wider, "I hope I shall have an open mind, and I shall certainly take the greatest pleasure in conferring in the most serious way with my colleagues at the other end of the city with regard to what is the right thing to do at the time concerning this great matter."

Most of the women seemed buoyed by Wilson's remarks. Even Paul left the White House saying the president "had swept aside the last obstacle which he previously had placed in the way of the Federal amendment." Harriot Blatch, however, was less convinced. "Ah, no," she said, "he didn't listen to us." And yet later that day, the resolution was introduced in both the House of Representatives and the Senate.

Pressure from other camps also mounted before year's end. On December 15, Wilson entertained visits from two more delegations of women, neither carrying banners nor accompanied by bands, as had become the custom. Josephine Jewell Dodge led a group of some two hundred antis, members of her National Association Opposed to Woman Suffrage. Shaw led a delegation four times that size, from NAWSA, paying respects during the organization's annual convention in Washington. The president did not commit himself further to either group, the *New York Times* reported. "He said nothing to the women opposed to suffrage," the article said. "To the suffragists he explained that he already had under consideration a request that he change his original position in opposition to a Federal amendment."

Malone was back in the news just before Christmas, when he spoke at the closing session of the NAWSA convention. Catt was also on the program but the star was Malone, who appeared before an audience that included President Wilson's daughter Margaret. The *New York Tribune* reported that his remarks injected a grim note on war preparedness into the convention's suffrage "love feast."

"Many people are prevented from joining suffrage because they think it is a peace-at-any-price organization," Malone said. "That is not true at all. We suffragists are organized to protect the home from the enemy in society. If the time comes when it is endangered by an enemy from without we must be ready to protect the home, then, too, by force of arms if necessary." The newspaper quipped that half the house applauded and that "the other half looked peace-at-any-price."

John O'Hara Cosgrave    Robert Schuyler    Edgar Sisson    Robert H. Davis

Mark Sullivan    Isador Michaels    Amos Pinchot    Woodrow Wilson

J.A.H. Hopkins    David I. Walsh    E.A. Rumely    John Spargo

Virgil Hinshaw    Edward House    William Channing
Gannett    George Gordon Battle

9

# "It May Move Like a Glacier, But . . ."

## 1916

Two fronts, two factions, two dramatically disparate approaches to achieving one objective. That, in sum, was how the American women's suffrage movement functioned for all of 1916.

On January 10, New York lawmakers introduced suffrage amendment measures in both houses of the New York legislature, prompting the arrival in Albany of an "advance guard" of suffragists to renew their campaign. Downstate, on January 27, at the Waldorf Astoria Hotel in New York City, President Wilson made time under some duress to meet again with members of Alice Paul's Congressional Union. At first, there was confusion over whether the women had an appointment and the president was unwilling to make room for them in his schedule. The situation was resolved only after the women refused to leave until they saw him. Wilson then welcomed them with a profuse apology for any inconvenience or embarrassment the muddle had caused.

At the meeting, the women pressed Wilson for support of the federal amendment, to which he gave his standard reply about the rights of states. But he also gave the same blink of hope he had offered at the meeting in December, when their representatives had presented the monster petition. However slowly his mind worked, he told the group in New York, it still remained "open."

Wilson also confessed that he had not yet kept his December promise to consult with congressional and party leaders about the federal amendment, but said that he fully intended to do so. He also hoped the suffragists would understand the delay, given the more urgent legislative matters that had been the focus of his annual address. "There are things," he said, "that cannot wait."

"But I want always to be absolutely frank," he added. "My own mind is still convinced that we ought to work this thing out state by state." Then he urged the women not to become discouraged. There had been progress. "It may move like a glacier," he acknowledged, "but when it does move, its effects are permanent."

In the February issue of the *Masses*, Eastman commented on how much he admired the growing political prowess of the suffragists led by Paul, and how effective they had been in exerting pressure on the US House and Senate in its push to get the federal suffrage question brought to the floor. Even the president had noticed, Eastman said, and offered as evidence the way Wilson had phrased his regrets over not being able to include mention of the federal suffrage amendment in his most recent State of the Union address. In declining, Wilson had nonetheless seemed impressed by the size and scope of that 18,000-foot-long petition and the widespread backing it represented.

How much things had changed since 1914, Eastman wrote, when congressmen had attacked suffrage as a "pleasant diversion." Only two years later, he said, these same federal legislators were feeling "the menace or the actual impact of woman's political power." The women of the Congressional Union, Eastman wrote, "seem to us already to have the political wisdom which will come to all women after they have had a little political experience."

Among some of the suffragists, gratitude to Eastman for his support, and especially for the October–November 1915 suffrage issue of the *Masses*, prompted a small group led by his sister, Crystal, to set out to raise $2,500 to help him finance the economically fragile monthly. "He has been accustomed to shouldering most of his own expenses," said Alice Carpenter, the fund's treasurer, "and we suffragists want to show our appreciation of his work by helping him along."

Middleton's suffrage plays found small performance venues. In Buffalo, Isadore Michaels offered his home for an evening of the playwright's one-acts, starring husband and wife, Middleton and La Follette. The public library in Chevy Chase, Maryland, featured local talent in *Back of the Ballot*, presented as the entertainment after a meeting about war preparedness.

The Men's League was well represented when Paul's organization met in New York City with US Representative John Carew, a New York Democrat and member of the House Judiciary Committee. The Columbia professors Charles Beard and Robert Livingston Schuyler were present, along with a dozen men less familiar to the fray. All pressed Carew to push the suffrage amendment through the committee and get it back into the House for consideration and a vote.

Other members of the Men's League, in their new guise as part of the newly formed New York State Woman Suffrage Party, made the newspapers for serving on the men's floor committee of the first suffrage social event of the season, a Mardi Gras Ball in Madison Square Garden held Tuesday, March 7. Some twenty thousand attendees came and went in relays, dressed in everything from elegant eveningwear to simple shirtwaists and men's suits. Originally, the organizers had asked that everyone don a bright suffrage yellow ten-cent crepe paper costume, but the fire marshal nixed the idea. They delayed the ball's start time long enough for the women who had spent the day lobbying the legislature in Albany to return and participate. The Grand March featured Laidlaw, Peabody, Reid, Brown, Strong, Creel, and Melville, who stepped to the music of Philip De Sousa's band.

—◁○▷—

It took three months, but by March 14, the New York State Assembly at last passed the new suffrage bill. The Senate, however, was stalled. The women prepared to go back to Albany to push again for action—six hundred of them from across the state, and many of their husbands. Laidlaw was quoted in the *Christian Science Monitor* saying that the Men's League was asking every one of the 544,457 men who had voted yes on the suffrage amendment in November 1915 "to gain one convert to the cause between now and the election of 1917." That, he said, would assure passage. Laidlaw said voters were being won over every day, especially in the college districts, where, he predicted, the vote for suffrage would be even stronger than it was in 1915.

The *New York Times* reported on April 5 that as soon as discussion in the legislature was imminent, a huge force of women would descend on Albany, this time with "many men from the Men's League in tow." On April 4, the Men's League had passed resolutions, one mailed to each member of the state Senate, urging an immediate end to the delays. A similar resolution went to Senator Elon Brown, the prime source of the blockage.

On April 10, the New York Senate passed the measure by the needed two-thirds majority, thirty-three votes in favor, ten opposed. That action prepared the way for favorable action by the legislature the following year, which in turn would ensure a new voter referendum on the amendment in November 1917. Laurels for the victory went to the "brilliant legislative work" of Vira Boarman Whitehouse and Harriet Laidlaw, assisted by the Albany district chairwoman, Helen Leavitt. Credit, too, went to "organizations throughout the State, through delegations, mass meetings, letters, and telegrams. 6,000 from the 9th district alone." As recorded in Harper's history of woman suffrage, the last sentence in a full paragraph of gratitude went without elaboration to the state's Men's League, saying only that it "gave invaluable help."

No contract shall be binding unless made in writing and signed by the President and Secretary.

**HONORARY VICE-PRESIDENTS**

SANFORD W. ABBY, Canandaigua
REV. WALDO ADAMS AMOS
HON. ROBERT ADAMSON
ROBERT P. BELL
HON. WILLIAM S. BENNET
Z. R. BROCKWAY, Elmira
WALSTON H. BROWN
CHARLES C. BURLINGHAM
JAMES S. CLARKSON
DOCTOR C. M. CULVER, Albany
JUDGE JOSEPH P. DALY
WILLIAM A. DELANO
EDWARD T. DEVINE
PROF. JOHN DEWEY
THOMAS F. FENNELL, Elmira
DOCTOR SIMON FLEXNER
G. E. FRANCIS, Syracuse
REV. W. C. GANNETT, Rochester
FREDERICK S. GREENE
JUDGE CHARLES L. GUY
SWINBURNE HALE
GEORGE HARVEY
HAMILTON HOLT
THOMAS W. HOTCHKISS
HON. FREDERICK C. HOWE
WILLIAM DEAN HOWELLS
FRANCIS C. HUYCK, Albany
WILLIAM M. IVINS
ALEXANDER D. JENNEY, Syracuse
GEORGE F. KUNZ
ALFRED G. LEWIS, Geneva
GEORGE R. LUNN, Schenectady
HOWARD MANSFIELD
EDWIN MARKHAM

# MEN'S LEAGUE
# FOR
# WOMAN SUFFRAGE

## OF THE STATE OF NEW YORK

11 BROADWAY
NEW YORK CITY

377

HONORARY PRESIDENT
GEORGE FOSTER PEABODY

PRESIDENT
JAMES L. LAIDLAW

VICE-PRESIDENTS
OSWALD GARRISON VILLARD
F. R. HAZARD          MAX EASTMAN

TREASURER
WARD MELVILLE

SECRETARY
R. C. BEADLE

**HONORARY VICE-PRESIDENTS**

REV. J. HOWARD MELISH
JOHN E. MILHOLLAND
PROF. HERBERT E. MILLS, Poughkeepsie
JOHN MITCHELL
HON. JOHN MURPHY
FREDERICK NATHAN
NORMAN S. NELSON
HON. JOHN B. OLMSTED, Buffalo
HON. HERBERT PARSONS
REV. JOHN P. PETERS
GEORGE A. RICKER, Buffalo
PROF. JAMES H. ROBINSON
GILBERT E. ROE
WILLIAM J. SCHIEFFELIN
PROF. NATHANIEL SCHMIDT, Ithaca
PROF. HENRY R. SEAGER
JEFFERSON N. SELIGMAN
H. H. SEYMOUR, Buffalo
PROF. V. G. SIMKHOVITCH
NELSON E. SPENCER, Rochester
NELSON S. SPENCER
CARLETON SPRAGUE, Buffalo
PRES. LANGDON C. STEWARDSON, Geneva
REV. PAUL MOORE STRAYER, Rochester
HON. CHAS. H. STRONG
PROF. W. P. TRENT
JUDGE WM. M. WADHAMS
HON. BYRON S. WAITE, Yonkers
ROBERT K. WALTON
RICHARD WELLING
NORMAN WHITEHOUSE
WILLIAM G. WILLCOX
THEODORE WILLIAMS
RABBI STEPHEN S. WISE

303 Fifth Avenue
Rooms 2016-2017
April 7, 1915.

---

## MEN'S LEAGUE FOR WOMAN SUFFRAGE

OF THE STATE OF NEW YORK

JAMES L. LAIDLAW, PRESIDENT

GEORGE FOSTER PEABODY
HONORARY PRESIDENT

WARD MELVILLE
TREASURER

R. C. BEADLE
SECRETARY

### THE CAMPAIGN COMMITTEE

GILBERT E. ROE
CHAIRMAN

CHARLES S. PEABODY
EXECUTIVE COMMITTEE

FRANK HARMAN BLACK
ORGANIZATION COMMITTEE

## OFFICE OF THE PUBLICITY COMMITTEE

GEORGE CREEL, CHAIRMAN

HEADQUARTERS: 303 FIFTH AVENUE
TELEPHONE MADISON SQUARE 6370

FRANKLIN P. ADAMS
SAMUEL HOPKINS ADAMS

NEW YORK, August 12    1915.

---

Two Men's League letterheads, 1915–1916, and a request to be reimbursed from George Creel, dated April 7, 1915. (Harriet B. Laidlaw Collection, Schlesinger Library, Radcliffe Institute, Harvard University)

No contract shall be binding unless made in writing and signed by the President and Secretary.

# MEN'S LEAGUE
# FOR
# WOMAN SUFFRAGE

## OF THE STATE OF NEW YORK

11 BROADWAY
NEW YORK CITY

377

HONORARY PRESIDENT
GEORGE FOSTER PEABODY

PRESIDENT
JAMES L. LAIDLAW

VICE-PRESIDENTS
OSWALD GARRISON VILLARD
F. R. HAZARD    MAX EASTMAN

TREASURER
WARD MELVILLE

SECRETARY
R. C. BEADLE

303 Fifth Avenue
Rooms 2016-2017
April 7, 1915.

| | | | |
|---|---|---|---|
| 1 | — | American Writing Mach Co. | $ 3.50 |
| 2 | — | Stenographic work | 1.50 |
| 3 | — | Eva Rea | 18.00 |
| 4 | — | Tybring & Co. (table) | 10.00 |
| 5 | — | Stamps | 6.00 |
| 6 | — | Telephone Boy | 1.00 |
| 7 | — | J J Morris (desk and filing case) | 23.00 |
| | | As per vouchers attached | $65.00 |

Voucher No 166
Applied 1-2-3-5-6 — Office Expense
4-7 — Furniture and Fixtures
Pay $65.00

Payment Approved

Check Drawn to the

order of George Creel to reimburse
him for cash advance for above items
vouchers covering which are attached.

Received Payment the sum of $65. in
full for advances made up to and
including April 7th 1915.

April...........1915

Around the same time, Democrats preparing for the party's national convention began discussing a suffrage plank for the 1916 campaign platform. A letter to Wilson from a Pittsburgh suffragist, Jennie Bradley Roessing, suggested two ideas: one favoring the enfranchisement of women and another acknowledging the right of women to participate in government, expressing favor for giving them the vote.

———◆———

Parade plans were again brewing in New York City, but the theme for the May 13 event this time was not suffrage. It was war preparedness, the far heavier question on everyone's mind. Preparedness was also the subject of a colloquy with the president in which Eastman and Wise participated, along with the New York settlement house leader, Lillian Wald. All expressed opinions against militarization, on behalf of themselves and the members of major labor unions. Villard, too, although not present, was part of this group. Excitement over military adventure, Eastman told the president, comes from the leisure and upper classes, not from the workers who have little profit to reap.

The *New York Sun's* cascade of headlines about the parade captured the size and character of what took place—the somber and earnest mood, the procession without banners, costumes, or any of the customary folderol:

## 142,000 MARCH IN PARADE FOR DEFENCE; 1,000,000 MORE LOOK ON AND CHEER FLAG IN IMPRESSIVE OUTBURST OF PATRIOTISM

—

## PREPAREDNESS DEMONSTRATION GREATEST TURNOUT IN THE CITY'S HISTORY

—

## EARNEST MARCHERS ENTHUSE GEN. WOOD

—

## SPIRIT OF COUNTRY REVEALED AS BANDS PLAY THE NATIONAL ANTHEM

—

## WOMEN WALK TO SHOW METTLE OF AMERICA

—

## MRS. ROOSEVELT CHEERED IN LINE—
## THOMAS EDISON LEADS NAVAL BOARD

By June, however, the mounting national preoccupation with war did not stop the Congressional Union from threatening to rally against the Democrats in Congress—those who represented the twelve states where women had the vote—if they did not act to pass the federal suffrage amendment. The *New York Times* dismissed the salvo as no more than a bluff from the "suffrage Extreme Left" that was likely to have "as much effect on the election as the evolutions of one Jersey mosquito on the movements of the satellites of Jupiter."

—◦▸—

Democrats preparing for their convention in St. Louis continued to debate the language of a suffrage plank. Henry F. Hollis of New Hampshire was among five senators who sent letters to the president with suggested ideas and language. Hollis enumerated the administration's achievements in domestic affairs and called for "further social and economic legislation." Someone had penciled out his more radical proposals, including one for "full suffrage rights for women." Other proposals on suffrage emphasized the rights of states. In the end, "Woman Suffrage" ended up the twentieth of twenty-three planks that the party voted to accept on June 14. It was offered in one simple sentence: "We recommend the extension of the franchise to the women of the country by the States upon the same terms as to men."

Five days later, Wilson wrote to Carrie Chapman Catt at her request to clarify his own position in light of the adopted plank, "though I had not thought that it was necessary to state again a position I have repeatedly stated with entire frankness," he said. "The plank received my entire approval before its adoption and I shall support its principle with sincere pleasure. I wish to join with my fellow Democrats in recommending to the several states that they extend the suffrage to women upon the same terms as to men."

Sara Bard Field, she of the 18,000-foot-long petition, wrote to protest Wilson's interpretation of the plank, as relayed by another member of the Congressional Union who had visited the president at the White House on June 21. In that meeting, Wilson held to his long-standing position and his unwillingness to push for federal action, saying he opposed the matter by both conviction and political tradition. She quoted him as telling his visitor that forcing a federal amendment on the states would do more harm to the cause than good. Field added to this recounting that she hoped his inaction on the federal initiative would not hurt the party in the November elections.

The published memoirs of Harriot Blatch recount what happened when she joined a delegation of four women from the Congressional Union whom Wilson received on July 24. What an uphill, fruitless battle so far the New York State amendment fight had been, she recalled telling him. "I am sixty years old, Mr. President," she said, "I have worked all my life for suffrage, and I am determined that I will never again stand up on the street corners of a great city appealing to every Tom, Dick, and Harry for the right of self-government. When we work for a Federal Amendment, we are dealing at last with men who understand what we are talking about and can speak to us in our own tongue. We are not asking for an easy way to win the vote. It is not easy to amend the United States Constitution. We are asking for a dignified way; and we ought to be able to rely on the chivalry of our representatives, particularly of the southern representatives, to accord to women a self-respecting method of working out their enfranchisement."

She said the president was unmoved. He could not push ahead of the party, he said, where the major opposition came from the south. The "Negro question," the white Southern fear of a black voting majority, was the major block. Blatch argued that giving the vote to Southern women would not decrease the proportion of black to white voters. Wilson said he knew that, but the congressmen did not. Blatch suggested a census that would demonstrate the actual figures. Wilson answered quietly that in two states, the black vote would preponderate.

Blatch then told him that his continued refusal to support the federal amendment would cost him the vote of the women of the West. Wilson replied that he found this unimaginable in such a time of crisis, especially "given the great political issues dividing the Parties at the present moment." Blatch and her small delegation then left, convinced that the president would take no action in favor the federal amendment. "The only alternative," she wrote, "was to change Presidents."

In August, Edward Mandell House, Wilson's informal adviser, reassured the president that he had done well not to come out in favor of the federal amendment. As to the unequivocal support for the measure that his Republican opponent, Charles Evans Hughes, was now touting, "It would not surprise me," House wrote, "if Hughes's actions would cost him the election if nothing else did." In the long run, House advised, "your position is better for the suffrage cause."

On September 2, before a crowd of some fifteen thousand supporters on the lawn of Wilson's summer home in Long Branch, New Jersey, the president accepted his party's nomination for a reelection bid. There had been a good bit of back and forth among his close advisers and Democratic legislators as to whether he should mention suffrage in that address. His vice president, Thomas Reilly Marshall, counseled against any mention of the women's vote. In the end, Wilson followed that advice.

"I have too much confidence in the good sense and public spirit of the women of the country to believe that they will act as unjustly as some of their number are predicting," Wilson told Marshall, who responded, "If all the women who don't want the ballot in the equal suffrage states will vote for you, you can carry them. I know. I've campaigned there twice." In any event, as Wilson explained in a letter to Ellen Duane Davis, the great granddaughter of Benjamin Franklin, he would not alter his position favoring states' rights simply because Hughes had come out so boldly for the federal amendment. As Wilson had told Villard during the 1912 campaign against Theodore Roosevelt's similar move, he said again that he would never want to be perceived as a mere "angler for votes."

Disappointment at NAWSA over the suffrage planks of both parties led Carrie Chapman Catt, who took over the presidency of the organization from Shaw in 1915, to call an "emergency convention" for early September in Atlantic City. Catt invited both Hughes and Wilson to address the gathering. Hughes was to be out west and could not attend, but the president said he would try. It was suggested that he appear on September 8, but by August 11, Wilson wrote to say he would need more time to confirm. He had a prior commitment in Kentucky to accept "for the nation the gift of the Lincoln birthplace." He told Norman Hapgood, who pressed Wilson to make the New Jersey trip, that the specter of a major railroad strike in Kentucky also threatened to detain him. To Catt, Wilson wrote, "But I shall try."

September 8 was expected to be "the most important day of the convention," the *New York Times* reported, because the delegates would be discussing a major controversy then besetting NAWSA. It pitted Catt, who continued to support Wilson's abiding view that suffrage was a matter for the states, against the hard push of Paul and her Congressional Union for NAWSA to focus its energy and resources more fully on the federal fight.

The Congressional Union also refused to relent in its decision to oppose Wilson and the Democrats in the November elections. As the group's vice chairman, Lucy Burns, told the *New York Times*, the Democrats "for four years treated with open contempt the movement for the enfranchisement of women. They have not only opposed the Federal suffrage amendment, but have refused to allow it to be discussed and voted by the Representatives of the people." Burns went on, "President Wilson opposed the Federal suffrage amendment without giving it due consideration in the first place, and he has now continued his opposition through sheer unwillingness to admit a bad error of judgment and tactics. Women will certainly not return to power a party that has denied them justice."

At the time, Hapgood, who was on Creel's publicity committee, was also serving as vice president of the Independent Wilson League, which put him in regular contact with the president and his aides. In late August, he had told Wilson that his campaign organization had begun to spend "a good deal of time" on "the women situation." He conveyed to Wilson the dismissive view of Anna Howard Shaw about Alice Paul's National Woman's Party, an outgrowth of the Congressional Union. Hapgood summarized Shaw's comments for the president, saying NAWSA's members understood the suffrage debate thoroughly; the Woman's Party membership was enthusiastic, but was "without much knowledge on the subject." He went on to explain that both Catt and Shaw planned to fight hard for a suffrage convention resolution, condemning the Woman's Party's actions. An appearance by Wilson in Atlantic City would greatly help their efforts to attract majority support. "The most useful speech for us," Hapgood quoted Shaw as saying, "would be one with some general topic, that should include a tactful expression of his attitude toward women's suffrage, and also include an account of some of the things done by the administration that many of the women know nothing about."

Wilson wrote back to Hapgood on August 30, again expressing his hope to get to Atlantic City if the threatened railroad strike did not "bog him down." On September 4, with the start of the convention two days away, he confirmed that he would attend as asked on September 8.

The Men's League, for its part, sent ten official delegates to the gathering. Among them were Peabody; Greene; Nathan, on behalf of the International Men's League; and the presidents of the New Jersey, Pennsylvania, and Connecticut leagues, all representing, in the reckoning of the *Times*, "an active membership of from 6,000 to 8,000." By September of 1916, the *Times* added, men's leagues for women's suffrage had formed in thirty-five states.

In a 1920 memoir, Maud Wood Park, a Boston suffragist who would soon become NAWSA's own top congressional "front door" lobbyist ("front door" to acknowledge the suffragists' practice of never using the more familiar back-door, backroom political lobbying tactics of men), remembered well the crowd's reaction to Wilson's Atlantic City speech. The delegates listened as he held out the sure promise of victory and urged those assembled to exercise a little more patience. Park said everyone was listening "as if life hung on his words." Wilson said:

> I hardly know how to conduct myself when I have not come to fight against anybody, but with somebody. I have come to suggest, among other things, that when the forces of nature are steadily working and the tide is rising to meet the moon, you need not be afraid that it will not come to its flood. We feel the tide; we rejoice in the strength of it; and we shall not quarrel in the long run as to the method of it. Because, when you are working with masses of men and organized bodies of opinion, you have got to carry the organized body along. The whole art and practice of government consists not in moving individuals, but in moving masses. It is all very well to run ahead and beckon, but, after all, you have got to wait for the body to follow. I have not come to ask you to be patient, because you have been, but I have come to congratulate you that there was a force behind you that will beyond any peradventure be triumphant, and for which you can afford a little while to wait.

A few days after the convention, Peabody and Wise discussed the speech by letter. Peabody had been present for the president's address, he told Wise, having spent "the most of two days" at the NAWSA meeting. "I thought the President fine and think his speech one that will have continuing influence upon those who are led to think by clearness of expression." Peabody's support for Wilson had not wavered. He found Hughes's position on suffrage dubious, especially given his reaction as governor of New York when Peabody asked him to include an appeal for suffrage in his message to the New York legislature. "He was absolutely unbending in his lack of sympathy," Peabody recalled in his letter to Wise, adding, "In 1915, when we were making desperate efforts in New York State, which you so valiantly championed, Justice Hughes did not take the trouble to come to New York to vote."

Park, in her memoir, said she and those assembled in Atlantic City took Wilson's address to be his first intimation of a willingness to support a federal amendment. Catt, at a crowded basement meeting afterward, called for a four-front strategy. First, she recommended resolutions pushing for federal action from the legislatures of states that had already granted women the vote. Second, she advocated for an intensification of efforts to win suffrage for women in the states that were actually in play, with New York high on her list. Third, in the states that were not so far along in their campaigns, she suggested that women try for at least the right to vote for presidential electors, which, Park's memoir explained, would mean that legislatures could grant this without taking the question to a vote of the electorate. And last, in the few single-party states in the South, she told delegates to push for suffrage in the primaries—effectively the equivalent of an election. Park said Catt then asked for a promise of total secrecy. Disclosure would cause the plan to fail.

Also, immediately after the convention, Shaw let Hapgood know how pleased she had been with Wilson's address, which he duly reported to the president. Hapgood said she especially liked how the president had realized "the character of the women who are in our organization," and the way he had shown respect for "our intelligence." Anna Johnson, a popular fiction writer whose novels appeared under the name Hope Daring, soon asked Wilson for a signed copy of excerpts from the address because a group she represented, the Writers Equal Suffrage League, wanted to put the copy up for auction to help defray league expenses. Wilson immediately asked Tumulty, his aide, to select passages for her.

Hapgood wrote the president again with another enclosure, this one from John Dewey's wife, Alice Chipman Dewey, who had sent Hapgood a letter in response to the president's address. On the stationery of the Congressional Union, she announced her resignation from its board and her intention to join Hapgood's Independent Wilson League. "As a non-voter," she wrote,

> I want on every occasion to register my protest against the injustice of my forcing myself to come to a decision of this kind. But women have convinced me that all women must stand together and I stand by the voters and am joining the Independent Wilson League for the sake of Woman Suffrage. You can readily see how difficult it is this year to walk in the dark and having nothing more than a flashlight to guide one over a long road. I trust that you will do everything possible to make Mr. Wilson's promise in regard to Woman Suffrage come to something real in less time than he himself suggested the other day at Atlantic City.

It was not long before House wrote Wilson to say that Hapgood was interested in a European ambassadorship for himself, should there be a vacancy. In the Wilson administration, several Men's League members had been under consideration for various positions, or had taken it upon themselves, as Villard had done in 1912, to suggest the names of possible appointees. Peabody's name came up less formally for ambassadorial appointments after he turned down the earlier offer of the post of Secretary of the Treasury. Villard himself, too, was mentioned, even at one point as an alternative to House in the role of Wilson's informal adviser, although Wilson had no apparent interest in Villard for such a position, nor did any of the president's close aides.

———◄○►———

NAWSA, in gearing up again for the new campaign, was in need of a fresh slogan. "Woman Suffrage Is Bound to Come" had outlived its usefulness. A twenty-five-dollar prize would go to the perfect tag line. League members on Creel's publicity committee dominated the judging: *Cosmopolitan* editor Edgar Sisson; Mark Sullivan of *Collier's*; John Cosgrave of the *New York World*; Robert Hobart Davis of *Munsey's*; and Frank Crowninshield of *Vanity Fair*, who had shared in *Puck's* February 20, 1915, suffrage issue about how the antis had converted him to the prosuffrage side by omitting any reference in their arguments to how many women worked outside the home. The winning entry:

## "THE WOMAN'S HOUR HAS STRUCK. WOMAN SUFFRAGE IS COMING."

Creel, meantime, issued a public scolding to any women who supported Hughes. In the "tapestried drawing room" of Gertrude and Amos Pinchot, a founder of the Progressive Party, Creel made an unseemly comparison that no doubt helped his statement make the press. He likened women "who are going around among the women voters betraying them to the Republican party" to the cow in the Chicago stockyards that kept "forever climbing up the runway to lead her sisters to the slaughter."

Hapgood reported to Wilson that Walter Lippmann would publish an article in the October 7 issue of the *New Republic* by the physician Alice Hamilton, the head of the Illinois Commission on Occupational Diseases. "As One Woman Sees the Issues" was the title of the essay, which sought to explain why a woman—a formidable woman in this case—would vote to reelect the president from her newly enfranchised state. Hamilton argued that Wilson had been clear on staying out of Mexico, while Hughes's reaction was so vague that it made her worry he might intervene. Hughes, like Wilson, was also indefinite on the European war, she said, but Hughes "conveys an intimation of greater aggressiveness, which makes me wary." She said Hughes also seemed to be wrong on other issues, namely,

Poster bearing the suffrage movement's 1916 slogan, chosen in a contest judged by Men's League members. (The National Women's Suffrage Publishing Co.)

protection, economy of administration, and appointment of experts to office. She also said she thought he seemed to be wrong on the federal amendment for women's suffrage, even though Hughes and the Republicans had come out in favor of it and the Democrats were still stuck on states' rights.

"It seems ungenerous for one who is already emancipated not to do all in her power to help emancipate the rest of womankind," Hamilton conceded, "and indeed I would gladly help, but not at the expense of measures which though perhaps no more important are immediately urgent and must be settled rightly now if we are to escape grave national disasters."

———◄○►———

On October 19, in Chicago, a mob raged outside the Congress Hotel as Wilson arrived to address some four thousand cheering nonpartisan women inside. The noisy protesters were mostly men, but there were women among them, too. They clashed with another group of demonstrators, silent ones, led by Paul and about a hundred members of her National Woman's Party. Cries of "Dishwashers!" "Where's your baby?" "Down with suffrascals!" and "Back to the kitchen" came at them. The *Chicago Tribune* reported on the mêlée, on its front page:

> Umbrellas, canes, hands and feet ripped them to bits and snapped their staffs. So violent was the attack on the handful of women that many were knocked down and trampled. Those who attempted to defend their banners were beaten on the knuckles until their grip relaxed. Hats were torn off. Hair fell in cascades. Hairpins jumped like Mexican beans on the pavement. Walls rose, tears fell, waists paired, stays creaked, and women were wild in Michigan avenue.

Wilson's automobile stopped only long enough for a "petulant tut tut or so," the *Tribune* said, then "rolled aloofly by" en route to the auditorium. The president entered the building with a campaigner's smile. On stage, he spoke of the need in politics to "get together" in both the national and international arenas. He never mentioned suffrage, but he did speak of the necessary role of women in American life. "Men have represented the principle of rivalry," he said, "the principle of commanding the services of others by superior powers of executive organization. They have gone out into the arena of business very much as they have gone out into the battlefield to make conquest of some place where they stand and control."

The spirit of the law, Wilson said, is to favor the dominant, "but it seems to me that the function of society now has another element in it, and I believe that it is the element which women are going to supply. It is the element of mediation, of comprehending and drawing the elements together. It is the power of sympathy as contrasted with the power of control." Society needs what women have, he said, "the power of interpretative understanding, of sympathetic comprehension."

On October 22, Creel spoke at a suffrage parade in Philadelphia, staged to welcome a giant Women's Justice Bell, drawn on wheels over the streets by "100 young women dressed in white, flowing garments, garlanded with daffodils." He appeared again later in the month at a Wilson mass meeting at Barnard College, sponsored by the Social Science League.

Creel's wife, Blanche Bates, was a close friend of Wilson's daughter Margaret, a relationship that had made the newspapers the preceding August, when the shaft of a carriage Creel was driving broke and hurled Margaret out of it and onto the ground. The three were on a picnic during a visit by the president's daughter to the Bates summer home near Ossining, New York. A local doctor treated her, and she made a full recovery.

Creel proved a passionate and energetic supporter of the president. His September 1916 paean, *Wilson and the Issues*, which the magazine the *Century* published in book form, took 167 pages to detail the president's positions on some of the most vexing issues of the period: retaliation against Mexico during the Border War; the sinking of the RMS *Lusitania*; war preparedness and national defense (Wilson was still against entering the war at that point); and American foreign policy. Creel included a personal defense of Josephus Daniels, US Secretary of the Navy, "the most maligned and most misunderstood man in the United States today."

Perhaps by request, perhaps by design, the one stunning omission in Creel's book was any mention of the suffrage debate, clearly one of the issues the president was grappling with in advance of the November ballot. Given Creel's simultaneous involvement with the Wilson campaign and the suffrage cause, the lapse is particularly glaring. As noted, between 1915 and 1917, Creel was running the Men's League's "Office of the Publicity Committee," as the League's printed stationery proclaimed in its letterhead, top and dead center. In the margins were the names of dozens of other well-known writers and editors who were in league with the League.

Support for Wilson was strong from other top Men's League officers, too. In the run-up to the election, Peabody sent Wilson repeated tidings of his support, including late-breaking news of the no doubt welcome interest in the president's reelection from Andrew Carnegie.

Villard, who acknowledged in his memoir that he was never on personally intimate terms with Wilson, was still in regular contact with Tumulty. Villard was in Washington often in those days. Since the sinking of the *Lusitania* in May

1915, he had become the *Evening Post*'s Washington correspondent, in addition to being its publisher. Malone spent the final days before the election in California, courting women and other groups of voters. The *Los Angeles Times* carried an item loaded with innuendo, reporting that Malone had been sent west to "stir up the workingmen for Wilson." "At home," it said, "Dudley Field Malone is one of the hottest little workingmen to be found on Manhattan Island. But his father-in-law, Senator James A. O'Gorman, is too busy to make any Wilson speeches."

———◦———

In November, Wilson narrowly won the election. He picked up victories in all the suffrage states except two, Illinois and Oregon. For an after-dinner talk at the Gridiron Club on December 9, he reflected on why the movement for women's suffrage was "becoming irresistible." The problems of "how to work out common rights, how to relieve common suffering" had become paramount, he said:

> Women feel further than we do and feeling, if it be comprehending, feeling goes further in the solution of problems than cold thinking does. The day of cold thinking, of fine spun constitutional argument is gone, thank God. We do not now discuss so much what the Constitution of the United States is as what the constitution of human nature is, what the essential constitution of human society is. And we know in our hearts that, if we ever find a place or a time where the Constitution of the United States is contrary to the constitution of human nature and human society, we have got to change the Constitution of the United States.

Among the guests at the president's first state dinner after reelection were cabinet members and their wives, along with Peabody and Creel. Colonel House had Creel on a short list that he shared with the president—"subject to your approval"—for prominent reporting positions with Curtis Publications, publisher of the *Saturday Evening Post*, which he had been asked to provide to editors. So cozy, the publishing houses kept proving to be with favored politicians. House also passed along a comment that the major issues in the next election would be prohibition and women's suffrage.

The year in suffrage rounded out sadly with a memorial service for Inez Milholland Boissevain, dead of pernicious anemia at the age of thirty. Max and Crystal Eastman both gave eulogies at her memorial service. Crystal recalled her dear friend's strong interest in internationalism, Max, her courageous feminism.

Willard D. Straight

Charles A. Lindbergh Sr.

Charles S. Whitman

John Purroy Mitchel

Charles B. Smith

Frank Vanderlip

Ogden Mills Reid

Jacob Gould Schurman

Rupert Hughes

Carl Jonas Nordstrom

George Notman

James W. Gerard

Robert Underwood
Johnson

Julius Frank

John A. Kingsbury

James Norman
deR. Whitehouse

# "Mr. President, How Long Must Women Wait for Liberty?"

## 1917

Every other matter and social cause shrunk in importance after the United States entered the World War. Yet that did not—could not—stop the New York suffragists from pressing for a state-level victory at the polls on November 6, in whatever way seemed appropriate to the times. Nor did it deter the activist flank of the movement in Washington, DC, from agitating for federal action, by means many considered less appropriate. Alice Paul's increasingly volcanic Congressional Union took on all of officialdom in the nation's capital, from the president to the local police. NAWSA leaders, in turn, clashed with Paul's forces, too.

On January 9, Sara Bard Field of Oregon led three hundred of the Congressional Union's members to the White House to present President Wilson with resolutions in memory of Inez Milholland Boissevain. The women also seized the opportunity to urge the president yet again to support the federal amendment publicly.

Wilson was not amused. "I had not been apprised that you were coming here to make any representations that would issue an appeal to me," he told them. "I had been told that you were coming to present memorial resolutions with regard to the very remarkable woman whom your cause has lost. I therefore am not prepared to say anything further than I have said on previous occasions of this sort." He then repeated his customary response, adding that he could not understand how anyone could fail to see that the Democrats were "more inclined than the opposition party to assist in this great cause."

On January 10, Harriot Blatch organized an "indignation meeting" to plan a new campaign that began the same day. The National Woman's Party stationed twelve "silent sentinels" at the two entrances to the White House so that the president would not be able to come or go without a direct encounter with one or more of them. The plan was to increase the number of picketers steadily until three thousand of them would surround the executive mansion. The front-page headline in the *New York Times* did not distinguish between the suffrage factions:

## SUFFRAGISTS WILL PICKET WHITE HOUSE

The timing may have been coincidental, but within a week, the president noticeably straightened up his prosuffrage posture. At a news conference on January 15, he told reporters that he personally believed in suffrage—and wanted it soon. For the first time, he said publicly that he regretted his failure to get a stronger suffrage plank included in the party's current platform, and added a new iteration of his reason for not pressing Congress about its inaction on the federal initiative. "I have got to take what my party says," Wilson told them. "I have to be satisfied for the time being with what I got then."

The president took further, but private, action on behalf of suffrage in the coming weeks. On January 23, he wrote to the governor of North Dakota, Lynn Joseph Frazier, asking Frazier to convey his "feeling of sincere gratification" that the state legislature had passed the same suffrage bill the Illinois legislature had approved, one that allowed women to vote in presidential elections and for municipal officials. "My interest in the extension of the suffrage to the women, is, as you know, very great," Wilson wrote, "and I feel that every step in this right direction should receive the most cordial endorsement and public recognition."

Two days later, he sent a similar message to Carrie Chapman Catt. "As you know," he said, "I have a real interest in the extension of the suffrage to the women, and I feel that every step in this direction should be applauded." On February 28, he wrote to the speaker of the Tennessee State Senate, William Riley Crabtree, to express an "earnest hope" that the Tennessee legislature would "reconsider" its vote rejecting an extension of the ballot to women. "Our party is so distinctly pledged to its passage," he wrote, "that it seems to me the moral obligation is complete."

Also noteworthy is an undated quotation from the president that appears in the 1924 chronicle of journalist David Lawrence about the eighteen years he spent covering Wilson's career. Lawrence points out how constant were the efforts of Wilson's daughters, Margaret and Janet, known as Jessie (his third daughter, Eleanor, came around much later), to persuade their father to change his mind on the suffrage question, as well as the esteem in which Wilson held Carrie Chapman Catt, Anna Shaw, and the author and free-thought advocate Helen Hamilton Gardener, great suffragists all. Lawrence quoted Wilson as explaining to a friend:

When I find two of my daughters such ardent suffragists, passionately devoted to the cause, and when I find also such refined cultured ladies as Mrs. Catt, Mrs. Shaw and Mrs. Gardener equally devoted and conscientious, I must concede that some of my prejudices were unreasonable, and that the desire for the ballot cannot be limited to the relatively few agitators. A cause which could enlist the enthusiastic, devoted, idealistic support of such ladies must be wholesome.

Although the provenance or timing is not offered, such a concession almost certainly would have happened during the winter of 1916–1917, as that is when Wilson stopped playing both sides in the suffrage debate.

———◇———

Not surprisingly, war dominated the preoccupations of the Men's League's founding quartet. Villard's communications with the White House in this period advocated repeatedly for disarmament. From his position on the NAACP's board, he also urged Wilson to include a statement in his inaugural address "against the barbaric system of lynching which prevails in various parts of this country." Peabody joined the attorney and legal scholar, George W. Kirchwey, warden of Sing-Sing and father of the suffragist Freda Kirchwey, in cofounding an Emergency Peace Federation, which had as its slogan, "Keep America Out of War and Its Intended Consequences." Wise wrote Wilson to say that from his pulpit at the Free Synagogue on Sunday morning, February 11, "I shall say that the country must stand behind you and will stand behind you," and that "the time has come for the American people to understand that it may become our destiny to have part in this struggle which would avert the enthronement of the law of might over the nations." He titled the sermon "America's Lincoln and Wilson's America" and said that Wilson's name would be "bracketed with the names of Washington and Lincoln, equal to the genius of the spirit of America and worthy to become the champion and servant of humanity."

Wise had recently come around, as Wilson had, and no longer flatly opposed US military intervention in Europe, but Eastman and Villard remained in the opposing camp. They were both members of a late February delegation to see the president from the American Union Against Militarism, led by the Progressive Party's Amos Pinchot. Eastman addressed the president on behalf of the group, offering "fervent support and admiration" for Wilson's advocacy of a

League of Nations. At this time, none of them appears to have used his access to the president to raise the subject of suffrage.

———◁◦▷———

Around March of 1917, the Congressional Union and the National Woman's Party merged. The new organization adopted fresh resolutions that their leaders wanted to present to the president. Wilson declined to meet with the women. In protest, they announced that on March 4, the day of Wilson's private inauguration for a second term—the public ceremony was a day later—they would summon ten thousand women to march around the White House, leaving picketers to remain at attention on site for three or four hours.

The turnout was low. "The drizzle had something to do with the fizzle," Wilson's presidential assistant, Thomas W. Brahany, explained. The entry in Brahany's diary for March 4 notes that two months had passed since the Congressional Union's "silent sentries" had first taken up their daily posts on the grounds of the White House. They had been at their stations every day, from ten o'clock in the morning until 4:30 in the afternoon. Brahany described them still as members of the Congressional Union, saying it was they who had opposed Wilson in the most recent election and were "the chief peddlers and promoters of the scandalous and utterly untrue stories circulated in the Middle West and Far West about the President's private life." These were tales making the rounds in the fall of 1915 that had him seeking forgiveness from his intended second wife, Edith Galt, who granted it. It was rumored that he had sent $15,000 to keep a woman with whom he had corresponded too ardently from making his letters public.

On March 4, from Brahany's up-close vantage point, he reviewed for his diary what had happened so far in the protest. On the sentinels' first day in position, he and two other presidential advisers, Tumulty and Rudolph Forster, the president's executive clerk, "held a Council of War and decided the best thing to do was ignore the women; that they would thrive on opposition." Yet on the first cold day, the president instructed his chief White House usher to offer the women respite in the lower corridor. They refused the gesture. "Instead," Brahany wrote, "a negro was employed to carry hot bricks to the gates for use on cold days."

It was raining hard when the larger wave of women arrived as planned, though by no means in the anticipated thousands. Not more than five hundred women took their places on the lawn. Most carried banners reading, "Mr. President, How Long Must Women Wait for Liberty?" "The rain beat their faces and the wind played havoc with the banners," Brahany wrote. "They presented a sorry sight but they went through with their program as well as they could." The police presence, he said, was the largest Washington had ever seen.

Anna Shaw found the antics of these suffragists embarrassingly destructive and got busy doing damage control among NAWSA's supporters. Ladies of the Social Registry, such as Alice Edith Binsse Warren of New York and Oyster Bay, were on her list. Shaw did what she could to distance NAWSA from its more militant relatives. Knowing that Warren was a Wilson devotee, Shaw assured her of NAWSA's support for the president. Of the Congressional Union, she wrote, "This little branch of Suffragists do not belong to the National Association and never will so long as they keep up their semi-militant practice, and I assure you no woman in the country can feel worse than I do over the foolishness of their picketing the White House and the folly of their performance on inauguration day." Shaw added that Wilson had done more for suffrage in the month of February than any previous president during his entire tenure. "I believe he is sincerely fighting with us," she wrote.

For NAWSA, maintaining the clear distinction between the two suffrage organizations became as much a problem in its dealings with US congressmen as it was in its communications with potential backers. As NAWSA began to lobby hard in the House and Senate for federal action, its lieutenants found themselves constantly having to answer for the "semi-militants," explaining that they came from a separate group, and that NAWSA believed in a wholly different approach.

In New York, the impending legislative votes in Albany became the state movement's focus. Suffragists would again need majority wins in both houses of the legislature to ensure the anticipated voter referendum in November. In New York City, a popular production company, the Washington Square Players, declared the week of March 11 "suffrage week" at the Comedy Theater near Broadway, and enlisted Dudley Field Malone as its featured "curtain raiser." It would not be long before the suffrage saga would confer on Malone a far more dramatic role.

At last, on March 12, there was cause for celebration. The state Senate—with only seven dissenting votes—followed the lead of the Assembly and voted in favor of the constitutional amendment. The November referendum was guaranteed. Ida Harper's official suffrage history would later praise George Creel for his actions during "that strenuous period." As the New York Men's League's publicity chairman, he worked closely with Vira Whitehouse, who chaired the League's umbrella organization, the New York State Woman Suffrage Party. Thirty years later, Creel would recall Whitehouse's conduct of the state campaign as "brilliant."

Following the vote in Albany, Whitehouse summarized where the campaign stood. "Woman suffrage has been coming East very fast since the beginning of 1917," she told the *New York Times*. Harriet Laidlaw added that the affirmative vote of New York's legislators reflected the "greater backing of suffrage sentiment in their districts" and the fact that support for suffrage nationwide had grown stronger, with votes in favor in the Electoral College leaping to 135 from 91 in only a few weeks. With a provocative twist, she also pointed out that given the growing force of female voters in Western states, how unappealing it would be for New York men to be "governed by the women of other states."

—◇—

Not three weeks later, on April 6, the expected happened. The United States entered the war in Europe. The New York State Woman's Suffrage Party immediately offered its services, announcing that on April 10 it would "set its campaign machinery to work at once" to recruit New York men for the Army and Navy. In several counties, the state suffrage party began taking a military census of all the men of New York who were over age twenty-one.

Creel, concerned about the form military censorship would take with the United States at war—and how and in what way it would impinge on press freedom—had already indicated to Wilson's closest aides that if there were to be a censorship office, he wanted to lead it. He drafted a memorandum of intent and sent it to the White House on April 11. "Censorship is a word to be avoided," the memo began. "It is offensive to Americans, and likewise misleading. While there is much that is properly secret, the total is small compared to the vast amount of information that it is right and necessary for people to have." Wilson was impressed with Creel's proposal. Four days later came news of Creel's appointment as head of the new US Committee on Public Information, the CPI.

There was a curious aspect to the announcement of Creel's appointment, as least from the vantage point of Men's League history. Even the longer articles about it in the New York newspapers omitted his concerted public efforts on behalf of suffrage. Yet he had been involved with the Men's League throughout the six years since 1911, and most heavily from 1915 to 1917, right up to the weeks before his CPI appointment. (When business pressures forced Robert Cameron Beadle to resign shortly before the New York campaign of 1917, Harper's official history notes, it was Creel who "ably filled the office of secretary.") The articles did note the active role Creel played in Wilson's presidential campaigns, as well as the ties of Creel's ostensibly antisuffrage wife, Blanche Bates, to Wilson's prosuffrage daughter Margaret.

Creel's major suffrage advocacy failed to warrant mention even in the report of his appointment in Villard's *Evening Post*. It is difficult not to wonder if, with Alice Paul's picketers still at the White House gates, it may have seemed the wiser course not to remind reporters that the morgues of their newspapers held clippings of Creel's earlier enthusiastic public support for her organization. In those archives, they would have found a chronicle of the admiration he had expressed for her group's more combative approach. They would also find references to the violence he said he wished he could have inflicted—immolation and mutilation were his images—on the New York state and federal legislators who had failed to support women's suffrage in earlier votes. "The Congressional Union can't go too far to please me" had been his published words.

———◄○►———

During the last full week of April, eight high-powered male supporters of suffrage invaded New York City's elite all-female Colony Club to urge support for the federal amendment and Rabbi Wise did his part to encourage support for suffrage among his colleagues at the assembly of the Eastern Council of Reform Rabbis, which was meeting at Temple Emanu-el. When the council's president, Dr. Joseph Silverman, objected to the assembly's even considering a suffrage resolution, Wise threatened to resign from the organization. Silverman had been warning against women polluting themselves in the cesspool of politics since as early as 1896, arguing that it would be against natural law for women to vote and of no benefit to the country. At the meeting, he contended it was inappropriate to bring politics into the assembly; Wise countered that suffrage was a moral, not a political, issue, which any such body should properly consider. "It is not our province," Silverman insisted, "even though, by a play of sophistry, the woman suffrage question may become twisted into a moral issue." The day after that exchange, Silverman gave a different explanation for his opposition. He told the *New York Tribune* that the time was wrong for suffrage. "With America at war, the people and the Legislature should concern themselves with conserving the defense of the nation." Let it wait until the war was over, he urged. Nonetheless, on April 26, the council passed a prosuffrage resolution. In Washington the same day, Malone, still serving as Wilson's appointee as Collector for the Port of New York, appeared before a US Senate committee to express his support for the federal amendment.

Wilson's mild hints in support of the national initiative gave way to bolder actions in the spring. On May 10, Helen Gardener, writing on behalf of NAWSA, asked if Wilson would allow her to tell Edward W. Pou, chairman of the Rules Committee, that the president supported the creation of a House suffrage committee. Wilson responded favorably and did her one better, writing on May 14 to Pou himself. "Of course, strictly speaking, it is none of my business," his note said, "and I have not the least desire to intervene in the matter, but I have a letter written in an admirable spirit from Mrs. Helen H. Gardener, in which she says that she has been told that you had said that you would report out a proposal for such a committee if I should approve." He added, "I heartily approve. I think it would be a very wise act of public policy, and also an act of fairness to the best women who are engaged in the cause of woman suffrage."

That same day, Wilson met for the first time in more than a year with a prosuffrage delegation, this one composed of men. Catt had written him a week earlier to let him know this newly assembled group would be asking to see him. It included representatives of the Progressives, Republicans, Socialists, Prohibitionists, and the Woman's Party who were to appear the following day before the House Judiciary Committee and the Senate Suffrage Committee. Only the Democrats were missing because David I. Walsh, the former governor of Massachusetts, who had been scheduled to join them, needed to cancel. "The results were very satisfactory," the Progressive representative, John Appleton Haven Hopkins of New Jersey, told the press. He said he found the president's interest in the federal amendment "very warm."

Pou responded to Wilson's letter, telling him that the rules committee would hold a hearing on the matter on the morning of May 18. "While I am convinced of the wisdom of favorable action," Pou wrote, "I doubt very much if a majority of the membership of the Committee on Rules is of like opinion." Actually, the resolution passed on June 6. Gardener then wrote Wilson on June 10 to enlist his help with an intractable committee member, James Thomas Heflin, a Democrat from Alabama. Wilson wrote to Heflin directly, too. Heflin replied that he believed suffrage was a matter for each state to decide. That said, he added, to consent to the formation of a committee did not require him to surrender his convictions. So he would no longer oppose its establishment. "Whenever I can serve you, call on me," he told the president. Wilson wrote back with "great pleasure," expressing his gratitude for "so public-spirited a view of the matter."

It took another two-and-a-half months for the House to establish its suffrage committee. The vote was 180 in favor, 107 opposed.

———◦———

At the end of May, Catt, as NAWSA's president, urged Alice Paul in an open letter to call off her pickets. "There is now clear proof that the presence of the pickets is hurting our cause in Congress," she wrote. Paul's supporters responded with disinterest and a counter, "It is a curious thing," said Abbie Scott Baker, chairman of the publicity committee for the National Woman's Party, "that since we began our campaign, in January, twenty-five members of Congress, who had been opposed to suffrage, have come over to our side."

In June and July, the picketers continued more aggressively. On June 20, a visiting mission from Russia was scheduled to arrive at the White House. Around two hundred and fifty people had gathered to watch the suffragists as they unfurled a provocative ten-foot-long banner, raising charges from the crowd of everything from lack of patriotism to outright treason. Members of the crowd tore the banner from its frame and ripped it to pieces before the arrival of the mission, to whom it was addressed, though its real targets were the president and his envoy to Russia, Elihu Root, who had served as war secretary in two previous administrations.

"To the Russian Mission," it read,

> President Wilson and Envoy Root are deceiving Russia. They say, "We are a democracy. Help us win a world war so that democracies may survive!"
>
> We, the women of America, tell you that America is not a democracy. Twenty million American women are denied the right to vote. President Wilson is the chief opponent of the national enfranchisement. Help us make this nation really free. Tell our government that it must liberate its people before it can claim free Russia as an ally."

The *Washington Post* clocked the altercation that ensued at a brief seven minutes, adding that the unfulfilled intent of the protesters had been to force their own arrest. Police officers stood by and watched, scribbling in their notebooks. Eventually, Police Superintendent Major Raymond W. Pullman arrived and warned the suffragists that it would be "unwise" to repeat their actions. In the next day's newspapers, Catt and Shaw denounced the women's conduct.

Banners appeared again at the White House gates on June 21, attracting a riotous crowd of some two thousand people. The police again laid low. Later in the afternoon, officers headed off a band of suffragists on their way from their headquarters at Cameron House to the White House. Preemptively, the police stripped the women of their banners, hoping to forestall another riot. The response of the district attorney, John E. Laskey, like that of the police, was to do no more than to take the matter under advisement, reluctant to take any action that might encourage the suffragists into martyrdom, as they "would welcome an opportunity to go on a 'hunger strike,'" the *Washington Post* reported.

On June 22, a capital policewoman arrived at the scene. She arrested Lucy Burns and Katherine Morey for blocking traffic, but they were released almost immediately, on their own recognizance. "They may be required to appear in police court," the *Washington Post* reported, "but this will depend on their own future conduct." The banners that day were hardly actionable; cleverly, the women had quoted President Wilson's war message to Congress: "We shall fight for the things we have always held nearest our hearts—for democracy—for the right of those who submit to authority to have a voice in their own government."

The next day, police officers took four more suffragists into custody and then released them just as quickly. A letter from Wilson to his prosuffrage daughter Jessie expressed a measure of exasperation. Of the picketers, he wrote, "They certainly seem bent upon making their cause as obnoxious as possible."

Overnight from June 24 to 25, all the typewriters at Cameron House vanished. "Tear her banner to shreds," the *Washington Post* offered in mocking lament, "drag her to police headquarters, tell her she is unpatriotic, even denounce her as a traitor—these things the suffragette views with a certain equanimity. But if you would have her fly into a rage—if you would 'get her goat,' as a man might say it—deprive her of her usual means of getting out her daily press statement."

On June 25, the police arrested twelve of eighteen picketers—the other six managed to evade the authorities—and charged them with unlawful assembly. Again, the women were released on their own recognizance, but this time, they were told to appear in police court for trial the next day. Conviction would mean either a fine, probably of twenty-five dollars, or, if the fine was not paid, a prison sentence of up to ten days. As the city's corporation counsel told the *Washington Post*, ten days would be too short a duration for a hunger strike to succeed.

On similar charges, on June 26, police arrested an additional nine "suffragettes," which the *Post* took to calling them, suggesting the militancy of their British counterparts. After court on June 27, six of those arrested declined to pay the fine and chose instead to accept three-day jail terms. With time served, that meant release the following morning. "Considering that it is jail," the Nevada suffragist Mabel Vernon told a reporter about her overnight stay, "we are very comfortably fixed."

Two more arrests occurred on June 28. The *Post* repeated how vigorously NAWSA and its president, Catt, had been condemning the Paul protests, emphasizing how small a minority Paul's forces were in the larger suffrage movement. "So changed is the situation in Congress," the *Post* said, "that the enemies of suffrage now are practically daring the suffrage advocates to bring the question to an issue on the floors of Congress." Rumors meant to discredit the picketers flew: that they had German backing, since this more militant approach did not cross the Atlantic until after the United States had entered the war; that there were anarchists in their midst.

In July, the picketing strategy shifted to one day a week, starting with July 4, when the women carried a banner quoting the Declaration of Independence. Their presence caused a riot, witnessed by several thousand people, but not by President Wilson, who had gone yachting on the Potomac. The incident landed thirteen of the suffragists in police custody, along with four men who scuffled with them in what the *Post* called a "knock down and drag out fight." The women chose jail over the alternative fine and were released on their own recognizance pending a court appearance the following morning. All but one of them pleaded not guilty to charges of disorderly conduct. Kitty Marion's charge was tussling with a War Department clerk. She said the clerk had tried to destroy copies of the *Suffragist* magazine, which she had been attempting to sell.

On July 6, Judge Alexander Mullowny found eleven of the women guilty. Defiantly, the women declined to pay the fine in favor of three days in jail. "I hate to do it," Judge Mullowny said in announcing the verdict, "but under the law there's nothing else for me to do." He even offered to advance the fine to any of them who did not have it. "I can't believe you'll go to prison," he said, "—ladies of education and refinement like you." A cordial exchange of views with the judge then followed, after which came the protesters' plans for a new picketing drive to start that same week.

On July 13, the *Washington Post* reported new demonstration plans afoot, possibly for Bastille Day, July 14, but Paul's group did not share the details. A failed "peace mission" to the militants earlier that week had brought the New York suffrage leaders Harriet Laidlaw and Narcissa Vanderlip to Washington as emissaries; they left "very much discouraged with the outlook for the referendum election in New York in November," not to mention "very angry at the militants" over the negative impact their demonstrations were having on prospective voters in New York.

Paul's forces reasoned that without Wilson's approval, without his considerable ability to persuade, there would be no movement toward the federal amendment in Congress. That was why they made the president their primary target. The women used the side doors of the White House, too, quietly forging relationships with sympathetic members of Wilson's inner circle. The 1920 memoir of Doris Stevens, one of Paul's organizers, offers word sketches of what must have been frustrating exchanges with close Wilson advisers. Edward House, for example, Stevens described as an "interesting but not unfamiliar type in politics. Extremely courteous, mild mannered, able, quickly sympathetic, he listens with undistracted attention to your request. His round bright eyes snap as he comes at you with a counter-proposal. It seems so reasonable. And while you know he is putting back upon you the very task you are trying to persuade him to undertake, he does it so graciously that you can scarcely resist liking it. He has the manner of having done what you ask without actually doing more than to make you feel warm at having met him." Stevens said that even though House was a supporter of the federal amendment, "his gentle, soft and traditional kind of diplomacy would not employ high-powered pressure."

As for Creel, a "suffragist of long standing," Stevens was quick to note, she and her colleagues called upon him "many times" to help with persuading Wilson to act "because his contact with the President was constant." Yet Creel, she said, hated her group's militant tactics because, at least in her view, "he knew we were winning and the Administration was losing." More likely, given Creel's much earlier nod of affirmation to the union's "not too card-indexy" approach, his first allegiance now was—had to be—to the president. Stevens described Creel as "a strange composite. Working at terrific tension and mostly under fire, he was rarely in calm enough mood to sit down and devise ways and means." Dialogue with him often went something like this:

> "But I talk to the President every day on this matter"—and "I am doing all I can"—and—"The President is doing all he can"—he would drive at you—without stopping for a breath.
> "But if you will just ask him to get Senator _____"
> "He is working on the Senate now. You people must give him time. He has other things to do."

Every suggestion the women offered, she said, Creel "just swept side."

The Bastille Day surprise proved to be the biggest shocker from the National Woman's Party to date. It culminated in the arrests of sixteen female picketers, among them, by tactical intention, women from every region of the country and several pedigreed New Yorkers. They included Eunice Dana Brannan, the sixty-two-year-old daughter of the late *New York Sun* editor Charles A. Dana, who was also the wife of an early Men's League supporter, John Winters Brannan, the respected Bellevue physician and president of the hospital's Board of Trustees; Florence Bayard, a daughter of Thomas F. Bayard, a former secretary of state and ambassador to Britain; Elizabeth Selden Rogers, a sister of a former secretary of war Henry L. Stimson and descendant of Roger Sherman, a signer of the Declaration of Independence; Alison Hopkins, the wife of the prominent Progressive Party member J.A.H. Hopkins, who had chaired New Jersey's Progressive State Committee in the last presidential campaign and was an important Wilson supporter; Matilda Gardner, wife of the journalist Gilson Gardner; and Doris Stevens, who, thanks to a romantic entanglement with a close Wilson ally, had pull of a different sort.

Each put up the requisite twenty-five dollars in fines and avoided a Saturday night and Sunday in jail. They appeared in court on Monday morning, July 16, before Judge Mullowny, who on Wednesday afternoon sentenced each of them to a sixty-day term at the workhouse in Occoquan, Virginia. There, they exchanged their dresses for prison gray. "It was an awkward ordeal," the *Washington Post* snipped. "Nearly all the ladies, being of wealth and distinction, usually had maids to attend to or help them out in such important details as dressing and undressing. But maids are not included in the Occoquan service, and the occasion was unceremonious."

The detention center allowed only close relatives to visit, as well as the women's legal counsel, who had raced down from New York City to testify on their behalf. He asked permission to defend them in court, but also from President Wilson, at whose pleasure he served. It was Dudley Field Malone.

As the suffragists settled in at the workhouse, into Wilson's office trooped the men who felt the women's plight most personally. Gilson Gardner, the Washington correspondent for the Scripps newspapers, sought an appointment to appeal for "the president's personal attention." Gardner said he took what he had been told as fact, that the matter had been handled without the president's personal attention, and that Wilson had not understood "the ultimate bad effects" that the publicity from jailing women of such high standing in a workhouse for sixty days would bring. "I am sure that the President will agree with me as to the political unwisdom of this procedure," Gardner wrote, explaining further that the repercussions of the court's ill-conceived judgment would tend to put the burden of responsibility on Wilson himself, "unless he personally intervenes at this time, and corrects this great blunder." Gardner added, "merely for the sake of frankness," that his wife was among the detainees. "I am willing that all allowances be made for this fact, and that my suggestion be weighed entirely on its merits."

Malone, although scheduled for a five-minute meeting in the late afternoon of Tuesday, spent a full forty-five minutes with Wilson "to the derangement of the President's regular afternoon motor ride." So perturbed was Malone as he left the White House that he forgot about the taxi he had ordered and instead walked rapidly back to his room at the Shoreham Hotel. The *New York Times* carried the rumor that Malone had threatened to resign his coveted post as port collector "over the attitude of the National Administration and the Washington Police toward the participants in this latest militant demonstration." Malone declined to confirm or deny this, or to make any statement at all about his meeting with Wilson. The *Washington Post* report included one additional detail: "The President is said to have refused to interfere."

The *Times* report included a lengthy reflection on Malone's state of mind, "the indignation he felt over the manner in which the suffragists had been treated. It stood out in his trembling voice, his nervous energy, and his emphatic statements."

Without reference to his meeting with the president, Malone told reporters that every American citizen had the right to petition for a redress of grievances and that to interfere with that right was "a breach of constitutional guarantees." He said he had witnessed the Bastille Day demonstration on Saturday, and had returned to Washington on Tuesday to testify in the local police court. The sixteen women had not created a disturbance, he said, adding that a single policeman— or he himself—could have dispersed the crowd that had gathered around them.

———◦———

Not public knowledge at the time was a likely impetus for Malone's impassioned crusade. Amorous letters had been passing between Malone and Doris Stevens at least since 1916. Hers would be sent to Malone in care of the Lambs Club, the theatrical society to which he belonged; his, from New York, went to her on the stationery of the Lambs or the Hotel Knickerbocker. The first letter of Malone's to survive is dated August 12, 1916. Words and phrases like "my own beautiful Love," "sweetheart," "dear love," "not a single day has gone by which I have not sent a wire and a letter," appear in the missive, along with "in the great pure truth and warmth of your love, Doris, no burden seems impossible to carry." The letter includes Malone's vow of absolute fidelity to Stevens during a number of forthcoming "stag days" in New York. "I say this, love of my heart, not because you need such assurance for your faith in me is great and wonderful, but just to show you how *I want to be* just filled inside and hugged outside in the power of your love, and quite alone to think of my brilliant and glorious girl, and just to revel in the joy that has cheered my old heart and made it young again."

At the time, Malone was still married to the former Patricia O'Gorman, and would continue to be through his unsuccessful run for governor of New York in 1920. His wife did not divorce him until 1921. Malone and Stevens, who had by then moved to Paris, married that year.

—◦—

On July 18 came another emissary from the contingent of aggrieved husbands, J.A.H. Hopkins, the Wilson supporter who had been part of the multiparty delegation in favor of the federal amendment that had visited Wilson in May. Hopkins also conferred with the president for forty-five minutes. Afterward, he told reporters how "deeply shocked at the whole affair" Wilson was and that "on learning the circumstances" he had "only one thought, namely to straighten the matter out."

Hopkins also tested the waters on the "advisability of urging the Susan B. Anthony suffrage amendment as an emergency war measure," the *Post* reported, saying that Wilson was considering it. Hopkins added that he had promised to canvass Congress to assess where support for the measure stood. The two men also discussed a pardon for the prisoners, an idea that Hopkins said appealed to Wilson in principle; but since it was unlikely to stop the picketing, he probably would not offer it.

Malone, meanwhile, was quoted in the press saying that he was pushing for an appeal of the suffragists' sentence and, the *Washington Post* reported, was "said to have offered to act as counsel regardless of the effect it might have on his government position." The newspaper added that those urging the appeal were really after a determination of who had ordered the police to break up the Bastille Day picketing and arrest the sixteen women. Gardner, the journalist, said he had information that the instructions had come from higher-ups, which the district police commissioner, Louis Brownlow, vigorously denied. "We are acting entirely on our own responsibility," Brownlow told the *Washington Post.*"

Hopkins followed up his White House meeting immediately with a letter to Wilson that included a careful calculation, provided by the suffragists, of the likely pro-amendment votes in the House and the Senate. Out of a total of ninety-six senators, fifty had promised to vote yes, including twenty-eight of forty-three Republicans and twenty-two of the fifty-three Democrats. That left forty-six senators, the reported noted, from which fourteen more votes could be drawn if the amendment were to become an administration measure.

The House figures held similar promise. Out of the 435 possible votes in the House, promises had been given by 139 of the 215 Republicans, 74 of the 215 Democrats, and four of the five Independents. That left seventy-six Republicans, 141 Democrats, and one Independent—218 in all—from whom to draw the needed seventy-three additional votes.

Wilson checked the calculations with the US Postmaster, Albert Sidney Burlson. "How nearly do you think it is likely to be accurate?" Wilson asked in a letter sent, in the words he closed with, "In haste."

Another meeting about the arrests took place on July 18, this one at the Shoreham. Among its participants were "others interested" along with Malone and a top New York attorney, George Gordon Battle, whom Malone had engaged to represent the women as legal adviser in case of an appeal, the *New York Times* reported. A cagey line followed their names: "They were joined by George Creel, Chairman of the Committee on Public Information, but it was said afterward that Mr. Creel just happened to be present, and did not take part in the conference."

The next day, July 19, Wilson indeed issued a pardon of the imprisoned women. The *Washington Post* offered speculation from Wilson's friends as to why the reprieve had been offered—that Wilson had been moved by reports of small children who needed their mothers, or that he hoped the pardons would blunt the reams of sensational publicity feeding into the activists' strategy. The suffragists saw another reason, the *Post* said: They insisted that Wilson "had become convinced that the country was aroused over the workhouse sentences."

It took some effort, but in the end, Malone and Hopkins persuaded the Occoquan women to accept the pardons and shift their full attention to both houses of Congress. Malone impressed upon them that the president's action was tantamount to his admission that they had suffered an injustice. The women balked, because for them, a pardon signified that a crime had been committed, and they had committed none. All the same, after three gruesome nights, they left the workhouse. From Philadelphia, Anna Shaw, who had cabled the president to urge the protesters' release, expressed her gratitude to the president.

———◦———

Commissioner Brownlow, in his 1958 autobiography, devotes two pages to his version of the Occoquan episode, tracing Wilson's reaction after he issued the pardon. "Mr. Wilson was highly indignant," Brownlow recalled. "He told me that we had made a fearful blunder, that we never ought to have indulged these women in their desire for arrest and martyrdom, and that he had pardoned them and wanted that to end it. I was obliged to tell him that the women had refused to accept his pardon. He was more indignant than ever when he found that they were still in prison despite his pardon, and his temper was not improved when I told him that the attorney general, Thomas Watt Gregory, had ruled that a pardon wasn't an effective pardon until it was accepted." Brownlow took full responsibility for the arrests. "At the end, he asked me not to make any further arrests until after notifying him, making it plain that he would never consent and that he wished to be advised if I, knowing his dissent, nevertheless intended to take further action."

On July 20, the *New York Tribune* managed to get comment from Alice Paul, who was being treated at Johns Hopkins Hospital in Baltimore for a kidney ailment. "Picketing will continue," she said, "and sooner or later the President will have to do something definite. Oh yes, picketing has accomplished just exactly what we wanted it to accomplish, and picketing is going to end in forcing the issue."

"The sentence was monstrous," she went on, "sixty days for blocking traffic! And we didn't block it! If we could only have appealed the case!" She also said that Malone would absolutely not resign his administration post, and that he had "only contemplated doing so if he were not allowed to retain that position and act for the pickets, should their case be appealed." In the end, there would be no appeal of the sentence because the proceedings involved no legal irregularities.

As to the amendment's prospects in Congress, the *Post* offered its own calculation, reinforced by "private admissions of the leaders of both houses" that if a vote were called in late July of 1917, the measure would surely fail. The *Post* also said that unnamed prosuffrage senators thought the altercations at the White House fence had set the cause back "at least several years." With war legislation keeping Congress so busy, the best that suffrage supporters could hope for would be to get the measure on the Senate calendar, which could at least mean the possibility of action during the winter legislative session of 1917–1918.

———◦———

The picketing resumed immediately. Alison Hopkins was at the gates the next day with a banner reading:

## WE DO NOT ASK PARDON FOR OURSELVES
## BUT JUSTICE FOR ALL AMERICAN WOMEN

Over the coming weeks, rain or shine, there were more demonstrations and more pickets at the White House gates, all of which the police studiously ignored. Malone sought an early afternoon interview with House on July 26, but he didn't arrive at House's home until after ten o'clock in the evening and kept House awake until nearly midnight. An entry for that day in House's diary describes what transpired. Malone recounted his July 17 exchange with the president, calling it "distressing" because of Wilson's inaction on suffrage. House found Malone's diatribe "not a pleasant thing to hear." Malone expressed the view that the president could "bring about national suffrage almost immediately if he was sincerely for it."

Malone told House that the president had said he did not think it right to go to Congress and demand that Congress act on the amendment. Malone said he had countered, asking Wilson "why he considered it right to demand of Congress practically all the important legislation he had gotten through." House wrote in his diary that he thought Wilson had erred in giving Malone such a reason, that the president "should have stated the truth."

Over the years, House said, he had learned never to argue with the president when he gave "evasive or foolish reasons" for a given action, "reasons I know are not the real ones." Instead, House's tactic was to go silent. "The President understands that I know he is talking nonsense, and my method is far more effective." House reflected further that Malone's action had caused a breach with the president that was bound to widen. "It is a pity that a man of Dudley's remarkable talents should not use them to better advantage. He is temperamentally unable to do sustained work," House wrote, adding that he had also urged Malone not to resign—at least not for the present. When Malone asked why, House told him that he thought it would be better for him and better for the president if there were no apparent breach between the two of them, especially given Malone's now prominent role in the suffrage drama at the gates. Malone did not promise.

House reported to Wilson, saying only that he had asked Malone not to resign and that Malone had given no definite promise, but House also added his concern over Malone's state of mind and his reflection on the impact of what Malone might do next. Malone "is standing on the brink and I am afraid that his political, domestic and religious affairs are about to crumble," House wrote. "The loss of his friendship, if indeed, it is lost, may cause you to doubt if any can endure. Such a dénouement must bring suspicion upon all, even upon those who wish nothing but an opportunity to serve you and the country well."

———◦———

There was more Congressional Union picketing in August, alongside the lobbying efforts in Congress by representatives of both the National Woman's Party and NAWSA. In New York, campaign momentum for the state constitutional amendment intensified, too. Vira Whitehouse sent a letter to Wilson asking him to offer a "friendly statement" on behalf of the New York amendment drive. Her New York State Woman Suffrage Party was planning a campaign conference at the end of August, she wrote, and she could use his good word. Her husband, the stockbroker James Norman de Rapelye Whitehouse, was the Men's League's treasurer at the time, succeeding Ward Melville.

Wilson quickly wrote back with a statement on August 14, expressing his pleasure in her impression of "a growing sentiment in the State of New York in favor of woman suffrage" and his interest in the results of her Saratoga conference. "May I not express the hope," he added, "that the conference will lead to a very widespread interest in your campaign and that your efforts will be crowned with the most substantial and satisfactory success?"

In Washington, Wilson received thoughtful letters of protest both for and against the way the Washington police had handled the August ruckuses. The journalist Henry Noble Hall, who had a strong international following, wrote to Wilson on August 15 to describe what he had witnessed that day and the day before, both in front of the White House and at suffrage headquarters. Crowds including servicemen, he said, had violently attacked the suffragists, whom the police then moved in to protect.

"The temper of the crowd was directed exclusively against the seditious and despicable banners carried by the women, and not in any way against their persons," Hall wrote. "Indeed I saw several instances of chivalrous regard for the women, several men interposing themselves to receive blows which would otherwise have fallen upon the suffragettes." He said he had witnessed "many women and men of mature years" openly applauding when younger people tore down the banners. "Frequently I heard the sentiment expressed that women who are capable of parading some of the most obnoxious banners must either be traitors or degenerates," he wrote. Especially galling to him at a time of war with Germany was a banner inscription referring to the nation's leader and commander in chief as "Kaiser Wilson." That, he said, effectively gave aid and encouragement to the enemy. "It does seem," Hall wrote, "that an indignant public should be allowed to deal with such banners according to the dictates of their patriotism without police interference. Today it was not the public that was protected, it was the women who held up to ridicule and contempt the President of the United States."

Wilson's reply to Hall was a courteous two sentences. He thanked him for his letter, which, the president said, "expresses not a little of my own concern and I hope sincerely that the matter you refer to is now being more wisely and more successfully handled." On August 23, six more picketers wound up at Occoquan.

Doris Stevens's memoir records a markedly different view of these events. The policemen did nothing to help the women during the confrontations, she writes, and by their inaction effectively incited the crowd. She also offers an explanation for her party's decision to escalate its rhetoric: "We did not regard Mr. Wilson as *our* president," Stevens wrote. "We felt that he had neither political nor moral claim to our allegiance. War had been made without our consent. The war would be finished and very likely a bad peace would be written without our consent. Our fight was becoming increasingly difficult—I might almost say desperate. Here we were, a band of women fighting with banners, in the midst of a world armed to the teeth."

Stevens said the organization no longer had any expectation of sympathy from the public. "The truth was not pleasant," she wrote, "but it had to be told." The offensive banner the women had carried read:


KAISER WILSON
HAVE YOU FORGOTTEN HOW YOU SYMPATHIZED
WITH THE POOR GERMANS BECAUSE THEY
WERE NOT SELF-GOVERNED?
20,000,000 AMERICAN WOMEN ARE NOT SELF-GOVERNED.
TAKE THE BEAM OUT OF YOUR OWN EYE.

———◇———


From Little Falls, Minnesota, came an "open letter" to Wilson from the Republican congressman Charles August Lindbergh, father of the aviator (who was a fifteen-year-old boy at the time.) The senior Lindbergh was a committed suffragist who believed that it was simply wrong to exclude women from the vote, that voting was their absolute fundamental right, as he had declared in a public statement in the House two years earlier. Over the course of many pages, the congressman gave Wilson his eyewitness account of the mobs of uniformed soldiers, sailors, and civil service employees who had swarmed the "defenseless women" and committed at least three "illegal and indefensible" acts. Lindbergh included the testimony of another eyewitness and a review of the history of the republic going back to John Quincy Adams. He also sent the text of a resolution of the Non-Partisan League, which had happened to be meeting in Washington on the third day of rioting. Representative John M. Baer of North Dakota, whose party was the Non-Partisan League, had introduced this call for justice for the suffragists in the House of Representatives.

"It is impossible to see, Mr. President," Lindbergh wrote, "how you could escape from direct responsibility for these things even if you desired to do so." The president, he said, could have dissipated the mobs with a single command, "yet they continued for three days in their mad work uninterrupted." If the women were violating the law of the land, he asked, could they not at least have a "fair and impartial trial on charges that will properly present the issues involved before a court of some degree of respectability which will hear and determine those issues in harmony with the great principles of democracy upon which our government is founded?"

———◄○►———

In New York, two days before the Suffrage Campaign Conference was to start in Saratoga, Whitehouse wrote back to Wilson, pointing out politely that the message the president had offered was a little too ambiguous. Would he consider redrafting it? By return mail, Wilson added two unequivocal sentences to his original note:

> I hope that the voters of the State of New York will rally to the support of woman suffrage by a handsome majority. It would be splendid vindication of the principle of the cause in which we all believe.

Whitehouse wrote the president again to express her appreciation. "At present we are suffering from the very general disapproval of the course of the pickets, over whom, of course, we have no control and whose methods we deeply deplore. Your message should help as much as anything to show the voters of New York State the fair attitude to take."

At Saratoga, Governor Charles S. Whitman, New York City Mayor John Mitchel, and the Democratic congressman Charles B. Smith all gave speeches, urging voters to pass the proposed state constitutional amendment. All predicted victory on November 6. As the result of a volunteer operation of near-military proportions across every district in the state, NAWSA had obtained the signatures of nearly one million New York women on a petition that confirmed their desire to vote. Speakers roundly denounced the Washington picketers.

The *New York Tribune* said the male delegates had "turned their faces bravely from the racetracks" to sit through all three of the first day's sessions. Laidlaw led the Men's League's contingent of influential backers, which included Frank Vanderlip, the president of the National City Bank of New York and husband of Narcissa Vanderlip; Ogden Mills Reid of the *New York Tribune*, whose wife, Helen Rogers Reid, was the treasurer of the state suffrage campaign organization; and Whitehouse's husband, Norman de R. Whitehouse. In addition to Mitchel, Whitman, and Smith, among the speakers were the president of Cornell University, Jacob Gould Schurman, and the Honorable James W. Gerard, who had been the US Ambassador to Germany until the declaration of war.

The reporter Sarah Addington was in Saratoga for the *New York Tribune*, describing what she saw as "a veritable crusade," "a holy cause," a moment "fraught with the responsibility of the last state campaign for woman suffrage in the Empire State (for the New York women will never again take state action to get the vote if November 6 does not bring them victory)." Especially striking, she said, was the "pent-up spirit of the thousand women" that greeted the address of Carrie Chapman Catt, which made it seem "as if the ardor of all the generations of suffragist had suddenly sprung forth in one gigantic flame." The antis were also well represented in the form of a number of "husbands of the opposition" who "picked up and left their spouses to grumble alone about woman's place," Addington said. She was struck by the longing looks of one woman toward Laidlaw as he sat on the platform, wishing her spouse were more like the husband of Mrs. Laidlaw, who had to be "the luckiest woman in the world." Indeed, years later, women who had worked for suffrage with Laidlaw would memorialize him not only as "the picturesque and fearless champion whose high spirit heartened the weary and brought recruits and new strength to the ranks," but as one to whom much more was owed than to "all the women put together."

In her article, Addington was quick to note that Narcissa Vanderlip had equally good fortune in her husband, Frank. In his speech to the delegates, Vanderlip referred to himself playfully as a "victim of indirect influence." When his quip brought a round of applause he found far too embarrassingly generous, he turned to his wife for a reassuring smile and a hand to hold. "If that's indirect influence," a Saratoga youth called out, "I want some."

Election Day was only two short months away. Whitehouse closed the proceedings with a poignant thought. "We've learned to work together, to respect each other, to love each other," she said, "and we'll miss the struggle. But we'll be glad to miss it, won't we?" She turned to the row of officers on the platform. All of them nodded yes.

———◦———

Given the violence of August in Washington and the president's continued inaction on the federal initiative, Malone's resignation became inevitable. He tendered it by letter on September 7, writing to the president at length, reminding Wilson of how diligently he had campaigned for his reelection in the western suffrage states, and how hard he had worked to respond to the arguments of seven million female voters against the failure of the Democratic Party to support passage of a federal suffrage amendment. He made a point of recalling particularly his work for Wilson in California, where women had carried the vote for him. This was despite Hughes's declared support for the federal constitutional amendment when Wilson had not offered his. Malone had promised the women of the west that he would "spend all my energy, at any sacrifice to myself, to get the present Democratic Administration to pass the Federal Suffrage Amendment," he wrote to Wilson, "but the present policy of the Administration, in permitting splendid American women to be sent to jail in Washington, not for carrying offensive banners nor for picketing, but on the technical charge of obstructing traffic, is a denial even of their constitutional right to petition for, and demand the passage of the Federal Suffrage Amendment. It therefore now becomes my profound obligation actively to keep my promise to the women of the West."

Malone then explained why the federal measure had become a necessity. More than twenty states effectively disallowed the possibility of amending their constitutions, meaning that only federal action could enable the enfranchisement of the women of those states. Even "in the midst of the great war," Malone noted, England and Russia had assured women of the vote. Should the United States not do likewise and thus "maintain our democratic leadership in the world"? He also reiterated, as he had advised the president on July 17, that to turn the country's women into voters was an "urgent war measure," a first step toward their "national emancipation." He went on:

> But unless the government takes at least this first step towards their enfranchisement, how can the Government ask millions of American women educated in our schools and colleges, and millions of American women in our homes, or toiling for economic independence in every line of industry, to give up by conscription their men and happiness to a war for Democracy in Europe, while these women citizens are denied the right to vote on the policies of the Government which demands of them such sacrifice?

Wilson himself was pivotal in the quest to get Congress to act, Malone said, "for the whole country gladly acknowledges, Mr. President, that no vital piece of legislation has come through Congress these five years except by your extraordinary and brilliant leadership."

Malone went on for several more pages, reviewing all he had done in Wilson's service, "with the most respectful affection and unshadowed devotion," he wrote. He traced his efforts back to Wilson's run for governor of New Jersey, and forward to all that Malone had accomplished as a Wilson governmental appointee. "It is no small sacrifice now for me, as a member of your Administration, to sever our political relationship," he said. "But I think it is high time that men in this generation, at some cost to themselves, stood up to battle for the national enfranchisement of women." Thus he framed his resignation as a way "to keep my promises made in the West and more freely to go into this larger field of democratic effort."

Newspapers all over the country covered the Malone resignation on their front pages, citing in headlines that the cause was the administration's foot-dragging on the federal suffrage amendment. House's diary entry for September 10 records how keenly the president felt this loss of friendship and support from Malone, the last man he would have suspected of disloyalty. House offered again his sense that Malone was simply not himself, an excuse that House thought the president was ready to accept.

Accolades poured in for Malone, even a cable from Whitehouse, despite her dismay with the picketers he had championed. "Although we disagree with you on the question of picketing," she wrote, "every suffragist must be grateful to you for the gallant support you are giving our cause and the great sacrifice you are making for it." In comments to the *New York Times*, Harriet Laidlaw proclaimed Malone's resignation "an act worthy of one of the finest knights of chivalry," but one she doubted would have a salutary effect on the New York campaign. Samuel Untermyer added, "Malone is too much identified with the picketing in Washington to help the party's cause in this State." All the same, Untermyer said, just getting the suffrage issue before the public, given these otherwise "stirring times," was positive in and of itself.

The poet Alice Duer Miller, a regular columnist for the *New York Tribune*, was moved to keenly insightful verse:

> *Some men believe in suffrage*
> *In a peculiar way*
> *They think it just and fair and right—*
> *Or so they always say*
> *And others work and speak for it,*
> *And yet you'll sometimes find*
> *Behind their little suffrage speech*
> *A little axe to grind.*
> *They put their Party interests first,*
> *And suffrage well behind.*
>
> *Of men who care supremely*
> *That justice should be shown,*
> *Who do not balk at sacrifice,*
> *And make the cause their own,*
> *I know, I think, of only one,*
> *That's Dudley Field Malone.*

In an editorial, the *New York Times* acknowledged Malone's "efficient," "excellent" work as port collector, a man whose "intense and ardent temperament has now concentrated itself on woman suffrage, notably on that direct-action emanation of it whose martyrs are sent to the workhouse." It would be unbecoming, the *Times* said, for Malone to continue to hold office under Wilson while supporting "this small Extreme Left, disowned by almost all the other suffragists," women who had made it their mission to annoy his boss. The editorialist scoffed at Malone's stated reason for his resignation—his wish to honor a commitment to the voting women of the West. The western women voters would never have held him to "so chivalrous and romantic an engagement," the *Times* said, because it is not the administration's responsibility to "pass" amendments, and in any event, the "Washington fanatics" had already spoiled the amendment's chances for success. On top of that, the westerners knew that "in the face of the supreme duties and trials which war lays upon the nation, woman suffrage is for the moment a slight and negligible thing."

To replace Malone as collector, President Wilson appointed Byron Newton, who was then assistant secretary of the treasury. Newton raised the ire of Alice Duer Miller with his expression of an un-feminist view. "When women attempt to leave their own realm and do man's work in a man's way," Byron was quoted as saying, "they lose their power in the world, just as men would become ridiculous if they should attempt to invade the realm which nature and civilization have set apart for women."

Miller's retort: "Before again attempting to help in a military census, in selling a Liberty Loan, in working in munitions factories or in replacing men in any work, we hope women will ask expert advice from Mr. Newton as to whether or not they were designed by God, Nature and civilization for such work." Her *coup de grâce*:

> The former Collector of the Port, Dudley Field Malone, resigned his post because the Administration was not taking a sufficiently active stand on woman suffrage. The new Collector is a violent anti-suffragist. If the Administration becomes more aggressive in its suffrage policy, will Mr. Newton show the same sincerity and courage that Mr. Malone showed—and resign?

————◦————

For the New York suffrage movement, the next harbinger was not a good one. It came from Maine. Despite endorsements for a state suffrage amendment from President Wilson, former president Theodore Roosevelt, two former senators, and a former attorney general, Maine's voter referendum failed resoundingly on September 10, by a vote of nearly two to one. The Maine state campaign manager, Deborah Knox Livingston, gave seven reasons for the defeat: not enough time to educate the public; the "natural prejudice" of the people of Maine against anything new; no declared support from either political party; a very light vote; the militants in Washington; the war; and the opposition's control of the "purchasable vote," that is, votes made possible by paying for them in money or in favors or offers of positions. She estimated that the antis had controlled between 15,000 and 20,000 of these votes, significantly tipping the balance.

In Washington, one of Maine's Republican congressmen, Ira G. Hersey, held the picketers wholly responsible for the loss. Before the election, he said, everywhere he traveled across the state, he would ask men whom he knew to be suffrage supporters how they planned to vote. Of those, he estimated that tens of thousands of them would refuse to vote, despite their prosuffrage views, and many others would vote against the measure as a rebuke to the picketers, especially for the "Kaiser Wilson" banners.

The antis, of course, relished their victory, predicting that as Maine went, so would go New York on November 6. Malone seized the moment to emphasize why the result in Maine made passage of the federal amendment so crucial. It had taken the forces for suffrage in Maine twenty years to get the measure on the ballot, he said, and the state's antiquated legislative structure would mean another twenty years before there was even a shot at doing so again. The only way the women of Maine could be enfranchised, he said, would be for the US constitution to allow it.

On September 16, the *New York Tribune* reproduced a map created by the *Woman Citizen*, a publication NAWSA had established with the Leslie bequest. It showed the national suffrage picture in graphic form. In eleven states, women had full voting rights (Washington, Oregon, California, Nevada, Idaho, Utah, Arizona, Montana, Wyoming, Colorado, Kansas). In six, they could vote in presidential elections (Illinois, Indiana, Ohio, Michigan, North Dakota, Nebraska). In one, they had primary election voting privileges (Arkansas). From Maine all the way down the eastern seaboard with a westward swish across the south, was a swath of black nothingness all the way to New Mexico. (Maine, New Hampshire, Vermont, Rhode Island, Massachusetts, New York, Pennsylvania, New Jersey, Maryland, West Virginia, Virginia, Kentucky, North Carolina, Tennessee, North Carolina, South Carolina, Georgia, Florida, Alabama, Mississippi, Louisiana, Texas, Oklahoma, New Mexico.) Five states not highlighted on the map had given women municipal suffrage, the legend explained. Four had given bond suffrage, and seventeen, school suffrage.

The *Boston Globe*, in its analysis of the Maine defeat, pointed out that all the states where women had voting rights were well to the western side of the country, none closer to the East Coast than Ohio, with its presidential-election-only allowance. The eastern front remained "unpierced." The newspaper reminded readers that New York, New Jersey, and Massachusetts (and Pennsylvania, which it neglected to mention) had defeated previous referenda. The Missouri River, the effective suffrage frontier line, the *Globe* said, had become "an astonishingly wide stream."

———◁○▷———

The somber war mood greatly influenced the choreography of a prereferendum parade down Fifth Avenue on October 27. Other than the bands and marching delegations of supporters, plans called for very few echoes of suffrage parades past. "Time was when suffrage organizations vied with one another in devising picturesque headgear for their parades, and the aim was to transform Fifth Avenue into a moving mass of brilliant yellow, or purple or white coloring," the *New York Tribune* observed. "The war has changed all that, as it has the whole tone of the suffrage campaign." This time, "black hats," "no spats" would be the dress code for the marchers, who were to be divided not by profession or organization, but by the kinds of service they were ready to offer the state. Grace Carley Harriman, the wife of the financier Oliver Harriman, accepted the chairmanship of the division for the "Mothers and Wives of Soldiers and Sailors," the *Tribune* reported; Helen Annan Scribner, wife of the book publisher Arthur H. Scribner, organized the "Tax-Paying Women." One group was to escort the weighty million-signature petition that women across the state had signed to signify their desire to vote.

Throughout October, the New York campaign trotted out its most impressive male allies in a series of "Men's Experience Meetings" at all the usual venues: Carnegie Hall, Cooper Union, and Madison Square Garden for the major ones. At Carnegie Hall, the featured speakers were Samuel Untermyer; Governor R. Livingston Beeckman of Rhode Island; the commissioner of corrections, John A. Kingsbury; the chairman of the State Industrial Commission, John Mitchell; Dr. Frederick Peterson of the "Normal Women Are Not Neurotic" pamphlet; and others of like standing. On tap for later meetings and venues were Malone, Wise, Jacob Gould Schurman, and William Jennings Bryan.

The philanthropist Katrina Trask, Peabody's future wife, at last came around to full-hearted support for the cause, just in time to offer a prereferendum endorsement. Her essay for the *Woman Citizen*, published October 13, was one that the publication's editors had urged her to write. She explained that she had never been against the suffrage cause, nor had she refused to sign on because of the militancy, which she abhorred. It was because she differed with NAWSA's belief that political freedom should precede the "spiritual emancipation" of women. Trask had felt the spiritual must come first—until the war.

"Now, however, the whole aspect of life has changed; the whole world, for three-and-a-half years, has been in a mad upheaval," she wrote. "One's theories and one's ideals must wait for fulfillment upon the issue of this tragic crisis. Meanwhile we must adapt ourselves to the crisis and seek all practical helps to meet it." Obtaining the franchise, she argued, "has become a necessity." She went on to elaborate what in essence had become the most persuasive of the wartime prosuffrage arguments:

The vote is a practical equipment. The vote will help women in their work; it is a national asset, valuable in this emergency.

Men are going to the war: they will return, God Help them, disabled and impaired. Women must loyally take the active work, the vital responsibility for the common good; and as suffrage gives to so many of them strength for this task, they ought to have it.

Women have been called upon to share in every possible preparation, in every national endeavor, and they have answered with a quick and eager affirmative.

As the franchise gives them a sense of surety and security, a feeling of cooperation with the Government which they are so quick to serve, it should not be denied them.

—◁◦▷—

As the day of the referendum neared, Whitehouse appealed to Wilson for support once again. Knowing the president could not leave Washington, she asked if he would be willing to receive a delegation from her state suffrage party that would begin its visit with an introduction from her and end with a statement from him on why he believed New York voters should support the state amendment. Wilson agreed and Whitehouse wrote to Tumulty on October 13 with possible dates and her plans for orchestrating the encounter. A delegation of about one hundred women were to travel from New York by special train and of them, about eight or ten would be designated to meet with the president, offering a short introductory speech about the state of the suffrage movement and "the work women are called upon to do in this war." His response would be immediate and reported at once to the rest of the delegation. The meeting date was set for October 25, eleven days before the state amendment ballot.

"Of course we want to arouse the greatest possible public interest in this interview, because we believe it can do more than any one thing to help win our campaign," Whitehouse wrote to Tumulty. She was mindful of the continuing succession of arrests and releases, court dates, protests, jailing—twice, of Alice Paul herself—the solitary confinements, the hunger strikes, and all the publicity the National Woman's Party's actions were still generating, despite efforts by Creel to get the newspapers to play down the events. Since July, Wilson had offered no further pardons.

Wilson wrote to Carrie Chapman Catt the same day, expressing his "very deep interest" in the New York campaign and his hope that "no voter will be influenced in his decision with regard to this great matter by anything the so-called pickets may have done." They may have "laid themselves open to serious criticism," he wrote, but they represented so small a fraction of the women in the country urging adoption of women's suffrage "that it would be most unfair and argue a very narrow view to allow their actions to prejudice the cause itself." He ended, "I am very anxious to see the great State of New York set a great example in this matter." Catt was pleased, writing back that the letter "quite fills the need in the New York State Suffrage campaign." She made the letter public the following day.

Two Men's League leaders, Rabbi Wise and Frederic C. Howe, the commissioner of immigration of the Port of New York, injected the war note into their rallying cries at Cooper Union on October 15. Wise said he was so weary of agitating for something that "should be a commonplace of a democratic government" that he would not blame women if, "in case the men fail them on November 6, they would refuse to participate in the prosecution of this war." His denunciation of recent antisuffrage comments from Elihu Root, the former secretary of state, provoked challenge from the floor.

"Why are you for war, then?" Wise was asked.

"I am not for war," he shouted back. "I am for war against war and Kaiserism, so that we can make peace for the world, and I want the women to vote so they can make the world safe for peace." Howe, who was presiding, had earlier advised the women to stop petitioning for the vote and demand it instead—in case the referendum failed. "Leave the shops and the stores and the factories until you get it," he urged. "You've been patient and lady like long enough."

On October 25, the scheduled White House meeting with the New York suffrage delegation took place. Whitehouse, too, sounded the war note, saying that although prosuffrage sentiment in New York was now "very marked," the multitudinous details of entering the war had overshadowed it. Many men, she said, did not even realize that suffrage for women of the state was up for a vote in two weeks' time.

"The confusion is due to the difficulty we have found in carrying on an active campaign, because," Whitehouse told the president, "while there has never before been so large a number of people on record in the State in favor of any measure as the 1,013,800 women enrolled for Suffrage, these very women, almost without exception, are engrossed in serving their country." She cited such endeavors as selling Liberty Bonds, supporting the Hoover Food Campaign, and volunteering for the Red Cross. Women, she said, "go into the factories and are ready to work in the fields. In fact, Mr. President, they are ready to give—they are now giving—the very support to this country which has led the statesmen of our Allies"—she named Canada, England, Russia, and France, all of which had been at war three years longer than the United States—"to declare that war could not be carried on without such active support on the part of the women." Like Trask, she noted that under current conditions, to give women the vote "has become not only a question of justice, but one of expediency."

Wilson responded with a long, carefully crafted reply. He spoke of the world's slow political reconstruction that "this war is going so to quicken the convictions and the consciousness of mankind with regard to political questions that the speech of reconstruction will be greatly increased. And I believe that, just because we are quickened by the questions of this war, we ought to be quickened to give this question of woman suffrage our immediate consideration."

He said he was giving both his personal and his party endorsement, not only because the country depended on women "for a large part of the inspiration of its life," but also because it depended on their "suggestions of service, which have been rendered in abundance and with the distinction of originality."

The usually dismissive *New York Times* called out from a front-page headline the next day:

## SUFFRAGE TO FORE
### TIME FOR STATES TO ACT ON WHAT
### IS NOW A FUNDAMENTAL QUESTION.

PRAISES WOMEN'S SERVICE
AND WISHES GODSPEED TO NEW
YORK DELEGATION OF WOMEN
ASKING SUPPORT.

For the first time, Wilson altered his oft-repeated insistence that women's suffrage was a matter for the states. "I perhaps may be touched a little too much by the traditions of our politics, traditions which lay such questions almost entirely upon the States," he acknowledged, "but I want to see communities declare themselves quickened at this time and show the consequence of the quickening." To honor the extraordinary war service that American women had been rendering, the remarkable work they had been doing, he urged the voters of New York "to set a great example by voting for woman suffrage."

◄◦►

"Patriotism, not propaganda" was how the *New York Tribune* characterized the suffrage parade of October 27, calling it the sign of a "new era" for the move-

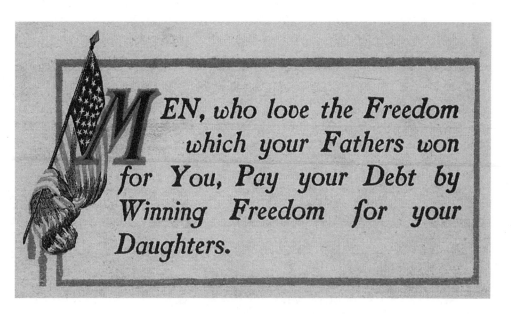

Suffrage campaign illustration. (Miller NAWSA Scrapbooks, 1897–1911, Section 16, No. 9, pp. 82–83, Library of Congress, Rare Book and Special Collections Division)

ment. The American flag came first, the yellow suffrage banner thereafter. The choreography emphasized how giving women the vote would help America.

The *Tribune* noted the roar of the crowd as Anna Howard Shaw and Carrie Chapman Catt first came into view, then "bands, banners and slogans, women and then more women: gray-haired, many of them; 'Vogue' covers, some of them, lame a few of them, colored women, a wee little Japanese and the men." An all-male guard of honor brought up the brigades of women bearing the reams of petitions,

> swinging along, for all the world to see as if they were enjoying marching "with the girls." Perhaps they were. At any rate, they were doing it, and not the least among them were Judge William H. Wadhams, Justice Charles L. Guy, Hamilton Holt, Robert Underwood Johnson, Samuel Untermyer, Commissioner Charles H. Strong, James Lees Laidlaw, and James Byrne.

The band struck up the tune of the giant new hit "Over There," as Harriman's contingent of mothers, sisters, and wives of soldiers and sailors appeared in formation. Their presence moved the crowd like nothing else, creating, in the words of the Manhattan borough president, Marcus M. Marks, "the most impressive showing for suffrage that could have been made."

A woman in the crowd burst forth with her own rendition of the George M. Cohan lyrics. "It's 'Over Here' for the mothers," she yelled out and then began to sing,

> *"The suffs are coming, the suffs are coming, and we won't give up until it's over, over here."*

———◦———

Imagine the emotional intensity of the days before the New York ballot on Tuesday, November 6. In Washington, more than a score of women from Paul's party were threatening to storm the Washington district jail, demanding that their still incarcerated sisters be classified political prisoners, not criminals. After sixty days in jail, a third of which they had spent in solitary confinement, most of the women were released November 3, but not Alice Paul, who remained in the jail's psychiatric wing, despite no evidence of mental imbalance during professional evaluations.

In Chicago, Max Eastman caused a kerfuffle with the words he spoke in support of the White House picketers, whom the Chicago Political Equality League, Eastman's host, had already gone on record to denounce. "Just Can't Keep Out of a Scrap," the *Chicago Tribune* tut-tutted in a headline. "Merely Mentions Those White House Pickets and—Zowie!!"

Du Bois again appealed to "every single black voter" in New York and throughout the United States to support the suffrage amendment, despite the abiding bitterness that black voters might harbor toward white women, and despite the "naïve assumption" among white women "that the height of his ambition is to marry them," their "artificially-inspired fear of every dark face, which leads to frightful accusations and suspicions," and their "sometimes insulting behavior toward him in public places."

At the eleventh hour, newspapers like the *New York Tribune* helped make the case for state suffrage. Women were not seeking the ballot as a reward for the patriotic service they had provided, the newspaper said, but "as a further means of rendering service." War work, in fact, had to a great extent overtaken the suffragists' ability to campaign for the referendum, making the rallying efforts of 1917 so different—and who knew if less or more effective—than those that had failed in 1915. This round, the *Tribune* said, the "fireworks" and "trappings" that had made the previous round such a "brilliant demonstration" were left behind in favor of "canvasses and street meetings and hosts of small meetings before every kind of audience under the sun. There's nothing spectacular about a hearing before a church committee, but the suffragists have had plenty of them, and they unquestionably make votes." New in 1917 was the courting of soldiers, which took campaigners into homes and on personal visits to military camps.

A two-column ad touting the high-level political support for suffrage ran in all the newspapers the day before the election, placed by Whitehouse's New York State Woman Suffrage Committee. It featured Woodrow Wilson, Theodore Roosevelt, Governor Whitman, Mayor Mitchel—prominent figures of all the political parties—and offered sharp expressions of amendment support. In the same ad was listed a twenty-member "Men's Advisory Board," chaired by Vanderlip. It included two names that had been on the Men's League roster since the start: Peabody and Untermyer.

◄○►

The New York State amendment giving women the vote passed in a "sweeping victory," granting suffrage to every eligible woman citizen in New York over the age of twenty-one as of January 1, 1918. The *New York Sun* put the winning majority at more than ninety thousand votes. New York became the fourteenth state in the union to endorse women's suffrage and a pivotal one for dispelling the East Coast hex.

To the New York State Woman Suffrage Party and its many section leaders, the *New York Tribune* accorded the greatest credit. Among those acknowledged were two of the Men's League's most loyal members: Laidlaw, who had "worked side by side with his wife during the long struggle," and Vanderlip, who headed the Men's Advisory Committee and had "stood beside Mrs. Vanderlip since the beginning in her fight for the vote."

Although a similar suffrage referendum in Ohio failed that day, the strength of the New York victory especially, along with wins in North Dakota, Indiana, Michigan, Nebraska, and Rhode Island, had local leaders predicting—accurately, as it turned out—that the results would influence Congress in favor of hastening acceptance of the federal measure.

Even the hostile *New York Times* flashed news of the victory from its "signal lights," although its editorial board could not have been more grudging or ungenerous in its response to the win. It attributed the referendum's success to the low turnout, the limits of the candidates on the ballot for several offices, and "the indifference of the opposition and the enthusiasm of the faithful." The editorial also noted by how great a margin this "startling innovation in the polity of the State" had been rejected in 1915, whereas in 1917, "by a much smaller one, when the world is afire, it seems to have been adopted." The editorial added in conclusion:

> The *Times* will not pretend to rejoice at the result to which it made no effort to contribute. May the experiment, if it is to be made, disappoint the fears and predictions of its adversaries. May the women justify by their behavior their fitness for the ballot. And, all division removed, may the feminists give henceforth the full measure of their strength and energy to the cause of freedom and democracy!

And so the feminists did, with the full measure of their strength and energy. For a rally at Cooper Union the next day, on the platform sat the women to whom so much was owed, among them Shaw, Catt, and Whitehouse. Also on stage were Laidlaw, representing the Men's League and clearly held in equivalent esteem, and the featured speaker, Judge Wadhams, another movement supporter.

It was possibly the largest crowd ever to pour into that ever-crowded venue by 1917, a gathering that set a new high for enthusiasm and elation, the *New*

New York State Suffrage Party campaign ad in all the newspapers. (*New York Sun,* November 5, 1917, p. 2, Chronicling America, Library of Congress)

*York Times* said, in a place "where emotion is not usually mute or unexpressed." Unanimously, clamorously, and in short order, those assembled adopted three resolutions: first, to renew the appeal to Congress to submit the federal suffrage amendment to the states; second, to thank President Wilson for his help in the New York campaign, and to "urge him to extend further aid to our cause," specifically by including a statement in favor of the amendment in his annual message to Congress; and third, to thank the press for "its valuable service."

And what of the legions of volunteers, the workers? Ida Harper's history of the movement concedes that it would have been impossible to record accurately the names of the thousands upon thousands of women who had served the movement during its New York campaigns, "and it would be equally impossible to mention the names of the men who helped. Behind many a woman who worked there was a man aiding and sustaining her with money and personal sacrifice." The New York campaign, the history adds, had made the moniker "suffrage husbands" a "title of distinction."

At Cooper Union, Gertrude Brown, of the state party, sparked "a burst of cheers" as she introduced Laidlaw as "the head of those men who have given their lives, their efforts and their fortunes to this cause." His response perfectly summarized a decade of concerted male engagement expressly on behalf of women, organized action that has proved to be an historical phenomenon, one without precedent or anywhere near as effective a contemporary parallel. "Mrs. Brown is right," Laidlaw told the crowd. "The women did it. But not by any heroic action, but by hard, steady grinding and good organization."

"We men, too, have learned something," he said, "we who were auxiliaries to the great woman's suffrage party.

"We have learned to be auxiliaries."

A Coda

# "The Least Tribute We Can Pay Them"

## 1918–1920

The afternoon of November 8, 1917, Dudley Malone addressed five hundred women at a celebration organized by Alva Belmont in the ballroom of the Ritz Carlton Hotel in New York. At the mention of President Wilson's name, one woman emitted a hiss that Malone quickly moved to quash. "Ladies," he said, "I hope no one ever can or ever will hiss the head of the nation. We can only educate him." He blamed bad advice and the unavoidable isolation of the presidency for Wilson's lack of action on the federal suffrage amendment. He also said that the "very substantial victory we have won in New York is not due to the belated efforts of the gentlemen of the Cabinet, but to the men and women in New York who love liberty." Applause greeted Malone's special acknowledgment of Anna Shaw, Carrie Chapman Catt, and Vira Whitehouse for their efforts in bringing success to the New York referendum. Then, he added: "But it cannot be denied that the women who dared by their picketing to dramatize the injustice done American women did much to aid in winning the victory."

Picketing was a legal tactic, he said, although he also conceded that it was fair to question the use of it as a matter of taste. The time for division in the movement over such differences was over, however; they needed to be cast aside. "Men never succeed unless they stand together," he said, "and women will do no better. You are going to have victory, but don't sweetly ask for anything. Demand it." The yield in contributions that day was a healthy $5,000.

The same day, the newspapers announced that Mary Ritter Beard, wife of the Men's League activist Charles Beard, had organized a new group called the Committee of One Thousand. Its first plan was to take the train to Washington to appeal directly to Wilson for the immediate release of the thirty-one arrested picketers, including Alice Paul, who had been imprisoned in the Washington district jail since October 20 and on a hunger strike since October 30. Creel advised the president to decline to see them, and Wilson took his advice. Yet on that day, the president did meet with Catt and a delegation from NAWSA.

Malone, in his address at the Ritz, also added his protest to an outcry from across the country over the force-feeding of Paul, which had begun in the seventy-third hour of her refusal to eat. Malone traveled to the capital after the New York event and managed to obtain Paul's transfer out of the jail's psychopathic ward and into its hospital. As her counsel, he argued that it was illegal to detain her in the psychiatric unit when she had not been declared insane. On November 9, Tumulty advised the president that it would soon be time to consider seriously what to do about Paul and her fellow protesters.

At some point in "the latter part of Miss Paul's imprisonment," according to Doris Stevens's memoir, the journalist David Lawrence paid a late-night jailhouse visit to Paul and her fellow picket inmates. Lawrence was the longtime newspaper chronicler of Wilson's career, known for his close ties to the administration and "equally known," Stevens wrote, for his habit of ascertaining the position on important questions of leaders of various constituencies and "keeping intimately in touch with opinion in White House circles at the same time."

Lawrence's report of the visit appeared on the front page of Villard's *New York Evening Post* on November 27. "Anybody who imagines that the women in jail are just 'silly women' with no idea of what they are driving at, is very much mistaken," he wrote. "They have a very definite idea and a very definite plan. I frankly told them I didn't agree with them, that I believed it was all absolutely unnecessary, and that woman suffrage would succeed in this country, not because of their efforts, but in spite of them." He also reviewed their conditions in jail and the apparent state of their health.

In her memoir, Stevens puts a different cast on the story, recounting what she had learned from her imprisoned colleagues about that late-night interview. Lawrence, she said, insisted that he had come of his own volition and not as a White House emissary, and that among the things he and Paul discussed was her insistence that the women be treated as political prisoners. Lawrence responded that the administration could easily have rented a comfortable house for their detention, but to do so would have opened the White House to having to extend the same privilege to every prisoner confined for political opinions, and that was out of the question. Stevens took this to mean that the demand of the jailed picketers to be treated as political prisoners had actually encouraged the administration to choose to take at least some action on behalf of the federal amendment as "the lesser of two evils."

Stevens said Lawrence then offered a suggestion, one that did not appear in his published report of the jailhouse visit: Would Paul agree to stop the picketing if the administration could get the amendment passed through one house of Congress in the coming session, then have it sent to the nation in the 1918 elections on that record and, if the measure was upheld, pass through the other house the following year? Paul responded by repeating, as adamantly as ever, that only passage of the amendment through the full Congress would end the agitation.

"Since Mr. Lawrence disavows any connection with the Administration in this interview," Stevens surmised, "I can only remark that events followed exactly in the order he outlined; that is, the Administration attempted to satisfy the women by putting the amendment through the House and not through the Senate."

At the very least, Lawrence indeed proved prescient about the course of events. On November 27, the same day his article appeared in the *Post*, Judge Mullowny summarily ordered the release of a visibly weakened Paul in the twenty-third day of her hunger strike and the fifth week of her seven-month sentence. Twenty-one of her hunger-striking colleagues were freed with her; the other nine picketers, who were not hunger striking, remained behind bars.

As Paul left the jail, reporters asked her if the picketing would resume. The response the newspapers carried contained more portent than it likely appeared to have at the time, given the unreported exchanges with Lawrence. "We hope that no more demonstrations will be necessary," Paul told reporters, "that the amendment will run steadily on to passage and ratification, without further suffering. But what we do depends on what the Administration does. We have one aim: The immediate passage of the Federal amendment. As for picketing, we are well pleased at what it has accomplished."

———◦———

Wilson did not heed the request the New York suffragists had made of him in their moment of triumph on the day after the state referendum. His State of the Union address on December 4 did not include a push for Congress to pass the federal amendment for women's suffrage. Suffrage, in fact, did not even rate a mention.

There were other affirming developments, however. On December 29, Creel, who had worked closely with Vira Whitehouse in the "great success in the New York suffrage campaign," appointed her to a special position, based in Switzerland, to promote the American position in the war through speeches, the distribution of literature, and other "informative activities." In 1920, she published a book about those experiences, *A Year as a Government Agent.* Everyone, she said without being more specific, presumed she was a spy. The very name of Creel's agency, the Committee on Public Information, certainly had that scent. But she always maintained that was not her role.

On January 9, 1918, Wilson met with the Democratic members of the House suffrage committee, after which the *New York Times* reported:

## WILSON BACKS AMENDMENT FOR WOMAN SUFFRAGE

The Democrats had crafted a carefully worded statement. It read: "The committee found that the President had not felt at liberty to volunteer his advice to members of Congress in this important matter, but when we sought his advice he very frankly and earnestly advised us to vote for the amendment as an act of right and justice to the women of the country and of the world."

The next evening, after five hours of debate, the House adopted the amendment by the exact two-thirds majority required for it to pass, 274 to 136. The Senate defeated the measure by two votes in the first attempt. The rest of the year swept by.

Wilson's next State of the Union address came on December 2, 1918, three weeks after the Allies signed the armistice with Germany that ended the fighting on the Western Front. This time the president's message included a suffrage passage:

> And what shall we say of the women—of their instant intelligence, quickening every task that they touched; their capacity for organization and cooperation, which gave their action discipline and enhanced the effectiveness of everything they attempted; their aptitude at tasks to which they had never before set their hands; their utter self-sacrifice alike in what they did and in what they gave? Their contribution to the great result is beyond appraisal. They have added a new lustre to the annals of American womanhood.

The least tribute we can pay them is to make them the equals of men in political rights as they have proved themselves their equals in every field of practical work they have entered, whether for themselves or for their country. These great days of completed achievement would be sadly marred were we to omit that act of justice. Besides the immense practical services they have rendered the women of the country have been the moving spirits in the systematic economies by which our people have voluntarily assisted to supply the suffering peoples of the world and the armies upon every front with food and everything else that we had that might serve the common cause. The details of such a story can never be fully written, but we carry them at our hearts and thank God that we can say that we are the kinsmen of such.

It took another six months, but by June 4, 1919, both houses of Congress voted to pass the Susan B. Anthony amendment. The process of state-by-state ratification progressed, culminating fourteen months later in the needed three-quarters majority, that is, ratification in thirty-six of the forty-eight states. On August 18, 1920, after seventy-two years and one month of unrelenting effort since Seneca Falls, and forty years since the women's suffrage amendment was first introduced in Congress, the women citizens of the United States had the vote.

—◦►—

Scholars remain divided over which factors had the greatest impact on bringing about this long-awaited outcome. As the historian Barbara Steinson points out, Paul's forces attributed victory to their dogged persistence, to the way they exposed to ridicule the administration's hypocrisy as it fought for democracy abroad while denying it to such a huge sector of the population at home. NAWSA leaders were certain that their own strategic trifecta had provided a pivotal element: the effects generated by the wartime heroism of American women, NAWSA's persistent lobbying efforts on Capitol Hill, and the great momentum from the "critical New York triumph."

As for the importance of Wilson's influence, there is disagreement, along a scale, from scholars who find it negligible to those who say it absolutely mattered. There is consensus, however, that both NAWSA's forces and Paul's believed that the president's potential to sway the votes of congressmen and senators was indispensable. Both organizations invested concerted effort in trying to win his favor. The record clearly documents the same.

Yet Steinson also notes how much the general climate toward suffrage had changed during the period leading up to the last congressional votes, and how, in the same period, the number of states with women on their voting rolls had also grown. She cites the work of Anne F. Scott and Andrew Scott, whose 1975 study of House and Senate voting patterns concludes that the greatest influence over the prosuffrage decisions of congressmen came not from the president's one-sentence notes or nudges of encouragement or gentle pressure, nor from his public statements in support of the measure, but from the will of the respective constituencies of these congressmen. This was especially true where voters had already granted the ballot to women through state constitutional amendments. More than ninety percent of representatives and senators from suffrage states supported the federal amendment, the researchers concluded, while slightly over fifty percent of those from nonsuffrage states supported the measure.

In the closing months of 1917, the late-breaking addition of increasing support from the largest delegation in the House of Representatives—that of New York, with its forty-three seats—provided unmistakable help in tipping the congressional balance. Oklahoma (eight seats), Michigan (thirteen seats), and South Dakota (three seats) all supplied a boost as their state amendments passed in 1918. Those figures underscore the wisdom of NAWSA, the Scotts and Steinson point out, in insisting that the state-by-state initiatives needed to continue in tandem with the federal suffrage campaign. At the same time, the support for the federal amendment from legislators from nonsuffrage states also increased steadily, indicating the general change in attitude toward the federal measure.

———◦———

To the *New York Times* on June 15, 1919, Carrie Chapman Catt explained why the fight for women's suffrage had taken more than half a century of "concerted, never-ceasing effort." She spoke of the struggle it had been to counter—if not eradicate, for they persist as impediments to full equality even today—some deeply entrenched attitudes about the nature and role of women. In the beginning, she said, the entire world, including women, "believed confidently that women were mentally, physically, morally, spiritually, inferior to men, with minds incapable of education, capacities too rudimentary to permit of their even looking after their own property, bodies too feeble to perform the simplest tasks for which men earned wages." Second, there was the "cave man" view of women as property, which men clung to for the sake of domination. "In the refined, educated man this primitive instinct developed into a chivalrous, high-minded spirit of protection," Catt wrote. To even suggest that women could look after themselves or their own property "served as a reflection upon man's honesty or ability to do it for her. To propose that women should speak in public implied that they had ideas which could not be expressed by their natural protectors."

Third, she said, was "pure politics," the "most prolific source of the delay." Both state and federal constitutions require that lawmakers submit an amendment aimed at enfranchising a given class to the electors "before the class to be enfranchised has received its vote." And last was the hurdle created by "an iniquitous system" loaded with individuals, corporations, and groups who "have found it to be a certain protection to their selfish interests, when threatened by legislation, to be on good terms with the parties in power and with leading men of Legislatures and Congress." All of those interests, she said, had been the movement's persistent nemesis.

She also explained why no one group, not even NAWSA, could claim sole credit for the suffragists' long-fought triumph. "Some pronounce it evolution," she said. "True, it is evolution.

> But behind the evolution there have been evolutors—hundreds, thousands of them, who, in order to push the demand for woman suffrage forward, gave every possibility of their lives to the cause. All that they had and all that they were went to the service of woman's emancipation. Although women were the chief workers, there have been men who, like the women, lived in strictest economy so that there should be more to give to the woman's cause. A long array of such noble souls rises in memory as one looks backward over the years; women who had the vision of the righteousness of the quality of rights between the sexes; men who dared to espouse a despised cause.

A full century later, scholars may still debate which group or organization among the myriad suffrage entities deserved the greatest credit for the movement's ultimate success. But no one challenges that the victory belongs to the women who fought for it from all directions for a very long time. The efforts of the men Catt so graciously acknowledged, the "men who dared to espouse a despised cause," have been all but forgotten, remanded to the historical bin. The men sought no recognition or credit for themselves, which is evident from their discreet behavior in the aftermath of victory. This also accounts in part for why the record of the good energy and actions they brought to the battlefield has been mostly lost, except when summoned for posterity by an appreciative wife.

A case in point is a tribute from Maud Nathan, who recalled in her 1933 memoir how her husband, Frederick, not only gave her every encouragement but "tangible evidence of his support on all occasions." She wrote of his willingness to march in the 1911 parade, his leadership in creating the international men's league, and, movingly, of so much more:

> In all the work that I did for the cause, my husband was at my side, aiding and abetting me. When we took a motor trip through New York State, in order to attend the annual convention for the State Suffrage League, which was held that year at Cornell University, Ithaca, my husband always helped to secure a crowd of listeners whenever I stopped to make a speech. He helped to distribute literature and whenever he was in the midst of a throng he led the applause and cheering. At the time that the suffrage amendment was voted upon in New York, my husband was an invalid, but he insisted upon being wheeled in his chair to the polls so that he could have the gratification of voting in favor of it.
>
> This has peculiar significance for me. It was the last vote he ever cast.

———◄○►———

I set out to write this book with the belief that the Men's League for Woman Suffrage deserved to have the record of its efforts gathered, documented, and preserved for the sake of the larger story—to have its role opened to evaluation within the wider context of one of the greatest social movements of the nineteenth and early twentieth centuries. The Men's League's active period was relatively brief, not quite a decade in a seventy-two-year struggle. Given the difficulty women have faced in efforts to uncover and promote understanding of their own fine history and achievements, it follows that the contributions and comportment of these men—no matter how superb—have been allowed to slip through history's grasp. Women's suffrage is a women's story, after all.

This is not to say that the women leading the suffrage movement were unappreciative of what these important figures of society did for the movement alongside their other progressive interests and their perches at companies, churches and synagogues, newspapers and magazines, at universities, and in government, political parties, the bar, the judiciary, and the military. This text includes all the known expressions of gratitude from various women leaders over the years, along with those recorded in memoirs and the press, and the acknowledgments in Harper's history of the women's suffrage movement. Yet almost no detail enlivens these mentions.

It is the specifics of this particular "cooperating organization" of men in the movement, as R.C. Beadle described it, that my research sought to provide. In the process of studying the efforts its members made on behalf of women, however, it became clear to me that something more emerged alongside of it, a significant although apparently unconscious aspect of their contribution, especially given the much more rigidly defined role expectations of the women and men of a century ago. As the New American Woman emerged and began to gain acceptance, the Men's League, with its modern beat on chivalry, displayed a worthy model of a New American Man, however unheralded in its day. This is evident not only in the League members' actions, but in the apparently unquestioning willingness of such men to surrender their alpha position in life's social queue and to agree, as they had done in the New York suffrage parade of 1913, to subordinate themselves publicly to the leadership of women. They brought up the rear. They did not merely lend their names, or sign an appeal, or do what was most convenient for busy men of affairs. They did not demand or choose the tasks that would have provided personal recognition or useful social or professional opportunities. They responded concretely to what the movement needed from them, even the goofy stuff. Indeed, of all the exceptional direct and indirect acts of commitment these men performed, to me, the League's finest achievement emerges from how its members used their ready trappings of privilege, influence, money, or power to serve a "despised" woman's cause. It comes through in the way they stayed in the background as the movement's handmaidens, its "auxiliaries," to borrow Laidlaw's perfect choice of word. Never, in prior or subsequent memory, has such an august group of men coalesced in quite the same way to advance any other women's cause. Think of the current campaigns for pay equity or the protection of reproductive rights or the fights against sexual trafficking and assault. More broadly, for people in positions of power or privilege who seek to further the work of a social cause that is not directly their own, the League provides a worthy prototype.

It is not clear if the men themselves recognized the novelty and stimulating power of their creation or if they deliberately chose to leave their work undersung. They seem to have been more than willing to allow their fine experiment to mist away. This especially stands out by way of omission in so many of the memoirs and autobiographies of various League members. These books sometimes mention the writer's interest in suffrage in a general way, but rarely do they refer to the Men's League by name. For the New Yorkers, if there is reference at all, it is to the way the writer amiably endured the humiliation of the 1911 parade. There is very little about the workings of the organization itself. Wise and Villard are among those who pointed out the 1911 march without reference to their own considerable public and private suffrage advocacy. Villard's most potent memory, he said, was a parade banner the men had to hand back that day because it read, "Men have the votes. Why not we?" He never mentions the Men's League's existence, let alone his rightful claim to having been its conceptualizer and midwife.

The self-published memoir of the Californian John Hyde Braly does include an entire chapter titled "My Part in the Battle for Woman's Suffrage," but of the men's autobiographies that had commercial circulation, only two contain reflective passages about suffrage. Eastman's appropriates his own magazine story of the League's founding from 1912 and offers his meditations on being a suffrage orator, supporter, and a feminist mama's boy; and George Middleton's expounds on the influence that the emergence of the modern woman had on his work as a playwright. Creel, who was among the movement's fiercest male gladiators, glosses over his suffrage work for the League between 1914 and 1917, before his wartime appointment to the Wilson administration. His memoir mentions his suffrage speeches and articles but offers little more. None of the books by New Yorkers describes how unprecedented it was for an all-male League to have an all-prowomen mission (Braly's California group comprised men and women) or how its members sparked and cultivated a nationwide movement of thousands more men of every social class who were willing to crusade for women with little or no thought to the embarrassment it initially caused them.

Nor do the men reflect on the phenomenon the Men's League for Woman Suffrage was—and remains—in the annals of male-female relations in the fight

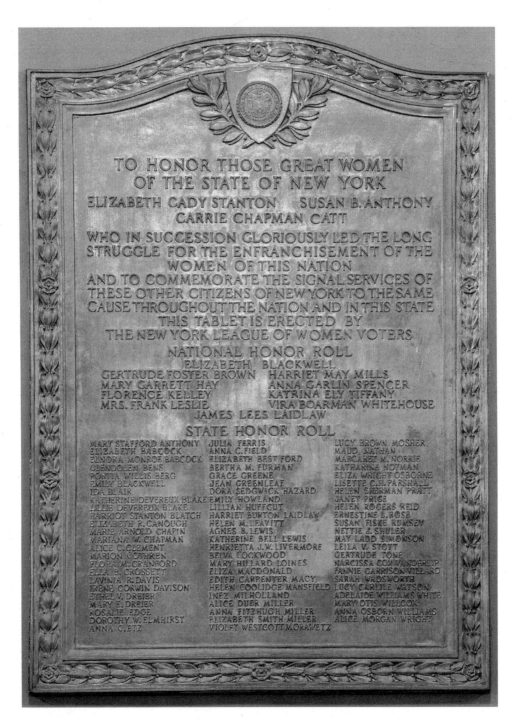

Bronze tablet erected by the Tenth Suffrage Anniversary Committee of the New York League of Women Voters in the New York State Capitol, Albany, November 22, 1931. (Courtesy of the New York State Capitol)

for a social cause perceived to be a women's cause. Perhaps they had no sense of the remarkable work they had done. Perhaps it all seemed too small, too brief, or tertiary in importance among the myriad other achievements and engagements of their large lives.

Was their participation as "suffragents" lost in recall because of the fullness of the subsequent twenty, thirty, forty, or fifty years in most of their lives? Or was the downplaying deliberate, a postchivalrous response to obscure their role in the great women's epic, as good allies should; that certainly has been the effect. It would be consistent with the League's performance throughout the period of its existence that the men preferred to stay in the historical shadows.

Of the scores of prominent league members from New York who populate the pages of this book and its endnotes, only Laidlaw's obituary in the *New York Times* mentions the Men's League by name and his major role in its leadership and administration. Neither Villard's nor Eastman's makes any note of the League or of either man's noteworthy support for the suffrage cause. Dudley Field Malone's obituary quotes him as saying that he was proudest of two things in his life: how much he looked like Winston Churchill and his appointment as Wilson's Third Assistant Secretary of State the same day Franklin D. Roosevelt became secretary of the Navy and Joseph E. Davies became Commissioner of Corporations. Two phrases in the article mention suffrage, one to cite the reason he resigned as port collector, and the other to note his marriage and divorce from Doris Stevens. The obituary makes much more of Malone's subsequent Hollywood law practice than of his valiance in Washington on behalf of the women's cause.

The single known official remnant of the men's contribution to the struggle in New York hangs in the lobby on the State Street side of the Capitol building in Albany. It appears on a bronze memorial plaque created to honor the state's great suffragists, first unveiled in Washington in 1931. One man's name appears among those of eighty women named on the tablet's "National Honor Roll" of "those great women of the State of New York": James Lees Laidlaw. The New York League for Women Voters, which evolved from NAWSA, requested his inclusion. Harriet Laidlaw, perhaps not coincidentally, was the group's chair at the time.

It seems fitting in this centennial period to provide the men of the Men's League of Woman Suffrage with at least this modest platform, not only to augment the historical record but to salute them.

Men's League Suffrage Parade delegation marches into Union Square, 1915 Suffrage Parade, New York City. (C. Catt Collection, Bryn Mawr College Library)

# Suffragent Portraits List and Credits

Grateful acknowledgment to the following institutions and repositories for providing the yearbook-style portraits that appear at the start of each chapter. Most are in the public domain and permission has been earnestly sought or obtained for all others. Portraits are listed in order of appearance, left to right.

CHAPTER 1, PAGE 10:

William Lloyd Garrison (Library of Congress, Prints and Photographs Division)

Israel Zangwill (Library of Congress, Prints and Photographs Division)

W.E.B. Du Bois (From the visual materials of the National Association for the Advancement of Colored People records, Library of Congress)

Stephen S. Wise (Photo by Pirie MacDonald, Pirie MacDonald Collection New-York Historical Society)

H.G. Wells (Photo by Alvin Langdon Coburn, Library of Congress, Prints and Photographs Division)

Thomas Hardy (Photo by Herbert Rose Barraud, Wikimedia Commons)

Bertrand Russell (Google Images)

John S. Crosby (From his undated address, "The Mission of Henry George," courtesy of the Science, Industry and Business Library, New York Public Library)

Oswald Garrison Villard (Library of Congress, Prints and Photographs Division)

John Dewey (Photo by Underwood and Underwood, Library of Congress, Prints and Photographs Division)

George Harvey (Library of Congress, Prints and Photographs Division)

Charles Sprague Smith (From *The World's Work: A History of Our Time*, Vol. XX [Garden City, NY: Doubleday, Page and Company, 1910], p. 12860, Wikimedia Commons)

Charles F. Aked (California Suffrage Centennial Celebration, courtesy of University of California Berkeley)

Frederick Douglass (Library of Congress, Prints and Photographs Division)

William M. Ivins (L. Alman & Company, postcard by the Rotograph Company)

Melville Stone (Photo by W.J. Root, Wikimedia Commons)

CHAPTER 2, PAGE 22:

Max Eastman (George Grantham Bain Collection, Library of Congress, Prints and Photographs Division)

Stewart Woodford (George Grantham Bain Collection, Library of Congress, Prints and Photographs Division)

J. Howard Melish (Brooklyn Historical Society)

Samuel J. Barrows (New York Public Library Digital Collections)

David J. Brewer (Miller NAWSA Suffrage Scrapbooks, 1897–1911; Scrapbook 8, p. 130, Library of Congress, Rare Book and Special Collections Division)

William Dean Howells (Library of Congress, Prints and Photographs Division)

Rollo Ogden (Courtesy of the *New York Times*)

Finley Peter Dunne (Photo by Thorn, Library of Congress, Prints and Photographs Division)

John Wesley Hill (Courtesy of Carnegie-Vincent Library of Lincoln Memorial University)

George Foster Peabody (Photo by Pach Brothers, Yaddo Records 1870–1980, Humanities and Social Sciences Library, Manuscripts and Archives Division, New York Public Library)

Charles Beard (George Grantham Bain Collection, Library of Congress, Prints and Photographs Division)

John B. Stanchfield (Courtesy of Booth Library, Chemung County Historical Society)

Barton Aylesworth (University Historic Photograph Collection, Colorado State University, Archives and Special Collections)

Nathaniel Schmidt (Miller NAWSA Suffrage Scrapbooks, Scrapbook 9, p. 82, Library of Congress, Rare Book and Special Collections Division)

Charles C. Burlingham (Harris and Ewing Collection, 1912, P.A.S. Titanic, Library of Congress, Prints and Photographs Division)

Arthur Levy (Leeds) (From *History of the Class of 1907*, published by the Columbia College class and courtesy of Columbia University, Biography Number 52)

Julius Mayer (Library of Congress, Prints and Photographs Division)

CHAPTER 3, PAGE 42:

Edwin Markham (Library of Congress, Prints and Photographs Division)

John Punnett Peters (Courtesy of St. Michael's Church, New York City)

Ben B. Lindsey (Library of Congress Prints and Photographs Division, ca. 1912)

William Gordon VerPlanck (From the Miller family camp, Fossenvue, courtesy of the Geneva Historical Society)

Robert Owen (Harris and Ewing Collection, Library of Congress, Prints and Photographs Division)

Clarence Mackay (George Grantham Bain Collection, Library of Congress, Prints and Photographs Division)

Raymond Robins (George Grantham Bain Collection, Library of Congress, Prints and Photographs Division)

Samuel Untermyer (George Grantham Bain Collection, Library of Congress, Prints and Photographs Division)

Hamilton Holt (George Grantham Bain Collection, Library of Congress, Prints and Photographs Division)

Robert H. Elder (George Grantham Bain Collection, Library of Congress, Prints and Photographs Division)

John Hyde Braly (From the frontispiece of Braly's self-published autobiography, *Memory Pictures: An Autobiography* [Los Angeles: The Neuner Company, 1912], digitized by Google)

Charles L. Guy (*New York State Red Book*, compiled by Edgar L. Murlin [Albany, NY: James B. Lyon, 1897], pp. 149f and 404, courtesy of the New York State Education Department, Manuscript Collections, NYSED PRI 3837 plus Senate, 1896–1997, Folder 9)

William E. Borah (Harris and Ewing Collection, Library of Congress, Prints and Photographs Division)

John E. Milholland (Courtesy of the Ticonderoga Historical Society)

Herbert Parsons (George Grantham Bain Collection, Library of Congress, Prints and Photographs Division)

Jesse Lynch Williams (In a photograph by Byron of New York, from Table L of a dinner to honor Mark Twain on his seventieth birthday at Delmonico's on December 5, 1905; Museum of the City of New York, Harper and Bros., 1905)

CHAPTER 4, PAGE 68:

Robert Cameron Beadle (George Grantham Bain Collection, Library of Congress, Prints and Photographs Division, Flickr Commons Project, 2009)

James Lees Laidlaw (Courtesy of Schlesinger Library, Radcliffe Institute, Harvard University, from the memorial book, *James Lees Laidlaw* [Privately printed, 1932])

Simon Flexner (George Grantham Bain Collection, Library of Congress, Prints and Photographs Division)

Frederick Nathan (From Maud Nathan's memoir, *Once Upon a Time and Today* [New York: G.P. Putnam's Sons, 1933], p. 53)

George Creel (Library of Congress, Prints and Photographs Division)

Harvey Washington Wiley (Library of Congress, Prints and Photographs Division)

James Brady (George Grantham Bain Collection, Library of Congress, Prints and Photographs Division, Flickr Commons Project)

Peter J. Brady (George Grantham Bain Collection, Library of Congress, Prints and Photographs Division)

George Middleton (Photo by Arnold Genthe, Arnold Genthe Collection, Library of Congress, Prints and Photographs Division)

Witter Bynner (Photo by Carl Van Vechten, courtesy of the Carl Van Vechten Trust, Museum of the City of New York)

Vladimir Simkhovitch (University Archives, Rare Book and Manuscript Library, Columbia University in the City of New York)

Harold Spielberg (From Members of the Assembly, 1910, in the *New York Red Book of 1910* [Albany, NY: William Press], courtesy of the Irma and Paul Milstein Division of United States History, Local History and Genealogy, New York Public Library)

Richard Le Gallienne (Library of Congress, Prints and Photographs Division)

Upton Sinclair (George Grantham Bain Collection, Library of Congress, Prints and Photographs Division)

Arthur Brisbane (Library of Congress, Prints and Photographs Division)

Norman Hapgood (George Grantham Bain Collection, Library of Congress, Prints and Photographs Division)


CHAPTER 5, PAGE 84:


Dudley Field Malone (Library of Congress, Prints and Photographs Division)

Edwin Mead (Photo by George Hastings, Boston, Harvard Square Library)

Lincoln Steffens (Photo by Pirie MacDonald, Library of Congress, Prints and Photographs Division)

Louis D. Brandeis (George Grantham Bain Collection, Library of Congress, Prints and Photographs Division)

Frederick S. Greene (from Harry Worcester Smith, *A Sporting Family of the Old South* [Albany, NY: J.B. Lyon Co., 1936], p. 56)

Winter Russell (Class of 1906, Pusey Library, Harvard University Archives)

Frederic C. Howe (Frontispiece photo by William M. Vanderweyde, from Howe's memoir, *The Confessions of a Reformer* [New York: Charles Scribner's Sons, 1925])

Joel Elias Spingarn (From the visual materials of the National Association for the Advancement of Colored People records, Library of Congress)

Gardner Hale (From the visual materials of the George Middleton Papers, Library of Congress, Prints and Photographs Division)

A.S.G. Taylor (Underwood and Underwood, from the collection of the Norfolk Historical Society)

Swinburne Hale (Class of 1905, Pusey Library, Harvard University Archives)

Algernon Crapsey (Courtesy of the Department of Rare Books, Special Collections and Preservation, University of Rochester River Campus Libraries)

Will Irwin (Library of Congress, Prints and Photographs Division)

Joseph Fels (George Grantham Bain Collection, Library of Congress, Prints and Photographs Division)

William Sulzer (Library of Congress, Prints and Photographs Division)

Theodore Roosevelt (Photo by Pach Brothers, 1913, Library of Congress, Prints and Photographs Division)

Charles Edward Russell (From the visual materials of the National Association for the Advancement of Colored People records, Library of Congress)

Charles S. Thomas (Underwood and Underwood, Library of Congress Prints and Photographs Division)

William A. De Ford (From the *Ottawa Daily Republic*, August 26, 1912, p. 1)

Gilson Gardner (From *Everybody's Magazine*, October 1920, Vol. XLIII, No. 4, p. 71)

Ward Melville (Courtesy of the Ward Melville Heritage Organization, Stony Brook, Long Island, New York)

William F. "Buffalo Bill" Cody (Library of Congress, Prints and Photographs Division)

James Tanner (Courtesy of James Marten, from his book, *America's Corporal: James Tanner in War and Peace* [Athens, GA: University of Georgia Press, 2014]. Tanner's official portrait as national commander-in-chief of the G.A.R. Roll of the Fortieth National Encampment of the Grand Army of the Republic [Philadelphia: Town Printing, 1906])

Herbert Warbasse (Photo by Gardner and Co., from the *Brooklyn Eagle*, August 28, 1912, p. 1)

Donald MacKenzie MacFadyen (Class of 1910: Donald B. Sinclair; 1910; Historical Photograph Collection, Student Photograph Albums, Box 123; Princeton University Archives, Department of Rare Books and Special Collections, Princeton University Library)

George E. Green (Photo by J.B. Lyon, from *The Convention Manual of Procedure, Forms and Rules for the Regulation of Business in the Seventh New York State Constitutional Convention 1915*, p. 301, General Research Division, New York Public Library, Astor, Lenox and Tilden Foundations)

Samuel Merwin (George Grantham Bain Collection, Library of Congress, Prints and Photographs Division)

Martin Glynn (National Photo Co., Library of Congress, Prints and Photographs Division)

W.S. Moore (Courtesy of the Photo Section, Naval History and Heritage Command, US Navy, Washington Navy Yard, DC.)

Gifford Pinchot (George Grantham Bain Collection, Library of Congress, Prints and Photographs Division)

William A. Delacey (Detail from photo of Harris and Ewing Collection, Library of Congress, Prints and Photographs Division)

Selden Allen Day (From *United Service*, Series 3, Vol. 1 [January–June 1902], p. 112, courtesy of the Science, Industry and Business Library, General Collection, New York Public Library)

CHAPTER 7, PAGE 138:

Adolph Lewisohn (Digital Collection of the Museum of the City of New York)

Floyd Dell (Photograph by Marjorie Jones, 1921, Floyd Dell Papers, Box 28, FL. 824, Newberry Library)

Theodore Dreiser (Theodore Dreiser Papers, Kislak Center for Special Collections, Rare Books and Manuscripts, University of Pennsylvania Libraries)

Gilbert E. Roe (George Grantham Bain Collection, Library of Congress, Prints and Photographs Division)

William H. Howell (Photo by Doris Ulmann, Library of Congress, Prints and Photographs Division)

Frederick Peterson (University Archives, Rare Book and Manuscript Library, Columbia University in the City of New York)

Walter Lionel George (Photo by Henry Walter [H. Walter] Burnett, vintage bromide print, 1910–1920, National Portrait Gallery, London)

Franklin P. Mall (Portrait in "A Memorial to Franklin Paine Mall," from the book *Contributions to Embryology*, Vol. IX, No. 27-46 [Washington: Carnegie Institution of Washington, Gibson Brothers Press, 1920], p. 1)

Frederick Davenport (Harris and Ewing Collection, Library of Congress, Prints and Photographs Division)

Edwin Björkman (Photo by Arnold Genthe, Arnold Genthe Collection, Library of Congress, Prints and Photographs Division)

Theodore Douglas Robinson (National Photo Company Collection, Library of Congress, Prints and Photographs Division)

Carl Lincoln Schurz (Photo by Pirie MacDonald, Pirie MacDonald Collection, New-York Historical Society)


CHAPTER 8, PAGE 154:

Calvin Tomkins (from the *Brooklyn Daily Eagle*, November 19, 1911, p. 3)

Anthony Fiala (Photo by Charles J. Dampf, from Fiala's book, *Polar Ice* [New York: Doubleday, 1906], p. 3)

Isaac Marcosson (Clarence K. Streit Papers, Library of Congress, Prints and Photographs Division)

Walter Lippmann (Photo by Pirie MacDonald, Walter Lippmann Papers [MS326], Manuscripts and Archives, Yale University Library)

Charles Burnham (Billy Rose Theater Division Collection Photograph File, New York Public Library Digital Collections)

Charles H. Strong (From *The Lance 1980*, p. 140, courtesy of Nash Library Archives, Gannon University, Erie, PA)

Frank Crowninshield (George Grantham Bain Collection, Library of Congress, Prints and Photographs Division)

Thomas E. Rush (From the book edited by Joshua Lawrence Chamberlain, *New York University: Its History, Influence, Equipment and Characteristics* [Boston, MA: R. Herndon Co., 1903], p. 379)

Irving Burdick (1900 Sheffield Scientific School Class Book [Ybc 900 1], courtesy of Manuscripts and Archives, Yale University Library)

Charles Frederick Adams (Harris and Ewing Collection, Library of Congress, Prints and Photographs Division)

George W. Kirchwey (Underwood and Underwood, purchased via eBay)

Leo M. Klein (From the *New York Sun*, September 26, 1915, p. 63, Chronicling America, Library of Congress)

Ray Stannard Baker (George Grantham Bain Collection, Library of Congress, Prints and Photographs Division)

William Harman Black (George Grantham Bain Collection, Library of Congress, Prints and Photographs Division)

William H. Wadhams (George Grantham Bain Collection, Library of Congress, Prints and Photographs Division)

Irvin S. Cobb (George Grantham Bain Collection, Library of Congress, Prints and Photographs Division)


CHAPTER 9, PAGE 176:

John O'Hara Cosgrave (Photo by Arnold Genthe, Arnold Genthe Collection, Library of Congress, Prints and Photographs Division)

Robert Schuyler (University Archives, Rare Book and Manuscript Library, Columbia University in the City of New York)

Edgar Sisson (Passport photo, from Edgar Sisson's book One Hundred Red Days [New Haven, CT: Yale University Press, 1931], p. 429)

Robert H. Davis (Photo by Ray Lee Jackson for NBC, from the Robert H. Davis Papers [NBC photo credit], Manuscripts and Archives Division, New York Public Library, Astor, Lenox and Tilden Foundations)

Mark Sullivan (Harris and Ewing Collection, Library of Congress, Prints and Photographs Division)

Isador Michaels (From the book *Men of Buffalo: A Collection of Portraits of Men Who Deserve to Rank as Typical Representatives of the Best Citizenship* [Chicago: A.N. Marquis and Co., 1902])

Amos Pinchot (George Grantham Bain Collection, Library of Congress, Prints and Photographs Division)

Woodrow Wilson (National Photo Company Collection, Library of Congress, Prints and Photographs Division)

J.A.H. Hopkins (Harris and Ewing Collection, Library of Congress, Prints and Photographs Division)

David I. Walsh (National Photo Company Collection, Library of Congress, Prints and Photographs Division

E.A. Rumely (Edward A. Rumely Collection, PH088, Box 1, Special Collections and University Archives, University of Oregon Libraries, Eugene, Oregon)

John Spargo (George Grantham Bain Collection, Library of Congress, Prints and Photographs Division)

Virgil Hinshaw (From the *College Patriot: The Organ of the Intercollegiate Prohibition Association*, Vol. 1, No. 4, December 15, 1903, p. 26, digitized by Google)

Edward House (George Grantham Bain Collection, Library of Congress, Prints and Photographs Division)

William Channing Gannett (Courtesy of the Rochester Regional Libraries Council)

George Gordon Battle (Photo by Pach Brothers, 1909)


CHAPTER 10, PAGE 194:


Willard D. Straight (George Grantham Bain Collection, Library of Congress, Prints and Photographs Division)

Charles A. Lindbergh Sr. (Harris and Ewing Collection, Library of Congress, Prints and Photographs Division)

Charles S. Whitman (*New York Times*, Pictures Section, cover, December 27, 1914, via Chronicling America, Library of Congress)

John Purroy Mitchel (George Grantham Bain Collection, Library of Congress, Prints and Photographs Division)

Charles B. Smith (Harris and Ewing Collection, Library of Congress, Prints and Photographs Division)

Frank Vanderlip (Harris and Ewing Collection, Library of Congress, Prints and Photographs Division)

Ogden Mills Reid (Library of Congress, Prints and Photographs Division)

Jacob Gould Schurman (National Photo Company Collection, Library of Congress, Prints and Photographs Division)

Rupert Hughes (George Grantham Bain Collection, Library of Congress, Prints and Photographs Division)

Carl Jonas Nordstrom (Passport photo via Ancestry.com)

George Notman (At Inlet Camp, Ausable Lakes, 1911, Keene Valley, NY, P-1062 [002], Keene Valley Library, New York)

James W. Gerard (Harris and Ewing Collection, Library of Congress, Prints and Photographs Division)

Robert Underwood Johnson (Engraving by Timothy Cole from Pirie MacDonald photograph, Library of Congress, Prints and Photographs Division)

Julius Frank (Courtesy of Susan Schwartz, great-granddaughter of Julius Frank)

John A. Kingsbury (Photo by Pach Brothers, ca. 1920, Library of Congress, Prints and Photographs Division)

James Norman deR. Whitehouse (Encore Images)

# Notes

## AN INTRODUCTION

1    *"from the curb to the building line"*   "3,000 Women in March for Votes; and 89 Men Trail Along to Help the Cause of Equal Suffrage," *NY Sun*, 7 May 1911, p. 1.

1    *"even pilots with steamboats"*   "Three Thousand Women in March for Votes," *NY Sun*, and also, "March for Ballot," *Washington Post*, 7 May 1911, p. 1.

2    *"teaching the theory and practice of government"*   People's Institute Records, New York Public Library, Humanities and Social Science Library, Manuscripts and Archive Division. Accessed 28 April 2016. https://www.nypl.org/sites/default/files/archivalcollections/pdf/peoplesinst.pdf.

3    *In England, John Stuart Mill's*   See Michael S. Kimmel and Thomas E. Mosmiller, *Against the Tide: Pro-Feminist Men in the United States, 1776–1990, A Documentary History* (Boston: Beacon Press, 1992), for which I am especially grateful. Part I covers the period before Seneca Falls in 1848 and includes essays on the rights of women starting with Paine's "An Occasional Letter on the Female Sex" in 1775. Specifically on suffrage, Part IV begins with Frederick Douglass's "The Rights of Women" (*North Star*, 28 July 1848, reprinted in Kimmel and Mosmiller, *Against the Tide*, pp. 211–212), followed by William Lloyd Garrison's "Intelligent Wickedness" (*NY Daily Tribune*, 7 September 1853, and in Kimmel and Mosmiller, *Against the Tide*, pp. 212–214), Theodore Parker's "A Sermon on the Public Function of Women" in 1853, and Ralph Waldo Emerson's "Woman: A Lecture Read before the Woman's Rights Convention" (Boston, 20 September 1855, reprinted in *Emerson's Complete Works*, Riverside ed. [Boston: Houghton Mifflin, 1883–1893] and in Kimmel and Mosmiller, *Against the Tide*, pp. 217–220). From across the Atlantic came John Stuart Mill's "On Liberty: The Subjection of Women," originally published in 1859 (London: Longman, Green, Reader, and Dyer, 1869). (British Library, accessed at http://www.bl.uk/collection-items/the-subjection-of-women-by-j-s-mill, 5 January 2016.) See also Michael S. Kimmel, "From Conscience and Common Sense to 'Feminism for Men': Pro-Feminist Men's Rhetorics of Support for Women's Equality," *International Journal of Sociology and Social Policy*, Vol. 17, No. 1, 2, 1997, pp. 8–34, in which (p. 23) he describes the Men's League as "the nation's first explicitly pro-feminist men's organization."

3    *a Young Men's Woman Suffrage League*    See meeting notices in the *Christian Union*, Vol. X, No. 7, 19 August 1874, p. 121; *Common Sense*, Vol. 1, No. 16, 29 August 1874, p. 183; *NY Times*, 24 September 1847, p. 10, 5 November 1874, p. 8; 19 November 1874, p. 8, 21 April 1875, p. 12; and *Voice of Peace*, Vol. 1, No. 8., November 1874, p. 115. Among the names mentioned as speakers and members were Philip Hecht, John Malony, Waldorf Philips, George Kilmer, S.S. Nash, and J.H.K. Wilcox, who served as the organization's president.

3    *"You won't get any dinner"*    "New York Women in Huge Parade Demand Ballot," *Chicago Tribune*, 7 May 1911, p. 1.

3    *"jeers, whistles"*    George Middleton, *These Things Are Mine: The Autobiography of a Journeyman Playwright* (New York: MacMillan, 1947), p. 125.

3    *In the last decade-long lap*    New York granted the vote in 1917 after these Western and Midwestern states: Wyoming in 1890, Colorado in 1893; Utah in 1896; Washington in 1910; California in 1911; Michigan, Kansas, Oregon, and Arizona in 1912, and Montana and Nevada in 1914.

3    *No known source to date*    See what most reports rely on: Max Eastman, "Early History of the Men's League for Woman Suffrage," *The Woman Voter*, October 1912, p. 17. There is also a second one by Eastman's successor: R.C. Beadle, "The Men's League for Woman Suffrage," *The Trend*, Vol. 6, No. 2, 13 November 1913, pp. 266–275.

5    *We get little more than some of the men's names*    Ida Husted Harper, ed., *The History of the Woman Suffrage Movement*, Vol. VI (New York: NAWSA, 1922), p. 476, in describing legislative action in New York State, said, "The Men's League gave invaluable help." Further references to the New York League appear on pages 475–477, 484–485, and 673–675. On page 484: "From 1910 to 1917, the Men's League for Woman Suffrage was an influential factor in the movement in New York." About the men's delegation in the Suffrage Day Parade of 1911, a passage on page 486 erroneously refers to the march of 1910 but the men first marched in the next year's parade, in 1911. "New York Women in Huge Parade Demand Ballot . . . Crowd Jeers Mere Men Marchers," *Chicago Tribune*, 7 May 1911, p. 1; also, "Big Crowds Cheer Suffragist Parade . . . Men Also in Line of March," *NY Tribune*, 7 May 1911, p. 1; also "Women Parade and Rejoice at End," *NY Times*, 7 May 1911. Coverage in 1910 makes no mention of male marchers, which would have been particularly noteworthy, as it proved the following year. The newspaper estimates of the number of men in the 1911 march vary from 80 to 200. Page 674 very briefly describes how the New York League became the model for other state leagues, characterizing it as an "association of influential men" and saying further of it and the dozens of other state Men's Leagues it spawned: "In every state, the men were of so much prominence as to give much prestige to the movement."

5    *Drawing on biographical sketches*    See, for example, "Dr. John Dewey Dead at 92; Philosopher a Noted Liberal," *NY Times*, 2 June 1952, pp. 1, 21; "Dr. S.S. Wise

Is Dead; Leader in Zionism," *NY Times*, 20 April 1949, pp. 1, 28; "Max Eastman Dies; Author, Radical and Expert on Bolshevism, Dies," *NY Times*, 26 March 1969, pp. 1, 47; Villard did not make the *Times* front page but equally did not mention his founding efforts for the League: "Oswald G. Villard Dies at Age of 77," *NY Times*, 2 October 1949, p. 80.

5    *these "Mere Men"*   Typical for the period was the coverage of the 6 May 1911 Suffrage Day Parade in New York City. For example, "New York Women in Huge Parade Demand Ballot . . . Crowd Jeers Mere Men Marchers," *Chicago Tribune*, 7 May 1911, p. 1, and, "Big Crowds Cheer Suffragist Parade . . . Men Also in Line of March . . . ," *NY Tribune*, 7 May 1911. Only the *NY Times* was straightforward: "Women Parade and Rejoice at the End . . . ," *NY Times*, 7 May 1911.

5    *these "Suffragents"*   For example, *NY Sun*, 16 January 1910, p. 11; *Washington Times*, 24 January 1910, p. 17; and dozens of other references in the newspapers. From "Cresskill Studies of the Jersey Hen. Mr. Robinson Opines That She Has Something of the Nature of Woman After All," *NY Times*, 23 July 1911, p. 4: "Are there any suffragents among fowls or birds?" asked Mr. Agnew. "What are they?" Mr. Robinson inquired. "Male birds that do the chores about the house, the cooking and all that." "Oh, yes," replied Mr. Robinson. "The male robin is a suffragent. Mrs. Robin makes him help out in the hatching very frequently, and instead of sporting around on the lawns the old man has to cover the eggs and keep them warm while Mrs. Robin attends meetings." Whereupon another vote was taken on the suffragist question and the women lost again.

6    *In Britain, male supporters*   "Men for Woman Suffrage," *Essex County Herald*, 12 April 1907, p. 1: "A vigorous campaign of meetings for men only will be started in the fall." See also "The Men's League for Women's Suffrage," *Women's Franchise*, 27 June 1907, p. 9: "The men's league is now entering upon the fourth month of its existence and, all things considered, has every reason to be satisfied with the progress that has been made."

6    *Men in Holland*   "Men's Equal Suffrage League," *Logansport Pharos Tribune*, 23 October 1908, p. 7. "A men's league for woman suffrage has been formed in Holland and the Lutheran church in that country has given women a vote in all church affairs."

6    *On this side of the Atlantic*   "Men Form Club to Help Women. Chicago Has First Organization of Its Kind to Advance Universal Suffrage. Founders in Earnest. One Member Says It Is Beginning of Vast Movement in the City and State," *Chicago Tribune*, 13 January 1909, p. 9.

8    *And yet more than once, an invited male speaker*   See, for example, Richard Barry, "A Political Promise from Women," *Pearson's Magazine*, Vol. 23, No. 2, February 1910, pp. 143–158. Barry followed up with a Pearson's piece on the antis in March: Richard Barry, "Why Women Oppose Woman's Suffrage," *Pearson's Magazine*, Vol. 23, No. 3, pp. 319–331. Richard Barry, "What Women Have Actually Done Where

They Vote: A Personal Investigation into the Laws, Records and Results of the Four Equal-Suffrage States of America: Colorado, Idaho, Utah, and Wyoming," *Ladies' Home Journal*, November 1910, pp. 15–16, 68–19; and *Lady's Realm*, Vol. 29, Issue 171, January 1911, pp. 271–278. In a precede, the magazine's editor, Edward Bok, said that although from a policy standpoint *Ladies' Home Journal* opposes woman suffrage, "it stood prepared and ready impartially to print the results of Mr. Barry's investigation no matter which side the investigation favoured. What the *Ladies' Home Journal* wanted was to get at the actual truth from the actual authoritative records of the States. And these, it believes are presented in Mr. Barry's article." Also, see "Feminism and the Facts," *NY Times*, 19 January 1914, p. 8; C.A. Woodward, Letter, "A Case for Feminism," *NY Times*, 22 January 1914, p. 10; "Indignant Feminists Reply to Prof. Sedgwick," *NY Times*, 15 February 1914, p. 4; Dr. Simon Flexner, "Anatomy Is Not a True Guide," *NY Times*, 15 February 1914, p. 4; Dr. Frederick Peterson, Pamphlet, "Normal Women Not Neurotic" (New York: National American Woman Suffrage Association, March 1914); Dr. Frederick Peterson, "Woman's Uplift Means Man's Uplift," *NY Times*, 15 February 1914, p. 4; Dr. Franklin P. Mall, "Women Students Above the Average," *NY Times*, 15 February 1914, p. 4; "Talk on Feminism Stirs Great Crowd," *NY Times*, 18 February 1914, p. 2. Also George Middleton, "What Feminism Means to Me," Speech delivered at Cooper Union, 17 February 1914. George Middleton Papers, Manuscript Division, Library of Congress, reprinted in Kimmel and Mosmiller, *Against the Tide*, pp. 358–359.

8    *Eastman had his respect*   A. Scott Berg, *Wilson* (New York: Berkley, 2013), p. 495 (Kindle version). Berg reports that when the postmaster general stopped distribution of eighteen periodicals after the United States entered World War I in 1917, Eastman, Amos Pinchot, and John Reed all wrote to the President asking if this was really necessary. Wilson wrote to the postmaster, saying, "These are very sincere men and I should like to please them." The PG, however, did not relent. This occurred a good five years after Eastman first met the then governor while he was campaigning for the Presidency for the first time in 1912. Berg cites Woodrow Wilson to A.S. Burleson, 13 July 1917, enclosed with Eastman, Pinchot, and Reed to Woodrow Wilson, 12 July 1917, 43:164–166n; WW to Max Eastman, 18 September 1917, 44:210–211.

9    *on "terms of intimacy"*   James Kerney, *The Political Education of Woodrow Wilson* (New York: The Century Company, 1926), p. 409. "Creel, who, in the war days, as chairman of the Committee on Public Information, was on terms of intimacy with Wilson, seeing him almost daily."

CHAPTER I

11    *"taxed to the limit of my strength"*   Oswald Garrison Villard to Anna Howard Shaw, 7 January 1908. Oswald Garrison Villard Papers, Houghton Library, Harvard University, MS Am 1323 (3494).

11      *"but have feared that if I did suggest it"*   Letter, Oswald Garrison Villard to Anna Howard Shaw, 7 January 1908. Oswald Garrison Villard Papers, 1872–1949, MS Am 1323 (3494), Houghton Library, Harvard University.

12      *his "maiden speech"*   Villard, *Fighting Years*, p. 105. Also, "Education v. Citizenship," "Woman's Column 1896," Vol. IX, New York and Boston, 14 January 1896. Accessed at http://archive.org/stream/WomansColumn1896/TheWomensColumn 1896_djvu.txt, 30 January 2015. Radcliffe had existed since 1879. Harvard School of Education began admitting women in 1920 and the medical school in 1945; "Younger Element Comes to the Front and Is Much in Evidence," *Boston Globe*, 15 January 1896, p. 5.

12      *Villard used the occasion*   Villard, *Fighting Years*, p. 105. Also, "Education v. Citizenship," "Woman's Column 1896," Vol. IX, New York and Boston, 14 January 1896. Accessed at http://archive.org/stream/WomansColumn1896/TheWomensColumn 1896_djvu.txt, 30 January 2015.

12      *Frederick Douglass, the prominent abolitionist*   Frederick Douglass, "The Rights of Women," *North Star*, 28 July 1848, reprinted in Kimmel and Mosmiller, *Against the Tide*, pp. 211–212, ". . . we are free to say that in respect to political rights, we hold woman to be justly entitled to all we claim for man. We go farther, and express our conviction that all political rights which it is expedient for man to exercise, it is equally so for woman. . . ."

12      *His last public act the day of his death*   Obituary, "Death of Fred Douglass," *NY Times*, 21 February 1895, pp. 1, 3. See also Editorial, "Heckling the Hecklers," *The Crisis*, Vol. 3, No. 5, March 1912, pp. 195–196, about the intensity of Douglass's support for the cause.

12      *Villard's maternal grandfather addressed the fourth women's suffrage convention*   William Lloyd Garrison, "Intelligent Wickedness," Speech at the Fourth National Women's Rights Convention, Cleveland 1853, reprinted in the *NY Tribune*, 7 September 1853, Kimmel and Mosmiller, *Against the Tide*, pp. 212–214. "So then, I believe, that as man has monopolized for generations that all the rights which belong to woman, it has not been accidental, not through ignorance on his part, but I believe that man has done this through calculation, actuated by spirit of pride, a desire for domination which has made him degrade woman in her own eyes, and thereby tend to make her a mere vassal. It seems to me, therefore, that we are able to deal with the consciences of men. . . ."

12      *A bold handful of other prominent men*   See also: Frederick Douglass, "The Rights of Women," *North Star*, 28 July 1848, reprinted in Kimmel and Mosmiller, *Against the Tide*, pp. 211–212; Ralph Waldo Emerson, "Woman: A Lecture Read before the Woman's Rights Convention," Boston, 20 September 1855. Reprinted in *Emerson's Complete Works*, Riverside ed. (Boston: Houghton Mifflin, 1883–1893) and in Kimmel and Mosmiller, *Against the Tide*, pp. 217–220; and John Stuart Mill, *The Subjection of Women* (London: Longman, Green, Reader, and Dyer, 1869). British

Library, accessed at http://www.bl.uk/collection-items/the-subjection-of-women-by-j-s-mill, 5 January 2016.

12    *he joined other male supporters of suffrage in "An Evening with the New Man"*   "Men Champion Cause," *Washington Post*, 15 February 1902, p. 3. Speakers included the Civil Service Commissioner, John S. Crosby, "the noted exponent of single taxation," and former senator Frank G. Cannon of Utah. Also, "New Man's Views on Woman Suffrage," *Washington Times*, 15 February 1902, p. 1. The other prosuffrage male speakers were William Dudley Foulke, a New York attorney transplanted to Indiana, where he became a state senator, civic reformer, and biographer, and was one of the first presidents of the American Woman Suffrage Association.

12    *In the* Washington Post   "Men Champion Cause: Woman Suffragists Not Alone in Their Battle," *Washington Post*, 15 February 1902, p. 3.

13    *And in the* Washington Times   "New Man's Views on Woman Suffrage," *Washington Times*, 15 February 1902, p. 1. In that speech, Villard examined the key role the Woman's Municipal League in New York City played in 1901 in defeating the corrupt forces of Tammany Hall.

13    *"an appeal to the Legislature"*   Letter, Anna Howard Shaw to Oswald Garrison Villard, 7 January 1908. Oswald Garrison Villard Papers, 1872–1949, MS Am 1323 (3494), Houghton Library, Harvard University.

13    *Villard's "close and binding" relationship*   D. J. Humes, *Oswald Garrison Villard: Liberal of the 1920s* (Syracuse, NY: Syracuse University Press, 1960), pp. 6–7.

13    *"It gives me joy to remember"*   Harper, *History of Woman Suffrage*, Vol. V, p. 244; also cited in Humes, *Oswald Garrison Villard*, p. 7.

13    *the militant British suffragette Anne Cobden-Sanderson*   Coverage of Mrs. Cobden-Sanderson's visit extends from the end of October 1907 to the end of January 1908, including: *Chicago Tribune*, 24 October 1907, p. 9; 2 November 1907, p. 1; 3 November 1907 p. A8; *NY Evening Post*, 7 November 1907, p. 10; *Atlanta Constitution*, 26 November 1907, p. 9; *NY Sun*, 26 November 1907, p. 4; *NY Times*, 26 November 1907, p. 2; *NY Evening World*, 27 November 1907, p. 3; *NY Times*, 27 November, p. 6 (Editorial); *Manchester Guardian*, 28 November 1907, p. 12; *Boston Globe*, 6 December 1907, p. 15; *NY Evening Post*, 7 December 1907, p. 4; *Boston Globe*, 8 December 1907, p. 31; *Washington Post*, 8 December 1907, p. 17; *NY Tribune*, 11 December 1907, p. 4; *NY Times*, 11 December 1907, p. 10; *Washington Post*, 12 December 1907, p. 3; *NY World*, 13 December 1907 (Miller NAWSA Suffrage Scrapbooks, 1897–1911; Scrapbook 1907–1908, p. 31; Library of Congress, Rare Book and Special Collections Division); *NY Tribune*, 13 December 1907, p. 5; *NY Times*, 13 December 1907, p. 6; *NY Sun*, 13 December 1907, p. 2; *NY Times*, 15 December 1907, p. 12; *NY Tribune*, 15 December 1907, p. 9; *Chicago Tribune*, 16 December 1907, p. 7; *Boston Globe*, 2 January 1908, p. 14; *Times of India*, 4 January 1907, p. 10; *NY Evening Post*, 10 January 1908, p. 4; *NY Herald*, 12 January 1908, p. 4; *NY Evening Post*, 24 January 1908, p. 4.

13    *Her conviction had put her away in the clothes of a jail bird* "Plans of the Suffragettes," *NY Sun*, 26 November 1907, p. 4.

13    *"years ahead of American women"* "Suffragists in America," *Manchester Guardian*, 18 November 1907, p. 12.

13    *American counterparts had not yet embraced* "Plans of the Suffragettes," *NY Sun*, 26 November 1907, p. 4.

13    *"We believe in doing real things"* "Plans of the Suffragettes," *NY Sun*, 26 November 1907, p. 4.

13    *"too ultra-refined"* "Ask for Pardon to Save a Vote," *Chicago Tribune*, 3 November 1907, p. A8.

13    *eventual victory demanded* "Thinks We Don't Care for Politics," *NY Times*, 26 November 1907, p. 2.

14    *"steeps herself in the degradation of luxury"* "Rich Women Mere Spenders," *Chicago Tribune*, 16 December 1907, p. 7. See also her own, Anne Cobden-Sanderson, "American Impressions," *The Independent*, Vol. 64, 20 February 1908, pp. 392–395.

14    *"timid conventionality of thought"* "Woman Suffrage: To the Editor of the Times," *London Times*, July 1908. See also "Our 'Idle Rich' Women Scolded," *Port Jervis (NY) Evening Gazette*, 12 October 1908. In a letter read at NAWSA's 60th anniversary convention in Buffalo in October of 1908, she said her rebuke of America's "idle rich" was not exaggerated in the least, this time making clear she meant the driving force behind the antisuffrage movement. In the United States, as in Britain, where the opposition was led by the novelist Mary Augusta Ward, who published as "Mrs. Humphry Ward" after her journalist husband Thomas Humphry Ward. The idle rich, she said, "represent the spirit of feudalism combined with modern imperialism, the two most retrograde elements in English politics today."

14    *one who "has no time to think"* "Rich Women Mere Spenders," *Chicago Tribune*, 16 December 1907, p. 7.

14    *she said, "I don't want to be uncomplimentary"* "Thinks We Don't Care for Politics," *NY Times*, 26 November 1907, p. 2.

14    *"I shall be glad to become a member of it"* Letter, Anne Miller to Oswald Garrison Villard, 3 December 1907. Miller NAWSA Suffrage Scrapbooks, 1897–1911; Scrapbook 1907–1908, p. 27; Library of Congress, Rare Book and Special Collections Division.

14    *"the greatest suffragist crusade"* "The Suffragists," *NY Times*, 11 December 1907, p. 10.

14    *"The house shook with applause"* "She Is 'The Cobden' Now. And She Thinks Some American Women Hopeless from High Living," *NY Sun*, 13 December 1907,

p. 2. Blatch was the founder that year of the evening's cosponsor, the Equality
League of Self-Supporting Women.

14  *"idle luxurious lives"*  "She Is 'The Cobden' Now. And She Thinks Some American
Women Hopeless from High Living," *NY Sun*, 13 December 1907, p. 2.

14  *They also devoted several paragraphs*  "Women Give a Dare: Ask Watchorn to Hear
Speaker He Says He Will Deport," *Washington Post*, 12 December 1907, p. 3.

16  *so many timid people so afraid of consequences*  "Eve Back in Garden. Mere Man
Quails at Interurban Woman Suffrage Meeting," *NY Tribune*, 15 December 1907,
p. 9.

16  *"So far as Mrs. Sanderson is concerned"*  Letter: Villard to Anna Howard Shaw, 7
January 1908. Oswald Garrison Villard Papers, 1872–1949, MS Am 1323 (3494),
Houghton Library, Harvard University. See also, "Boycott in Bosom of Family,"
*Chicago Tribune*, 2 November 1907, p. 1. In this article she is cited as having spent
two months in prison, but in "Thinks We Don't Care for Politics," *NY Times*, 26
November 1907, p. 2, she gives the dates of her incarceration as one month, from
October 23, 1906, to November 23, 1906.

16  *"to enlist the sympathy of the men of America"*  "Suffragists in America," *Manchester
Guardian*, 18 November 1907, p. 12.

16  *"Nearly all of our most distinguished men"*  "Says Britain Is Far Ahead. Its Public
Men Favor Woman Suffrage," *Boston Globe*, 8 December 1907, p. 31.

16  *in Britain early in 1907*  "Men for Woman Suffrage," *Essex County Herald*, 12 April
1907, p. 1: "A vigorous campaign of meetings for men only will be started in the
fall." See also "The Men's League for Women's Suffrage," *Women's Franchise*, 27
June 1907, p. 9: "The men's league is now entering upon the fourth month of
its existence and, all things considered, has every reason to be satisfied with the
progress that has been made."

16  *"some excellent names on it"*  Letter, Villard to Anna Howard Shaw, 7 January 1908.
Oswald Garrison Villard Papers, 1872–1949, MS Am 1323 (3494), Houghton
Library, Harvard University.

16  *"create the very foundation"*  Editorial, *NY Evening Post*, 24 January 1908, p. 4.

16  *to be of any real use*  Letter, Shaw to Villard, 6 February 1908. Oswald Garrison
Villard Papers, 1872–1949, MS Am 1323 (3494), Houghton Library, Harvard
University.

17  *"some of our over-zealous women"*  Letter, Shaw to Villard, 6 February 1908. Oswald
Garrison Villard Papers, 1872–1949, MS Am 1323 (3494), Houghton Library,
Harvard University.

17  *"all the protection that is legitimately possible"*  PWW 18:3–4, "An Interview." From
the *Royal Gazette*, Hamilton, Bermuda, 2 March 1908, portions of which were
reprinted in the *Jersey City Evening Journal*, 10 March 1908.

17  *"a dead letter"*  PWW 18:3–4, "An Interview." From the *Royal Gazette*, Hamilton, Bermuda, 2 March 1908, portions of which were reprinted in the *Jersey City Evening Journal*, 10 March 1908.

17  *"after the names were collected"*  Letter, Shaw to Villard, 6 February 1908. Oswald Garrison Villard Papers, 1872–1949, MS Am 1323 (3494), Houghton Library, Harvard University.

17  *"whose names would really carry weight"*  Letter, Villard to Shaw, 13 February 1908. Oswald Garrison Villard Papers, 1872–1949, MS Am 1323 (3494), Houghton Library, Harvard University.

17  *"provided someone turned up"*  Eastman, "Early History," p. 17.

18  *Wise not only rejected the idea*  "Rev. Dr. Wise Surprises Emanu-el Trustees; Speaks of a Call when They Flatly Deny. NO ACTION, OFFICERS SAY. Portland Rabbi Tells His Congregation That He Stipulated for Perfect Freedom in the Pulpit," *NY Times*, 6 January 1906, p. 5.

18  *He then established*  The congregation is now known as the Stephen Wise Free Synagogue.

18  *Affairs of state and social justice*  Urofsky, *A Voice That Spoke for Justice*, pp. 4–5.

18  *The essay compared Lincoln's role*  Urofsky, *A Voice That Spoke for Justice*, pp. 6, 373n10, citing Stephen S. Wise, "Abraham Lincoln," *Literary Review*, 1, August 1889.

18  *her invitation to speak on the subject*  Letter, Stephen S. Wise, Temple Beth Israel, Portland, Oregon, to Eva Dye, 20 March 1906. American Jewish Archives, Cincinnati, Ohio. Wise declines an invitation to speak in Oregon City on equal suffrage because of his impending move to New York. But he notes that if he gives an address on suffrage in Portland, he might be able to repurpose it for her. He signs, "Wishing I could serve you better, with cordial greetings and every hope for the triumph of your cause, I am. . . ." See also Wise's 2 February 1907 "Statement on Suffrage: The Field of Their Activity, the Position Taken on Suffrage by Rabbi Wise," published in "Prominent Speakers in Favor of Woman Suffrage." Sophia Smith Collection, Women's History Archive at Smith College.

18  *"a whole network of fallacies"*  "Mr. Zangwill on Women's Suffrage," *The Jewish Exponent*, 10 July 1908, p. 5. The timing, the publishing venue and the Men's League subject matter strongly suggest this was the article Wise sent, though it was no longer in the envelope. Oswald Garrison Villard to Stephen S. Wise, 23 July 1908. Follow-up with further published comments from Israel Zangwill, Mary A. Ward, and Anne Cobden-Sanderson, titled "Woman Suffrage," *The Times* (London) circa 12 July 1908. Stephen S. Wise collection, Robert D. Farber University Archives & Special Collections, Brandeis University.

19  *street-level organizers*  Angela V. John and Claire Eustance, "Shared Histories, Differing Identities," in *The Men's Share? Masculinities, Male Support and Women's Suffrage*

in *Britain, 1890–1920* (London and New York: Routledge, 1997), pp. 1–37. The authors' scholarly analysis of the British league indicates as many as a thousand men joined British Men's League for Women's Suffrage over the seven years of its existence and that its composition was much like that of its American counterpart.

19    *voters "might become a political danger"*   "Woman Suffrage," *Irish Times*, 10 July 1908, p. 7.

19    *"cannot be trusted with a vote"*   "Woman Suffrage," *London Times*, 9 July 1908, p. 9.

20    *the "political machinery"*   "Woman Suffrage," *London Times*, 10 July 1908, p. 9.

20    *"the rest should be comparatively easy"*   Letter, Villard to Wise, 23 July 1908. Stephen S. Wise collection, Robert D. Farber University Archives & Special Collections, Brandeis University.

20    *"woman's suffrage in our backward country"*   Letter, Harriot Stanton Blatch to Wise, 11 September 1908. Stephen S. Wise collection, Robert D. Farber University Archives & Special Collections, Brandeis University. Also noted in Wise's autobiography, *Challenging Years*, p. 110, one paragraph that represents the only reference he makes to his suffrage involvement. "As early as 1908 on the request of Harriot Stanton Blatch," he writes, "I joined with a small group to secure the right to vote for women in the United States and the battle to secure full citizenship for women was at times as exciting here in the United States as it was in England. Our suffragettes were not always treated with chivalry in the national capital any more than on the streets of New York and men who supported them were subject to what now sound like rather amusing jibs that questioned our masculinity." The group was not the Men's League, which hadn't yet formed, but the Equal Franchise Society, led by Mrs. Clarence (Katherine Duer) Mackay.

20    *"than it has yet been"*   "New Suffrage Society: Mrs. Clarence Mackay Heads a New Body to Get Votes for Women," *NY Times*, 24 December 1908, p. 6.

20    *"English Suffragette"*   "Pack Carnegie Hall for Mrs. Snowden," *NY Times*, 5 December 1908, p. 1.

20    *"remarkable" suffrage movement*   Charles F. Aked, "The Woman Movement in England," *North American Review*, Vol. 188, No. 636, November 1908, pp. 650–658.

21    *Other prominent men*   Press coverage of the Society's launch also touted the names of the attorney and politician John B. Stanchfield, and the general manager of the *Associated Press*, Melville E. Stone. All but Ogden, Stanchfield, and Stone also became founding Men's League members, too. See "Constitution and Charter Members of the Men's League for Woman Suffrage of the State of New York 1910," Yale University Library, Okr40M29m.

21    *"women on equal terms with men"*   "Equal Rights Society Aims to Advance Measures for the Extension of the Franchise," *NY Times*, 21 February 1909, SM2, p. 2.

21    *a headline that affirmed the women's wise choice*   "Well-Known Men Advocate It: George Harvey, Rabbi Wise and Others Contend That Women Should Vote," *NY Times*, 21 February 1909, SM2, p. 2.

21    *"indirect influence by charm and personality"*  Dewey's jumping-off point was a particularly controversial article that had appeared in the October 1908 issue of *American* magazine, titled "The Adventitious Character of Woman." The writer, the University of Chicago sociologist, W.I. Thomas, asserted that the twentieth-century woman had been reduced to nothing more than an ornament who, to exercise influence, had only personal charm and the instinct to "make a flash" at her disposal. See W.I. Thomas, "The Adventitious Character of Woman," *American Magazine*, Vol. LXVI, No. 6, October 1908, pp. 523–530.

21    *"—that is, rule of the people"*  "Well-Known Men Advocate It: George Harvey, Rabbi Wise and Others Contend That Women Should Vote," *NY Times*, 21 February 1909, SM2, p. 2

## CHAPTER 2

23    *a project "on foot"*  Letter, Max Eastman to Annis Eastman, 1 February 1909. Max Eastman Collection I, Box 10, Lilly Library, Indiana University.

23    *among their close friends*  Special thanks to Christoph Irmscher, the author of a forthcoming biography of Max Eastman (Yale University Press) for this from his introduction, and for many kindnesses.

23    *a 1905 graduate of Williams College*  "News of Colleges Fellowships," *NY Evening Post*, 2 May 1908.

23    *John Dewey's protégé*  Letter, Max Eastman to his mother, the Rev. Dr. Annis Eastman, 21 January 1910, Max Eastman Collection I, Box 9, Lilly Library, Indiana University. "Dewey and Woodbridge both say the Plato essay is enough for a dissertation—so I shall perfect only that—not write about Aristotle and I guess I shall pull thro' in my usual way—again what I have done always—not what I do or what I am really going to do." See also, "Young Elmiran Creates a Stir," *Elmira Star-Gazette*, 10 February 1910, p. 11, which says he is taking a leave of absence from his work at Columbia, presumably as Dewey's assistant and a philosophy instructor. See also, Letter, Max to Mother, 19 May, 1910. Max Eastman Collection I, Box 9, Lilly Library, Indiana University: "I passed my exam, mamsey, and survived the comet—so I've done all I 'laid out' to for this year and I'll be strolling home in a little while."

23    *establishing the NAACP*  The NAACP was founded February 12, 1909. The organization's website (naacp.org) lists as founding members Oswald Garrison Villard, John Dewey, William Dean Howells, Lincoln Steffens, Arthur Spingarn, and Charles Edward Russell. All these names appear frequently or at least sporadically as active Men's League members.

23    *national notice for his published work*  Max Eastman, "Patriotism: A Primitive Ideal," *International Journal of Ethics*, Vol. 16, No. 4, July 1906, pp. 472–486; Max Eastman, "The Poet's Mind," *North American Review*, March 1908, pp. 417–425; Max Eastman, "The Art of Healing," *Atlantic Monthly*, May 1908; 101, 000005; pp. 644–651.

24    *Eastman too had the idea for a men's league*    The item was not located in the *NY Herald* or any other New York newspaper between 1907 and 1909, nor in the Max Eastman archive at Indiana University.

24    *"more or less of a league"*  Eastman, "Early History," pp. 17–18.

24    *"nothing to do but go ahead and organize"*  Eastman, "Early History," pp. 17–18.

24    *"we have hopes of them"*  "More Sound Reasons Advanced for Giving Women the Ballot: Max Eastman Answers Some of the Arguments Raised against Equal Suffrage Movement," *Elmira Star-Gazette*, 20 February 1909, p. 4.

24    *and wherever else they might be needed*  Villard to Shaw, 13 February 1908. Oswald Garrison Villard Papers, 1872–1949 (MS Am 1323). Houghton Library, Harvard University.

25    *"resolved upon Woman's Suffrage"*  "More Sound Reasons Advanced for Giving Women the Ballot: Max Eastman Answers Some of the Arguments Raised against Equal Suffrage Movement," *Elmira Star-Gazette*, 20 February 1909, p. 4.

25    *"civic wonders"*  Eastman, "Early History," pp. 17–18.

25    *in such a ridiculous light*  Eastman, "Early History," pp. 17–18. Eastman named the attorney as Hector S. Tyndale.

25    *"this new movement all over the world"*  Letter, Mother to Max, 21 February 1909. Max Eastman Collection I, Box 9, 1908–1909, Lilly Library, Indiana University.

25    *Eastman must have "captured"*  Eastman, "Early History," pp. 17–18.

25    *main financial backer*  Max Eastman, *Enjoyment of Living* (New York: Harper and Brothers, 1948), p. 308.

25    *"its early standing before the public"*  Eastman, "Early History," pp. 17–18.

25    *"work which women cannot do"*  "The Men's League for Women's Suffrage," *Common Cause*, 29 April 1909, reprinted in Kimmel and Mosmiller, *Against the Tide*, pp. 198–199.

26    *"first time a man ever held that position"*  "Mrs. MacKay Pleads for Equal Suffrage," *NY Times*, 16 January 1909, p. 18.

26    *"the movement for woman suffrage is spreading"*  William Hemingway, "Campaigning for Equal Franchise," *Harper's Weekly*, Vol. 53, No. 2725, 13 March 1909, pp. 14–16. The article puts the date of the Political Equality League's founding at 21 December 1908 at Mackay's home.

26    *Eastman obsessed over a suffrage speech*  Letter, Max to Mother, 13 and 16 April 1909. Max Eastman Collection I, Box 9, 1908–1909, Lilly Library, Indiana University. The speech was 17 April 1909 at 5 p.m.

26    *"open to reason"* Eastman, "Early History," pp. 17–18.

26    *He invited them to join the League*  Letter, the Rev. Dr. Annis Eastman to Anne Fitzhugh Miller, [July 1909], requesting names of men to be sent copies of an

enclosure, Max Eastman's circular inviting men to join the Voters' Woman Suffrage League & Constitution of this men's organization to support woman suffrage. Miller NAWSA Suffrage Scrapbooks, 1897–1911; Scrapbook 7, p. 106, July 1909; Library of Congress, Rare Book and Special Collections Division. The letter reads:

Dear Sir,

We write to ask you to become a member of our Voters' Woman Suffrage League. The league is to consist of men only, and we hope to have among its members from two to five prominent citizens in each senatorial district of the state. We have already over fifty such men in New York City.

We feel that an organization of men supporting the enfranchisement of women will have a peculiarly strong influence both upon those who regard the cause as trivial, and upon those who are moved only by opinions that are reinforced by ballots. In this position we have the support of the leading women advocates of the cause.

The league will not hold meetings, nor for the present do active work. It will simply make its existence and membership known, and be represented at important meetings and legislative hearings by such prominent members as are willing to appear.

There will be nominal dues of $1.00 a year for membership. Beyond this, we ask nothing of you but your name and influence.

We enclose a copy of our "Constitution," and if the cause and our method of supporting it appeal to you, we ask that you sign it and return it to the Secretary as soon as possible.

26    *one hundred prominent names*  Eastman, "Early History," pp. 17–18.

26    *Daniel De Leon delivered a major address*  Daniel De Leon, "Woman's Suffrage: An Address Delivered by Daniel De Leon under the Auspices of the Socialist Women of Greater New York, Mary Papelsky, Presiding, Cooper Union, May 8, 1909" (New York: New York Labor News Company, 1911).

26    *on the newspaper's front page*  "Male Suffragettes Now in the Field. The Deeper Notes to Join the Soprano Chorus for Women's Votes. Birth of an Uplift Idea. Scope of Operations Will Determine How Far Advanced This Movement Is to Be," *NY Times*, 21 May 1909, p. 1.

26    *"very delicate handling"*  Eastman, "Early History," pp. 17–18.

27    *In addition to listing the names*  "Male Suffragettes Now in the Field," *NY Times*, 21 May 1909, p. 1. The full text:

The battle cry of freedom for women, hitherto ringing only in soprano and contralto, is soon to be deepened and increased in volume by the voices of 100 or more men.

Among the notable men who have paid $1 and joined—for their plan is to get such weighty names as will bring to bear "a peculiarly strong influence" upon such as regard the cause flippantly—are: Oswald Garrison Villard, William Dean Howells, Charles Sprague Smith, Director of the People's Institute; the Reverend J. Howard Melish of Brooklyn, Profs. Vladimir Simkhovitch, John Dewey, and Charles Beard of Columbia, Dr. Samuel J. Barrows, Rabbi Stephen S. Wise, Charles J. Strong, Charles C. Burlingham, William M. Ivins, Col. George Harvey, Profs. James H. Robinson, William P. Trent, Richard Miller, Dr. Simon Flexner, Dr. John Brannan, Charles B. Reed, Louis Ehrich, and George F. Kunz. And then the Secretary, he who conceived the idea and is now fostering it—Max Eastman by name, versed in sociological matters, a philosophy instructor, and candidate for a Ph.D. at Columbia. Moreover, he is a writer.

Mr. Eastman, like most of the other members of the league, is strong for all enterprises of human uplift.

He pushed forward his idea on the strength of his conviction that suffrage should be given to women, but that it could not be won for them in a country where everything is decided with the ballot, unless they had allies among the voters. So he appealed to men in Columbia, and elsewhere whom he thought would be interested, and intends eventually to make this a State league, with many branches.

From Mr. Eastman's account, there is one curious feature of this organization. It is this: The league will do no active work of any kind, at least for the present, but will simply announce itself, also its membership, and then stand pat. This fact seems at first sight to put it far below the Suffragettes, whose watchword is activity, but the league has not yet announced in what way it will make its presence felt.

It now has twenty-eight members, but expects soon to have a great many more than that, and the original plan was to hide it under a bushel until there were a full hundred members. Then to throw the announcement, with all its imposing list of names, into the camp of anti-suffragists like a bomb.

Membership in the league is open to every voter in the city.

27   *"whose watchword is activity"*   "Male Suffragettes Now in the Field," *NY Times*, 21 May 1909, p. 1.

27   *"a private rebuff"*   Eastman, *Enjoyment of Living*, p. 308.

27   *"brief and caustic resignation"*   Eastman, "Early History," pp. 17–18.

27      *"—I wish I could"*   Letter, Max to Mother, 23 May 1909. Max Eastman Collection I, Box 9, 1908–1909, Lilly Library, Indiana University. Also mentioned verbatim in Eastman, "Early History," pp. 17–18.

27      *ready to go public*   Eastman, "Early History," pp. 17–18.

27      *summer of 1909*   Letter, the Rev. Dr. Annis Eastman to Anne Fitzhugh Miller, requesting names of men to be sent copies of an enclosure, Max Eastman's circular inviting men to join the Voters' Woman Suffrage League & Constitution. Miller NAWSA Suffrage Scrapbooks, 1897–1911; Scrapbook 7, p. 106, July 1909; Library of Congress, Rare Book and Special Collections Division. The early adopters included those already named—Ivins, Wise, Peabody, Villard, Dewey, Burlingham, Harvey, Beard, Melish, and Smith—plus John Mitchell, Edward T. Devine, William Jay Schleffelin, William Dean Howells, Hamilton Holt, Dr. Simon Flexner, Dr. Julius Rudisch, Prof. Vladimir Simkhovitch, Prof. Dickinson S. Miller, Prof. James H. Robinson, Prof. W.P. Trent, Prof. James Shotwell, Prof. W.P. Montague, Rev. Thomas C. Hall, Rev. Leighton Williams, the Rev. Dr. John P. Peters, Charles and Josiah Strong, Nelson Spencer, Louis R. Ehrich, William Adams Delano, Charles B. Reed, John E. Milholland, Charles Rann Kennedy, Edwin Markham, Edmond Kelley, George F. Kunz, John Mead Howells, Henry S. Marlor, Robert H. Elder, and William H. Ingersoll.

27      *"my first speech"*   Suffrage Speeches Complete. Max Eastman Collection II, Box 20, Lilly Library, Indiana University. Eastman's handwritten note in blue pencil identifies this as "what must be the ms. of my first speech at Ontario." But actually the speech to the Monroe County Suffrage Association took place in the Rochester neighborhood of Charlotte and in any event he had spoken on suffrage at NYU in April.

27      *"favoring woman suffrage"*   "Encouragement for Suffragists. County Association Annual Meeting in Charlotte. Men's League Best of All. Nothing Can Do More Good Than the Favor of Such Men as Are Now on the Side of Equal Franchise, Says State Organizer," *Rochester Democrat and Chronicle*, 15 June 1909. "Political Equality Club in Convention," *Rochester Post-Express*, 14 June 1909, p. 8.

27      *keynote speaker*   Eastman, *Enjoyment of Living*, p. 310.

28      *week after week*   First speech at Monroe County, 14 June 1909. Suffrage Speeches Complete. Max Eastman Collection II, Box 20, Lilly Library, Indiana University.

28      *"The speech was to last forty-five minutes"*   Eastman, *Enjoyment of Living*, p. 310.

28      *his hand-written notes sprawl*   Suffrage Speeches Complete. Max Eastman Collection II, Box 20, Lilly Library, Indiana University. Noted in blue on manuscript of his first speech at Monroe County, 14 June 1909.

28    *"like a river between high banks"* Eastman, *Enjoyment of Living*, pp. 313–314. By Ontario, he meant Charlotte in Monroe County.

28    *The address of Harriet May Mills*    "Encouragement for Suffragists. County Association Annual Meeting in Charlotte. Men's League Best of All. Nothing Can Do More Good Than the Favor of Such Men as Are Now on the Side of Equal Franchise, Says State Organizer," *Rochester Democrat and Chronicle*, 15 June 1909, p. 2.

28    *fireworks or finesse*    "Max Eastman on Humor," undated, unidentified. Max Eastman Collection, Box I, Lilly Library, Indiana University. Noted in his hand as "from St. Louis." It described Eastman at the podium as "a mixture of Nat Goodwin, Sol Smith Russell, Mark Twain, Artemus Ward and Bill Nye, but with more personality—sheer personality than anyone of them, save perhaps Goodwin."

28    *convention in Troy*    Eastman, *Enjoyment of Living*, pp. 313–314. See also Max Eastman, "Who's Afraid? Confessions of a Suffrage Orator," *The Masses*, November 1914, pp. 7–9. About speechmaking, Eastman says: Speeches must have only one dimension: they must start at the beginning and flow to the end. "You cannot spread it out, or carry it back and forth, or take it here and there," he wrote later, "You can not dig around under it. A speech should be rapid, clear and energetic, and make one main point. It should run like a river between high banks, and the floods of emotion adding to its force, but never widening the territory it covers. . . . Only once, perhaps twice in a lifetime can a person accomplish this extemporaneously," he continued, but one can never do so "by taking successive starts from a series of penciled notes. The more impassioned the language, the more it will in these circumstances tend to expatiate and meander. . . . A speech that is well memorized can, by trick and art, be made to deceive the hearer completely and make him reverently marvel at the talent that can enable a man to stand up unprepared and pour out perfectly phrased felicities as easily and as comfortably and as confidently as less gifted people talk lusterless commonplaces. . . . This obvious, yet for some strange reason esoteric piece of good sense is what I learned in that purgatory at Ontario. I learned it all at once, in a lump, without instruction and without hesitance or self-persuasion."

29    *telephone in their ballots*    Peter Finley Dunne, "Mr. Dooley on Woman's Suffrage," *American Magazine*, Vol. 63, June 1909. Reprinted in Kimmel and Mosmiller, *Against the Tide*, pp. 236–239.

29    *university's faculty since 1904*    Max Eastman, "John Dewey," *Atlantic*, December 1941, pp. 671–685. As his student and protégé for three years (from 1908 to 1912) during this period at Columbia, Eastman's much later insights are noteworthy. "In general, ideas were sprouting up through the bricks at Columbia in those days, and Dewey's mind was happy there. Also he found it easier, while living in New York, to play a part in civic movements of national scope, to be a factor in the nation's political life, as is appropriate to a philosopher who believes that the truth of an idea lies in its practical effect."

| 29 | *"ticking perkily up in the back"* "Mrs. Clarence H. Mackay Shows Devotion to the Cause," *Boston Globe*, 27 July 1909, p. 7. |
|---|---|

29    *"other personal expenses"* "Professor Dewey with Suffragists. Declares Right to Own Realty Carries with It Women's Moral Right to Ballot. They Control Tariff. Columbia University Pedagogue Asserts Man Who Gives Pay to Wife Weekly Is Ideal," *NY Times*, 7 July 1909, p. 5.

29    *the enfranchisement of women* "Professor Dewey with Suffragists. Declares Right to Own Realty Carries with It Women's Moral Right to Ballot," *NY Herald*, 27 July 1909, p. 5.

29    *female teachers feminized boys* "Begins Campaign. Dr. Dewey Speaks for Mrs. Mackay's Society at Columbia," *NY Tribune*, 27 July 1909, p. 3. Dewey was quoted as saying, "Hall is entitled to speak of the boys he knows, but for my part I haven't met any mollycoddles from the public schools. The boys who come here might have a little more of the feminine quality without injuring them at all. I confess there are some things in Dr. Hall's contentions that I cannot understand. I cannot see why if contact with study and the higher education makes a woman masculine her influence when she becomes a teacher should be to make the boys effeminate weaklings."

30    *"regulating the consumption"* "Professor Dewey Tells Why Women Should Have the Vote," *Christian Science Monitor*, 27 July 1909, p. 8.

30    *She also double-checked her son's notes* Letter, Mother to Max, 11 July 1909. Max Eastman Collection I, Box 9, Lilly Library, Indiana University. Annis writes to Max, telling her about the letters she has sent out and how little response there has been, likely due to the vacation period. Also, the return response, under Max Eastman's name, carried her Elmira address, not League headquarters, which initially was Max's apartment in Greenwich Village.

30    *"make the affirmative vote a majority"* "Voter's League for Woman Suffrage," *Woman's Journal*, 7 August 1909, Issue 32, p. 126.

30    *"will prove invaluable"* "Voter's League for Woman Suffrage," *Woman's Journal*, 7 August 1909, Issue 32, p. 126.

30    *convention of October 1909* "Convention of State Woman Suffrage Association Will Meet Next Week at Troy," *NY Evening Post*, 13 October 1909, p. 5. The convention took place October 20–23.

30    *"the jolliest bunch of reformers"* Eastman, *Enjoyment of Living*, p. 315.

32    *"familiar assertions"* "The Minority Report on Equal Suffrage," *Harper's Weekly*, 26 April 1879. "Women are inexperienced, and depend upon the other sex; they can not enforce the laws which they make; very few of them wish the suffrage; the change should be made slowly, and if at all, by the States; it would increase the number of voters by the millions, and there are but thirty-thousand petitioners." And the counters: "Inexperience is true of every voter when he first

votes, and if it be a valid objection, it would have prevented any extension of suffrage. Incapacity for military duty may be considered when incapable men are disfranchised for the same reason. Impotence to enforce laws supposes women as women arrayed against men in passing laws, and this contradicts the assertion of the dependence of women and their unwillingness to assume political burdens. The majority concede that women may be properly enfranchised in any State when they desire it. But if women are fit to decide a fundamental question in politics, for what public question are they unfit? And if the change ought to be made by the States, is it not plain that when two-thirds of Congress and three-fourths of the States have voted for it, there must be a large number in other States favorable to it, so it can never be forced upon unwilling communities, while the prevention of unjust discrimination by States against large classes of people is a matter of national concern, and a constitutional amendment may be deemed necessary if shown to be required by constitutional principles."

32    *popular thought*    "State Convention Closes," *Troy Daily Times*, 23 October 1909, p. 2. "Says Women Need New Arguments," *Elmira Star-Gazette*, 27 October 1909, p. 9. See also the manuscript and typescript dated October 1910 (not the same speech), "The World Is Full of Suffrage Arguments." Max Eastman Collection II, Box 20, Lilly Library, Indiana University.

32    *"the way we get things in America"*    "State Convention Closes," *Troy Daily Times*, 23 October 1909, p. 2.

32    *"the largest audience"*    "Woman Suffragists of NY State: Report of Annual Convention at Troy by Mrs. C.T. Johnson, President of Holley Political Equality Club," *Holley Standard*, 25 November 1909, p. 1.

32    *"to speak with Mrs. Snowden"*    Letter, Max to Mother, 26 October 1909. Max Eastman Collection I, Box 9, Lilly Library, Indiana University.

32    *"the most eminent asset"*    Eastman, *Enjoyment of Living*, p. 314.

32    *"the sensation of the year"*    Eastman, *Enjoyment of Living*, p. 314.

33    *"his three-cornered life scheme"*    Eastman, *Enjoyment of Living*, pp. 313–314.

33    *"a line of persistent ones"*    "Great Throng Hears Mrs. Pankhurst. Carnegie Hall Filled to Overflowing and Hundreds in the Street Fail to Gain Admission," *NY Times*, 26 October 1909, p. 1.

33    *"Sitting as a distinguished guest"*    Letter, Max to Mother, 28 October 1909. Max Eastman Collection I, Box 9, Lilly Library, Indiana University.

33    *"I think of her when I wake up"*    Letter, Max to Mother, 28 October 1909. Max Eastman Collection I, Box 9, Lilly Library, Indiana University.

33    *"spoken of with Washington and Lincoln"*    Letter, Max to Mother, 28 October 1909. Max Eastman Collection I, Box 9, Lilly Library, Indiana University.

33    *"not a rabid suffragist"*    William Howard Taft, "Address to the Students of the State Institute and College at Columbus, Mississippi, 2 November 1909," *Presidential*

*Addresses and State Papers of William Howard Taft from March 4, 1909 to March 4, 1910* (New York: Doubleday, Page and Co., 1910), pp. 396–398.

33    *"800 as pretty girls as could be found"*  "For Friendship of the South Taft Appeals," *Atlanta Constitution*, 3 November 1909, p. 1.

34    *"however altruistic that class"*  Taft, "Address to the Students," pp. 396–398.

34    *his disappointing comment*  "Why and When Should a Woman Marry. President Taft's Speech Widely Discussed at National Capital. Many Leaders in Social Circles Hold Pronounced Views as to the Duty of a Girl," *Washington Post*, 5 November 1909, p. 3.

34    *"nothing to fear"*  Letter to the Editor, "Taft's Speech to Girls. Can Their Future Vote Open More Avenues of Self-Support?" *NY Times*, 6 November 1909, p. 6.

34    *"made decided headway"*  "Talked About in Hotel Lobbies," *Washington Post*, 6 November 1909, p. 6.

34    *"vigor and energy"*  "Votes for Women. Since Election Day Organized Movements Having Woman's Suffrage for Their Object Are Everywhere Active and Plan Long Campaign," *NY Times*, 7 November 1909, SMS p. 2.

35    *"the sinews of war"*  "Votes for Women. Since Election Day Organized Movements Having Woman's Suffrage for Their Object Are Everywhere Active and Plan Long Campaign," *NY Times*, 7 November 1909, SMS p. 2.

35    *The place was packed*  Postcard, Max to Mother, 8 November 1909. Max Eastman Collection I, Box 9, Lilly Library, Indiana University.

35    *"that fiery and eloquent apostle"*  "Buffalo Paper Lauds Elmiran," *Elmira Star-Gazette*, 15 November 1909, p. 9.

35    *"But so it fell out"*  Eastman, *Enjoyment of Living*, p. 315.

35    *"beautiful, cloistered saints"*  "Someone Will Be Killed While Suffrage Battle Is On," *Buffalo Courier*, 13 November 1909, p. 8.

36    *further the development of women*  "Someone Will Be Killed While Suffrage Battle Is On," *Buffalo Courier*, 13 November 1909, p. 8.

36    *in the Garden of Eden*  "Someone Will Be Killed While Suffrage Battle Is On," *Buffalo Courier*, 13 November 1909, p. 8.

36    *the extent of their political slavery*  "Fails to See President. Mrs. Snowden Calls at White House," *Boston Globe*, 23 November 1909, p. 4.

36    *"the modern style of chivalry"*  "Hostesses and Guests Are Occupied with Attractive Round of Social Affairs. Every Day and Evening Filled with Teas, Luncheons, Dinners and Bridge with Now and Then a Lecture for More Serious Hours," *Buffalo Courier*, 14 November 1909, p. 58.

36    *slow drips*  Letter, Max to Mother, 16 November 1909, Max Eastman Collection I, Box 9, Lilly Library, Indiana University. "I enclose $36.00 which is all the treasury is good for so far. Don't deduct the money for stamps from what you

are hereby paid, but just keep that record and it'll go in next time I balance the accounts."

36    *filled Carnegie Hall*    "Suffragists Hear Harvard Criticised. The Rev. Dr. Anna Shaw Raps the University for Barring a Woman Law Student," *NY Times*, 18 November 1909, p. 7.

36    *"the platform was filled"*    "Suffragists Hear Harvard Criticised. The Rev. Dr. Anna Shaw Raps the University for Barring a Woman Law Student," *NY Times*, 18 November 1909, p. 7. Dr. Barton Aylesworth of Denver was another speaker in Carnegie Hall. He told of all the good the right to vote had meant for women of Colorado. He assured those assembled that enfranchising women in no way had become "a consumer of time needed in the home."

36    *"votes to set things right"*    "Suffragists Begin. Open with Big Guns. Mrs. Belmont Starts Great Meeting at Carnegie Hall," *NY Tribune,* 18 November 1909, p. 3.

37    *"I'm not sure there ever was any Mrs. Peabody"*    Letter, Max to Mother, 16 November 1909. Max Eastman Collection I, Box 9, Lilly Library, Indiana University.

37    *and close friend, Spencer Trask*    See generally, Louise Ware, *George Foster Peabody: Banker, Philanthropist, Publicist* (Athens, GA: University of Georgia Press, 1951), pp. 150–151, inter alia. Peabody's marriage to Katrina Trask took place shortly before her death. She was the guiding spirit behind Yaddo, the Trask estate at Saratoga Springs that was becoming the important artists' retreat it is now.

37    *"an inevitable reflection"*    Item, *Brooklyn Eagle*, 5 December 1909, p. 2. Peabody had lived in Brooklyn for years before retiring upstate.

37    *"City Club the 29th"*    Letter, Max Eastman to Anne Fitzhugh Miller, 19 November 1909. Miller NAWSA Suffrage Scrapbooks, 1897–1911; Scrapbook 8, p. 118; Library of Congress, Rare Book and Special Collections Division.

37    *executive secretary of the statewide organization*    "To Boom Woman Suffrage," *NY Sun*, 24 November 1909, p. 5. Arthur S. Levy ("1910 law," later known as Arthur S. Leeds Jr.) was named vice-president, and a postgrad named Read Lewis its secretary and treasurer. Levy's name change is listed in a "redirect" in Columbia University archival records, emailed in a conversation with Kat Thornton, 12 January 2016.

37    *accepted the presidency*    "People of Note," *Lowell Sun*, 27 November 1909, p. 6.

39    *their favorite sons*    For example: "A New 100 to Help Women: Men's Suffrage League Started at Last. George Foster Peabody Is the President. William Dean Howells One of the Vice Presidents—A Big Campaign Is Planned. If Interested, You May Join," *NY Sun*, 30 November 1909, p. 6; "Men Enter Fight: League for Woman Suffrage Made State-wide," *NY Tribune*, 30 November 1909, p. 5; "Men for Woman Suffrage: Prominent New Yorkers in League for Active Work for the Cause," *NY Times*, 30 November 1909, p. 5; "More Than 100 Noted Men Join

Suffrage Cause: Form League to Push War for Women's Votes," *NY Herald*, 30 November 1909, p. 5; "Elmira Men in Society: Former Mayor Brockway, Attorney Thomas F. Fennell and Max Eastman Are Officers of New League," *Elmira Star-Gazette*, 30 November 1909, p. 10; "Cornell Men in Suffrage Crusade: Professor Schmidt and Tommy Fennell Members of League for Woman Suffrage," *Ithaca Daily News*, 30 November 1909, p. 4; "Men Cry 'Votes for Women' William Dean Howells Aids New Suffrage Club; Object of Organization Will Be to Stand Sponsor for Crusade to Get Ballot Rights," *Brooklyn Eagle*, 30 November 1909, p. 20; "Voters' League for Woman Suffrage. Organized in NYC Last Evening— George Foster Peabody President. Carlton Sprague on Advisory Committee," *Buffalo Courier*, 30 November 1909, p. 5; "Noted Men for Equal Suffrage: Voters League for Enfranchising Women Is Formed in NYC. Genevans Are Members," *Geneva Daily Times and Courier*, 30 November 1909, p. 1.

39    *"dog whips on mere men"*   "Strenuous Suffragette Approves of Horsewhipping Men Sometimes," *Williamsport Gazette-Bulletin*, 1 December 1909, p. 1.

39    *"get to work at once"*   "Men for Suffrage in Spite of Whips," *Williamsport Gazette-Bulletin*, 1 December 1909, pp. 1–2.

40    *"it has not been the fault of the executive committee"*   Eastman, "Early History," pp. 17–18.

40    *Dewey presided as platform chair*   "Beware Ye Prison! No Suffrage Joke. If Mrs. Pankhurst Dies There Women May Get Votes," *NY Tribune*, 1 December 1909, p. 4.

40    *he deflected the most common arguments*   Justice David J. Brewer, "Summing Up the Case for Woman Suffrage," *Ladies' World*, December 1909. Reported in *Woman's Journal*, 27 November 1909, p. 192.

40    *speech in Ulster County*   "Addresses Delivered by Justice David J. Brewer & Mr. Warner Van Norden on July 4th, 1908" (New York: Mohonk Lake, Ulster County).

40    *"adapted to present conditions"*   "Her Vote Would Tone Us Up. Eastman, Friend of Suffrage, So Appeals to Men," *NY Sun*, 3 December 1909, p. 6.

41    *"you ride right over those things"*   Letter, Max to Mother, 3 December 1909. Max Eastman Collection I, Box 9, Lilly Library, Indiana University.

41    *Charles Evans Hughes*   "Governor Listens to Woman Suffragists," *Syracuse Post Standard*, 23 December 1909, p. 2.

41    *form their own local chapters*   "News Notes," *Twentieth Century Magazine*, January 1910, Vol. 1, No. 4, p. 386.

41    *the Men's League itself*   The speeches that survive in published or unpublished form include the following: Suffrage Speeches Complete, Max Eastman Collection II, Box 20, Folder II, Lilly Library, Indiana University, has numerous in unpublished

form, including iterations of "Man and the Family," "Feminism," and "An Object Lesson for the Suffragists"; Unpublished, Max Eastman, mss., "The World Is Full of Suffrage Arguments," dated October 1910, Max Eastman, "Women and Democracy," *Woman's Journal*, 30 April 1910, which also appears, in part, in Harper, *History of Woman Suffrage*, Vol. V, 1900–1920, p. 285. Also, there are: Pamphlet, Max Eastman, "Suffrage and Sentiment," New York: Equal Franchise Society of New York City, 1909; Max Eastman, "Is Woman Suffrage Important?" *North American Review*, Vol. CXCIII, No. DCLXII, January 1911, pp. 61–71; Pamphlet, Max Eastman, "Values of the Vote: Address before the Men's League for Woman Suffrage of New York, 21 March 1912" (New York: Men's League for Woman Suffrage); and "The Bryn Mawr Chapter of the National College Equal Suffrage League," *The Lantern*, Spring 1913, No. 21, p. 99.

41    *"united martyrdom with money earning"*  Eastman, *Enjoyment of Living*, p. 316.

41    *"latest acquisition"*  Letter, Max to Mother, 6 December 1909. Max Eastman Collection I, Box 9, Lilly Library, Indiana University.

43    *"speculate about it until January"*  Letter, Max to Mother, 6 December 1909, Max Eastman Collection I, Box 9, Lilly Library, Indiana University.


CHAPTER 3

43    *added a "Mrs."*  "What Women Are Doing," *San Antonio Light*, 5 January 1910, p. 8. There was no Mrs. George Peabody at the time. Other members of the group the item mentioned were Carrie Chapman Catt, Ella H. Crossett, and Fanny Garrison Villard. E.C. Stanton, S.B. Anthony, M.J. Gage, and I.H. Harper, eds., *History of Woman Suffrage*, Vol. I (New York: Arno Press, 1969), pp. 456–457, adds the names of several other men as legislative committee members who were members of the original League, including Edwin Markham, the American poet; William Gordon VerPlanck (misidentified as Van Plank); the Reverend Doctor John D. Peters; William M. Ivins of the City Club; Rabbi Stephen S. Wise; and Oswald Garrison Villard. The Reverend Doctor Charles Aked's name does not appear on the original League charter and constitution. See also "Constitution and Charter Members of the Men's League for Woman Suffrage of the State of New York," Yale University Library, Okr40M29m.

43    *the initial 1910 League charter*  See "Constitution and Charter Members of the Men's League for Woman Suffrage of the State of New York," Yale University Library, Okr40M29m. See also, Stanton et al., *History of Woman Suffrage*, Vol. I, pp. 456–457.

45    *the birth of Christ*  Letter, Charles T. Hoy to Max, 30 March 1911, Max Eastman Collection I, Box 1, Correspondence 1911–1912, Lilly Library, Indiana University.

45     *he remained unmoved*    Stanton et al., *History of Woman Suffrage*, Vol. I, p. 457. At the meeting with the governor were Peabody, Villard, Fanny Garrison Villard, Crossett, Mrs. Frederick R. Hazard, and Anne F. Miller.

45     *"sainted rhetoric"*    Letter, Max to Mother, 16 January 1910, Max Eastman Collection I, Box 10, Lilly Library, Indiana University.

45     *"part of the time in jail"*    Letter, Max to Mother, 21 January 1910. Max Eastman Collection I, Box 10, Lilly Library, Indiana University. Also, Eastman, *Enjoyment of Living*, p. 316.

45     *led to her arrest*    See Linda J. Lumsden, *Inez: The Life and Times of Inez Milholland* (Bloomington: Indiana University Press, 2004).

45     *"What can we do to persuade you"*    Eastman, "An Object Lesson for the Suffragists," Suffrage Speeches Complete, Max Eastman Collection II, Box 20, Folder Two, Lilly Library, Indiana University.

46     *"in which women have no position"*    Eastman, "An Object Lesson for the Suffragists," Suffrage Speeches Complete, Max Eastman Collection II, Box 20, Folder Two, Lilly Library, Indiana University.

46     *"intimidating the scabs"*    Eastman, "An Object Lesson for the Suffragists," Suffrage Speeches Complete, Max Eastman Collection II, Box 20, Folder Two, Lilly Library, Indiana University.

46     *"criminally liable"*    Eastman, "An Object Lesson for the Suffragists," Suffrage Speeches Complete, Max Eastman Collection II, Box 20, Folder Two, Lilly Library, Indiana University.

46     *"working women themselves"*    Eastman, "An Object Lesson for the Suffragists," Max Eastman Collection II, Box 20, Suffrage Speeches Complete, Folder Two, Lilly Library, Indiana University.

46     *"upon the oppressed"*    Eastman, "An Object Lesson for the Suffragists," Max Eastman Collection II, Box 20, Suffrage Speeches Complete, Folder Two, Lilly Library, Indiana University.

46     *"disgrace"*    Letter, Max to Mother, 18 January 1910. Max Eastman Collection I, Box 10, Lily Library, Indiana University.

46     *"the finest in the land"*    Letter, Max to Mother, 16 January 1910. Max Eastman Collection I, Box 10, Lilly Library, Indiana University, in part repeated in Eastman, *Enjoyment of Living*, p. 315, where he adds: "I am so often asked how I came to be that 'ardent male suffragette' that I want to make sure I have explained the process. Underlying it all was my unqualified liking for women with brains, character and independence, a taste I share with Plato and Shakespeare and owe, as I suppose they did, to my mother's nature."

47     *"one-eyed jackasses"*    Letter, Max to Mother, 16 January 1910. Max Eastman Collection I, Box 10, Lilly Library, Indiana University.

47    *"saved the day"*   Letter, Max to Mother, 16 January 1910. Max Eastman Collection I, Box 10, Lilly Library, Indiana University.

47    *their traditional roles*   "For and Against Votes for Women. Suffrage Meeting Audience Sits Up and Takes Notice of Remarks by R. E. Connell," *Poughkeepsie Daily Eagle*, 13 January 1910, pp. 5 and 7.

47    *"with some discrimination"*   Letter, Max to Mother, 16 January 1910. Max Eastman Collection I, Box 10, Lilly Library, Indiana University.

47    *"well-received"*   "For and Against Votes for Women. Suffrage Meeting Audience Sits Up and Takes Notice of Remarks by R. E. Connell," *Poughkeepsie Daily Eagle*, 13 January 1910, pp. 5 and 7.

47    *"draw the same kind of crowd"*   Letter, Max to Mother, 16 January 1910. Max Eastman Collection I, Box 10, Lilly Library, Indiana University.

47    *"please don't"*   "Be a Sport on Suffrage. Max Eastman Says Take a Chance Even If You Don't Like Votes for Women," *NY Sun*, 22 January 1910, p. 5.

47    *"into the world"*   "Max Eastman. Says He's Sick of the Worn Out Arguments for Women's Suffrage," *Elmira Morning Telegram*, 23 January 1910, letters page. Also, "Be a Sport on Suffrage. Max Eastman Says Take a Chance Even If You Don't Like Votes for Women," *NY Sun*, 22 January 1910, p. 5.

47    *"as a regular business"*   Letter, Max to Mother, 23 January 1910 (postmark. Dated 22 January 1910). Max Eastman Collection I, Box 10, Lilly Library, Indiana University.

48    *"permitted to help"*   "Bribery and Women. Feminine Voters Are Fifty Times as Honest as Men Says Judge Lindsey," *Greensburg New Era*, 11 January 1910, p. 1.

48    *movement supporters*   "Suffragists in All Ranks. The Cry 'Votes for Women' Heard on All Sides," *NY Sun*, 30 January 1910, p. 6.

48    *making suffrage the topic*   Item, *NY Tribune*, 5 February 1910, p. 9.

48    *"Dogs of war"*   "Suffragists Hit at Own Meeting. Ministers Openly Attack Principles Involved in Double Ballot," *NY Herald*, 6 February 1910, p. 6.

48    *"minced no words"*   "Suffragists Hit at Own Meeting. Ministers Openly Attack Principles Involved in Double Ballot," *NY Herald*, 6 February 1910, p. 6. The clergymen were the Reverend Doctor Henry A. Stimson of the Manhattan Congregational Church and the Reverend Doctor Andrew F. Underhill of the (Episcopal) Church of the Ascension.

48    *"peril of the age"*   "Spat Over the Ladies' Votes," *NY Sun*, 6 February 1910, p. 7; "Suffragists Hit at Own Meeting. Ministers Openly Attack Principles Involved in Double Ballot," *NY Herald*, 6 February 1910, p. 6. See also, "Talk of Suffrage. Both Sides Heard," *NY Tribune*, 6 February 1910, p. 5.

48    *"Your time is up"*   "Suffragists Hit at Own Meeting. Ministers Openly Attack Principles Involved in Double Ballot," *NY Herald*, 6 February 1910, p. 6.

49     *"they have been proved unequalled"*   "Suffragists Hit at Own Meeting. Ministers Openly Attack Principles Involved in Double Ballot," *NY Herald*, 6 February 1910, p. 6.

49     *called the luncheon to a close*   "Suffragists Hit at Own Meeting. Ministers Openly Attack Principles Involved in Double Ballot," *NY Herald*, 6 February 1910, p. 6.

49     *"they may seem obvious"*   Newspaper ad for the February 1909 issue of *Pearson's Magazine*.

49     *"distressing part of our work"*   Richard Barry, "A Political Promise from Women," *Pearson's Magazine*, Vol. 23, No. 2, February 1910, pp. 143–158.

49     *Mackay in particular*   Richard Barry, "A Political Promise from Women," *Pearson's Magazine*, Vol. 23, No. 2, February 1910, pp. 143–158. Barry followed up with a *Pearson's* piece on the antis in March: Barry, "Why Women Oppose Woman's Suffrage," *Pearson's Magazine*, Vol. 23, No. 3, pp. 319–331.

50     *"it must fail"*   "Mrs. O.H.P. Belmont Erases Color Line: Wealthy Suffragette Leader Invites Negro Recruits," *San Francisco Call*, Vol. 107, No. 69, 7 February 1910, p. 1.

50     *Midtown Manhattan*   "People," *Washington Tribune*, 17 March 1910, p. 8. See also John Koegel, *Music in German Immigrant Theater: New York City, 1840–1940* (Rochester, NY: University of Rochester Press), p. 324. The cost of the Adolf Philipp's 57th Street Theater around that time was $32,000.

50     *NAWSA's presidency*   "People," *Washington Tribune*, 17 March 1910, p. 8.

50     *"critical to the cause"*   Kenneth Florey, *Women's Suffrage Memorabilia: An Illustrated Historical Study* (Jefferson, NC: McFarland and Company, 2013).

50     *"never could or would have said"*   "Editorial Notes," *Woman's Journal*, 29 January 1910, p. 1.

51     *Men's League members*   "The Suffrage Campaign. An Organizer Tells of Her Trip through the State," *Troy SemiWeekly Times*, 18 February 1910, p. 5 or 8.

51     *obliged him to take a leave from the philosophy department*   "Young Elmiran Creates a Stir," *Elmira Star-Gazette*, 10 February 1910, p. 11.

51     *"logical, fair, and yet a woman"*   Letter, Max to Mother, 23 January 1910 (postmark. Dated 22 January 1910). Max Eastman Collection I, Box 10, Lilly Library, Indiana University.

52     *no known remarks*   Letter, Mother to Max, 22 January 1910. Max Eastman Collection I, Box 9, Lilly Library, Indiana University.

52     *Equal Franchise Society*   "Urge Women's Votes at Albany Meeting," *NY Times*, 17 February 1910, p. 9. The men who shared her box had enough cachet to help garner publicity as they were singled out for mention in the press, including Mackay's husband, Clarence MacKay; Speaker and Mrs. James Wadsworth Jr.; Senator George A. Davis; and Assemblyman Lewis Stuyvesant Chanler.

52  *an absence*  "Urge Women's Votes at Albany Meeting," *NY Times*, 17 February 1910, p. 9.

52  *"not a few State officers"*  "Urge Women's Votes at Albany Meeting," *NY Times*, 17 February 1910, p. 9.

52  *buoyed the movement*  "Big Suffrage Meet: Every Seat Taken for Mass Meeting in Albany Tonight," *NY Call*, 16 February 1910, p. 4.

52  *"question our democracy"*  "All Albany Cheers Suffrage Fight: Campaign Starts with Giant Meeting Attended by Many Noted Personages," *NY Herald*, 17 February 1910, p. 4.

52  *"free from corruption and graft"*  "Albany Suffrage PowWow: Prof. Eastman Denounces Gaynor, Police and Courts," *NY Sun*, 17 February 1910, p. 2.

52  *and with more women*  For example, "Suffragists Meet: Big Turnout of Leaders at Albany Gathering," *Brooklyn Eagle*, 17 February 1910, p. 10; "Urge Women's Votes at Albany Meeting: Political Leaders Attend Big Gathering and Hear Suffrage Arguments and Pleas," *NY Times*, 17 February 1910, p. 9; "All Albany Cheers Suffrage Fight: Campaign Starts with Giant Meeting Attended by Many Noted Personages," *NY Herald*, 17 February 1910, p. 4; "Albany Suffrage PowWow: Prof. Eastman Denounces Gaynor, Police and Courts," *NY Sun*, 17 February 1910, p. 2.

52  *"glad of it"*  "Albany Suffrage PowWow: Prof. Eastman Denounces Gaynor, Police and Courts," *NY Sun*, 17 February 1910, p. 2.

54  *"between now and April"*  Letter, Max to Mother, 21 February 1910. Max Eastman Collection I, Box 10, Lilly Library, Indiana University.

54  *"not tepid about anything"*  "Urge Women's Votes at Albany Meeting," *NY Times*, 17 February 1910, p. 9.

54  *Eastman wrote his mother*  Letter, Max to Mother, 21 February 1910. Max Eastman Collection I, Box 10, Lilly Library, Indiana University.

54  *"death of 'em"*  Letter, Max to Mother, 25 February 1910. For more on Eastman's thinking about effective suffrage oratory, see Max Eastman, "Who's Afraid? Confession of a Suffrage Orator," *The Masses*, November 1914, pp. 7–8.

54  *teaching post at Columbia*  Letter, Max to Mother, 21 February 1910. Max Eastman Collection I, Box 10, Lilly Library, Indiana University.

54  *"amazement of all"*  Eastman, *Enjoyment of Living*, p. 315.

54  *"consist of writing"*  Eastman, *Enjoyment of Living*, p. 316.

55  *memoir says by chance*  See Villard, *Fighting Years*, pp. 216–217, where he says they met by chance on the return steamer from Bermuda, 5 March 1910. However, in Letter, Woodrow Wilson to Cleveland Hoadley Dodge, dated 18 February 1910, Wilson writes, "Mr. Villard, of the Evening Post, came down here by the steamer which came in this morning. . . ." Arthur S. Link, ed., *The Papers of Woodrow Wilson* (Princeton: Princeton University Press, 1966), Vol. 20, p. 141.

55 *combative board* PWW 20:141, Wilson from Bermuda to Cleveland Hoadley Dodge, 18 February 1910. See also John Milton Cooper Jr., *Woodrow Wilson: A Biography* (New York: Random House, 2009), pp. 89–32. See also A. Scott Berg, *Wilson* (New York: Random House, 2013), pp. 179–181. The battles were over his expansion plans and large donations that came with thick knotty strings attached that were being solicited independently by board members who opposed Wilson's leadership. See also PWW 17:609n1, Wilson to Villard, 26 January 1908, when, just as Villard and Shaw were hashing out the details for a Men's League, Wilson, from Bermuda, offered a similar invitation to Villard to come visit him, writing that he had not forgotten Villard's "kind invitation to come in and talk over the Democratic situation."

55 *fervent backers* Villard, *Fighting Years*, p. 217.

55 *"Governorship of New Jersey"* PWW 21:58–59, Oswald Garrison Villard to Woodrow Wilson, 22 August 1910.

55 *president of the United States* See Willis Fletcher Johnson, *George Harvey* (New York: Houghton Mifflin, 1929), chapter 12, "At the Lotos Club," pp. 111–115. See also PWW 16:300, Harvey's speech at the Lotos Club, 3 February 1906.

55 *Wilson's political career* "Boom for Dr. Wilson: Colonel Harvey Proposes Princeton's Head as Presidential Nominee," *NY Tribune*, 4 February 1906, p. 1; "Lotos Dinner for Wilson," *NY Sun*, 4 February 1906, p. 6; Julius Chambers, "Walks and Talks," *Brooklyn Eagle*, 5 February 1906, p. 24, and "Many New Attractions at Coney Island This Year" (erroneous headline), 1 April 1906, p. 13: "No recent event in the entire field of politics has awakened greater interest than the speech of Colonel George Harvey at a recent dinner at the Lotos Club, when the editor of *Harper's Weekly* suggested the name of President Woodrow Wilson of Princeton as the Democratic candidate for president in 1908. . . ." See also PWW 16:300, as cited in Cooper, *Woodrow Wilson*, p. 611n30.

55 *"The first was George Harvey"* Villard, *Fighting Years*, pp. 220–221. See also Kerney, *The Political Education of Woodrow Wilson*, p. 31.

55 *Assembly was scheduled to meet* "Urge Women's Votes at Albany Meeting," *NY Times*, 17 February 1910, p. 9.

55 *"advocates of the cause"* "Suffragists Invade Albany. Legislative Hearing on the Woman Suffrage Bill," *NY Sun*, 10 March 1910, p. 2.

56 *"are required to live"* "Women Argue on Suffrage. Albany Besieged by Suffragists and Anti-Suffragists," *NY Times*, 10 March 1910, p. 2.

56 *briefly looked in* "Suffragists Invade Albany. Legislative Hearing on the Woman Suffrage Bill," *NY Sun*, 10 March 1910, p. 2.

56 *produce from the electorate* "Memorial. Of the Woman Suffrage Legislative Committee of New York State to the Judiciary Committees of Senate and Assembly," *Progress*, March 1910, Issue 3, p. 2.

56    *"hope of its recovery"*   "Women Hold Albany. Suffragists and Anti at Hearing. Bill Advocated by Former Said to Have Suffered Most at Capital," *NY Tribune*, 10 March 1910, p. 9.

56    *"The Woman's Portion"*   Franklin H. Wentworth, "The Woman's Portion," an address delivered in Carnegie Hall, Sunday, 27 February 1910, under the auspices of the Women of the Socialist Party.

56    *"she is learning to cook"*   Frederic Arnold Kummer, "Votes for Women," *Smart Set*, Vol. 30, No. 3, March 1910, pp. 46–62.

57    *"equal rights for women"*   "Women Want Equal Rights: Enthusiastic Meeting at the League Building in Flushing," *Brooklyn Daily Star*, 17 March 1910, p. 1. Clipping with Flushing dateline, Newspaper clippings, Max Eastman Collection I, Lilly Library, Indiana University.

57    *Trade Union League*   "Suffragists to Hear Taft. Other Distinguished Men Will Address National Association," *Washington Herald*, 21 March 1910, p. 3.

57    *twenty-five men*   "Women Hiss Taft; Angry at Speech," *Chicago Tribune*, 15 April 1910, p. 1.

57    *"welcoming you to Washington"*   "Suffragettes Hiss Taft, Their Guest," *NY Times*, 15 April 1910, p. 1.

58    *"as members of the electorate"*   "Suffragettes Hiss Taft, Their Guest," *NY Times*, 15 April 1910, p. 1.

58    Times' *front-page headline*   "Suffragettes Hiss Taft, Their Guest," *NY Times*, 15 April 1910, p. 1.

58    *the* Post's *front-page headline*   "Taft Is Hissed by Suffragists. Women Resent Lack of Full Approval by Honor Guest. Rebuke Prompt in Coming," *Washington Post*, 15 April 1910, p. 1.

58    *"successful self-government is impossible"*   "Suffragettes Hiss Taft, Their Guest," *NY Times*, 15 April 1910, p. 1.

58    *"the keenest possible regret"*   Harper, *History of Woman Suffrage*, Vol. VI, "National Convention of 1910," pp. 269–274. (It reads in part: "At one point in his brief address there was apparently a slight hissing in the back part of the room. The President paused; Dr. Shaw sprang to her feet exclaiming, 'Oh, my children!' and the audience, which was excited and amazed, instantly became quiet and listened respectfully to the rest of his speech, but as he left the room, after shaking hands with Dr. Shaw, a few remained seated. As this incident attracted nation-wide comment and much criticism, it seems advisable to publish the proceedings in full.")

58    *became quiet and respectful*   Harper, *History of Woman Suffrage*, Vol. VI, "National Convention of 1910," p. 285.

58    *"Woman and Democracy"*   "Max Eastman on Woman Suffrage," *Woman's Journal*, 30 April 1910, p. 72. The speech appears in full in the *Woman's Journal* and in part

in *Harper's* history of the movement. It was also quoted in the *Washington Herald* the following day.

59      *"polls against it"*   "Women Cowards, Says Dorothy Dix. Writer Tells Suffragists They Must Fight More," *Washington Herald*, 17 April 1910, p. 2.

59      *"most ardent suffragist"*   "Sidelights on Suffrage People and Happenings," *Washington Times*, 17 April 1910, p. 2.

59      *prepared for the westernmost campaign*   John Hyde Braly, *Memory Pictures: An Autobiography* (Los Angeles: The Neuner Company Press, 1912), pp. 223–237. See also, Rockwell D. Hunt, "Some California Pioneers I Have Known," *The Quarterly: Historical Society of Southern California*, Vol. 30, No. 4, December 1948, pp. 294–295.

59      *parades between 1910 and 1913*   Eastman had speaking engagements in May at Wellesley College and in Geneva, NY. See "Mr. Max Eastman on Woman Suffrage," *Wellesley College News*, 4 May 1910, p. 5, and *Geneva Daily Times*, 6 May 1910, p. 5; *Geneva Gazette*, 19 May 1910.

59      *Harper explained this at length*   "Women Meet, Ignoring Rain," *NY Sun*, 22 May 1910, p. 5. About the significance of the parades, see Jennifer L. Borda, "The Woman Suffrage Parades of 1910–1913," *Western Journal of Communication*, Winter 2002, pp. 32+.

59      *continuous heavy showers*   "Women Meet, Ignoring Rain," *NY Sun*, 22 May 1910, p. 5.

59      *"held in the United States"*   "Suffrage Parade Has Police Guard," *NY Times*, 22 May 1910, p. 11.

59      *flowed into Union Square*   "Women March for Votes," *NY Tribune*, 22 May, 1910, p. 3.

60      *"identified themselves with the movement"*   Ida Husted Harper, "Militant Suffrage Here," *NY Sun*, 12 June 1910, p. 8.

60      *"a political issue"*   Harper, "Militant Suffrage Here," *NY Sun*, 12 June 1910, p. 8.

60      *Robert H. Elder*   "Women Meet, Ignoring Rain," *NY Sun*, 22 May 1910, p. 5.

60      *"vote on this bill"*   Harper, "Militant Suffrage Here," *NY Sun*, 12 June 1910, p. 8.

60      *"rather silly joke"*   Paul Kennaday, "Where Women Vote," *Outlook*, May 21, 1910, pp. 117–122.

60      *"upon the right side"*   William E. Borah, "Why I Am for Woman Suffrage," *Delineator*, Vol. 76, No. 85, pp.142–147, as found in Edith M. Phelps, *Selected Articles on Woman Suffrage* (Minneapolis: H.W. Wilson Co., 1912), pp. 59–64.

60      *they published this headline*   "The Suffrage Cause Invades the Men's Clubs," *NY Times*, 25 May 1910, p. 6.

61     *other suffrage groups*   "The Woman Suffrage Movement," *The Chautauquan*, Vol. 59, No. 1, June 1910, pp. 69–83.

61     *under the byline of*   Mrs. Barclay Hazard, "New York State Association Opposed to Woman Suffrage," *The Chautauquan*, Vol. 59, No. 1, June 1910, pp. 84–89.

61     *the* New York Tribune *told its readers*   "To Convert Mere Man: Great Suffrage Demonstration Planned for October 29," *NY Tribune*, 10 September 1910, p. 5.

61     *responded positively*   "Suffragists Dig Hold for the Antis," *NY Times*, 8 October 1910, p. 11.

61     *following two days*   "Women at Saratoga, Too. Suffragists Will Be on Hand at Republican Convention," *NY Tribune*, 25 September 1910, p. 2.

61     *newest organized ally*   "With Eulogy by Dr Eliot. Funeral of Mrs. Howe This Afternoon," *Boston Globe*, 20 October 1910, p. 3.

61     *"world they live in"*   Suffrage Speeches Complete, Max Eastman Collection II, Box 20, Lilly Library, Indiana University. Eastman notes in handwriting after the introductory section of the speech devoted to Howe that the rest came from his repertoire of standard remarks.

61     *two days later*   "Mrs. Eastman Has Stroke," *Elmira Star-Gazette*, 21 October 1910, p. 15.

62     *forever lost*   Letter, Mother to Max, 1 October 1910, Max Eastman Collection I, Box 9, Lilly Library, Indiana University.

62     *"nothing to say about it"*   From the manuscript of Christoph Irmscher's biography of Max Eastman, citing a letter from Crystal Eastman to her brother, 11 February 1911.

62     *"home of the community"* "Beautiful Memorial Service Is Held for Mrs. Eastman," *Elmira Star-Gazette*, 31 October 1910, p. 2.

62     *the "Man Suffragette"*   "Man Suffragists to Speak: Bazaar Gives Way to Nordica Concert," *NY Tribune*, 11 October 1910, p. 9.

62     *"the melancholy Dane"*   "Women Hold Convention," *NY Tribune*, 29 October 1910, p. 7. Joseph E. Daily, the former justice of the Illinois Supreme Court, had also been announced as a speaker, although there is no known coverage to confirm this. He was, however, with Eastman in Irvington on October 13 for the fall campaign opening of the Hudson River Suffrage League. See also, "Man Suffragette to Speak. Bazaar Gives Way to Nordica Concert—Campaign Upstate," *NY Tribune*, 11 October 1910, p. 9.

62     *"without bias"*   Item, *Cayuga Herald*, 25 November 1910, p. 4, column 3.

62     *"granting women the vote"*   Item, *Cayuga Herald*, 25 November 1910, p. 4, column 3.

62     *"it's absurd"*   Jesse Lynch Williams, "A Common Sense View of Woman Suffrage," reproduced as a NAWSA pamphlet reprint of his article in *Ladies' World*, December

1910. Lynch would go on to win the first Pulitzer Prize in drama in 1918 for his play, *Why Marry: A Comedy in Three Acts*, a work he dedicated to Harriet and James Lees Laidlaw. Jesse Lynch Williams, *Why Marry: A Comedy in Three Acts* (New York: Charles Scribner's Sons, 1914, 1918), new and revised edition published April 1918, reprinted September 1918 and February 1919. It was produced at the Astor Theater, 25 December 1917, directed by Roi Cooper Megrue.

62      *"men antis"*  "Men Suffragists Dine Mrs. Snowden, English Woman Leader Tells the Guests She Finds America Sympathetic to the Cause," *NY Times*, 14 December 1910, p. 6. Additional reports appeared on 14 December 1910 in the *NY Herald*, p. 7, and *Brooklyn Eagle*, p. 21. Among those singled out in the headlines were John Dewey and Dr. Simon Flexner, the physician and scientist. Other members of the host committee included Eastman, Villard, the editor Charles H. Strong, and Professor Vladimir Simkhovitch of Columbia.

64      *"and Wyoming"*  Richard Barry, "What Women Have Actually Done Where They Vote: A Personal Investigation into the Laws, Records and Results of the Four Equal-Suffrage States of America: Colorado, Idaho, Utah, and Wyoming," *Ladies' Home Journal*, November 1910, pp. 15–16; 68–19, and *Lady's Realm*, Vol. 29, Issue 171, January 1911, pp. 271–278.

64      *"in Mr. Barry's article"*  Barry, "What Women Have Actually Done Where They Vote," *Ladies' Home Journal*, November 1910, pp. 15–16, 68–19, and *Lady's Realm*, Vol. 29, Issue 171, January 1911, pp. 271–278.

64      *in favor of women voters*  Barry, "What Women Have Actually Done Where They Vote," *Ladies' Home Journal*, November 1910, pp. 15–16, 68–19, and *Lady's Realm*, Vol. 29, Issue 171, January 1911, pp. 271–278.

64      *"similar communities elsewhere"*  Barry, "What Women Have Actually Done Where They Vote," *Ladies' Home Journal*, November 1910, pp. 15–16; 68–19, and *Lady's Realm*, Vol. 29, Issue 171, January 1911, pp. 271–278.

64      *grown in the same period*  Ethel C. Macomber, "News of Fundamental Democratic and Economic Advance. Woman's Progress," *Twentieth Century*, Vol. 3, Issue 15, December 1910, pp. 273–275. The antisuffragists found the piece useful enough to turn it into a pamphlet and claim it as their own. See, Pamphlet, Richard Barry, "The Truth Concerning Four Woman-Suffrage States" (New York: National League for the Civic Education of Women, 1910).

64      *"are ignored"*  "The Truth versus Richard Barry," National American Woman Suffrage Association, undated.

65      *"Barry-Bok type"*  Item, *Literary Digest*, 26 November 1910, p. 971.

65      *"publisher of the same"*  Item, *Literary Digest*, 26 November 1910, p. 971.

65      *findings were hard science*  "Bad Report on Cities Where Women Vote. Investigator Found Flaunting Vice in Denver and Salt Lake and Bribery at the Polls," *NY Times*, 30 October 1910, p. 62.

65    *the featured speaker*  "Suffragists Storm Meeting of Antis; Demonstration Inside and Outside of Lyceum Theater Where Richard Barry Speaks," *NY Times*, 10 January 1911, p. 22.

65    *as soon as it appeared*  See Carrie Chapman Catt, "Mrs. Catt Answers Barry," *NY Times*, 3 November 1910, p. 3; Richard Barry, "Mr. Barry Answers Mrs. Catt," *NY Times*, 5 November 1910, p. 6; Unidentified authority, "A Hunch of a Cause," *NY Times*, 6 November 1910, p. 12; Alice Stone Blackwell, "Not Without Protest," *NY Times*, 14 November 1910, p. 8; "Mr. Barry and the Suffragists," *NY Times*, 22 November 1910, p. 10; "Suffragists Storm Meeting of Antis," *NY Times*, 10 January 1911, p. 22; "Dr. Aked Challenges Our Sense of Humor," *NY Times*, 11 January 1910, p. 5; Annie Nathan Meyer, "Mr. Barry's Statements Have Been Taken Up but Not Answered," *NY Times*, 19 January 1910, p. 8; Caroline I. Reilly, "The Woman Suffragist's Side of an Extended Debate," *NY Times*, 21 January 1911, p. 12; Alice Stone Blackwell, "Divorce and Suffrage," *NY Times*, 4 February 1911, p. 12.

65    *aide de camp, Robert Cameron Beadle*  Ware, *George Foster Peabody*, p. 148. The sole reference to Beadle in this biography identifies him in 1907 as Beadle's secretary. In the *Trend*, November 1913, he is described as secretary and treasurer of the American Stoker Company and general manager of the U.S. Stoker Corporation, both of which had Peabody connections.

65    *fifty different lines*  Obituary, "James L. Laidlaw, Dead of Pneumonia," *NY Times*, 10 May 1932, p. 21.

66    *senior thesis at Harvard*  Interview transcript, John Gabe, the Theodore Roosevelt Association, PBS, "The American Experience: The Story of Theodore Roosevelt." Accessed 1 July 2015, http://pbs.org/wgbh/americanexperience/features/interview/tr-gable.

66    *"would certainly do good"*  Letter, Theodore Roosevelt to Lillie Devereux Blake, 12 December 1898. Woman Suffrage Correspondence, 002619_001_0004. Schlesinger Library, Radcliffe Institute, Harvard University.

66    *"a very important matter"*  "He Angers Women. President Lukewarm in Support of Suffragists," *Washington Post*, 5 December 1908, p. 1.

66    *His wide-ranging remarks*  "Hot Campaign by T.R. Plans for a Whirlwind Dash into Every County," *Washington Post*, 30 September 1910, p. 3.

66    *gave Eastman grist for one his own major addresses*  Both the Men's League and NAWSA would reprint Eastman's article as a pamphlet under their imprints. Max Eastman, "Is Woman Suffrage Important?" *North American Review*, Vol. 193, No. 662, January 1911, pp. 60–71. JStor stable URL: http://jstor.org/stable/25106847. The article misdates the Poughkeepsie speech of Roosevelt. It took place on September 30, 1910, not September 29, 1910, when the *Washington Post* article about it appears. See also, Pamphlets, Max Eastman, "Is Woman Suffrage Important?" Men's League for Woman Suffrage, undated. Sophia Smith Collection, Women's

History Archive at Smith College. And the same pamphlet, also undated, by the National Woman Suffrage Publishing Company, National Woman's Party Papers, Pamphlets, 1850–1971. Schlesinger Library, Radcliffe Institute, Harvard University.

66    *"attending to their duties"*   "Hot Campaign by T.R. Plans for a Whirlwind Dash into Every County," *Washington Post*, 30 September 1910, p. 3.

67    *in politics or business*   Max Eastman, "Is Woman Suffrage Important?" *North American Review*, Vol. 193, No. 662, January 1911, pp. 60–71. The speech also appeared as a pamphlet published by the Men's League. Sophia Smith Collection, Women's History Archive at Smith College. And the same pamphlet by NAWSA via the National Woman Suffrage Publishing Company. National Woman's Party Papers, Pamphlets, 1850–1971, No. 53, undated. Schlesinger Library, Radcliffe Institute, Harvard University. Also JStor stable URL for the *North American Review* article: http://jstor.org/stable/25106847.

## CHAPTER 4

69    *"question before the public"*   "Women Suffragists Ready for Albany Demonstration," *Elmira Star-Gazette*, 18 February 1911, p. 1.

69    *"suffrage for women"*   "Women Heard at Albany," *NY Tribune*, 23 February 1911, p. 3 (continues from p. 1).

69    *Charles S. Thomas*   "A Word from Colorado" and "Lindsey Aids Suffragists," *NY Tribune*, 24 February 1911, p. 14.

69    *outside the home*   "Women Heard at Albany," *NY Tribune*, 23 February 1911, p. 3 (continues from p. 1).

70    *"whose parents are in trade"*   "Big Bazaar for Suffrage," *NY Sun*, 15 February 1911, p. 7.

70    *give them the vote*   "Big Bazaar for Suffrage," *NY Sun*, 15 February 1911, p. 7.

71    *press against it*   "Women Suffragists Ready for Albany Demonstration," *Elmira Star-Gazette*, 18 February 1911, p. 1.

71    *"governing Colorado"*   "Lindsey Women's Hero," *NY Tribune*, 25 February 1911, p. 7.

71    *before she was born*   "Elmiran Speaks at Albany Meeting," *Elmira Star-Gazette* (citing the *Albany Argus*), 28 February 1911, p. 9.

71    *declined to confirm or deny*   "Forbid Suffrage Rally in Apartment. But Owners Get No Satisfaction from Prof. Dewey of Columbia or Mrs. Dewey," *NY Times*, 25 February 1911, p. 2.

71    *"in a queer way"*   "Negro Suffrage Meeting," *The Anti-Suffragist*, Issue 3, March 1911, p. 4.

72    *"both big and vital"*   PWW 22:289–290, Clara Schlee Laddey and Mary Loring Colvin to Woodrow Wilson, 2 January 1911.

72      *"detaining me long"*    PWW 22:354–356, Interview, Virginia Tyler Hudson, "Wilson to Attempt to Kill Lobby," *NY Globe and Commercial Advertiser*, 17 January 1911.

72      *political lieutenant for the job*    See Villard to Wilson, PWW 22:83, 22, November 1910; PWW 22:101–102, 28 November 1910; PWW 22:127, 3 December 1910; PWW 22:287, 31 December 1910; Wilson to Villard, explaining why not, PWW 22:289, 2 January 1911.

72      *"on this side of the river"*    PWW 22:308, Wilson to Villard, 6 January 1911.

73      *only grew*    George Creel, *Rebel at Large: Recollections of Fifty Crowded Years* (New York: G.P. Putnam's Sons, 1947), p. 101. For a fuller treatment, see also, Stephen L. Vaughn, *Holding Fast the Inner Lines: Democracy, Nationalism, and the Committee on Public Information* (Chapel Hill: University of North Carolina Press, 1980), pp. 16–19.

73      *Denver's chief of police*    George Creel and Judge Ben B. Lindsey, "Measuring Up Equal Suffrage," *Delineator*, Issue 77, February 1911, pp. 85–86.

73      *Barry's points*    Letter to the editor, Annie Nathan Meyer to the *NY Times*, 19 January 1911, p. 8.

73      *"take it seriously"*    Letter to the editor, Caroline I. Reilly to the *NY Times*, 21 January 1911, p. 12.

73      *enthusiasm for suffrage*    Charles Larsen, *The Good Fight: The Life and Times of Ben B. Lindsey* (Chicago: Quadrangle Books, 1972), pp. 94–95. Although Lindsey's biographer devoted only two pages to the topic of suffrage, he did say that in the judge's heart, the cause was second only to issues of child welfare, for which work Lindsey is better remembered. By letter, Lindsey endorsed suffrage frequently and traveled east several times in 1910 and 1911 to speak on its behalf.

73      *"a personal report"*    Creel, *Rebel at Large*, pp. 145–147.

73      *"industrial victories"*    Clipping (newspaper unid.) Mary Gray Peck, "Contented Suffragists: Glowing Review of the Stockholm Congress." Miller NAWSA Suffrage Scrapbooks, 1897–1911; Scrapbook 9, pp. 93–94, June 12–17, 1911; Library of Congress, Rare Book and Special Collections Division.

74      *"a laughing matter"*    Clipping (newspaper unid.) Peck, "Contented Suffragists: Glowing Review of the Stockholm Congress." Miller NAWSA Suffrage Scrapbooks, 1897–1911; Scrapbook 9, pp. 93–94, June 12–17, 1911; Library of Congress, Rare Book and Special Collections Division.

74      *"fraternal delegates"*    "American Delegates to Stockholm Alliance," *Labor World*, 8 April 1911, p. 1.

74      *Beckman as president*    This international league photo did not run in the *NY Times* until July. Photo, "First International Men's League for Woman Suffrage," *NY Times*, 9 July 1911, p. 15.

74    *Hotel Astor, in April*   William F. McCombs, the Democratic National Committee chairman 1912–1916, whose support had helped Wilson get elected governor of New Jersey in 1910, must have been unaware of Wilson's familiarity with Wise. In August of 1911, he wrote the governor to say that Wise, "a very prominent Hebrew. He is for you," was planning to write an article about Wilson. PWW 23:259–260, McCombs to Wilson, 8 August 1911.

74    *"direction of right"*   PWW 22:585–586, Woodrow Wilson's address at the Astor Hotel for the fourth anniversary of the Free Synagogue, 24 April 1911. Reprinted *Newark Evening News*, 25 April 1911. See also, "Call Gov. Wilson Man with a Future," *NY Times*, 25 April 1911, p. 3; "Readjustment Going On: Politics and Religion Feel It, Says Governor Wilson," *NY Tribune*, 25 April 1911, p. 7.

75    *along with three other men*   "A Symposium on Woman Suffrage by George Foster Peabody, Prof. Vida D. Scudder, Alexander Harvey, Robert Herrick, Annie Nathan Meyer, Prof. John Dewey, Edith Wynne Matthison, Elbert Hubbard, Hamilton Holt, Charlotte Perkins Gilman, Theodore Schroeder, Upton Sinclair," *The International*, Vol. 3, No. 6, May 1911, pp. 93–94. See also, Arthur Levy, "The Poor Pretty Anti-Suffrage Arguments," *The International*, Vol. 3, No. 6, May 1911 p. 83. The other three were: Frederick A. Cook, Robert Herrick, and Alexander Harvey.

76    *"—not till then"*   "A Symposium on Woman Suffrage." *The International*, Vol. 3, No. 6, May 1911, pp. 93–94, reprinted in Jo Ann Boydston, ed., *John Dewey: The Middle Works, 1899–1924*, Vol. 6, 1910–1911 (Carbondale: Southern Illinois University Press), pp. 153–154. See also Robert B. Westbrook, *John Dewey and Democracy* (Ithaca: Cornell University Press, 1991), p. 167, in which Dewey's views are summarized, noting how little he actually wrote on the woman question, although his feminist views come through in his writing on co-education and teachers.

76    *then editor of* Collier's Weekly   "Suffrage News," *Brooklyn Daily Eagle*, 29 April 1911, p. 24.

76    *to take part in government*   "Brisbane Guest: Journalism His Subject at City Club," *Boston Globe*, 16 January 1909, p. 9.

76    *not even to Eastman's father*   From chapter 4 of Christoph Irmscher's manuscript for a forthcoming biography of Max Eastman. So Eastman did not march with the first League parade delegation.

76    *hesitant about joining them*   "Men for Suffrage Parade: Speakers at Men's League Meeting Tell Why Women Should Get the Vote," *NY Times*, 3 May 1911, p. 2. Also, "Equal Suffrage Men," *NY Sun*, 3 May 1911, p. 3.

77    *Under that headline*   "Big Crowds Cheer Suffragist Parade . . . Men Also in Line of March," *NY Tribune*, 7 May 1911, p. 1.

77    *the men who participated*   "Men for Suffrage Parade," *NY Times*, 3 May 1911, p. 2.

77    *put the number at one hundred*  Booklet, "Men's League for Woman Suffrage of the State of New York 1912" (New York: Men's League for Woman Suffrage), Library of Congress, Rare Books, HQ1236.Z9, Box 1, No. 30, Copy 1, RBSCD, p. 4. ("It mustered one hundred men in the Woman Suffrage parade in New York City last spring.")

77    *"hide a deep scowl"*  "Big Crowds Cheer Suffragist Parade . . . Men Also in Line of March," *NY Tribune*, 7 May 1911, p. 1.

77    *"was the kindest"*  "Big Crowds Cheer Suffragist Parade . . . Men Also in Line of March," *NY Tribune*, 7 May 1911, p. 1.

78    *from the sidelines*  "New York Women in Huge Parade Demand Ballot," *Chicago Tribune*, 7 May 1911, p. 1.

78    *"hurrahs rent the air"*  "Parade Makes Converts," *NY Tribune*, 7 May 1911 p. 6.

78    *"were the men"*  Bertha Damaris Knobe, "The March of 3,000 Women," *Harper's Weekly*, 20 May 1911, pp. 3, 8.

78    *"lined the sidewalks"*  Stanton et al., *History of Woman Suffrage*, Vol. I, p. 485.

78    *"questioned our masculinity"*  Stephen S. Wise, in his memoir, *Challenging Years*, p. 110, says: "Our suffragettes were not always treated with chivalry in the national capital any more than on the streets of New York and men who supported them were subject to what now sound like rather amusing jibs that questioned our masculinity." See also, diary entry, Stephen S. Wise, 4 May 1912, K-0002-002-002, Folder 104A, Stephen S. Wise Papers, Special Collections, Estelle and Melvin Gelman Library, George Washington University. Wise describes his experience on the second suffrage parade line in 1912, when the men were greeted by jeering from "male and female rowdies but with respect from the intelligent class of people."

78    *"council that he led"*  Harriet Burton Laidlaw, *James Lees Laidlaw, 1868–1932*, privately printed 1932, pp. 20–21.

80    *"deserted the ranks"*  Middleton, *These Things Are Mine*, p. 125.

80    *"a moment's cessation"*  Villard, *Fighting Years*, p. 199.

80    *"over again tomorrow"*  Villard, *Fighting Years*, p. 199.

80    *seventeen against*  Stanton et al., *History of Woman Suffrage*, Vol. I, p. 458.

80    *The poet Witter Bynner*  In the 1912 Men's League booklet, Bynner is listed as a member with a Gramercy Park address in the Twenty-Fifth Assembly District.

81    *"frank statement of my views"*  PWW 23:160, Wilson to Witter Bynner, 20 June 1911.

81    *Brooklyn's Kings County chapter*  "Men's Equal Suffrage League Opens Campaign," *Santa Ana Register*, 13 September 1911, p. 1. Also, "Suffragists Don't Agree on a Parade," *NY Times*, 27 September 1911, p. 13.

81    *campaign junctures*  W.E.B. Du Bois, "Forward Backward," *The Crisis*, Vol. 2, No. 6, October 1911, pp. 243–244. See also, "Heckling the Hecklers," *The Crisis*, Vol. 3, No. 5, March 1912, pp. 195–196 (in which the white suffragist Martha Gruening,

director of the Frederick Douglass Center, cites Celia Park Woolsey in responding to Shaw's statement); "Suffering the Suffragettes," *The Crisis*, Vol. 4, No. 2, June 1912, pp. 76–77; "Ohio," *The Crisis*, Vol. 4, No. 4, pp. 81–82; "Votes for Women," *The Crisis*, Vol. 4, No. 5, September 1912, p. 234; "A Suffrage Symposium," *The Crisis*, Vol. 4, No. 5, September 1912, pp. 240–247; "Hail Columbia!" *The Crisis*, Vol. 5, No. 6, April 1913, pp. 289–290; "Woman's Suffrage, *The Crisis*, Vol. 6, No. 1, May 1913, p. 29; "Votes for Women," *The Crisis*, Vol. 8, No. 4, August 1914, pp. 179–180; "Suffrage and Women," *The Crisis*, Vol. 9, No. 4, February 1915, p. 182; "Woman Suffrage," *The Crisis*, Vol. 9, No. 6, April 1915, p. 285; "Votes for Women," *The Crisis*, Vol. 10, No. 4, August 1915, p. 177; "Votes for Women: A Symposium by Leading Thinkers of Colored America," *The Crisis*, Vol. 10, No. 4, August 1915, pp. 178–192; "Woman Suffrage," *The Crisis*, Vol. 11, No. 1, November 1915, pp. 29–30; "Votes for Women," *The Crisis*, Vol. 15, No. 1, November 1917, p. 8; "Woman Suffrage," *The Crisis*, Vol. 19, No. 5, March 1920, p. 234. As cited in Garth E. Pauly, "W.E.B. Du Bois on Woman Suffrage: A Critical Analysis of his Crisis Writings," *Journal of Black Studies*, Vol. 3, No. 3, January 2000, pp. 383–410.

81    *rejoiced in the victory*    "Women Celebrate California Victory," *NY Times*, 14 October 1911, p. 13.

81    *greatest need of public schools*    "Giving Lectures First of Series," *Elmira Star-Gazette*, 23 November 1911, p. 14.

82    *"grow upon it"*    "Gives First of the Series of Lectures in the Schools," *Elmira Star-Gazette*, 23 November 1911, p. 14.

82    *"willing to work"*    "Gives First of the Series of Lectures in the Schools," *Elmira Star-Gazette*, 24 November 1911, p. 14.

82    *"best talks ever given us"*    Letter, Fredrick V. Burns, Syracuse Chamber of Commerce, to Max, 7 December 1911. Mas Eastman Collection I, Box I. Lilly Library, Indiana University.

82    *"a badge of slavery"*    "Max Eastman and Wife State Views about Marriage. Go through Ceremony but Does Not Believe in It," *Elmira Star-Gazette*, 1 December 1911, p. 9, and "Is Still a 'Miss' Wife of Prof. Max Eastman Scorns the Prefix 'Mrs.' Husband Upholds Views," *Syracuse Herald*, 2 December 1911, p. 5.

82    *"topic of public comment"*    "The Growler," *Elmira Star-Gazette*, 23 December 1911, p. 8.

82    *"Is Woman a Parasite?"*    Letter, Anna Howard Shaw to Rabbi Stephen S. Wise, 5 December 1911. Stephen S. Wise collection, Robert D. Farber University Archives & Special Collections, Brandeis University.

82    *"equally true of men"*    Letter, Anna Howard Shaw to Rabbi Stephen S. Wise, 5 December 1911. Stephen S. Wise collection, Robert D. Farber University Archives & Special Collections, Brandeis University.

82    *"orators of the day"*    "Villard Criticizes Harvard. Evening Post Editor Calls Barring Mrs. Pankhurst a Blunder," *NY Times*, 4 December 1911, p. 24.

82    *"as a closed shop"*   "Harvard Men Hear Mrs. Pankhurst," *Woman's Journal,* Vol. 42, No. 47, 9 December 1911.

82    *"October 19 to 23"*   "Women Gather and Plan for Equal Suffrage," *Christian Science Monitor,* 19 October 1911, p. 4.

83    *"playing with fire"*   Unsigned Editorial, "The Woman's Suffrage Congress," *Louisville Courier Journal,* 20 October 1911, p. 4.

83    *Peabody wrote a letter*   "Letters from the People," *Athens Banner,* 24 November 1911, p. 4.

83    *"her political activities"*   "Peabody Protests," *Woman's Journal,* 23 December 1911, Issue 42, pp. 2–3.

83    *"reform them alone"*   "Peabody Protests," *Woman's Journal,* 23 December 1911, Issue 42, pp. 2–3.

83    *"they feel of a just cause"*   "Distinguished Georgian Defends Suffrage," *Atlanta Constitution,* 3 December 1911, p. E2.

83    *"with both voice and pen"*   "Peabody Protests," *Woman's Journal,* 23 December 1911, p. 402.

83    *"lack of intellect"*   "Women Always Right; Also 'Gates of Hell,'" *NY Tribune,* 23 October 1911, p. 1.

CHAPTER 5

85    *home or business addresses*   "Men's League for Woman Suffrage of the State of New York 1912" (New York: Men's League for Woman Suffrage), Library of Congress, Rare Books, HQ1236.Z9, Box 1, No. 30, Copy 1, RBSCD. It lists the four "associate members" with New Jersey or Massachusetts addresses separately.

85    *The booklet also enumerates* "Men's League for Woman Suffrage of the State of New York 1912," New York: Men's League for Woman Suffrage. (Library of Congress, Rare Books, HQ1236.Z9, Box 1, No. 30, Copy 1, RBSCD.) Four "associate members" with New Jersey or Massachusetts addresses are listed separately.

85    *"woman to-day"*   Pamphlet, Charles Beard, "The Common Man and the Franchise" (New York: NAWSA, 1912), reprinted courtesy of the Men's League for Woman Suffrage and again reprinted in Kimmel and Mosmiller, *Against the Tide,* pp. 263–264. Also Gale Nineteenth Century Collections Online: http://tinyurl.galegroup.com/tinyurl/oyVU9

85    *And New York's immigration commissioner*   Frederic C. Howe, "Why I Want Woman Suffrage," *Colliers,* Vol. 48, Issue 18, March 16, 1912, pp. 15, 31. Later reprinted by NAWSA as a pamphlet titled, "What the Ballot Will Do for Women and for Men."

89    *"abdicate economic power"*   Frederic C. Howe, *The Confessions of a Reformer* (New York: Charles Scribner's Sons, 1925), pp. 232–235.

89    *"pertain to the common good"*   Pamphlet, Judge Ben B. Lindsey, "If I Were a Woman," reprinted from *The Housekeeper,* undated (1912 is noted in the text).

89 *"silly contention"* Edwin D. Mead, "Suffrage and Soldiering," *Woman's Journal*, Issue 8, 24 February 1912, p. 58.

89 *New York State Police* Villard notes in *Fighting Years* (pp. 242–243) that the historian and researcher Katherine Mayo, who did the legwork for his John Brown book, initiated the movement for a state police force in New York following a rash of ninety-one highway rapes. The official history of the state police cites the brutal murder in rural Westchester County of a construction foreman, Sam Howell. Mayo was a friend of Howell's employer, Moyca Newell. (See http://troopers.ny.gov/ Introduction/History/1917%2D1929/, accessed 13 June 2016.)

89 *published in 1910* Villard's John Brown book appeared several months after Du Bois's 1910 biography of Brown, exacerbating tension between the two men, although they continued to work together through the NAACP. There was an unsigned but savage review of Du Bois's work in Villard's the *Nation* that Du Bois knew to be Villard's own handiwork, and the editor's refusal to publish Du Bois's letter in response. Still their relationship developed into a "grudging mutual respect." See David Levering Lewis, *W.E.B. Du Bois: Biography of a Race*, 1868–1919, pp. 369–370.

90 *journalistic emergencies* Villard, *Fighting Years*, pp. 242–243.

90 *19 percent for the men* See John Henderson, http://www.icyousee.org/titanic.html, accessed 13 June 2016, Ithaca College. See also, Steven Biel, *Down with the Old Canoe: A Cultural History of the Titanic Disaster* (New York: Norton, 2012).

90 *"sets them apart"* See Emma Goldman, "Suffrage Dealt Blow by Women of Titanic: Emma Goldman Inquires to Know If Equality Is Demanded Only at Ballot Box— Human Nature Came into Own in Men," *Denver Post*, 21 April 1912; Alice Stone Blackwell, "The Lesson of the Titanic," *Woman's Journal*, 27 April 1912, p. 132; Inez Milholland, quoted in "Women First Barbarous," *NY Tribune*, 19 April 1912, p. 16; Anna Howard Shaw, quoted in "St. Louis Suffragists, Like Dr. Shaw, Decry the Women First Rule on the Sea," *St. Louis Post-Dispatch*, 24 April 1912, p. 10.

90 *"fighting the same battle"* W.E.B. Du Bois, "Heckling the Hecklers," *The Crisis*, Vol. 3, No. 5, March 1912, pp. 195–196.

91 *"application for membership"* W.E.B. Du Bois, "Suffering Suffragettes," *The Crisis*, Vol. 4, No. 2, June 1912, pp. 76–77.

91 *"defeat us every time"* Du Bois, "Suffering Suffragettes," *The Crisis*, Vol. 4, No. 2, June 1912, pp. 76–77.

91 *"high in counsel"* W.E.B. Du Bois, "Ohio," *The Crisis*, Vol. 4, No. 4, August 1912, pp. 181–182.

91 *"mean votes for black women"* "Woman Suffrage Number," W.E.B. Du Bois, *The Crisis*, Vol. 4, No. 5, September 1912, pp. 215, 240–247.

91 *under a facetious headline* Edward J. Ward, "Women Should Mind Their Own Business," *The Independent*, Vol. 70, No. 3264, June 22, 1911, pp. 1370–1371. Also, reprinted in Kimmel and Mosmiller, *Against the Tide*, pp. 262–263.

92    *"they should not do"*    Edward J. Ward, "Women Should Mind Their Own Business," *The Independent*, Vol. 70, No. 3264, June 22, 1911, pp. 1370–1371. Also, reprinted in Kimmel and Mosmiller, *Against the Tide*, pp. 262–263.

92    *"dip my pen"*    Middleton, *These Things Are Mine*, p. 126.

92    *Robert "Fighting Bob" La Follette*    George Middleton, "Votes for Woman Struggle Educates," *St. John's (New Brunswick) Globe*, 17 July 1912.

92    *presidential aspirations*    Kerney, *The Political Education of Woodrow Wilson*, p. 131.

92    *"reassurance and strength"*    PWW 23:561, Villard to Wilson, 1 December 1911, and PWW 23:589, Wilson to Villard, 9 December 1911.

92    *not fettered to big business*    "Wilson Is Minus the Big Fetters," *Galveston Daily News*, 12 January 1912, p. 1.

92    *Wilson ballyhoo*    See PWW 24:59, Villard to Wilson, 22 January 1912; PWW 24:72–74, 25–26, January 1912; "The Long and Short of the Wilson-Col. Harvey Exchange, Prompted by Watterson," *NY Evening Post*, 30 January 1912. See also the lengthiest rendering of the Wilson-Harvey imbroglio in Johnson, *George Harvey*, pp. 180–200.

92    *She reminded him about the suffrage sash*    Wilson's visit to the fair was September 3, 1911, *NY Sun*, 3 September 1911, p. 5; *NY Tribune*, 3 September 1911, p. 5.

93    *"will you openly do so"*    PWW 24:100, Edith Whitmore to Wilson, 31 January 1912, *NY Sun*, 10 February 1912, p. 4.

93    *"a just conclusion"*    PWW 24:140, Wilson to Edith M. Whitmore, 8 February 1912; also "Wilson's Mind Not Made Up on Suffrage," *NY Sun*, 10 February 1912, p. 4. See also PWW 24:179–181, "Report of After Dinner Remarks at Sussex Society at Hotel Astor," 19 February 1912. The speaker encouraged those present to corner the governor on the suffrage question and see if they could keep him from evading the question "with the same diplomatic skill" he had shown in the recent exchange chronicled in the press. There was no effort to do so. (Reprinted from *Newark Evening News*, 19 February 1912.) His response that day was almost identical to what he told the chair of Staten Island's suffrage party when she pressed to know if he would support suffrage if elected. At that point he said he found it a very difficult question that he was debating with himself. He told her, "I am honestly trying to work my way toward a just conclusion."

93    *"civilization itself will perish"*    Theodore Roosevelt, "Women's Rights; and the Duties of Both Men and Women," *Outlook*, 3 February 1912, pp. 262–266.

93    *"forced upon them"*    Theodore Roosevelt, "Women's Rights; and the Duties of Both Men and Women," *Outlook*, 3 February 1912, pp. 262–266.

93    *"I have ever seen"*    "Hits Roosevelt's Suffrage Views, Max Eastman Says Former President Is Much Like a Chameleon," unidentified newspaper article, dated 4 March 1912, Max Eastman Collection I, Box I, Lilly Library, Indiana University. The article notes Eastman's speech at the East End Baptist Church, 2 March 1912.

93     *"one step further"*   "Hits Roosevelt's Suffrage Views. Max Eastman Says Former President Is Much Like a Chameleon," unid. newspaper article dated March 4, 1912. Notes speech at the East End Baptist Church on Saturday, March 2, 1912.

94     *"interesting and illuminating"*   "Hits Roosevelt's Suffrage Views. Max Eastman Says Former President Is Much Like a Chameleon," unid. newspaper article dated March 4, 1912. Notes speech at the East End Baptist Church on Saturday, March 2, 1912.

94     *"as well as men"*   "Hits Roosevelt's Suffrage Views. Max Eastman Says Former President Is Much Like a Chameleon," unid. newspaper article dated March 4, 1912. Notes speech at the East End Baptist Church on Saturday, March 2, 1912. As for more activity in this period, prominent men led an elaborate three-county "trolley campaign" in Connecticut, which that state's female suffragists organized. Headliners included the journalist Lincoln Steffens and Louis D. Brandeis, the widely lauded litigator who would become an associate US Supreme Court justice under Wilson in 1916; Harvard and Vassar professors, along with many mainstays of the New York League, participated, including Beard and Eastman. See, for example, "Seeking Votes by Trolley in Connecticut," *NY Sun*, 18 February 1912, p. 5, and "Connecticut Suffragists. Women Made Trolley Campaign in Three Counties," *NY Evening Post*, 6 April 1912. In late March, the League sponsored its inaugural dinner at the Marseilles Hotel in Manhattan. Fifty men sat at tables in a sea of 350 women. Laidlaw presided, and both Eastman and Beard gave speeches considered good enough to become League pamphlets. See, "Reception and Dinner for Men's Suffrage League," *Brooklyn Eagle*, 10 March 1912, p. 37. Also, "Houn' Song for Suffragists. It Greets Mrs. C.P. Gilman at the Men's League Dinner," *NY Times*, 10 March 1912, p. 3. The pamphlets are titled "Values of the Vote" (Eastman) and "The Common Man and the Franchise" (Beard).

94     *"belittled everything we women have done"*   "Says Legislators Have Reviled Women," *NY Tribune*, 30 March 1912, p. 1.

94     *going on to the Senate*   "Suffrage Wins, Then Is Shelved," *NY Times*, 30 March 1912, p. 2.

94     *founding of the Men's League*   Eastman, "Early History," pp. 17–18.

94     *"no pay"*   Art Young, *Art Young: His Life and Times*, Young Press reprint, 2007, p. 275 (New York: Sheridan House, 1939): "I nominated Max Eastman, who had lately been ousted from a Columbia professorship for his outspoken opinions on the social conflict in classroom lectures. Max and I had met at a Jack London dinner, and we had discussed the possibility of building up the Masses into a magazine which would have the bold tone and high quality of Simplicissimus, Jugend, Steinlen's Gil Blas, and Assiette au Beurre, all of which were inspiring to the world's rising young artists. To show how Max could handle words and ideas, I read to the conference a magazine article he had written, describing with charming humor how he had organized the first Men's League for Woman's Suffrage

in New York. All the others acquiesced in the nomination, and we all signed a letter to Max, which said: "You are elected editor of the Masses, no pay."

95   *role in the League*   "Political Party to Aid Suffragettes. Men's League to Organize on Same Lines as Other Parties for Campaign. In All Election Districts. Nearly 500 Men Pledge Themselves to March in Parade Here on May 4," *NY American*, 14 April 1912.

95   *"head of the organization"*   "Political Party to Aid Suffragettes. Men's League to Organize on Same Lines as Other Parties for Campaign. In All Election Districts. Nearly 500 Men Pledge Themselves to March in Parade Here on May 4," *NY American*, 14 April 1912. This was on top of Laidlaw's position as head of the National Men's League, effectively combining their functions.

95   *"The Right of the Ballot"*   "News of Club and Social Events," *NY Tribune*, 28 April 1912, p. 5.

95   *upstate New York*   PWW 24:265, Woodrow Wilson to George Foster Peabody, 26 March 1912.

95   *on April 7*   "Wilson Delights Chamber's Guests . . . Prof. Eastman's Jollity," *Syracuse Herald*, 9 April 1912.

95   *as a suffragist*   Eastman, *Enjoyment of Living*, p. 386. See also, "Table of Honor at Chamber's Great Annual Banquet" and "A Memorable Banquet," *Syracuse Herald*, 9 April 1912, pp. 6, 8; "Few Control Politics Gov. Wilson Contends," *Syracuse Daily Journal*, 9 April 1912, p. 4; "Governor Wilson Favors Publicity of Funds Contributed for Pre-Convention Campaign," *Syracuse Post-Standard*, 9 April 1912, pp. 1, 6. Also, a reprint in PWW 24:307–308n4 adds the note about the extra 40 dollars Eastman earned by keeping Wilson laughing.

95   *his regular fee*   "Governor Wilson Favors Publicity of Funds Contributed for Pre-Convention Campaign," *Syracuse Post-Standard*, 9 April 1912, pp. 1, 6, also found as reprint in PWW 24:307–308n4.

95   *"personal elation"*   Eastman, *Enjoyment of Living*, p. 386.

96   *"stating his own"*   Eastman, *Enjoyment of Living*, p. 386.

96   *"smilingly friendly mood"*   Eastman, *Enjoyment of Living*, p. 386.

96   *"agitated for the vote"*   Kerney, *The Political Education of Woodrow Wilson*, pp. 32, 138–139, 471.

96   *"wittier than in their company"*   David Lawrence, *The True Story of Woodrow Wilson* (New York: George H. Doran, 1924), pp. 135–136.

96   *"worshiped, cared for and protected"*   Lawrence, *The True Story of Woodrow Wilson*, pp. 135–136.

96   *"masculinized women"*   Kerney, *The Political Education of Woodrow Wilson*, pp. 32, 138–139, 471.

96   *"disliked them"*   Lawrence, *The True Story of Woodrow Wilson*, pp. 135–136.

96     *"any conclusion"*   PWW 24:315–316, Reprint of a report in the *Pittsburgh Post*, 11 April 1912. The woman was Mary Ella Bakewell, secretary of the city's Free Kindergarten Association.

96     *In the* New York American   "Political Party to Aid Suffragettes. Men's League to Organize on Same Lines as Other Parties for Campaign. In All Election Districts. Nearly 500 Men Pledge Themselves to March in Parade Here on May 4," *NY American*, 14 April 1912.

97     *"why we have a parade"*   Harriot Stanton Blatch, "Why Suffragists Will Parade on Saturday," *NY Tribune*, 3 May 1912, p. 1.

97     *front-page notice*   "Host of Men to March in Big Suffrage Parade," *NY Tribune*, 3 May 1912, p. 1.

97     *"much less a petticoat"*   "Host of Men to March in Big Suffrage Parade," *NY Tribune*, 3 May 1912, p. 1.

97     *featured coverage*   "Men Will March," *NY Sun*, 3 May 1912, p. 3.

98     *"why shouldn't we"*   "Men Will March," *NY Sun*, 3 May 1912, p. 3.

98     *"parade for a principle"*   "Men Will March," *NY Sun*, 3 May 1912, p. 3.

98     *"they'll be marching"*   "Host of Men to March in Big Suffrage Parade," *NY Tribune*, 3 May 1912, p. 1. See also "20,000 Women, All Hats Alike, in Suffrage Parade; Mere Men in Line," *NY Evening World*, 4 May 1912, pp. 1–2.

98     *front-page headline*   "20,000 Women, All Hats Alike in Suffrage Parade," *NY Evening World*, 4 May 1912, pp. 1, 2.

98     *"except the clergy"*   Editorial, "The Heroic Men," *NY Times*, 3 May 1912.

99     *"unsympathetic multitude"*   Editorial, "The Heroic Men," *NY Times*, 3 May 1912.

99     *"endearing names"*   Editorial, "The Heroic Men," *NY Times*, 3 May 1912.

99     *"sympathy and admiration"*   Editorial, "The Heroic Men," *NY Times*, 3 May 1912.

100    *"unabashed in their convictions"*   "Suffrage Army Out on Parade: Perhaps 10,000 Women and Men Sympathizers March for the Cause," *NY Times*, 5 May 1912, p. 1. Among the dozens in formation were Villard, Laidlaw, Wise, Dewey, Eastman, Nathan, Holt, Le Gallienne, Professor Joel Elias Spingarn, Dr. Algernon Crapsey.

100    *"these estimates were much too large"*   "Suffrage Army Out on Parade: Perhaps 10,000 Women and Men Sympathizers March for the Cause," *NY Times*, 5 May 1912, p. 1.

100    *Waterproofing Company*   "Suffrage Army Out on Parade: Perhaps 10,000 Women and Men Sympathizers March for the Cause," *NY Times*, 5 May 1912, p. 1. Also "Host of Proud Men March for Women," *NY Tribune*, 5 May 1912, p. 3.

100    *on his behalf*   Theodore Roosevelt Center, Dickinson State University, Letter from TR to R.C. Beadle, 14 June 1912.

100    *"because I have two parents"*   "Host of Proud Men March for Women," *NY Tribune*, 5 May 1912, p. 3.

101     *"I learned by contrast"*    George Middleton, "Snap Shots," *La Follette's*, Vol. 4, No. 20, 18 May 1912, p. 6.

101     *police protection*    See "Still Criticise Police," *NY Tribune*, 7 May 1912; "Suffrage Inning Next," *NY Tribune*, 9 May 1912; "Suffragists Tell Waldo Their Woes," *NY Times*, 11 May 1912, p. 22; "Waldo Hears Mrs. Blatch Arraign the Department," *NY Telegraph*, 11 May 1912. None of the men were named in any article.

101     *"pit to gallery"*    "Big Carnegie Hall Rally Ends Parade," *NY Times*, 5 May 1912, p. 2.

101     *"oratorical fire"*    "Broadway Oratory at Night," *NY Times*, 5 May 1912.

101     *"I fail to see it"*    "Male Republic Archaic. Swinburne Hale Says Bi-Sexed Democracy Will Follow Men's Rule," *NY Times*, 19 May 1912, p. X5 (special thanks to Kat Thornton).

101     *"support to women"*    James Lees Laidlaw, "Men's Leagues—Why," *St. John's* (New Brunswick) *Globe*, 17 May 1912.

101     *throughout this period*    Item, unid. Schlesinger Library Woman Studies Collection, Women Suffrage Movement and New York City Suffrage Parade Newspaper Clippings. 00261-_166_0101_From_1_to_83. Circa 4 May 1912. Schlesinger Library, Radcliffe Institute, Harvard University. The New Hampshire Men's League reached one thousand members and both Connecticut and Oregon announced new chapters "all over the state" and planned a convention for July or August.

102     *"what they lack in political power"*    James Lees Laidlaw, "Men's Leagues—Why," *St. John's* (New Brunswick) *Globe*, 17 May 1912.

104     *"if she wanted to"*    "Feuds and Factions That Rend the Suffragettes," *NYC Press*, 2 June 1912.

104     *"was conducting it"*    "Feuds and Factions That Rend the Suffragettes," *NYC Press*, 2 June 1912.

104     *"read the enclosed treat"*    Letters, unid., undated, but estimated date of June 1912, friends to Max, Max Eastman Collection I, Box I, Lilly Library, Indiana University.

104     *"for the Youngsters"*    Letters, unid., undated, but estimated date of June 1912, friends to Max, Max Eastman Collection I, Box I, Lilly Library, Indiana University.

104     *city parade permit*    "Men Suffrage Parade. League Asks Permission to March Soon after Election," *NY Sun*, 28 June 1912.

105     *"from its official pamphlet"*    "A Socialist-Suffragist Parade," *NY Times*, 18 July 1912, p. 8.

105     *"get away from 'em anywhere"*    "Suffrage via Biograph," *NY Tribune*, 1 June 1912, p. 3. The *Tribune* attributed all three short films to Biograph but it appears to have been an Éclair Film Company production. See, with synopsis, "H.B. Francis Produces Fine Suffrage Picture for Éclair," *Motion Picture News*, Vol. 5, No. 21, 25 May 1912, p. 19.

105     *"great deal of pink coating"*    "Suffrage via Biograph," *NY Tribune*, 1 June 1912, p. 3.

105 *"'Votes for Women'"* "Mrs. Nathan Off on Suffrage Tour," *NY American*, 24 May 1912.

105 *"food propaganda"* "Humorous Side of Row That Is on in Chicago," *NY Evening World*, 14 June 1912, p. 2.

105 *Women's Clubs* "Persons in the News," *San Francisco Call*, 22 June 1912, p. 9.

106 *continued faith* Ware, *George Foster Peabody*, "Peabody and Wilson," pp. 161–173.

106 *New Jersey retreat* PWW 24:401–15, Wilson to Peabody, 15 May 1912; PWW 24:472, Peabody to Wilson, 12 June 1912; PWW 24:474, Wilson to Peabody, 13 June 1912; PWW 24:491, Wilson to George Foster Peabody, 21, 23 June, Wilson to Peabody, 21, 23 June, 1912.

106 *"their old estate"* Diary entry, Stephen S. Wise, 7 July 1912. See also Letters, Wise to George Foster Peabody, 8 July 1912; Peabody to Wise, 12 July 1912. Stephen S. Wise collection, Robert D. Farber University Archives & Special Collections, Brandeis University.

106 *"Wilson platform"* Letter, Peabody to Wise, 12 July 1912. Stephen S. Wise collection, Robert D. Farber University Archives & Special Collections, Brandeis University.

106 *"more than help"* Letter, Peabody to Wise, 12 July 1912. Stephen S. Wise collection, Robert D. Farber University Archives & Special Collections, Brandeis University.

106 *"term implies"* Letter, Wise to Peabody, 7 August 1912. Stephen S. Wise collection, Robert D. Farber University Archives & Special Collections, Brandeis University.

106 *"as a risk"* Letter, Peabody to Wise, 10 August 1912. Stephen S. Wise collection, Robert D. Farber University Archives & Special Collections, Brandeis University.

107 *"'coming of the Lord'"* "Roosevelt Named Shows Emotion," *NY Times*, 8 August 1912, pp. 1–2.

107 *"non-partisan attitude"* "Asks if Roosevelt Set Suffrage Trap," *NY Times*, 10 August 1912, p. 6.

107 *"doubled this Fall"* "Asks if Roosevelt Set Suffrage Trap," *NY Times*, 10 August 1912, p. 6.

107 *"all parties"* "Asks if Roosevelt Set Suffrage Trap," *NY Times*, 10 August 1912, p. 6.

108 *"no doubt it is true"* Diary entry, 14 August 1912; Letter, Villard to Susan Walker FitzGerald, 14 August 1912, Vol. 25–26, Oswald Garrison Villard Papers 1872–1949 (MS Am 1323). Houghton Library, Harvard University.

108 *Wilson replied* PWW 25:24–25, Villard diary entry, 14 August 1912 after meeting with Wilson at which they also discussed the situation in New York, the Navy, and the Negro.

108 *"voting citizen"* PWW 25:42, Woodrow Wilson to Eugene Noble Foss, 17 August 1912.

108   *"direct assistance of women"*   "Criticises Jane Addams," *NY Times*, 21 August 1912, p. 1.

109   *"to support the home"*   Theodore Roosevelt, "Mr. Roosevelt's Speech on Suffrage, Delivered at St. Johnsbury, Vermont, August 30, 1912." Accessed via 19th Century Collections, New York Public Library.

109   *across Long Island*   Stanton et al., *History of Woman Suffrage*, Vol. I, pp. 448–449.

109   *"colony attending"*   "Suffrage Rally Drew Crowd," *Brooklyn Daily Eagle*, 21 September 1912, p. 6.

109   *"money to hear and see"*   "None Braver Than These: Six Men Face Vaudeville Audience for Suffragettes," *NY Tribune*, 11 September 1912, p. 7. Other performers named were John S. Crosby, Arthur Levy, and A. Savage.

109   *The* Tribune*'s headline*   "None Braver Than These: Six Men Face Vaudeville Audience for Suffragettes," *NY Tribune*, 11 September 1912, p. 7.

109   *Peabody himself*   Telegrams, R.C. Beadle to Wise, 1 and 2 October 1912; Peabody to Wise, 2 October 1912. Stephen S. Wise collection, Robert D. Farber University Archives & Special Collections, Brandeis University.

110   *"the 'academic' sense"*   Ida Husted Harper, "Women Watching Syracuse," *NY Tribune*, 2 October 1912, p. 3.

110   *"take their place"*   Harper, "Women Watching Syracuse," *NY Tribune*, 2 October 1912, p. 3.

110   *ten long minutes*   "Wilson Heckled at Big Meeting in the Academy," *Brooklyn Eagle*, 20 October 1912, p. 1.

110   *"What is it, Madame"*   "Cheering Crowd Storms Wilson," *NY Times*, 20 October 1912, p. 4. See also "Wilson Heckled at Big Meeting in the Academy," *Brooklyn Eagle*, 20 October 1912, p. 1. PWW 25:435–440, esp. 438, "A Campaign Address at the Academy of Music in Brooklyn," 19 October 1912.

110   *"on this occasion"*   "Cheering Crowd Storms Wilson," *NY Times*, 20 October 1912, p. 4.

111   *friend and supporter*   PWW 25:449n1, Wilson to Norman Hapgood, 21 October 1912.

111   *"trifle for you"*   Diary entry, Stephen S. Wise, 28 October 1912. Stephen S. Wise collection, Robert D. Farber University Archives & Special Collections, Brandeis University.

111   *"matter of right"*   "An Appeal to Men," *Woman's Journal*, 26 October 1912, p. 341.

111   *the following June*   "Rich Program for the Men's League Conference in London," *Woman's Journal*, 26 October 1912, p. 343.

111   *US league*   Joseph O'Brien, "The Women's Congress," *Collier's*, Vol. 51, No. 20, 2 August 1913, pp. 7–8, 34.

112     *"movement of our times"*   Letter, Harriot Stanton Blatch to Wise, 7 November 1912. Stephen S. Wise collection, Robert D. Farber University Archives & Special Collections, Brandeis University.

112     *"political campaign"*   "Ten Suffrage States: Dr. Anna Shaw Jubilantly Predicts Fresh Conquests," *NY Times*, 7 November 1912, p. 10.

112     *federal Constitution*   "Ten Suffrage States: Dr. Anna Shaw Jubilantly Predicts Fresh Conquests," *NY Times*, 7 November 1912, p. 10.

112     *convention in Syracuse*   "Cause Mothered Sulzer," *NY Tribune*, 4 October 1912, p. 7.

112     *"by their paraders"*   "Great Victory for Suffrage Indicated," *NY Tribune*, 7 November 1912, p. 7.

112     *Grecian robes*   "Suffragettes in Chariots! Garbed in Grecian Robes," *NY American*, 19 October 1912.

113     *"long river of fire"*   "400,000 Cheer Suffrage March," *NY Times*, 10 November 1912, pp. 1, 8–9.

113     *"kept their peace"*   "20,000 Women in Suffrage Parade," *NY Sun*, 10 November 1912, p. 1.

113     *"told them noisily"*   "20,000 Women in Suffrage Parade," *NY Sun*, 10 November 1912, p. 1.

113     *pressing business*   "Suffragists to March To-Night 20,000 Strong in Torchlight Parade without Mr. Sulzer," *NY Herald*, 9 November 1912, and (noting Sulzer's participation) "Suffrage Will Own 'The Town' Tonight," *NY Sun*, 9 November 1912, p. 9. See also "Parade Not for Sulzer," *NY Tribune*, 9 November 1912, p. 6.

113     *"when it's for the cause"*   "Suffrage Will Own 'The Town' Tonight," *NY Sun*, 9 November 1912, p. 9.

113     *"women's organizations"*   "400,000 Cheer Suffrage March," *NY Times*, 10 November 1912, pp. 1, 8–9.

113     *"or a torch"*   "With the Men Marchers: Less Jeering from the Side Lines Than in Previous Parade," *NY Times*, 10 November 1912, p. 8.

114     *Laidlaw's wife, Harriet*   "Suffragettes in Chariots! Garbed in Grecian Robes," *NY American*, 19 October 1912.

114     *"a blessing to us"*   Theodora Bean, "The Greatest Woman in Suffrage and the Greatest Story Ever Written About Her," *NY Morning Telegraph*, 29 December 1912, Section Two, p. 1.

115     *"Mrs. Catt's feet"*   "Money Welcomes Mrs. Carrie Chapman Catt," *NY Tribune*, 20 November 1912, p. 9.

115     *political expression*   James Lees Laidlaw, "Statement at the National American Woman Suffrage Convention," Philadelphia, [23] November 1912. See Kimmel and Mosmiller, *Against the Tide*, pp. 262–263.

115　*one of the speakers*　See *NY Times*, 23 November 1912, p. 12, and *NY Tribune*, 23 November 1912, p. 6. Frederick C. Howe was among the speakers. Peabody was announced as a speaker the day before (*NY Tribune*, 21 November 1912, p. 7) but his name is not listed in subsequent reports.

115　*Jessie Lynch Williams*　"National Suffrage Convention Focuses All Eyes on Philadelphia," *Pittsburgh Post-Gazette-Sun*, 17 November 1912, p. 12. See also, "Women Defeat Unit Rule Plan," *Scranton Tribune-Republican*, 23 November 1912, p. 1.

115　*"work for the cause"*　"Convention Notes," *Woman's Journal*, November 30, 1912, Issue 48, p. 380.

115　*"use for bouquets"*　Ida Husted Harper, "Suffragists Discuss Presidential Booms," *NY Tribune*, 23 November 1912, p. 6.

115　*"turned on full"*　Harper, "Suffragists Discuss Presidential Booms," *NY Tribune*, 23 November 1912, p. 6.

116　*"over twenty-thousand"*　Ida Husted Harper, "Bewails Party Politics in Suffrage Cause," *NY Tribune*, 24 November 1912, p. 7.

116　*"depriving them of political expression"* Harper, *History of Woman Suffrage*, Vol. V, p. 349, reprinted in Kimmel and Mosmiller, *Against the Tide*, p. 272.

116　*over the defeat*　"Mrs. Belmont Beaten, Threatens to Resign," *NY Sun*, 24 November 1912, p. 1.

116　*did not desert the cause*　"Mrs. Belmont More in Sorrow than Anger," *NY Tribune*, 26 November 1912, p. 6.

116　*"noblest exposition on democracy"* Letter, Harriot Stanton Blatch to Wise, 7 November 1912. Stephen S. Wise collection, Robert D. Farber University Archives & Special Collections, Brandeis University.

116　*stage that night*　"Women Here Celebrate Suffrage Victories," *NY Tribune*, 14 November 1912, p. 7.

116　*came to naught*　"Cause to Hold Jubilee," *NY Tribune*, 7 November 1912, p. 7.

116　*"set back ten years"*　"Sulzer and the Suffragettes," *Washington Post*, 26 December 1912, p. 6.

117　*"decking out her house"*　"Keeping Peace Among Diplomats," *Boston Globe*, 30 November 1913, p. 44. The interview took place during Malone's first appointment in the Wilson administration as Third Secretary of State. She was quoted as saying that she was too busy decking out her home to consider the subject of suffrage. She also said that Malone had convinced her not to complete her studies at Barnard if she did not intend to take up a career other than matrimony. Malone replaced John Purroy Mitchel, who had been elected as New York City's next mayor.

117　*delay their union*　"Keeping Peace Among Diplomats," *Boston Globe*, 30 November 1913, p. 44.

117　*"his favorite subject"*　"Honor Mrs. Wilson in Great Waldorf Crush," *NY Tribune*, 22 December 1912, p. 6.

119    *"suffrage playlets"*    "Four Suffrage Playlets," *NY Dramatic Mirror*, 29 January 1913, p. 7.

119    *New York's Berkeley Theater*    Roland Lewis, "George Middleton," *Contemporary One-Act Plays* (New York: Charles Scribner, 1922).

119    *"dominated by her father"*    Middleton, *These Things Are Mine*, p. 132. La Follette starred in the one-night-only production, along with Alice Leigh and George Wilson.

119    *in later years*    See George Middleton, *One-Act Plays of Contemporary Life* (New York: Henry Holt and Co., 1913); "Four Suffrage Playlets," *NY Dramatic Mirror*, 29 January 1913, p. 7; "Brooklyn Theater Guild Gives One-Act Plays," *Brooklyn Standard-Union*, 12 March 1921, p. 5; and Roland Lewis, "George Middleton," *Contemporary One-Act Plays* (New York: Charles Scribner, 1922).

119    *"brilliant success"*    "Suffragist Sulzer Honored by Women," *NY Times*, 4 February 1913, p. 7.

119    *"'votes for women'"*    "600 Dine for Suffrage," *NY Tribune*, 4 February 1913, p. 7.

119    *The honoree was*    "Suffragist Sulzer Honored by Women," *NY Times*, 4 February 1913, p. 7.

120    *"long exercised the power"*    "Suffragist Sulzer Honored by Women," *NY Times*, 4 February 1913, p. 7.

120    *"constraints of office"*    Letter, Peabody to Woodrow Wilson, 20 March 1913, as cited in Ware, *George Foster Peabody*, p. 167.

120    *"American men are famous"*    "Suffrage Lasso Ready for Buffalo Bill," *NY Tribune*, 6 February 1913, p. 7.

121    *"women's enfranchisement"*    "Suffragette Parade at Washington Will Make Inauguration Look Like a Sideshow," *Des Moines Daily News*, 20 February 1913, p. 5.

121    *he took office*    "5,000 Women March for Equality; Demonstration at Capital Badly Hampered and Congress Is Asked to Investigate," *NY Times*, 4 March 1913, p. 5.

122    *respective houses*    "Men's League Protest," *Boston Globe*, 8 March 1913, p. 8.

122    *"it is a success"*    "Men in Police Attack. Take Up Suffragists' Plaint of 'No Protection,'" *Washington Post*, 10 March 1913, p. 2.

122    *during the parade*    "Suffrage Parade Hearings before a Subcommittee of the Committee on the District of Columbia of the United States Senate," Sixty-Third Congress, Special Session of the Senate Under S. Res. 499 of March 4, 1913, directing said committee to investigate the conduct of the district police and police department of the District of Columbia in connection with the Woman's Suffrage Parade on March 3, 1913, Part I.

124 *"equally with its men"* Telegram, Rabbi Stephen S. Wise to Corporal James Tanner, undated [9 March 1913]. Stephen S. Wise collection, Robert D. Farber University Archives & Special Collections, Brandeis University.

124 *"Happy Land"* W.E.B. Du Bois, "Hail Columbia!" *The Crisis*, Vol. 5, No. 6, April 1913, pp. 289–290, as cited in David Levering Lewis, *W.E.B. Du Bois: Biography of a Race, 1868–1919* (New York: MacMillan, 1994), p. 432.

124 *"disgusting in the main"* "Suffragists Odious. So Mr. Wheeler Explains Their Ill-Treatment in Washington," *NY Times*, 9 March 1913, p. 10.

124 *as odious as Mormonism* "Suffragists Odious. So Mr. Wheeler Explains Their Ill-Treatment in Washington," *NY Times*, 9 March 1913, p. 10.

125 *"hot wax if they want to"* "Suffragist Sulzer Honored by Women," *NY Times*, 4 February 1913, p. 7.

125 *hard labor for breaking windows* "2 Months for Suffragists," *NY Times*, 19 February 1913, p. 5.

125 *"Would it be wise and helpful"* Letter, Wise to Peabody, undated. Stephen S. Wise collection, Robert D. Farber University Archives & Special Collections, Brandeis University.

125 *OUR CAUSE HERE* Telegram, Peabody to Wise, 21 March 1913. Stephen S. Wise collection, Robert D. Farber University Archives & Special Collections, Brandeis University.

125 *"raids upon property"* Letter, Wise to Alice Lewisohn, 25 March 1913. Stephen S. Wise collection, Robert D. Farber University Archives & Special Collections, Brandeis University.

125 *"for our purpose"* Letter, Wise to Alice Lewisohn, 26 March 1913. Stephen S. Wise collection, Robert D. Farber University Archives & Special Collections, Brandeis University.

126 *"we are mongrels"* Max Eastman, "Gettes and Gists," *The Masses*, Vol. IV, No. VII, April 1913, Issue 23, pp. 5–6.

126 *"both now and eternally"* Eastman, "Gettes and Gists," *The Masses*, Vol. IV, No. VII, April 1913, Issue 23, pp. 5–6.

126 *"knows no race or sex"* W.E.B. Du Bois, "Woman's Suffrage," *The Crisis*, Vol. 6, No. 1, May 1913, p. 29.

127 *"separate existence necessary"* "Eastman and the Men's League," *Clinton Courier*, 29 October 1913, editorial page.

127 *"is past"* "Max Eastman and the Men's League," *Clinton Courier*, 21 May 1913, editorial page.

127 *"Society for the Prevention of Cruelty to Women"* "Everett P. Wheeler an Anti. His New Organization Will Work against Votes for Women," *NY Times*, 2 May 1913, p. 3.

127 *"possession of the congress"* Stanton et al., *History of Woman Suffrage*, Vol. I, pp. 856–858.

129　　*"sentiment of the Senators"*　　See PWW 28:60–61, Villard to Wilson, 21 July 1913; PWW 28:65, Wilson to Villard, 23 July 1913; PWW 28:163–165, Storey, Du Bois and Villard to Wilson, 15 August 1913; PWW 28:202, Wilson to Villard, 21 August 1913; PWW 28:239–240, Villard to Wilson, 27 August 1913; PWW 28:245–246, Wilson to Villard, 29 August 1913.

129　　*a Race Commission*　　Villard, *Fighting Years*, p. 236. For a fuller discussion of Villard's numerous exchanges with Wilson on the race issue and his fight on behalf of the NAACP of Wilson's segregationist policies meant to mollify Southern senators, see pp. 236–242.

129　　*such a commission*　　See PWW 28:60–61, Villard to Wilson, 21 July 1913; PWW 28:65, Wilson to Villard, 23 July 1913; PWW 28:163–165, Storey, Du Bois and Villard to Wilson, 15 August 1913; PWW 28:202, Wilson to Villard, 21 August 1913; PWW 28:239–240, Villard to Wilson, 27 August 1913; PWW 28:245–246, Wilson to Villard, 29 August 1913.

129　　*right versus wrong*　　PWW 28:316, Wilson to Villard, 22 September 1913; PWW 28:332, John Palmer Gavit to Villard, 26 September 1913; PWW 28:342–344, Villard to Wilson, 29 September 1913; PWW 28:348–350, John Palmer Gavit to Villard, 1 October 1913; PWW 28:352–353, Wilson to Villard, 3 October 1913; PWW 28:401–410, Villard to Wilson, 14 October 1913; PWW 28:413–414, Wilson to Villard, 17 October 1913; PWW 28:493–499n1, Trotter to Wilson, 6 November 1913.

129　　*too busy at home for public service*　　"Mrs. Shumway's Ten Reasons Why Women Do Not Need the Ballot," *Brooklyn Eagle*, 28 June 1913, p. 18.

129　　*"indirect influence"*　　"Voteless-Woman Is Debauched," Says Male Supporter of Cause, *Brooklyn Eagle*, 2 July 1913, p. 24.

129　　*announced their engagement*　　"Suffrage Romance: Warbasse to Wed," *Brooklyn Eagle*, 28 August 1912, p. 1.

130　　*"endurable position"*　　"Voteless-Woman Is Debauched," Says Male Supporter of Cause, *Brooklyn Eagle*, 2 July 1913, p. 24.

130　　*"the governor of his mate"*　　"Man Is Not All-Wise," Asserts Ward Melville, *Brooklyn Eagle*, 3 July 1913, p. 19.

130　　*"Peculiar to Itself"*　　"Mrs. Shumway Persists Woman Should Not Vote," *Brooklyn Eagle*, 7 July 1913, p. 22.

130　　*"For Cause"*　　"Men's League to Ride," *NY Tribune*, 17 June 1913, p. 6.

131　　*"convincing suffragette playlets"*　　"Men's League to Ride," *NY Tribune*, 17 June 1913, p. 6.

131　　*"myself on record"*　　PWW 28:67, Ellen Axon Wilson to Wilson, 23 July 1913.

131　　*"constitutional amendment"*　　"Senate Held in Siege," *Washington Post*, 1 August 1913.

131　　*"busily at work"*　　"Senate Held in Siege," *Washington Post*, 1 August 1913, p. 2.

131　　*the legislature in 1915*　　"Men's League to Ride," *NY Tribune*, 17 June 1913, p. 6.

131     *"favorite measures"*    "Full Report of the Frawley Committee," *NY Times*, 12 August 1913, p. 2.

131     *possible successors*    Correspondence between Villard and Peabody, July–August 1913. Oswald Garrison Villard Papers, 1872–1949, MS Am 1323 (3494), Houghton Library, Harvard University.

132     *"hero of the occasion"*    "Insurgent Women Work a Coup D' Etat," *NY Tribune*, 15 October 1913, p. 7.

132     *totaled $8,593*    "N.Y. Suffragists Elect Mrs. Brown as Head," *NY Tribune*, 17 October 1913, p. 7.

132     *detained her*    "Mrs. Pankhurst Is Barred Out," *NY Times*, 19 October 1913, p. 1, 2.

132     *"moral turpitude"*    "President Decides Case: Order for Release of Mrs. Pankhurst Given at His Direction," *NY Times*, 21 October 1913, p. 3.

132     *not to wait for evolution*    "Feted at Aldine Club," *NY Times*, 21 October 1913, p. 3. At the speakers' table with her were Blatch, Belmont, and several other women with a good selection of Men's Leaguers: Dewey, Untermyer, Hapgood, and the playwright and author Samuel Merwin.

132     *opposition to the cause*    Allison Guertin Marchese, *Hidden History of Columbia County, New York* (Charleston: The History Press, 2014), p. 27.

133     *earlier political skirmishes*    See Urofsky, *A Voice That Spoke for Justice*, p. 105, which says that Wise helped persuade Whitman to veto a bill "that would have exempted the canning industry from nearly all of the protective labor laws."

133     *served as vice-presidents*    R.C. Beadle, "The Men's League for Woman Suffrage of the State of New York," *The Trend*, Vol. 6, No. 2, November 1913, pp. 266–275. The ministers were Henry Ward Beecher, John W. Chadwick, A. P. Putnam and the professor, George Plympton. The group's name changed to the Brooklyn Woman Suffrage Association in 1883.

133     *"viewpoint in politics"*    Beadle, "The Men's League," pp. 266–275.

133     *"on and off the platform"*    Beadle, "The Men's League," pp. 266–275.

133     *"services as secretary"*    Eastman, "Early History," pp. 17–18. (It was Eastman's 1912 article that brought him to the attention of Art Young, who proposed Eastman's name to become editor of *The Masses*. His acceptance of the position and his work for the Men's League brought Eastman's short-lived academic career to a premature close.)

133     *"serious and faithful thought"*    Beadle, "The Men's League," pp. 266–275.

133     *"quality of names"*    Beadle, "The Men's League," pp. 266–275.

134     *"inspiring ideals"*    Beadle, "The Men's League," pp. 266–275.

134     *"the sobriquet of the 'Sphinx'"*    Beadle, "The Men's League," pp. 266–275.

134    *"in less than three years"*  Beadle, "The Men's League," pp. 266–275.

134    *"join its ranks"*  Beadle, "The Men's League," pp. 266–275.

134    *"takes away from it"*  "Dr. Wise Scores Parasite Women," *Woman's Journal*, 22 November 1913, p. 376. Also, "Urges Aid of Poor by State, Better Than Child Labor Laws, Says Dr. S.S. Wise," *Boston Sunday Post*, 16 November 1913, p. 7.

135    *"pale purple velvet"*  "Suffragists Flock to Washington," *NY Tribune*, 29 November 1913, p. 6. See also "Coiffeurs Stay, Despite Votes," *NY Tribune*, 2 December 1913, p. 7, in which the *Tribune's* later coverage reports—as if what it described was new—that there were "many beautifully gowned women" at the convention's reception at the Bellevue Hotel on December 2, and that several delegates showed up with short hair, all but two of whom were men. "Why shouldn't men be delegates to a woman suffrage convention?" the reporter asked rhetorically. "They are shy and retiring and so far have not spoken, so it is difficult to learn their names, but Mr. Taylor of Connecticut, is one of the brave souls, and Mr. Braley, of California, is another." The reporter surely meant A.S.G. Taylor, president of the Connecticut Men's League, and John Braly, a founder of the California Political Equality League.

135    *"Congressional committee"*  "Suffragists Flock to Washington," *NY Tribune*, 29 November 1913, p. 6. Names mentioned were: Colonel Selden Allen Day, U.S.A.; Judge William H. Delacey; the Reverend U.G.B. Pierce; Commodore W.S. Moore, U.S.N.; Gifford Pinchot; and Justice Stafford.

136    *It passed*  "Lost by His Stand," *Washington Post*, 3 December 1913, p. 2.

136    *Committee on Woman Suffrage*  House of Representatives, 63d Congress, 2d Session, Committee on Suffrage, Hearing Before the Committee on Rules, House of Representatives, Sixty-Third Congress, Second Session on Resolution Establishing a Committee on Woman Suffrage, December 3, 4, and 5, 1913 (Washington: Government Printing Office, 1914).

136    *enfranchisement of women in twenty-six years*  Marlee Newman, "National Woman Suffrage Procession," *HistoryNet*, accessed 24 July 2014 at http://www.historynet.com/womens-suffrage-movement.

136    *under law*  63d Congress, 2d Session, Committee on Suffrage, Hearing Before the Committee on Rules, House of Representatives, Sixty-Third Congress, Second Session on Resolution Establishing a Committee on Woman Suffrage, December 3, 4, and 5, 1913 (Washington: Government Printing Office, 1914), p. 186–187.

136    *"contempt of the opposite sex"*  House of Representatives, 63d Congress, 2d Session, Committee on Suffrage, Hearing Before the Committee on Rules, House of Representatives, Sixty-Third Congress, Second Session on Resolution Establishing a Committee on Woman Suffrage, December 3, 4, and 5, 1913 (Washington: Government Printing Office, 1914), p. 162.

136 *"give as well as take"* "'Antis' Now Lead. House Committee Turns from Suffragists, Says Reports," *Washington Post*, 5 December 1913, p. 2.

136 *"committee of its own"* PWW 29:21–22n1, "Remarks to a Delegation from the National Woman Suffrage Convention," 8 December 1913, citing also *NY World*, 9 December 1913.

136 *"upon the Congress"* PWW 29:21–22n1, "Remarks to a Delegation from the National Woman Suffrage Convention," 8 December 1913, citing also *NY World*, 9 December 1913.

CHAPTER 7

139 *"masculine assemblage"* "Suffragists Told to Use Dynamite," *NY Tribune*, 13 January 1914, p. 4.

139 *turkey trot* "Give Wide Choice in Dances," *NY Times*, 14 January 1914, p. 2.

139 *quip in a headline* "Families Will Be United at Suffrage Dansant," *NY World*, 18 January 1914.

139 *antis in the room* "Talk on Suffrage Stirs Eager Crowd," *NY Times*, 20 January 1914, p. 18. For the speeches, see *Yearbook of the Economic Club of New York*, vol. 4, 1913/14, pp. 81–139, via Hathi Trust, http://hdl.handle.net/2027/coo.31924056327376.

140 *front page of the* Times "Suffragists Hiss Opposing Debaters," *NY Times*, 27 January 1914, pp. 1–2. Elgin R.L. Gould was the chairman.

140 *"wide interest"* Pamphlet, R.C. Beadle, introduction to Gilbert E. Roe, "Discriminations against Women in the Laws of New York" (New York: National Woman Suffrage Publishing Company, 1914).

140 *"immense value"* Roe, "Discriminations against Women in the Laws of New York."

141 *women got a much worse deal* Roe, "Discriminations against Women in the Laws of New York." Roe said further that women could have their property confiscated as men can but have nothing to say about whether the public necessity for which it was taken was legitimate; that women were subject to the same punishment as men for committing crimes and yet had no say about what constitutes crime or what might excuse or mitigate it; that women were held to the same standard in contracts yet had no say in what makes a contract valid or void; that she had no vote in "the machinery of law by which her property rights or personal rights are determined"; that the law discriminated in favor of men for child custody rights, that the father's will was "supreme" in matters of religious instruction and training, and that men were favored over women in the appointment of executors and administrators. Husbands could serve on a jury on the strength of their wives' property ownership but the opposite did not hold. Descent and inheritance laws "notoriously" discriminated against women, as did laws of courtesy and dower

and those pertaining to mothers inheriting from their own children compared to fathers. In addition, the husband of a wife with no descendants was entitled to all her property but the wife of a husband with no descendants but who had a living father, mother, brother, sister or even nieces and nephews, entitled the wife to only half of his assets. In joint earnings, the law "grossly" discriminated against the wife. Roe had a few other examples on his list.

141   *"a lasting peace"*   See W. L. George, "Feminist Intentions," *Atlantic Monthly*, Vol. 112, No. 6, December 1913, pp. 721–732. Also, W. L. George, "What the Feminists Really Are Fighting For," *NY Times Sunday Magazine*, 14 December 1913, p. SM6.

141   *"men and women"*   See W. L. George, "Feminist Intentions," *Atlantic Monthly*, Vol. 112, No. 6, December 1913, pp. 721–732. Also, W. L. George, "What the Feminists Really Are Fighting For," *NY Times Sunday Magazine*, 14 December 1913, p. SM6.

141   *later in the month*   See W. L. George, "Feminist Intentions," *Atlantic Monthly*, Vol. 112, No. 6, December 1913, pp. 721–732. Also, W. L. George, "What the Feminists Really Are Fighting For," *NY Times Sunday Magazine*, 14 December 1913, p. SM6.

141   *"biological bosh"*   George MacAdam, "Feminist Revolutionary Principle Is Biological Bosh," *NY Times*, 18 January 1914, p. 50.

141   *"feminist movement"*   George MacAdam, "Feminist Revolutionary Principle Is Biological Bosh," *NY Times*, 18 January 1914, p. 50.

142   *"dominating brute"*   "Feminism and the Facts," *NY Times*, 19 January 1914, p. 8.

142   *"They accused Sedgwick of being"*   "Indignant Feminists Reply to Prof. Sedgwick," *NY Times*, 15 February 1914, p. 4.

142   *"precisely the same"*   Dr. Simon Flexner, "Anatomy Is Not a True Guide," *NY Times*, 15 February 1914, p. 4.

142   *NAWSA reproduced in pamphlet form*   Dr. Frederick Peterson, Pamphlet, "Normal Women Not Neurotic" (New York: National American Woman Suffrage Association, March 1914).

143   *"affirmation in others"*   Dr. Frederick Peterson, "Woman's Uplift Means Man's Uplift," *NY Times*, 15 February 1914, p. 4.

143   *"significant or determinative"*   Dr. William H. Howell, "Has Found Women as Able as Men," *NY Times*, 15 February 1914, p. 4.

143   *differences between them*   Dr. Franklin P. Mall, "Women Students above the Average," *NY Times*, 15 February 1914, p. 4.

143   *"—so does feminism"*   "Talk on Feminism Stirs Great Crowd," *NY Times*, 18 February 1914, p. 2. Also George Middleton, "What Feminism Means to Me," Speech delivered at Cooper Union, 17 February 1914. George Middleton Papers,

Manuscript Division, Library of Congress, reprinted in Kimmel and Mosmiller, *Against the Tide*, pp. 358–359.

143    *"not a handcuff"*   Middleton, *These Things Are Mine*, pp. 130–31.

143    *Wallace J. Benedict*   "Miss Eastman Seeks Divorce; Scorns Alimony," *Chicago Tribune*, 29 February 1916, p. 1. Middleton's autobiography notes that the line also appeared in her obituary, however, at least not in the *Times*: "Crystal Eastman, Radical Leader, Dies," *NY Times*, 29 July 1928, p. 25.

143    *"in relation to each other"*   Middleton, *These Things Are Mine*, pp. 131.

143    *"more expert hands"*   "Woman of Past a 'Clothes Horse,'" *NY Tribune*, 18 February 1914, p. 3.

144    *got the suit dismissed*   "Two Articles Related to the Associated Press Libel Suit against the Masses," *The Masses*, January 1914 and April 1914. See https://www.marxists.org/history/etol/writers/eastman/works/1910s/libel.htm, accessed 11 December 2015.

144    *"sarcastic shafts"*   "Max Eastman Raps Feminist Leaders," *NY Evening Call*, 18 February 1914, p. 2.

144    *Laidlaw pilgrimage*   "Campaigning in Montana. Mr. and Mrs. James L. Laidlaw in Whirlwind Tour," *NY Evening Post*, 25 February 1914.

144    *reprinted*   Max Eastman, "Her Right to Be Happy," *NY Evening Post*, 25 February 1914.

144    *"Mrs. Charles Tiffany"*   "Victory in New York in 1915. Reports of the Winning Fight for Suffrage from Every Nook and Corner of the Empire State," *NY Evening Post*, 25 February 1914.

145    *"he would urge this change"*   PWW 29:213–215, "Suffragists Snub President When He Refuses Them Aid," *NY World*, 3 February 1914.

145    *"not as a representative of his party"*   PWW 29:213–215, "Suffragists Snub President When He Refuses Them Aid," *NY World*, 3 February 1914.

145    *"gunning for votes then"*   PWW 29:213–215, "Suffragists Snub President When He Refuses Them Aid," *NY World*, 3 February 1914.

145    *"they went away angry"*   PWW 29:213–215, "Suffragists Snub President When He Refuses Them Aid," *NY World*, 3 February 1914.

145    *"making this recommendation"*   PWW 29:309–310, Wilson to John Avery McIlhenny, 4 March 1914.

145    *"unless he did certain things*   PWW 29:515–516, Entry from Edward Mandell House's diary of April 27, 1914. House's diary notes that Wilson wrote back to thank the woman and said, "he sincerely hoped they would."

145    *"both body and mind"*   PWW 30:225, John Randolph Thornton to Wilson, 29 June 1914.

146     *"cross examination"*    PWW 30:226–228, "Remarks to a Woman Suffrage Delegation," 30 June 1914.

146     *"I believe"*    PWW 30:240, Wilson to John Randolph Thornton, 1 July 1914.

146     *"personal questions"*    PWW 30:257n1, Letter from Josephine Marshall Jewell Dodge to Wilson, 4 July 1914.

146     *Creel was back in the news*    George Creel, "What Have Women Done with the Vote," *Century*, Vol. 87, No. 5, March 1914, pp. 663–671.

146     *a movement pamphlet*    Pamphlet, George Creel, "What Have Women Done with the Vote" (Hartford: Connecticut Woman Suffrage Association, undated).

146     *"women of the community"*    "Mayor Gill's Case. George Creel Defends Suffrage Vote in Seattle," *NY Times*, 3 April 1914, p. 10. See also "The Seattle Suffragists. Why Have They Re-Elected the Deposed Hiram Gill?" *NY Times*, 1 April 1914, p. 12.

146     *"disintegration of the home"*    "'Homes.' Mr. Creel Wishes to Know Which Ones Suffragism Threatens," *NY Times*, 18 April 1914, p. 10.

147     *danger could be assessed*    "'Homes.' Mr. Creel Wishes to Know Which Ones Suffragism Threatens," *NY Times*, 18 April 1914, p. 10.

147     *"hope of the Republic"*    "Suffrage Run Riot," *NY Times*, 27 April 1914, p. 10.

147     *two dozen of them dead*    PWW 30:38–39, Benjamin Barr Lindsey to Joseph Patrick Tumulty, 16 May 1914.

147     *publicity game*    Item, *Rock Island Argus*, 18 May 1914, p. 12.

147     *antisuffragist views*    "My Interviews with My Husband: Blanche Bates Intimately Talks with George Creel. Don't Agree about Woman Suffrage or How Children Should be Reared—Single Thing on Which They Do Agree Is That They Always Disagree," *Elmira Star-Gazette*, 3 February 1923, p. 10.

147     *Hazel MacKaye*    "To Pose for Suffrage. Eugen Boissevain Will Take Part in Tableaus at Armory," *NY Tribune*, 23 March 1914, p. 10.

147     *barefoot dancers*    "Five Thousand at Suffrage Pageant . . . Barefoot Dance a Feature," *Brooklyn Eagle*, 18 April 1914, p. 5.

147     *James E. Beggs*    Program, Pageant and Ball, April 17, 1914, 71st Regiment Armory, Men's League for Woman Suffrage of the State of New York in collaboration with the Equal Franchise Society, presents a Pageant, written and directed by Hazel MacKaye, pageant director of the Equal Franchise Society. Music composed by Bertha Remick. Score arranged by James E. Beggs. University of California-Davis Special Collections.

147     *women in history*    "Men's League for Woman Suffrage Plan a Pageant," *NY World*, 29 March 1914.

148     *financial success was guaranteed*    "Calves Man's Suffrage Test. Few Found Who Can Grace Colonial Costumes in Fete," *NY Sun*, 17 March 1914.

148    *"make it a success"*    "To Pose for Suffrage. Eugene Boissevain Will Take Part in Tableaus at Armory," *NY Tribune*, 23 March 1914.

148    *had become a partner*    "Five Thousand at Suffrage Pageant," *Brooklyn Eagle*, 18 April 1914, p. 5.

149    *told in allegory form*    See "Five Thousand at Suffrage Pageant," *Brooklyn Eagle*, 18 April 1914, p. 5; "Woman's Advance Told by Pageant," *NY Tribune*, 18 April 1914, p. 7; "Real Beauty Show in League Pageant; Handsomest of Their Sex Chosen for Suffrage Allegorical Scene. 500 People in Action. Commissioner Davis Leads Grand March with James Lees Laidlaw after Brilliant Performance," *NY Times*, 18 April 1914, p. 11.

149    *"dance of triumph"*    "Women's Advance told by Pageant," *NY Tribune*, 18 April 1914, p. 7.

149    *"if not paralyzing"*    Karen Blair, *The Torchbearers* (Bloomington: Indiana University Press, 1994), pp. 139–140.

149    *"injustice is harmful"*    "Adolph Lewisohn in Suffrage Speech. . . . Agrees with Geo. Creel," *NY Times*, 25 April 1914, p. 13.

149    *"tedious toddle"*    "Suffrage Day," Editorial, *NY Times*, 4 May 1914, p. A10. See also, "Woman Orators Are Preparing Speeches for Suffrage Day," *NY Evening World*, 1 May 1914. In the parade's stead, the suffragists held meetings all over town, assigning Laidlaw and his Men's League colleagues to the downtown business districts.

149    *That speech*    "Mayor Mere Man on Suffrage Day," *NY Tribune,* 2 May 1914, p. 9.

149    *written a century ago*    "Mitchel Jolts Suffrage: Mrs. Blatch Retorts at Big Carnegie Hall Meeting," *NY Times*, 3 May 1914, pp. 1, 12. See also, "Women to Keep Up Fight," *NY Tribune*, 14 May 1914, p. 18. Eastman spent Suffrage Day upstate in Utica, giving a keynote speech at a banquet where he also recruited for the League. The Laidlaws, who had an estate at Sands Point, organized smaller summer pageants, receptions, and mass meetings in nearby Hempstead and elsewhere up and down Long Island.

150    *"a hero and a scoundrel at the same time"*    Floyd Dell, "Feminism for Men," *The Masses*, Vol. V, No. 10; Issue No. 38, 10 July 1914, pp. 19–20.

150    *"ultimate hearing and sympathy"*    W.E.B. Du Bois, "Votes for Women," *The Crisis*, Vol. 8, No. 4, August 1914, pp. 179–180.

151    *as a charter member*    "Suffrage Advance to Rochester Is On," *NY Sun*, 8 October 1914, p. 8. Consultation 5 February 2016 with the Rockland County Historian indicates there was no John Calvin at the time but John Calvin Blauvelt fits the age range (he was ninety-one, not ninety-four but close) and particulars offered.

151    *"fire company"*    "Suffrage Advance to Rochester Is On," *NY Sun*, 8 October 1914, p. 8.

151 *for three days* "Suffrage Pilgrims Gain Many Converts," *NY Sun*, 12 October 1914, p. 6.

151 *"march on Syracuse"* "Suffrage Autoists Have Casualties," *NY Sun*, 11 October 1914, p. 18.

151 *Carrie Chapman Catt* "Leslie Million to Aid Suffrage," *NY Tribune*, 8 October 1914, p. 7.

152 *"traitors to their race"* PWW 31:328n2, Villard to Wilson with enclosures, 17 November 1914. See also "The President and Segregation," *NY Evening Post*, 13 November 1914, p. 8. See also, Christine A. Lunardini, "Standing Firm: William Monroe Trotter's Meetings with Woodrow Wilson, 1913–1914," *Journal of Negro History*, 64 (Summer 1979): 244–264, as cited in Gary Gerstle, "Race and Nation in the Thought and Politics of Woodrow Wilson," chapter 4 in John Milton Cooper Jr., ed., *Reconsidering Woodrow Wilson* (Baltimore: Johns Hopkins University Press, 2008), p. 120.

152 *"previously existed"* PWW 31:328n2, Villard to Wilson with enclosures, 17 November 1914. See also "The President and Segregation," *NY Evening Post*, 13 November 1914, p. 8.

152 *"vicinity of the White House"* PWW 31:328n2, Villard to Wilson with enclosures, 17 November 1914. See also "The President and Segregation," *NY Evening Post*, 13 November 1914, p. 8.

152 *"public opinion of the country"* PWW 31:329–330, Wilson to Mary M. Childs, 18 November 1914.

152 *Roe, Laidlaw, Wise, and Charles Strong* "Men Want Suffrage Amendment," *NY Times*, 10 December 1914, p. 8. Also present were Thomas H. More, William Harmon Black, Amos R. Pinchot, Bertram Cruger, and Irving E. Burdick.

153 *"65 Liberty St."* "Manhattan Club Doors Closed to Fair Reporters and Equal Rights Champions Distressed by Rule That Causes Woe," *NY Tribune*, 17 December 1914, p. 11.

153 *offered meeting space* Hilda Watrous Papers, notes on James Lees Laidlaw. New York State Library, NYSED, undated.

CHAPTER 8

155 *"were never equaled"* Harper, *History of Woman Suffrage*, Vol. VI, pp. 459–460.

155 *come November 2* "Suffrage Motion Wins," *NY Times*, 4 February 1915, p. 6.

155 *Mary Ritter Beard* "Suffrage Matinee Talks," *NY Times*, 12 January 1915, p. 7. Among others who spoke were George Creel, Witter Bynner, *Vanity Fair's* editor Frank Crowninshield, the explorer Anthony Fiala, and the financial investigator Isaac Marcosson.

155     *"'votes for women' organizations"*  "Vote Fight Camp in Beauty Parlor," *NY Tribune*, 12 January 1915, p. 4.

155     *"give up the ghost"*  "Vote Fight Camp in Beauty Parlor," *NY Tribune*, 12 January 1915, p. 4.

157     *The headline*  "It Must Be Defeated," *NY Times*, 6 February 1915, p. 10.

157     *"women don't"*  PWW 32:22–23, "Remarks to a Delegation of Democratic Women," and PWW 32:21–22, "Diary of Nancy Saunders Toy," 6 January 1915.

157     *renewed strength*  "Suffragists Lose Fight in the House," *NY Times*, 13 January 1915, p. 1.

157     *"get after"*  "Women to Watch Congress," *NY Times*, 23 January 1915, p. 10.

157     *"card indexy"*  "'Burn Them Alive,' He Says of Antis," *NY Tribune*, 23 January 1915, p. 16.

157     *"to please me"*  "'Burn Them Alive' He Says of Antis," *NY Tribune*, 23 January 1915, p. 16.

158     *federal initiative*  "To Raise Suffrage Fund," *NY Times*, 23 January 1915, p. 10. The other men named in various capacities were: Thomas L. Manson (husband of May Groot Manson, an important suffragist and philanthropist on the East End of Long Island; Thomas E. Rush, Calvin Tomkins, Charles Burnham, Leo M. Klein, Charles Frederick Adams, George W. Kirchwey, Irving E. Burdick, Joseph F. Daly, William Harman Black, and Roger Foster.

158     *"forcible and definite"*  "The Woman Suffrage Crisis," *NY Times*, 7 February 1915, p. 30.

158     *"admonitions of common sense"*  "The Woman Suffrage Crisis," *NY Times*, 7 February 1915, p. 30.

158     *the editorial could have easily appeared*  "The Conning Tower," *NY Tribune*, 8 February 1915, p. 6.

158     *"mediaeval monk"*  "The Woman Suffrage 'Crisis' in 'The Times,'" *NY Tribune*, 9 February 1915, p. 8.

158     *"masterful editorial handling"*  "The Woman Suffrage 'Crisis,'" *NY Tribune*, 12 February 1915, p. 8.

158     *banner headline*  "Should Women Vote in New York?" *NY Times*, 14 February 1915, pp. 75+.

158     *"anti-suffragists"*  "Thought It Was a Parody," *NY Times*, 14 February 1915, p. 86.

159     *Munsey Publications*  "Band-Wagon Biography," *NY Tribune*, 15 February 1915, p. 4. See also "Woman Suffrage Number," *Puck*, week ending 20 February 1915, p. 2 with full list.

160     *"suffrage is won"*  "Woman Suffrage Number," *Puck*, week ending 20 February 1915, pp. 1–2, 4–8, 12–16, 18–22, 25–27.

161     *"went smoothly"*   "Suffragists Draw 7,000 to Their Ball," *NY Times*, 17 February 1915, p. 7.

161     *"that life is made of"*   "George Middleton. A Volume of His Plays of Contemporary Life," *NY Times Book Review*, 7 March 1915, p. BR83.

161     *Schlesinger Library at Harvard*   Harriet Wright Burton Laidlaw Papers, A-63, Box 7: 122–144, Men's League for Woman Suffrage materials, 1915. Schlesinger Library, Radcliffe Institute, Harvard University.

161     *lengthy Creel essay*   George Creel, "Chivalry versus Justice: Why the Women of the Nation Demand the Right to Vote," *Pictorial Review*, March 1915. NAWSA hustled it out as a pamphlet the next month as George Creel. Chivalry versus Justice (New York: National Woman Suffrage Publishing Company, April 1915). Schlesinger Library, Women's History Collection, 002615_160_0748_From_1_to_6.

161     *"anti-equal-suffrage"*   "Who Only Are So Inspired. Search the Whole Forward Movement for an Anti-Equal Suffrage Person," *NY Times*, 28 March 1915, p. 34.

161     *"charitable lines"*   Alice Hunt Bartlett, "Otherwise Inspired. Anti-Suffrage Women Who Are Performing Social Service," *NY Times*, 2 April 1915, p. 10.

161     *"more closely in the future"*   Alice Hunt Bartlett, "Otherwise Inspired. Anti-Suffrage Women Who Are Performing Social Service," *NY Times*, 2 April 1915, p. 10.

162     *Greenwich Village*   "Catholic Women Sound Vote Call," *NY Tribune*, 10 April 1915, p. 7.

162     *"valuable asset"*   Editorial, [W.E.B. Du Bois], "Woman Suffrage," *The Crisis*, Vol. 9, No. 6, April 1915, Whole No. 54, p. 285.

164     *"his ideals and his country"*   Editorial, [W.E.B. Du Bois], "Woman Suffrage," *The Crisis*, Vol. 9, No. 6, April 1915, Whole No. 54, p. 285.

164     *disparaging publicity in the press*   See, for example: *NY Times* 18 April 1915, p. 14; *NY Tribune*, 21 April 1915, p. 14; *NY Times*, 25 April 1915, p. 30; *NY Times*, 2 May 1915, p. 1, 15, and C4; *NY Times*, 4 May 1915, p. 31 (three items); *NY Times*, 9 May 1915, p. 33; *NY Tribune*, 18 May 1915, p. 12; *NY Times*, 30 June 1915, p. 11 (two items); *NY Times*, 6 July 1915, p. 9; *NY Tribune*, 25 July 1915, p. 13; *NY Times*, 13 July 1915, p. 11; *NY Times*, 27 July 1915, p. 9.

164     *"strong suffrage speech"*   "Ideals of Women Higher Than Men's," *NY Times*, 7 April 1915, p. 7.

164     *"beautiful and lovely"*   "Ideals of Women Higher Than Men's," *NY Times*, 7 April 1915, p. 7.

164     *"such men as James L. Laidlaw"*   Sarah Addington, "The Man in the Street and Suffrage Tips. Eavesdropping Round to Campaign Corners. Here's What One Reporter Caught of the Spirit of the Men Who Vote in November," *NY Tribune*, 25 July 1915, IV, p. 14.

164     *"than with persuasion"*   Middleton, *These Things Are Mine*, pp. 131–132.

165    *"no matter how he thought now"* "Men Yield to Suffrage Call," *NY Tribune*, 30 July 1915, p. 14.

165    *"politics ever written"* Editorial, "'Votes for Women,'" *The Crisis*, Vol. 10, No. 4— Whole No. 58, August 1915, p. 177.

165    *National Association of Colored Women* "Votes for Women," *The Crisis*, Vol. 10, No. 4, August 1915, pp. 178–192.

165    *"political power"* "Suffragists to Gather: Council Fire Night Will Be Celebrated Tomorrow," *NY Times*, 5 August 1915, p. 4.

165    *"at the polls on November 2"* "Suffragists to Gather: Council Fire Night Will Be Celebrated Tomorrow," *NY Times*, 5 August 1915, p. 4.

165    *"suffrage strength"* "The Suffrage Fight," *Washington Post*, 2 October 1915, p. 6.

167    *"becomes a reality"* "The Suffrage Fight," *Washington Post*, 2 October 1915, p. 6.

167    *high state office holders* Letter and replies, Thomas W. Hotchkiss, campaign committee of the Men's League for Woman Suffrage, to public officials in states where women had the vote, 27 September 1915. Men's League for Woman Suffrage of the State of New York letters, 1915, MS 144, Woodson Research Center, Fondren Library, Rice University.

167    *"every turn of the agitation"* PWW 35:28, "A Press Release," 6 October 1915.

167    *"opposition to the measure"* PWW 35:28n2, "A Press Release," 6 October 1915. See also "Wilson Indorses Woman Suffrage," *NY Times*, 7 October 1915, p. 1, 4.

168    *having the vote* "Mrs. Galt Opposes Votes for Women," *NY Times*, 20 October 1915, p. 1.

168    *"suffrage support?"* Villard, *Fighting Years*, pp. 290–291.

168    *"democratic society"* Villard, *Fighting Years*, pp. 290–291.

168    *as it was necessary* For a full, excellently sourced reconsideration of Wilson's evolution on the suffrage question, see Victoria Bissell Brown, "Did Woodrow Wilson's Gender Politics Matter?" chapter 5 in John Milton Cooper Jr., ed., *Reconsidering Woodrow Wilson* (Baltimore: Johns Hopkins University Press, 2008), pp. 126–162, citing Christine A. Lunardini and Thomas J. Knock, "Woodrow Wilson and Woman Suffrage: A New Look," *Political Science Quarterly*, Vol. 95, Winter 1980–1981, pp. 655–671.

168    *"the bosses"* "Long Suffrage Campaign at an End; Leaders of Each Side Confident of Victory Tuesday," *NY Herald*, 17 October 1915.

168    *"his party"* "Wilson Indorses Woman Suffrage," *NY Times*, 7 October 1915, p. 1, 4.

168    *"in favor of suffrage"* "30,000 to Join Suffrage Line. . . . 5,000 Men Among Votes Volunteers," *NY Tribune*, 17 October 2015, p. 8.

169    *"parade of 1911"* "30,000 to Join Suffrage Line. . . . 5,000 Men Among Votes Volunteers," *NY Tribune*, 17 October 2015, p. 8. The article refers to Greene as

one of the "Noble Ninety-two" of the 1911 march. Men's League delegation estimates for that first parade outing range from eighty-nine to ninety-two to one hundred.

169     *"head Division A"*    "30,000 to Join Suffrage Line. . . . 5,000 Men Among Votes Volunteers," *NY Tribune*, 17 October 2015, p. 8.

169     *"constitutional amendment"*    "New Jersey Beats Suffrage by 46,278; While President Wilson Votes 'Yes,'" *NY Times*, 20 October 1915, pp. 1–2.

169     *and brothers*    "Suffrage Beaten Everywhere . . . Right to Vote in Next May's Preferential Election to Be Asked of the Legislature," *Trenton Evening Times*, 20 October 1915, p. 1.

169     *start time*    "Expects 10,000 Men in Suffrage March," *NY Times*, 20 October 1915, p. 2.

170     *"service to all mankind"*    "Mayor Now Sure Suffrage Will Win," *NY Times*, 23 October 1915, p. 4.

170     *"big impression on the crowd"*    "Three Hours in Review," *NY Times*, 24 October 1915, p. 1.

170     *under its own subhead*    "Men Marchers Were Brave," *NY Times*, 24 October 1915, p. 2.

170     "On next Election Day"    "Men Marchers Were Brave," *NY Times*, 24 October 1915, p. 2.

171     "Lizzie"    "Men Marchers Were Brave," *NY Times*, 24 October 1915, p. 2.

172     *"complete preparedness"*    "Suffrage Campaign to End in a Whirl," *NY Times*, 29 October 1915, p. 5.

172     *devoted its October–November issue to suffrage*    Max Eastman, "Who's Afraid? Confessions of a Suffrage Orator," *The Masses*, Vol. 7, No. 1, Issue 53, November 1915, pp. 7–9.

172     *"she isn't fit to live"*    Floyd Dell, "Adventures in Anti-land," *The Masses*, Vol. 7, No. 1, Issue 53, November 1915, pp. 5–6.

172     *the scholar's every point*    W.E.B. Du Bois, "Woman Suffrage," *The Crisis*, Vol. 11, No. 1, November 1915, pp. 29–30.

172     *help ensure against fraud*    "5,000 Women Picked for Working Polls. Suffragists Go Early to Bed as Men Volunteers Wind Up Their Campaign," *NY Times*, 2 November 1915, p. 4.

172     *their amendment, too*    "Women Win in Few Places," *NY Times*, 3 November 1915, pp. 1–2.

173     *"Franklin statue"*    "Suffrage Loses in NY by 180,000; Constitution Killed," *NY Tribune*, 3 November 1915, p. 1.

173     *Creel and Beard among the speakers*    "Antis Will Celebrate," *NY Times*, 11 November 1915, p. 7.

173     *"subject in his house"*    "Suffragists Call the President Weak," *NY Times*, 12 November 1915, p. 6.

173     *"than all the angels"*    "Suffragists Call the President Weak," *NY Times*, 12 November 1915, p. 6.

173     *Equal Franchise League*    "State Suffragists Will Consolidate," *NY Times*, 13 November 1915, p. 9.

173     *"forces made permanent"*    "State Suffragists Will Consolidate," *NY Times*, 13 November 1915, p. 9.

173     *"influence upon the nation"*    "Women Begin Anew Fight for Suffrage," *NY Times*, 1 December 1915, p. 13.

174     *"and they liked it"*    "Honor Mrs. Chapman Catt," *NY Times*, 2 December 1915, p. 6.

174     *"and a threat"*    "President Hears Suffrage Plea; Envoys Rejoice," *NY Tribune*, 7 December 1915, p. 5.

174     *"habit of the teacher"*    "President Hears Suffrage Plea; Envoys Rejoice," *NY Tribune*, 7 December 1915, p. 5.

174     *"full programme"*    Text of Woodrow Wilson's State of the Union Address to Congress, 7 December 1915, http://www.infoplease.com/t/hist/state-of-the-union/127.html, accessed 27 November 2015.

175     *"concerning this great matter"*    "President Hears Suffrage Plea; Envoys Rejoice," *NY Tribune*, 7 December 1915, p. 5.

175     *"he didn't listen to us"*    "President Hears Suffrage Plea; Envoys Rejoice," *NY Tribune*, 7 December 1915, p. 5.

175     *and the Senate*    "President Hears Suffrage Plea; Envoys Rejoice," *NY Tribune*, 7 December 1915, p. 5.

175     *convention in Washington*    "Wilson Hears Pleas of Pros and Antis," *NY Times*, 15 December 1916, p. 8.

175     *"Federal amendment"*    "Wilson Hears Please of Pros and Antis," *NY Times*, 15 December 1915, p. 8.

175     *"love feast"*    "Fight for Peace, Mrs. Catt Urges, Preparedness Issue Up at Suffragists' Love Feast. Dudley F. Malone Boosts Defences," *NY Tribune*, 20 December 1915, p. 9.

CHAPTER 9

177     *"advance guard"*    Stanton et al., *History of Woman Suffrage*, Vol. I, p. 476. See also "Suffrage Bills in State House," *NY Tribune*, 11 January 1916, p. 1.

177     *embarrassment the muddle had caused*    PWW 36:3–4, "Remarks in New York to a Suffrage Delegation," 27 January 1916.

177    *it still remained "open"*  PWW 36:3–4, "Remarks in New York to a Suffrage Delegation," 27 January 1916.

177    *"that cannot wait"*  PWW 36:3–4, "Remarks in New York to a Suffrage Delegation," 27 January 1916.

177    *"state by state"*  PWW 36:3–4, "Remarks in New York to a Suffrage Delegation," 27 January 1916.

177    *"effects are permanent"*  PWW 36:3–4, "Remarks in New York to a Suffrage Delegation," 27 January 1916.

178    *backing it represented*  "The President Impressed," *The Masses*, Vol. VIII, No. 4, Issue No. 56, February 1916, p. 11. Also, Item, *Commercial Advertiser* (Potsdam, NY), 18 January 1916, p. 4.

178    *"woman's political power"*  "The President Impressed," *The Masses*, Vol. VIII, No. 4, Issue No. 56, February 1916, p. 11. Also, Item, *Commercial Advertiser* (Potsdam, NY), 18 January 1916, p. 4.

178    *"little political experience"*  "The President Impressed," *The Masses*, Vol. VIII, No. 4, Issue No. 56, February 1916, p. 11. Also, Item, *Commercial Advertiser* (Potsdam, NY), 18 January 1916, p. 4.

178    *"by helping him along"*  "Suffragists Work to Rescue 'Masses,'" *NY Tribune*, 8 January 1916, p. 6.

178    *Middleton and La Follette*  Item, *Buffalo Evening News*, 28 January 1916, p. 11.

178    *war preparedness*  "Local News Briefs," *Washington Post*, 12 February 1916, p. 14.

178    *less familiar to the fray*  "Suffragists Lease New Quarters," *NY Tribune*, 30 January 1916, p. 7. Those named were Walter Ehrith, Robert Niles, James L. Johnson, James Gear, William Kelly, Charles Friedman, Thomas J. Shelley, Frederick Wilson, Frederick C. Hitchcock, Gus Gitterman, Ralph Korn, and Joseph Nayer.

178    *went in relays*  "Suffrage Dancers Overflow 'Garden,'" *NY Times*, 8 March 1916, p. 5.

179    *fire marshal nixed the idea*  "Suffragists to Give Ball," *NY Tribune*, 17 January 1916. Serving were Frank Crowninshield, Moncure Robinson, Henry Bull, Charles Wetmore, Bertram de. N. Cruger, and Charles B. Dillingham.

179    *to return and participate*  "Suffrage Dancers Overflow Garden," *NY Times*, 8 March 1916, p. 5.

179    *including many of their husbands*  "Suffrage Men in Albany Fight To-Day," *NY Press*, 16 March 1916. Among the husbands participating were Laidlaw, Ogden Mills Reid, Frederick Nathan, Norman de. R. Whitehouse, Edward van Zile, and Charles Nordstrom.

179    *would assure passage*  "Definite Plan to Get Enough Votes to Win Suffrage," *Christian Science Monitor*, 22 March 1916, p. 4.

179    *even stronger than it was*  "Definite Plan to Get Enough Votes to Win Suffrage," *Christian Science Monitor*, 22 March 1916, p. 4.

179 *"Men's League in tow"* "Women to Invade Albany. Suffragists Impatient Because Their Bill Is Neglected," *NY Times*, 5 April 1916, p. 24.

179 *source of the blockage* "Women to Invade Albany. Suffragists Impatient Because Their Bill is Neglected," *NY Times*, 5 April 1916, p. 24. See R.C. Beadle's letter to the editor of the *NY Tribune* about Brown's opposition, 22 March 1916, p. 10.

179 *amendment in November 1917* "Pass Suffrage Bill in Senate, 33 to 10," *NY Times*, 11 April 1916, p. 1.

179 *"6,000 from the 9th district alone"* Stanton et al., *History of Woman Suffrage*, Vol. I, p. 476.

179 *"gave invaluable help"* Stanton et al., *History of Woman Suffrage*, Vol. I, p. 476.

182 *giving them the vote* PWW 36:484–485, Jennie Bradley Roesing to Wilson, 14 April 1916.

182 *everyone's mind* "1,600 Women Will Parade by Sitting," *NY Sun*, 3 May 1916, p. 14. See also "142,000 March in Parade for Defence," *NY Sun*, 14 May 1916, p. 1.

182 *major labor unions* PWW 36:635–647, "A Colloquy," 8 May 1916.

182 *profit to reap* PWW 36:639, Eastman, as official representative of labor, in an address to Wilson, 8 May 1916.

183 *"Leads Naval Board"* "142,000 March in Parade for Defence," *NY Sun*, 14 May 1916, p. 1.

183 *"satellites of Jupiter"* Editorial, "Suffrage By Threat," *NY Times*, 22 June 1916, p. 10.

183 *"rights for women"* PWW 37:169n1, Albert Sidney Burleson to Wilson, 7 June 1916.

183 *rights of states* For correspondence with Wilson over the suffrage plank, see PWW 37:199, 10 June 1916; PWW 37:208–209, 12 June 1916; PWW 37:237n1, 16 June 1916; PWW 37:266, 19 June 1916; PWW 37:329, 29 June 1916; and PWW 37:375–376n1, 7 July 1916.

183 *"terms as to men"* "Political Party Platforms," Democratic Party Platform of 1916, 14 June 1916, http://www.presidency.ucsb.edu/ws/?pid=29591, accessed 23 November 2015.

183 *"extend the suffrage to women"* Letter, Woodrow Wilson to Carrie Chapman Catt, 19 June 1916. Manuscripts, Archives and Rare Books Division, New York Public Library.

184 *November elections* PWW 37:375–376, Sara Bard Field to Wilson, 7 July 1916, citing also, "Suffrage First Slogan of the Women in West," *NY Evening Post*, 21 June 1916, p. 9, and "Wilson and Suffrage," 21 June 1916, p. 16. Also Doris Stevens, *Jailed for Freedom: The Story of the Militant American Suffragist Movement* (New York: Boni and Liveright, 1920), p. 43. The visitor was Mrs. D.E. Hooker

of Richmond, Virginia, who came as part of a delegation representing the 60,000 member Virginia Federation of Labor.

184    *"their enfranchisement"*   Harriot Stanton Blatch, *Challenging Years: The Memoirs of Harriot Stanton Blatch* (New York: G.P. Putnam's Sons, 1940), pp. 268–269. Also PWW 37:426–427n1,2,3,4, Wilhelmina Caroline Giner Van Winkle to Wilson, 7 July 1916.

184    *"at the present moment"*   Blatch, *Challenging Years*, pp. 268–269. Also PWW 37:426–427n1,2,3,4, Wilhelmina Caroline Giner Van Winkle to Wilson, 7 July 1916.

184    *"change Presidents"*   Blatch, *Challenging Years*, pp. 268–269. Also PWW 37:426–427n1,2,3,4, Wilhelmina Caroline Giner Van Winkle to Wilson, 7 July 1916.

184    *"for the suffrage cause"*   PWW 37:535, Colonel Edward Mandell House to Wilson, 6 August 1916.

185    *"I've campaigned there twice"*   PWW 37:516, Thomas Reilly Marshall to Wilson, 2 August 1916, and PWW 37:517, Wilson to Marshall, 3 August 1916. For the rest of the suffrage-related correspondence with Wilson in this short period, see PWW 37:425–427n1,2,3,4, Wilhelmina Caroline Ginger Van Winkle to Wilson, 7 July 1916; PWW 37:490n1, 27 July 1916 and PWW 347:490, 27 July 1916, exchange between Wilson and Joseph Patrick Tumulty; PWW 37:502–504, Mary Wilson Thompson to Wilson, 30 July 1916; PWW 37:513–514, Letter from John Humphrey Small to Wilson, 2 August 1916; PWW 37:515, Letter from Josephus Daniels to Wilson, 2 September 1916; PWW 37:518, Wilson to Mary Wilson Thompson, 3 August 1916; PWW 37:522–533, Ellen Duane Davis to Wilson 3 August 1916; PWW 37:529, Wilson to Ellen Duane Davis, 5 August 1916; PWW 37:532–533, Irving Fisher to Wilson, 5 August 1916; PWW 37:535, Edward Mandell House to Wilson, 6 August 1916; PWW 37:536–537, Wilson to Jane Jefferson Club of Colorado, 7 August 1916.

185    *"angler for votes"*   PWW 37:529, Wilson to Ellen Duane Davis, 5 August 1916.

185    *"emergency convention"*   "Suffragists at Atlantic City," *Boston Globe*, 3 September 1916, p. 41.

185    *"Lincoln birthplace"*   "Wilson to Talk to Suffragists," *NY Times*, 12 August 1916, p. 9.

185    *threatened to detain him*   PWW 38:117, Wilson to Norman Hapgood, 30 August 1916.

185    *"But I shall try"*   "Wilson to Talk to Suffragists," *NY Times*, 12 August 1916, p. 9.

185    *"day of the convention"*   "Wilson to Talk to Suffragists," *NY Times*, 5 September 1916, p. 5.

186   *"Representatives of the people"*   "Congressional Union Bitter against Wilson," *NY Times*, 12 August 1916, p. 9.

186   *"denied them justice"*   "Congressional Union Bitter against Wilson," *NY Times*, 12 August 1916, p. 9.

186   *"the women situation"*   PWW 38:87, Norman Hapgood to Wilson, 28 August 1916.

186   *"knowledge on the subject"*   PWW 38:87, Norman Hapgood to Wilson, 28 August 1916.

186   *"know nothing about"*   PWW 38:86–87, Norman Hapgood to Wilson, 28 August 1916.

186   *"bog him down"*   PWW 38:117, Wilson to Norman Hapgood, 30 August 1916.

186   *he confirmed that he would attend*   "Wilson to Talk to Suffragists," *NY Times*, 5 September 1916, p. 5.

186   *"6,000 to 8,000"*   "Wilson to Talk to Suffragists," *NY Times*, 5 September 1916, p. 5.

186   *thirty-five states*   "Wilson to Talk to Suffragists," *NY Times*, 5 September 1916, p. 5. The three other presidents were Champlayne Riley of the New Jersey League, Wilmer Atkinson of Pennsylvania's, and A.S.G. Taylor of Connecticut's.

187   *"as if life hung on his words"*   Maud Wood Park (1920, 1960, 2009 Qontro.com reprint), *Front Door Lobby* (Boston: Beacon Press), chapter 1.

187   *"a little while to wait"*   Woodrow Wilson, "Address at the Suffrage Convention, Atlantic City, New Jersey," 8 September 1916. Online by Gerhard Peters and John T. Woolley, the American Presidency Project. http://www.presidency.ucsb.edu/ws/?pid=65395, accessed 24 December 2015.

187   *"by clearness of expression"*   Letter, Peabody to Wise, 12 September 1916. Stephen S. Wise collection, Robert D. Farber University Archives & Special Collections, Brandeis University.

187   *"come to New York to vote"*   Letter, Peabody to Wise, 12 September 1916. After Hughes's term as New York's governor ended in 1910, he moved to Washington to become an associate justice fo the US Supreme Court. Stephen S. Wise collection, Robert D. Farber University Archives & Special Collections, Brandeis University.

187   *support a federal amendment*   Maud Wood Park (1920, 1960, 2009, Qontro.com reprint), *Front Door Lobby* (Boston: Beacon Press), chapter 1.

188   *high on her list*   Park, *Front Door Lobby*, chapter 1.

188   *vote of the electorate*   Park, *Front Door Lobby*, chapter 1.

188   *cause the plan to fail*   Park, *Front Door Lobby*, chapter 1.

188   *"our intelligence"*   PWW 38:178–179, Hapgood, with Anna Howard Shaw enclosure, to Wilson, 16 September 1916.

188    *"to select passages for her"*   PWW 38:52n1,2, Anna Johnson to Wilson, 24 October 1916; Wilson asked Tumulty to pick suitable excerpts c. October 25, 1916 (TL, WP, DLC).

188    *"at Atlantic City"*   PWW 38:175n1, Alice Chipman Dewey to Norman Hapgood, 15 September 1916.

188    *should there be a vacancy*   PWW 38:349–350, Edward Mandell House to Wilson, 5 October 1916.

189    *the president's close aides*   See, for example, PWW 34:378n2, 30 August 1915. Wilson to his wife, Edith, referencing a dispatch from George Laughlin of the *NY Herald* with rumor that Villard had replaced Edward Mandell House as Wilson's adviser. Also, PWW 35:192, 12 November 1915 Wilson to House.

189    *John Cosgrave of the* New York World   "Suffragists Will Go to Atlantic City, Strike or No," *NY Tribune*, 1 September 1916, p. 7.

189    *worked outside the home*   Frank Crowninshield, "An Editor's Conversion," *Puck*, 20 February 1915, p. 26.

189    *The winning entry*   "Women's Hour Has Struck," *Arkansas City Daily Traveler*, 7 September 1916, p. 4.

189    *"sisters to the slaughter"*   "Creel Scolds Women Who Support Hughes," *NY Tribune*, 18 October 1916, p. 5.

189    *enfranchised state*   PWW 38:273–276, Norman Hapgood to Wilson, 25 September 1916. See also, Alice Hamilton, "As One Woman Sees the Issues," *New Republic*, Vol. 8, Issue 101, 7 October 1916, pp. 239–241.

191    *"grave national disasters"*   Hamilton, "As One Woman Sees the Issues," *New Republic*, Vol. 8, Issue 101, 7 October 1916, pp. 239–241.

191    *National Woman's Party*   PWW 38:481n1, "An Address in Chicago to Nonpartisan Women," 19 October 1916. See also, "Storm Hall to See Wilson," *Chicago Tribune*, 20 October 1916, various, pp. 1, 2, 3, 4, and 6.

191    *"were wild in Michigan avenue"*   "Banners Torn; Hughes Women Lose Battle," *Chicago Tribune*, 20 October 1916, p. 1.

191    *"where they stand and control"*   "President Sees Hand of Woman Molding Nation's Destiny; Does Not Mention Suffrage," *Chicago Tribune*, 20 October 1916, p. 2.

191    *"with the power of control"*   "President Sees Hand of Woman Molding Nation's Destiny; Does Not Mention Suffrage," *Chicago Tribune*, 20 October 1916, p. 2.

191    *"sympathetic comprehension"*   "President Sees Hand of Woman Molding Nation's Destiny; Does Not Mention Suffrage," *Chicago Tribune*, 20 October 1916, p. 2.

192    *"garlanded with daffodils"*   "8,000 March in Philadelphia," *NY Times*, 23 October 1916, p. 4.

192    *Social Science League*    "'Cabinet Day' on Van," *NY Tribune*, 25 October 1917, p. 8.

192    *a full recovery*    "Margaret Wilson Is Hurled from Carriage," *NY Tribune*, 8 August 1916, p. 3.

192    *American foreign policy*    George Creel, *Wilson and the Issues* (New York: The Century Company, 1916).

192    *"United States today"*    Creel, *Wilson and the Issues*, p. 88.

192    *particularly glaring*    Creel, *Wilson and the Issues*.

192    *in league with the League*    Letterhead dated [1915] Men's League for Woman Suffrage of the State of New York. Schlesinger Library Woman Studies Collection, 002685_006_0275_From_1_to_11. It lists Peabody as honorary president, Beadle as secretary, Gilbert Roe as chairman of the Campaign Committee, Peabody as head of the executive committee, and Frank Harman Black as head of the organization committee. Creel appears as chairman of the "Office of the Publicity Committee." Among the names along the left-hand column are Walter Lippmann, Will Irwin, Eastman, Samuel Merwin, Middleton, Ogden Reid, Charles Edward Russell, Villard, William Allen White, Williams, Young, and other writers and journalists along with many members of the Players Club.

192    *from Andrew Carnegie*    PWW 38:23–24n1, Peabody to Wilson, 10 August 1916; PWW 38:549, 28 October 1916; PWW 38:620–621, Peabody to Wilson, 6 November 1916; PWW 38:625, Wilson to Peabody, 10 November 1916.

192    *with Tumulty*    Villard, *Fighting Years*, p. 256: "As far as Mr. Wilson is concerned, I saw him only rarely and never was on anything approaching an intimate footing. He never sent for me or talked with me informally about politics or affairs. If I influenced him during this period it was through my letters in the Evening Post and my daily contacts with Joe Tumulty, for whom I retain to this day a great liking and respect. . . ."

193    *"make any Wilson speeches"*    "Pen Points," *Los Angeles Times*, 6 November 1916, p. 114.

193    *"Illinois and Oregon"*    See Brown, "Did Woodrow Wilson's Gender Politics Matter?" p. 146, where Brown notes the significance of Wilson's sweep of Western states, "which could mean that the party leadership no longer dictated obedience to the South. At the same time, women's support for Wilson reputedly put him over the top in California and thereby secured his victory. This naturally strengthened his loyalty to those women who had, themselves, been enfranchised by the state approach and had turned away from the 'belligerent' Paul to vote for Wilson, his peace platform and, presumably, his approach to woman suffrage." (Citing John Milton Cooper Jr., *The Warrior and the Priest* [Cambridge: Harvard University Press, 1983], p. 250, and Christine A. Lunardini, *From Equal Suffrage to Equal Rights* [New York: New York University Press, 1986], pp. 101–102.)

193     *"of the United States"*   PWW 40:196, "After-dinner Speech to the Gridiron Club," 9 December 1916.

193     *Peabody and Creel*   "Society," *Washington Post*, 13 December 1916, p. 7.

193     *"subject to your approval"*   PWW 40:375, Colonel Edward Mandell House to Wilson, 31 December 1916.

193     *prohibition and women's suffrage*   PWW 40:173–5, Colonel Edward Mandell House to Wilson, 5 December 1916.

193     *courageous feminism*   "Will Honor Noted Woman," *Daily Long Island Farmer*, 20 December 1916, p. 1.

## CHAPTER 10

195     *entered the World War*   Harper, *History of Woman Suffrage*, Vol. VI, p. 478. From the chapter on New York: "Early in 1917 the entire organization was well developed and suffrage work was at its height when it was suddenly stopped short by the entrance of the United States into the World War. At once everything else became of secondary importance."

195     *"in this great cause"*   "Suffragists Will Picket White House," *NY Times*, 10 January 1917, p. 1.

196     *surround the executive mansion*   "Picket Line of 3,000," *Washington Post*, 11 January 1917, p. 1.

196     *front-page headline*   "Suffragists Will Picket White House," *NY Times*, 10 January 1917, p. 1.

196     *"with what I got then"*   PWW 40:473, "Press Conference," 15 January 1917.

196     *"endorsement and public recognition"*   PWW 40:549, Wilson to Lynn Joseph Frazier, 23 January 1917.

196     *"should be applauded"*   PWW 41:13, Wilson to Carrie Chapman Catt, 25 January 1917.

196     *"the moral obligation is complete"*   PWW 41:299, Wilson to William Riley Crabtree, 28 February 1917.

197     *"must be wholesome"*   Lawrence, *The True Story of Woodrow Wilson*, p. 136.

197     *"parts of this country"*   PWW 41:8, Villard to Wilson, 24 January 1917, and PWW 41:281, Villard and NAACP members to Wilson, 14 February 1917.

197     *"Its Intended Consequences"*   "Pacifists Start Anti-War Fight," *NY Tribune*, 7 February 1917, p. 3.

197     *"servant of humanity"*   PWW 41:180–181, Rabbi Stephen S. Wise to Wilson, 9 February 1917.

197   *advocacy of a League of Nations*   PWW 41:305–308, Address of Max Eastman to Wilson, 28 February 1917.

198   *"with the fizzle"*   Diary entry, Thomas W. Brahany, 4 March 1917. PWW 41:329–330.

198   *"the President's private life"*   Diary entry, Thomas W. Brahany, 4 March 1917. PWW 41:329–330.

198   *making his letters public*   For a fuller recounting, see Cooper, *Woodrow Wilson: A Biography*, pp. 301–303.

198   *"use on cold days"*   Diary entry, Thomas W. Brahany, 4 March 1917. PWW 41:329-330.

198   *"Wait for Liberty"*   Diary entry, Thomas W. Brahany, 4 March 1917. PWW 41:329-330.

199   *Washington had ever seen*   Diary entry, Thomas W. Brahany, 4 March 1917. PWW 41:329–330.

199   *"inauguration day"*   PWW 41:399, Anna Howard Shaw to Alice Edith Binsse Warren, 9 March 1917.

199   *"fighting with us"*   PWW 41:399, Anna Howard Shaw to Alice Edith Binsse Warren, 9 March 1917.

199   *wholly different approach*   Park, *Front Door Lobby*, chapter 2.

199   *"curtain raiser"*   "Suffrage Week at Theater," *NY Tribune*, 11 March 1917, p. 2.

199.  *referendum was guaranteed*   "State Will Vote on Suffrage Again," *NY Times*, 12 March 1917, p. 1.

199   *"strenuous period"*   Stanton et al., *History of Woman Suffrage*, Vol. I, p. 485.

199   *"brilliant"*   Creel, *Rebel at Large*, p. 173.

200   *"women of other states"*   "Suffragists See Victory," *NY Times*, 14 March 1917, p. 10.

200   *"Army and Navy"*   "Suffragists Out to Get Recruits," *NY Times*, 11 April 1917, p. 13.

200   *over age twenty-one*   Stanton et al., *History of Woman Suffrage*, Vol. I, p. 478.

200   *"for people to have"*   PWW 432:39, A Memorandum by George Creel, 11 April 1917.

200   *the CPI*   PWW 42:43, Wilson to Josephus Daniels, 12 April 1917 and PWW 42:52, Josephus Daniels diary entry, 13 April 1917.

200   *before his CPI appointment*   "Creel to Direct Nation's Publicity," *NY Times*, 15 April 1917, p. 1; "Creel Heads Press Bureau," *NY Sun*, 15 April 1917, pp. 1–2; "George Creel, Magazine Writer, Will Censor Nation's War News," *NY Tribune*, 15 April 1917.

200   *"ably filled the office of secretary"*   Harper, *History of Woman Suffrage*, Vol. VI, p. 485.

201   *prosuffrage daughter Margaret*   "Creel to Direct Nation's Publicity," *NY Times*, 15 April 1917, p. 1.

201   *Villard's* Evening Post   "The Nation's Publicity Bureau," *NY Evening Post*, 24 May 1917, p. 5.

201   *his published words*   "'Burn Them Alive' He Says of Antis." *NY Tribune*, 23 January 1915, p. 16.

201   *male supporters of suffrage*   "Men Give Suffrage Reasons," *NY Times*, 25 April 1917, p. 13. The speakers were Richard Billings, James Cushman, George L. Shearer, Abram Flexner, James Byrne, Herbert Parsons, George W. Perkins, and Willard D. Straight.

201   *"twisted into a moral issue"*   "Clash on Suffrage at Rabbi's Council," *NY Times*, 24 April 1917, p. 11.

201   *"defense of the nation"*   "Dr. Silverman Explains His Opposition," *NY Tribune*, 25 April 1917, p. 9.

201   *prosuffrage resolution*   "Clash on Suffrage at Rabbi's Council," *NY Times*, 27 April 1917, p. 11.

201   *the federal amendment*   "Suffragists Assail Selection of Root. Object to Him Going to Russia—Malone Speaks at Hearing," *Washington Post*, 27 April 1917, p. 7.

201   *House suffrage committee*   PWW 42:269–270, Helen Hamilton Gardener to Wilson, 10 May 1917.

201   *cesspool of politics* See "The Mission of Woman," *NY Times*, 16 November 1896, p. 8; "Rabbi Against Suffragettes," *NY Times,* 30 January 1909, p. 5; "Does New York Want Woman Suffrage?" *NY Times*, 28 November 1909, p. SM12; and "Suffragists Hear Varying View of Their Status in Community," *NY Tribune*, 20 November 1913, p. 7.

202   *"cause of woman suffrage"*   PWW 142:293, Wilson to Edward W. Pou, 14 May 1917.

202   *written him a week earlier*   PWW 42:237–238n1, Carrie Chapman Catt to Wilson, 7 May 1917.

202   *"very warm"*   "Suffragists May Move In," *Los Angeles Times*, 15 May, 1917, p. 12; "Suffragists See Wilson," *NY Times,* 15 May 1917, p. 12; "President Tells Suffragists His Mind Is 'To Let,'" *NY Tribune*, 15 May 1917, p. 8. "Wilson's Mind 'To Let' on Suffrage," *Boston Globe*, 15 May 1917, p. 13. Other group members were Dr. E.A. Rumely, independent Republican and vice president of the *NY Mail*; John Spargo, a Socialist author; and Virgil Hinshaw of the Prohibitionists.

202   *"is of like opinion"*   PWW 142:320–320n1, Edward W. Pou to Wilson, 17 May 1917.

202   *Heflin directly, too*   PWW 42:474–475, Helen Hamilton Gardener to Wilson, 10 June 1917; PWW 42:497, Wilson to James Thomas Heflin, 13 June 1917.

202   *"call on me"*   PWW 43:36, James Thomas Heflin to Wilson, 28 June 1917.

202 *"view of the matter"* PWW 43:71n1, Wilson to James Thomas Heflin, 2 July 1917.

203 *107 opposed* Cong. Rec., 65th Cong., 1st. sess., p. 7384, as cited in PWW 142:320–320n1.

203 *"over to our side"* "Suffragists Refuse to Call Off Pickets from White House," *NY Tribune*, 30 May 1917, p. 9.

203 *"Russian Mission"* "Flaunt Fresh Banner," *Washington Post*, 21 June 1917, p.1.

203 *denounced the women's conduct* "Flaunt Fresh Banner," *Washington Post*, 21 June 1917, p. 1.

204 *"go on a 'hunger strike'"* "Brave Third Day Riot," *Washington Post*, 22 June 1917, p. 1.

204 *"future conduct"* "Move Along, Pickets," *Washington Post*, 23 June 1917, p. 1.

204 *"in their own government"* "Move Along, Pickets," *Washington Post*, 23 June 1917, p. 1.

204 *just as quickly* "Bar Cells to Pickets," *Washington Post*, 24 June 1917, p. 2.

204 *"obnoxious as possible"* PWW 42:560561n1, Wilson to Jessie Woodrow Wilson Sayre, 22 June 1917.

204 *"daily press statement"* "New Pickets on Duty," *Washington Post*, 25 June 1917, p. 2.

204 *strike to succeed* "Arrest 12 Pickets," *Washington Post*, 26 June 1917, p. 1.

204 *British counterparts* "Take 9 More 'Suffs,'" *Washington Post*, 27 June 1917, p. 2.

205 *"comfortably fixed"* "Suffragettes in Jail," *Washington Post*, 28 June 1917, p. 1.

205 *"floors of Congress"* "Plot of 'Suffs' Fails," *Washington Post*, 29 June 1917, p. 2.

205 *in their midst* "'Suffs' War Menace," *Washington Post*, 30 June 1917, p. 2.

205 *one day a week* "Women to Picket One Day a Week," *Washington Post*, 2 July 1917, p. 3.

205 *yachting on the Potomac* "Militants in Riot; 13 Held for Trial," *Washington Post*, 5 July 1917, p. 1.

205 *"drag out fight"* "Militants in Riot; 13 Held for Trial," *Washington Post*, 5 July 1917, p. 1.

205 *attempting to sell* "Militants Argue Case," *Washington Post*, 6 July 1917, p. 2; and "Has Choice of Trial," *Washington Post*, 8 July 1917, p. 2.

205 *refinement like you* "Militants Go to Jail," *Washington Post*, 7 July 1917, p. 2.

205 *that same week* "Defiant 'Pickets' Plan New Drive," *Washington Post*, 9 July 1917, p. 2.

205 *"at the militants"* "Surprise by Pickets," *Washington Post*, 13 July 1917, p. 2.

206 *"having met him"* Stevens, *Jailed for Freedom*, p. 263.

206    *"high-powered pressure"*  Stevens, *Jailed for Freedom*, p. 267.

206    *"suffragist of long standing"*  Stevens, *Jailed for Freedom*, p. 267

206    *"the Administration was losing"*  Stevens, *Jailed for Freedom*, p. 267.

206    *"ways and means"*  Stevens, *Jailed for Freedom*, p. 267.

206    *"other things to do"*  Stevens, *Jailed for Freedom*, p. 267.

206    *"just swept aside"*  Stevens, *Jailed for Freedom*, p. 267.

207    Judge Mullowny  "Pickets Amuse Court," *Washington Post*, 17 July 1917, p. 12.

207    *"occasion was unceremonious"*  "Sixteen Militants Begin 60-Day Term," *Washington Post*, 18 July 1917, p. 1.

207    *Dudley Field Malone*  "Suffragists Take 60-Day Sentence; Won't Pay Fines," *NY Times*, 18 July 1917, pp. 1, 5. Also, "Sixteen Militants Begin 60-Day Term," *Washington Post*, 18 July 1917, p. 1.

207    *"the ultimate bad effects"*  PWW 43:201–202n1, Gilson Gardner to Wilson, 17 July 1917.

208    *"this great blunder"*  PWW 43:201–202n1, Gilson Gardner to Wilson, 17 July 1917.

208    *"entirely on its merits"*  PWW 43:201–202n1, Gilson Gardner to Wilson, 17 July 1917.

208    *"latest militant demonstration"*  "Suffragists Take 60-Day Sentence; Won't Pay Fines," *NY Times*, 18 July 1917, pp. 1, 5.

208    *Malone declined to confirm*  "Suffragists Take 60-Day Sentence; Won't Pay Fines," *NY Times*, 18 July 1917, pp. 1, 5.

208    *"refused to interfere"*  "Sixteen Militants Begin 60-Day Term," *Washington Post*, 18 July 1917, p. 1.

208    *"his emphatic statements"*  "Suffragists Take 60-Day Sentence; Won't Pay Fines," *NY Times*, 18 July 1917, pp. 1, 5.

208    *"constitutional guarantees"*  "Suffragists Take 60-Day Sentence; Won't Pay Fines," *NY Times*, 18 July 1917, pp. 1, 5.

208    *gathered around them*  "Suffragists Take 60-Day Sentence; Won't Pay Fines," *NY Times*, 18 July 1917, pp. 1, 5.

208    *Hotel Knickerbocker*  Letters between Doris Stevens and Dudley Field Malone, especially 12 August 1915 to September 1922. Doris Stevens Papers, Box 22, No. 5. Schlesinger Library, Radcliffe Institute, Harvard University.

209    *"seems impossible to carry"*  Letter, Malone to Stevens, 12 August 1915, Box 22, No. 5. Schlesinger Library, Radcliffe Institute, Harvard University.

209    *"made it young again"*  Letter, Malone to Stevens, 12 August 1915, Box 22, No. 5. Schlesinger Library, Radcliffe, Harvard University.

209 *"to straighten the matter out"* "Militants' Plight Shocks President," *Washington Post*, 19 July 1917, p. 1.

209 *"emergency war measure"* "Militants' Plight Shocks President," *Washington Post*, 19 July 1917, p. 1.

209 *"government position"* "Militants' Plight Shocks President," *Washington Post*, 19 July 1917, p. 1.

209 *"entirely on our own responsibility"* "Militants' Plight Shocks President," *Washington Post*, 19 July 1917, p. 1.

210 *an administration measure* PWW 43:212–213, A.J.H. Hopkins to Wilson, 18 July 1917.

210 *seventy-three additional votes* PWW 43:212–213, A.J.H. Hopkins to Wilson, 18 July 1917.

210 *"In haste"* PWW 43:212–213, Wilson to Postmaster Albert S. Burleson, 19 July 1917.

210 *George Gordon Battle* "Wilson, Shocked at Jailing Militants, May Advocate 'Votes for Women' as Part of War Emergency Program," *NY Times*, 19 July 1917, p. 1.

210 *"did not take part in the conference"* "Wilson, Shocked at Jailing Militants, May Advocate 'Votes for Women' as Part of War Emergency Program," *NY Times*, 19 July 1917, p. 1.

210 *"workhouse sentences"* "Fight of the Militants Taken to Congress," *Washington Post*, 20 July 1917, p. 1.

210 *both houses of Congress* "Fight of the Militants Taken to Congress," *Washington Post*, 20 July 1917, p. 1.

210 *gratitude to the president* "Pardon Pleases Shaw," *Washington Post*, 20 July 1917, p. 1.

211 *"until it was accepted"* Louis Brownlow, *A Passion for Anonymity: The Autobiography of Louis Brownlow, Second Half* (Chicago: University of Chicago Press, 1958), pp. 78–79, as cited in PWW 43:201–202n1, Gilson Gardner to Wilson, 17 July 1917.

211 *"intended to take further action"* Brownlow, *A Passion for Anonymity*, pp. 78–79, as cited in PWW 43:201–202n1, Gilson Gardner to Wilson, 17 July 1917.

211 *"forcing the issue"* "Pickets 'Obliged to Wilson'; But They'll Picket Again," *NY Tribune*, 21 July 1917, p. 14.

211 *"only have appealed the case"* "Pickets 'Obliged to Wilson'; But They'll Picket Again," *NY Tribune*, 21 July 1917, p. 14.

211 *"should their case be appealed"* "Pickets 'Obliged to Wilson'; But They'll Picket Again," *NY Tribune*, 21 July 1917, p. 14.

211 *would surely fail* "Fight of the Militants Taken to Congress," *Washington Post*, 20 July 1917, p. 1.

211 *"at least several years"* "Fight of the Militants Taken to Congress," *Washington Post*, 20 July 1917, p. 1.

211    *the winter legislative session of 1917–1918*   "Fight of the Militants Taken to Congress," *Washington Post*, 20 July 1917, p. 1.

212    *"not a pleasant thing to hear"*   PWW 43:290, Diary of Colonel Edward Mandell House, 26 July 1917.

212    *"if he was sincerely for it"*   PWW 43:290, Diary of Colonel Edward Mandell House, 26 July 1917.

212    *"should have stated the truth"*   PWW 43:290, Diary of Colonel Edward Mandell House, 26 July 1917.

212    *"far more effective"*   PWW 43:290–291, Diary of Colonel Edward Mandell House, 26 July 1917.

212    *Malone did not promise*   PWW 43:290–291, Diary of Colonel Edward Mandell House, 26 July 1917.

213    *"serve you and the country well"*   PWW 43:283n1, Colonel Edward Mandell House to Wilson, 26 July 1917.

213    *"most substantial and satisfactory success"*   PWW 43:462n1–462n2, Wilson to Vira Whitehouse, 14 August 1917.

213    *"fallen upon the suffragettes"*   PWW 43:477–478, Henry Noble Hall to Wilson, 15 August 1917.

213    *"traitors or degenerates"*   PWW 43:477–478, Henry Noble Hall to Wilson, 15 August 1917.

214    *"Kaiser Wilson"*   PWW 43:477–478, Henry Noble Hall to Wilson, 15 August 1917.

214    *"President of the United States"*   PWW 43:477–478, Henry Noble Hall to Wilson, 15 August 1917.

214    *"more successfully handled"*   PWW 44:12n1, Wilson to Henry Noble Hall, 21 August, 1917.

214    *wound up at Occoquan*   "Protest for Pickets. Militants Meet at Cameron House Tonight to Aid Prisoners," *Washington Post*, 20 August 1917, p. 1.

214    *"armed to the teeth"*   Stevens, *Jailed for Freedom*, pp. 123–124.

214    *"but it had to be told"*   Stevens, *Jailed for Freedom*, pp. 123–124.

214    *The offensive banner*   Stevens, *Jailed for Freedom*, p. 127.

214    *"open letter"*   PWW 44:108–116, Charles A. Lindbergh to Wilson, 27 August 1917.

215    *two years earlier*   Bruce L. Larson, *Lindbergh of Minnesota: A Political Biography* (New York: Harcourt, Brace, Jovanovich, 1971, 1973), p. 206.

215    *"defenseless women"*   PWW 44:108–116, Charles A. Lindbergh to Wilson, 27 August 1917.

215    *"illegal and indefensible"*   PWW 44:108–116, Charles A. Lindbergh to Wilson, 27 August 1917.

215    *suffragists in the House of Representatives*    PWW 44:108–116, Charles A. Lindbergh to Wilson, 27 August 1917.

215    *"upon which our government is founded"*    PWW 44:108–116, Charles A. Lindbergh to Wilson, 27 August 1917.

215    *"in which we all believe"*    PWW 44:62, Wilson to Vira Boarman Whitehouse to Wilson, 27 August 1917.

216    *"fair attitude to take"*    PWW 44:79, Vira Boarman Whitehouse to Wilson, 28 August 1917.

216    *"bravely from the racetracks"*    "Suffragists Hear Mayor Denounce Picketing," *NY Tribune*, 30 August 1917.

216    *Norman de R. Whitehouse*    "Suffragists Hear Mayor Denounce Picketing," *NY Tribune*, 30 August 1917. Other men on hand included Captain Rupert Hughes, a novelist and film director as well as a military officer; and, from upstate, Carl Jonas Nordstrom of Lake George, and from Ogdensburg, George Notman and the town's mayor, Julius Frank.

216    *until the declaration of war*    "Suffragists Hear Mayor Denounce Picketing," *NY Tribune*, 30 August 1917.

216    *"does not bring them victory"*    Sarah Addington, "Plans for Last Suffragist State Vote Campaign Laid at Saratoga," *NY Tribune*, 2 September 1917, p. 9.

216    *"pent-up spirit of the thousand women"*    Addington, "Plans for Last Suffragist State Vote Campaign Laid at Saratoga," *NY Tribune*, 2 September 1917, p. 9.

216    *"one gigantic flame"*    Addington, "Plans for Last Suffragist State Vote Campaign Laid at Saratoga," *NY Tribune*, 2 September 1917, p. 9.

216    *"luckiest woman in the world"*    Addington, "Plans for Last Suffragist State Vote Campaign Laid at Saratoga," *NY Tribune*, 2 September 1917, p. 9.

216    *"new strength to the ranks"*    Harriet Burton Laidlaw, *James Lees Laidlaw, 1868–1932*, privately printed 1932, p. 85, citing *The League of Women Voters Bulletin*, May 1932.

216    *"all the women put together"*    H.B. Laidlaw, *James Lees Laidlaw*, p. 99.

217    *"I want some"*    Addington, "Plans for Last Suffragist State Vote Campaign Laid at Saratoga," *NY Tribune*, 2 September 1917, p. 9.

217    *All of them nodded yes*    Addington, "Plans for Last Suffragist State Vote Campaign Laid at Saratoga," *NY Tribune,* 2 September 1917, p. 9.

217    *had not offered his*    PWW 44:167–168, Dudley Field Malone to Wilson, 7 September 1917.

217    *"women of the West"*    PWW 44:167–168, Dudley Field Malone to Wilson, 7 September 1917.

217    *"midst of the great war"*    PWW 44:167–168, Dudley Field Malone to Wilson, 7 September 1917.

218     *"maintain our democratic leadership"*    PWW 44:167–168, Dudley Field Malone to Wilson, 7 September 1917.

218     *"national emancipation"*    PWW 44:167–168, Dudley Field Malone to Wilson, 7 September 1917.

218     *"demands of them such sacrifice"*    PWW 44:167–168, Dudley Field Malone to Wilson, 7 September 1917.

218     *"brilliant leadership"*    PWW 44:167–168, Dudley Field Malone to Wilson, 7 September 1917.

218     *run for governor of New Jersey*    PWW 44:167–168, Dudley Field Malone to Wilson, 7 September 1917.

218     *"democratic effort"*    PWW 44:167–168, Dudley Field Malone to Wilson, 7 September 1917.

218     *federal suffrage amendment*    For example, "Malone Breaks with Wilson Over Suffrage. Resigns Position Because Wilson Will Not Back Anthony Bill. Attacks Policy of Government. Declares Promises Have Not Been Kept. Cites His Service," *NY Tribune*, 8 September 1917, p. 1.

218     *ready to accept*    PWW 44:185, Diary entry of Colonel Edward Mandell House, 10 September 1917.

219     *"sacrifice you are making for it"*    "Malone's Action Called Chivalrous by New York Woman. Suffragist Wire Congratulations for 'Glorious Act' Despite Stand on Pickets," *NY Tribune*, 9 September 1917, p. 14.

219     *"finest knights of chivalry"*    "Suffragists See No Aid in Malone," *NY Times*, 9 September 1917, p. 8.

219     *"party's cause in this State"*    "Suffragists See No Aid in Malone," *NY Times*, 9 September 1917, p. 8.

219     *"stirring times"*    "Suffragists See No Aid in Malone," *NY Times*, 9 September 1917, p. 8.

219     "That's Dudley Field Malone"    Alice Duer Miller, "To Dudley Field Malone," *NY Tribune*, 16 September 1917, p. B3.

219     *"all the other suffragists"*    "The Resignation of Collector Malone," *NY Times*, 9 September 1917, p. 22.

220     *"negligible thing"*    "The Resignation of Collector Malone," *NY Times*, 9 September 1917, p. 22.

220     *secretary of the treasury*    "Byron Newton Chosen for Port Collector," *NY Times*, 18 September 1917, p. 9.

220     *"have set apart for women"*    "To Byron R. Newton," *NY Tribune*, 14 October 1917, p. B3.

220     *"for such work"*    "To Byron R. Newton," *NY Tribune*, 14 October 1917, p. B3.

220 *"—and resign"* "To Byron R. Newton," *NY Tribune*, 14 October 1917, p. B3.

221 *tipping the balance* "Maine Suffrage Defeat Analyzed," *Christian Science Monitor*, 18 September 1917, p. 9.

221 *"Kaiser Wilson" banners* "Lays Maine Defeat to 'Picketing,'" *NY Times*, 16 September 1917, p. 6.

221 *constitution to allow it* "Suffragists Calm in the Face of Defeat," *NY Times*, 12 September 1917, p. 9.

221 *school suffrage* "The Maine Election—and Suffrage," *NY Tribune*, 16 September 1917, p. D3.

222 *"unpierced"* "The Eastern Front Still Unpierced," *Boston Globe*, 11 September 1917, p. 6.

222 *"astonishingly wide stream"* "The Eastern Front Still Unpierced," *Boston Globe*, 11 September 1917, p. 6.

222 *"tone of the suffrage campaign"* "Suffragists Bar Spats in Parade," *NY Tribune*, 30 September 1917, p. 3.

222 *ready to offer the state* "Suffragists Bar Spats in Parade," *NY Tribune*, 30 September 1917, p. 3.

222 *"Tax-Paying Women"* "Noted Men to Tell Why They Favor Suffrage," *NY Tribune*, 3 October 1917, p 16.

222 *"Men's Experience Meetings"* "Noted Men to Tell Why They Favor Suffrage," *NY Tribune*, 3 October 1917, p 16.

222 *William Jennings Bryan* "Noted Men to Tell Why They Favor Suffrage," *NY Tribune*, 3 October 1917, p 16.

223 *"has become a necessity"* Katrina Trask, "Woman Suffrage a Practical Necessity," *Woman Citizen*, 13 October 1917, pp. 368–369.

223 *"should not be denied them"* Trask, "Woman Suffrage a Practical Necessity," *Woman Citizen*, 13 October 1917, pp. 368–369.

223 *support the state amendment* PWW 44:335, Vira Whitehouse to Wilson, 8 October 1917.

224 *"to do in this war"* PWW 44:384, Vira Whitehouse to Joseph Tumulty, 13 October 1917.

224 *"set a great example in this matter"* PWW 44:372, Wilson to Carrie Chapman Catt, 13 October 1917.

224 *"State Suffrage campaign"* PWW 44:391, Carrie Chapman Catt to Wilson, 16 October 1917.

224 *"prosecution of this war"* "Wise Suggests Strike Would Win Suffrage," *NY Tribune*, 16 October 1917.

224 *"safe for peace"* "Tells Dissatisfied to Quit Country," *NY Times*, 16 October 1917, p. 13.

224 *"lady like long enough"*   "Wise Suggests Strike Would Win Suffrage," *NY Tribune*, 16 October 1917, p. 4.

225 *"but one of expediency"*   PWW 44:440–441, "An Address to the President," Vira Boarman Whitehouse, 25 October 1917.

225 *"our immediate consideration"*   PWW 44:441–443, "A Reply," Wilson to the NY State Woman's Suffrage Party delegation, 25 October 1917.

225 *"distinction of originality"*   PWW 44:441–443, "A Reply," Wilson to the NY State Woman's Suffrage Party delegation, 25 October 1917.

225 *front-page headline*   "Suffrage to Fore," *NY Times*, 26 October 1917, pp. 1, 24.

226 *"voting for woman suffrage"*   "Suffrage to Fore," *NY Times*, 26 October 1917, pp. 1, 24.

226 *a "new era"*   "Country First Is Keynote of Suffragists," *NY Tribune*, 28 October 1917, p. 8.

227 *"The suffs are coming"*   "Country First Is Keynote of Suffragists," *NY Tribune*, 28 October 1917, p. 8.

227 *political prisoners, not criminals*   "Militants to Take Demands to Jailer," *Washington Post*, 3 November 1917, p. 7.

227 *"professional evaluations"*   "Pickets Fed by Force," *Washington Post*, 9 November 1917, p. 1. See also Stevens, *Jailed for Freedom*, p. 226, concerning her correspondence with Paul's prison physician.

228 *tut-tutted in a headline*   "Just Can't Keep Out of a Scrap. Merely Mentions Those White House Pickets and—Zowie!!" *Chicago Tribune*, 4 November 1917, p. 15. This was also the year Eastman ran afoul of the Espionage Act and the US Postal Service stopped the mailed distribution of the August 1917 issue of *The Masses* because of two controversial cartoons and an Eastman editorial it included. He, Floyd Dell, and several cartoonists and contributors were indicted for sedition on November 19, charged with conspiracy. Malone, who with Doris Stevens was also a social friend of Eastman's, served as his defense attorney throughout the 1918 proceedings. See "Radicals Form Body to Fight Suppression of Press by P.O.," *NY Call*, 14 July 1917. See also PWW 44:468 and 470, Letter to Wilson from Upton Sinclair, 30 October 1917. A footnote explains that the Postmaster General considered the content of the *Masses* to be "rank treason" and Eastman himself "no better than a traitor." See also, "7 on Masses Staff Indicted for Sedition," *NY Tribune*, 20 November 1917, p. 14, and "Radicals Have Final Fling before Sedition Bill Is Law," *NY Tribune*, 10 May 1918, p. 8.

228 *"in public places"*   W.E.B. Du Bois, "Votes for Women," *The Crisis*, Vol. 15, No. 1, November 1917, p. 8.

228 *"rendering service"*   "Suffragists Neglect Cause to Help Country in Crisis," *NY Tribune*, 4 November 1917, p. 13.

228 *"unquestionably make votes"*   "Suffragists Neglect Cause to Help Country in Crisis," *NY Tribune*, 4 November 1917, p. 13.

228    *Peabody and Untermyer*   For example, Advertisement, "See What They Say!" *NY Tribune*, 5 November 1917, p. 9.

229    *ninety thousand votes*   "Suffrage Won for 2,000,000 Women of N.Y.," *NY Sun*, 7 November 1917, p. 1.

229    *"fight for the vote"*   "Suffrage Leaders Worked Faithfully For Victory Here," *NY Tribune*, 7 November 1917, p. 5.

229    *Rhode Island*   "The Women's Victory," *Boston Globe*, 8 November 1917, p. 10.

229    *federal measure*   "Hylan and Tammany Ticket Win; Suffrage Carries City and State. New York Gives Ballot to Women," *NY Tribune*, 7 November 1917, p. 1.

229    *"freedom and democracy"*   Editorial, "Woman Suffrage," *NY Times*, 7 November 1917, p. 12.

231    *"its valuable service"*   "Women Citizens Pledge Votes to Nation's Welfare," *NY Times*, 8 November 1917, p. 1.

231    *"title of distinction"*   Harper, *History of Woman Suffrage*, Vol. VI, p. 484.

231    *"fortunes to this cause"*   "Women Citizens Pledge Votes to Nation's Welfare," *NY Times*, 8 November 1917, p. 1.

231    *"to be auxiliaries"*   "Women Citizens Pledge Votes to Nation's Welfare," *NY Times*, 8 November 1917, p. 1.

## A CODA

233    *"winning the victory"*   "Talk of Dropping Capital Pickets," *NY Times*, 9 November 1917, p. 13.

233    *"Demand it"*   "Talk of Dropping Capital Pickets," *NY Times*, 9 November 1917, p. 13.

234    *hunger strike since October*   "Demand Release of Pickets," *NY Times*, 9 November 1917, p. 13.

234    *Wilson took his advice*   PWW 44:551n1, George Creel to Wilson, 9 November 1917.

234    *a delegation from NAWSA*   PWW 44:556n2, Diary entry of Josephus Daniels, 9 November 1917.

234    *from across the country*   "Pickets Fed by Force," *Washington Post*, 9 November 1917, p. 1.

234    *her fellow protesters*   PWW 44:559–560 Memorandum, Joseph Tumulty to Wilson, 9 November 1917.

234    *"at the same time"*   Stevens, *Jailed for Freedom*, pp. 226–227.

234    *"but in spite of them"*   Lawrence, "For and Against Suffrage Pickets," *NY Evening Post*, 27 November 1917, pp. 1, 5.

235     *"the lesser of two evils"*    Stevens, *Jailed for Freedom*, pp. 226–227.

235     *would end the agitation*    Stevens, *Jailed for Freedom*, pp. 226–227.

235     *"not through the Senate"*    Stevens, *Jailed for Freedom*, pp. 226–227.

235     *about the course of events*    See Sally Hunter Graham, "Woodrow Wilson, Alice Paul, and the Woman Suffrage Movement," *Political Science Quarterly*, Vol. 98, No. 4, Winter, 1983–1984, pp. 665–679, especially 677–679, and the excellent summation of the mixed scholarly opinion on the role of the picketing in Wilson's conversion in Ross A. Kennedy, ed., *A Companion to Woodrow Wilson* (West Sussex, UK: Wiley-Blackwell, 2013), chapter 18, "Wilson and Woman Suffrage," by Barbara J. Steinson, pp. 343–363.

235     *remained behind bars*    "Suffrage Pickets Freed from Prison," *NY Times*, 28 November 1917, p. 13.

235     *"it has accomplished"*    "Suffrage Pickets Freed from Prison," *NY Times*, 28 November 1917, p. 13.

236     *"New York suffrage campaign"*    "Mrs. Whitehouse Is Going Abroad for Government," *NY Times*, 30 December 1917, p. 1.

236     *that was not her role*    Vira B. Whitehouse, *A Year as a Government Agent* (New York: Harper and Brothers, 1920), p. 10.

236     *"and of the world"*    "Wilson Backs Amendment for Woman Suffrage," *NY Times*, 10 January 1918, p. 1.

236     *274 to 136*    PWW 45:565, Helen H. Gardener to Joseph Tumulty, 10 January 1918. See also, Cong. Record, 65th Cong. 2d sess., pp. 762–811.

237     *"kinsmen of such"*    "Woodrow Wilson, December 2, 1918," State of the Union Address, accessed at http://www.infoplease.com/t/hist/state-of-the-union/130.html, 19 December 2015.

237     *"critical New York triumph"*    Kennedy, *A Companion to Woodrow Wilson*, chapter 18; Steinson, "Wilson and Woman Suffrage," p. 353.

238     *House and Senate voting patterns*    Anne F. Scott and Andrew MacKay Scott, *One Half the People: The Fight for Woman Suffrage* (Champaign: University of Illinois Press) (reprint 1982).

238     *supported the measure*    Ross A. Kennedy, *A Companion to Woodrow Wilson* (West Sussex, UK: Wiley-Blackwell, 2013), chapter 18, "Wilson and Woman Suffrage," by Barbara J. Steinson, p. 353, citing Anne F. Scott and Andrew MacKay Scott, *One Half the People: The Fight for Woman Suffrage* (Philadelphia: Lippincott, 1975).

238     *tipping the congressional balance*    Also in 1917, North Dakota, Nebraska, and Rhode Island passed presidential suffrage by legislative enactment and Arkansas secured primary suffrage by legislative enactment. (Scott and Scott, *One Half the People*,

pp. 166–167, citing NAWSA, *Victory: How Women Won It* [New York: H.W. Wilson CO., 1940], Appendix 4, pp. 161–164.)

238    *passed in 1918*   Also in 1918, Texas secured primary suffrage by legislative enactment.

238    *attitude toward the federal measure*   Scott and Scott, *One Half the People* (Philadelphia: Lippincott, 1975), tables, pp. 161–163.

239    *"by their natural protectors"*   "Why Suffrage Fight Took 50 Years," *NY Times*, 15 June 1919, p. 82.

239    *"Legislatures and Congress"*   "Why Suffrage Fight Took 50 Years," *NY Times*, 15 June 1919, p. 82.

239    *"despised cause"*   "Why Suffrage Fight Took 50 Years," *NY Times*, 15 June 1919, p. 82.

240    *the last vote he ever cast*   Maud Nathan, *Once Upon a Time and Today* (New York: G.P. Putnam's Sons, 1933), pp. 179–180.

242    *"Why not we"*   Villard, *Fighting Years*, p. 199.

242    *"My Part in the Battle"*   Braly, *Memory Pictures*, pp. 223–263.

242    *but offers little more*   Creel, *Rebel At Large*, pp. 145–146, 148, 154, 173.

244    *leadership and administration*   "James L. Laidlaw, Dead of Pneumonia," *NY Times*, 10 May 1932, p. 21.

244    *noteworthy support for the suffrage cause*   "Oswald G. Villard Dies at Age of 77," *NY Times*, 2 October 1949, p. 80; "Max Eastman Dies; Author and Radical," *NY Times*, 26 March 1969, pp. 1, 47.

244    *on behalf of the women's cause*   "Dudley F. Malone Dies in California," *NY Times*, 6 October 1950, p. 25.

244    *One man's name appears*   "James L. Laidlaw Dead of Pneumonia," *NY Times*, 10 May 1932, p. 21.

244    *chair at the time*   "Honor Pioneers in Women's Rights," *NY Times*, 16 April 1931, p. 5. The plaque is now displayed in the State Capitol at Albany in the State Street lobby.

# Bibliography

ESSAYS AND ARTICLES

Aked, Charles F. "The Woman Movement in England." *North American Review*, Vol. 188, No. 636 (November 1908), pp. 650–658.

Alonso, Harriet Hyman. "Gender and Peace Politics in the First World War: United States: The People's Council of America." *International History Review*, Vol. 19, No. 1 (February 1997), pp. 83–102.

Atkinson, Wilmer. "Nuts to Crack." Philadelphia: Men's League for Woman Suffrage, 1916. Sophia Smith Collection, Women's History Archive at Smith College, reprinted in Kimmel and Mosmiller, *Against the Tide*, pp. 270–271.

Beard, Charles. "The Common Man and the Franchise." Men's League for Woman Suffrage, 1912, reprinted n.d. New York: National Woman Suffrage Publishing Co. (Also in Kimmel and Mosmiller, *Against the Tide*, pp. 263–264.)

Benedict, William. Unpublished letter to the *New York Times*, February 8, 1915, from Harriet B. Laidlaw Papers, Schlesinger Library, Radcliffe Institute, Harvard University, reprinted in Kimmel and Mosmiller, *Against the Tide*, pp. 249–250.

Borda, Jennifer L. "The Woman Suffrage Parades of 1910–1913: Possibilities and Limitations of an Early Feminist Rhetorical Strategy." *Western Journal of Communication*, Vol. 66, No. 1 (Winter 2002), pp. 25–52.

Brewer, David J., and Warner Van Norden. "Addresses Delivered at Lake Mohonk Mountain House by Justice David J. Brewer and Mr. Warner Van Norden," July 4, 1908, Mohonk Lake, Ulster County, NY.

Bzowski, Frances Diodato. "Spectacular Suffrage: Or, How Women Came Out of the Home and into the Streets and Theaters of New York City to Win the Vote." *New York History*, Vol. 76, No. 1 (January 1995), pp. 56–94.

Clarke, James Freeman. "Woman Suffrage." Woman Suffrage Leaflet 2, No. 14, February 15, 1889, reprinted in Kimmel and Mosmiller, *Against the Tide*, pp. 234–235.

Creel, George. "What Have Women Done with the Vote?" *The Century*, Vol. 87 (March 1914), pp. 663–671. (Reprinted by the Connecticut Woman Suffrage Association.)

———. "Chivalry versus Justice: Why the Women of the Nation Demand the Right to Vote." *Pictorial Review*, March 1915. (Reprinted April 1915 by the National Woman Suffrage Publishing Company.)

Crothers, Samuel McChord. *Meditations on Votes for Women* [excerpt]. Boston: Houghton Mifflin, 1914.

Daniels, Doris. "Building a Winning Coalition: The Suffrage Fight in New York State." *New York History*, Vol. 60, No. 1 (January 1979), pp. 58–80.

Debs, Eugene V. "Woman—Comrade and Equal." From *Writings and Speeches of Eugene V. Debs* (1915). New York: Hermitage, 1948, reprinted in Kimmel and Mosmiller, *Against the Tide*, pp. 250–252.

Dell, Floyd. "Feminism for Men." *The Masses*, Vol. 5, No. 10, July 1914, pp. 19–20. modjourn.org, accessed July 8, 2014.

————. "Adventures in Anti-land." *The Masses*, November 1915, Vol. 7, No. 1, Issue 53. modjourn.org, accessed July 8, 2014.

Douglass, Frederick. "The Rights of Women." *North Star*, July 28, 1848, reprinted in *History of Woman Suffrage*, Vol. I, and in Kimmel and Mosmiller, *Against the Tide*, pp. 211–212.

Du Bois, W.E.B. "Votes for Women." *The Crisis*, Vol. 15, No. 1, November 1917, reprinted in Kimmel and Mosmiller, *Against the Tide*, pp. 253–254. modjourn.org, accessed July 8, 2014.

Dunne, Finley Peter. "Mr. Dooley on Woman's Suffrage." *American Magazine*, Vol. 63 (June 1909), reprinted in Kimmel and Mosmiller, *Against the Tide*, pp. 236–239.

Eastman, Max. "Woman's Suffrage and Sentiment." The Equal Franchise Society of New York City, 1909.

————. "Women and Democracy." (Speech) National American Convention of 1910.

————. "Is Woman Suffrage Important?" *North American Review*, Vol. 193, Issue 662 (January 1911), pp. 60–71.

————. "The Unlimited Franchise." *Atlantic Monthly*, Vol. 108, No. 1 (July 1911), pp. 46–51.

————. "The Values of the Vote." Men's League for Woman Suffrage, March 21, 1912.

————. "The Early History of the Men's League." *The Woman Voter* (October 1912), pp. 17–18.

————. "Who's Afraid? Confessions of a Suffrage Orator." *The Masses*, Vol. 7, No. 1, Issue 53 (October–November 1915), pp. 7–9. modjourn.org, accessed July 7, 2014. Also reprinted in Kimmel and Mosmiller, *Against the Tide*, pp. 265–269.

Ellis, A. Caswell. "Why Men Need Equal Suffrage for Women." *War Messages to the American People*, No. 3. New York: National Woman Suffrage Publishing, 1918, reprinted in Kimmel and Mosmiller, *Against the Tide*, pp. 255–257.

Emerson, Ralph Waldo. "Woman: A Lecture Read before the Woman's Rights Convention," Boston, September 20, 1855. Reprinted in *Emerson's Complete Works*, Riverside ed., Boston: Houghton Mifflin, 1883–1893, and in Kimmel and Mosmiller, *Against the Tide*, pp. 217–220.

Fraser, Samuel. "What Are You Going to Do November Second?" An address before the Livingston County Granges, Geneseo, NY, 1914, reprinted in Kimmel and Mosmiller, *Against the Tide*, pp. 245–247.

Garrison, David Lloyd [age 8]. "Suffrage and ?S" *The Woman's Journal* (April 24, 1913), reprinted in Kimmel and Mosmiller, *Against the Tide*, p. 243.

Garrison, William Lloyd. "Intelligent Wickedness," *New York Daily Tribune* (September 7, 1853), and reprinted in *History of Woman Suffrage*, Vol. I, and in Kimmel and Mosmiller, *Against the Tide*, pp. 212–214.

Garwood, Omar Elvin. c. 1915. "Fifteen Reasons Why I Am in Favor of Universal Equal Suffrage," Schlesinger Library, Harriet B. Laidlaw Papers, Schlesinger Library, Radcliffe Institute, Harvard University, reprinted in Kimmel and Mosmiller, *Against the Tide*, pp. 269–271.

Graham, Sally Hunter. "Alice Paul and the Woman Suffrage Movement." *Political Science Quarterly*, Vol. 98, No. 4 (Winter 1983/1984), pp. 665–679.

Huff, Robert A. "Anne Miller and the Geneva Political Equality Club, 1897–1912." *New York History*, Vol. 65, No. 4 (October 1984), pp. 325–348.

Hunt, Rockwell D. "Some California Pioneers I Have Known." *The Quarterly: Historical Society of Southern California*, Vol. 30, No. 4 (December 1948), pp. 294–295.

Julian, George W. "The Slavery Yet to Be Abolished: Delivered at Various Points in Michigan and Iowa in the Year 1874." Reprinted in *Later Speeches on Political Questions with Select Controversial Papers*, ed. Grace Julian Clarke. Indianapolis: Carlon and Hollenbeck, 1889, and in Kimmel and Mosmiller, *Against the Tide*, pp. 224–226.

Kenton, Edna. "The Militant Women—and Women." *The Century* (November 1913), pp. 12–20.

Kimmel, Michael. "Real Men Join the Movement." *Ms*, Vol. 8, No. 3 (November–December 1997), pp. 52–59.

———. "Is It the End of Men, or Are Men Still in Power? Yes!" *Boston University Law Review*, Vol. 93, No. 3 (May 2013), pp. 689–697.

Laidlaw, James Lees. "Statement at National American Woman Suffrage Convention (1912)." Reprinted in *History of Woman Suffrage*, Vol. 5, and in Kimmel and Mosmiller, *Against the Tide*, pp. 262–263.

Lerner, Elinor. "Jewish Involvement in the New York City Woman Suffrage Movement." *American Jewish History*, Vol. 70, No. 4 (June 1981), pp. 442–461.

Lunardini, Christine A., and Thomas J. Knock, "Woodrow Wilson and Woman Suffrage: A New Look." *Political Science Quarterly*, Vol. 95, No. 4 (Winter 1980/1981), pp. 655–671.

Marcellus, Jane. "Southern Myths and the Nineteenth Amendment: The Participation of Nashville Newspaper Publishers in the Final State's Ratification." *Journalism and Mass Communication Quarterly*, Vol. 87, No. 2 (Summer 2010), pp. 241–262.

Massachusetts Men's League for Woman Suffrage. *Massachusetts Men's League for Woman Suffrage*. Boston: T. Todd, printers, 1911. Suffrage Collection, Series I, United States, Box 11, Folder 12. Sophia Smith Collection, Women's History Archive at Smith College.

Middleton, George. "What Feminism Means to Me." Speech delivered at Cooper Union, New York City, February 17, 1914. George Middleton Papers, Manuscript Division,

Library of Congress, reprinted in Kimmel and Mosmiller, *Against the Tide*, pp. 358–359.

Oshinsky, David. "The Crayon Was Mightier Than the Sword." *New York Times* (September 4, 1988). Describes Men's League for Woman Suffrage as a "virtually memberless group," p. 2.

Palmer, Robert, Hon. "Why Men Should Support Woman Suffrage." *The Conservative and Unionist Women's Franchise Review* (December 1912), p. 239.

Parker, Theodore. "A Sermon of the Public Function of Woman—Preached at the Music Hall, March 27, 1853." Reprinted in *Additional Speeches, Addresses and Occasional Sermons, Vol. 2*, Boston: Little Brown, 1855, and in Kimmel and Mosmiller, *Against the Tide*, pp. 214–217.

Pinar, William F. "The NAACP and the Struggle for Anti-Lynching Legislation, 1897–1917." In *The Gender of Racial Politics and Violence in America: Lynching, Prison Rape, and the Crisis of Masculinity*, pp. 623–682. New York: Peter Lang, 2001.

Randolph, A. Phillips. "Woman Suffrage and the Negro." *Messenger*, Vol. 1, No. 2 (November 1917), reprinted in Kimmel and Mosmiller, *Against the Tide*, pp. 254–255.

Rhodes, Arthur Neil. *Women's Suffrage and Intemperance* [excerpt]. Minneapolis: McIntire and Dahlen, 1914.

Schaffer, Ronald. "The New York City Woman Suffrage Party, 1909–1919." *New York History*, Vol. 43, No. 3 (July 1962), pp. 269–287.

Steffens, Lincoln. "Woman Suffrage Would Increase Corruption (1917)." From *Anti-Suffrage Arguments Answered*, Harriet B. Laidlaw Papers, Schlesinger Library, Radcliffe Institute, Harvard University, reprinted in Kimmel and Mosmiller, *Against the Tide*, pp. 272–273.

Stewart, Jane A. "Woman's Widening Way." *Journal of Education*, Vol. 76, No. 7 (1892; August 22, 1912), p. 175.

Szajkowski, Zosa. "The Jews and New York City's Mayoralty Election of 1917." *Jewish Social Studies*, Vol. 32, No. 4 (October 1970), pp. 286–306.

Terrell, Robert H., Hon. "Our Debt to Suffragists" (circa 1915). Library of Congress, Mary C. Terrell Collection, reprinted in Kimmel and Mosmiller, *Against the Tide*, pp. 252–253.

Testi, Arnaldo. "The Gender of Reform Politics: Theodore Roosevelt and the Culture of Masculinity." *Journal of American History*, Vol. 81, No. 4 (March 1995), pp. 1509–1533.

Villard, Oswald Garrison. "Women in the New York Municipal Campaign of 1901: Delivered by OGV at the National Suffrage Convention Held at Washington, DC, Feb. 14, 1902." In O.G. Villard, C.C. Catt, and National American Woman Suffrage Association Collection (Library of Congress), *Women in the New York Municipal Campaign of 1901*. Boston, MA: J. Youngjohn, 1902.

———. "Loyalty and the Editor." *Forum* (August 1, 1928), pp. 278–286.

Ward, Edward J. "Women Should Mind Their Own Business." New York: National Woman Suffrage Association, 1912, reprinted in Kimmel and Mosmiller, *Against the Tide*, pp. 240–242.

Wise, Rabbi Stephen S. "Statement on Suffrage." *The Field of Their Activity: The Position Taken on Suffrage by Rabbi Wise*, 2 February 1907. Sophia Smith Collection, Women's History Archive at Smith College, reprinted in Kimmel and Mosmiller, *Against the Tide*, pp. 260–261.

Zangwill, Israel. "Reception to Men Suffragists" (speech). *The Suffragette* (November 1, 1912).

## BOOKS

Anonymous. *Pamphlets in Favor of Woman Suffrage*, Vol. 3. Undated. (reprint)

Anonymous. *Pamphlets in Favor of Woman Suffrage*. Vol. 4. Undated. (reprint)

Antler, Joyce. *The Journey Home: Jewish Women and the American Century*. New York: Free Press, 1997.

Bausam, Ann. *With Courage and Cloth: Winning the Fight for a Woman's Right to Vote*. Washington, DC: National Geographic, 2004.

Berg, A. Scott. *Wilson*. New York: Berkeley Books, 2013.

Bernstein, Patricia. *The First Waco Horror: The Lynching of Jesse Washington and the Rise of the NAACP*. College Station, TX: Texas A&M University Press, 2005.

Biel, Steven. *Independent Intellectuals in the United States: 1910–1945*. New York: New York University Press, 1992.

Birmingham, Stephen. *The Grandees*. New York: Syracuse University Press, 1971.

Blair, Karen J. *The Torchbearers: Women and Their Amateur Arts Associations in America, 1890–1930*. Bloomington: Indiana University Press, 1994.

Blatch, Harriot Stanton. *Mobilizing Woman-Power*. Minneapolis: Filiquarian, 1918. (reprint)

———. *A Woman's Point of View: Some Roads to Peace*. New York: The Woman's Press, 1920.

———, and Alma Lutz. *Challenging Years: The Memoirs of Harriot Stanton Blatch*. New York: G.P. Putnam's Sons, 1940.

Boydston, Jo Ann, ed. *John Dewey: The Middle Works, 1899–1924*. Carbondale: Southern Illinois University Press, 1978.

Clift, Eleanor. *Founding Sisters and the Nineteenth Amendment*. New York: John Wiley and Sons, 2003.

Cooney, Robert P.J. *Winning the Vote: The Triumph of the American Woman Suffrage Movement*. Santa Cruz, CA: American Graphics Press, 2005.

Cooper, John Milton, Jr., ed. *Reconsidering Woodrow Wilson: Progressivism, Internationalism, War and Peace*. Baltimore: Johns Hopkins University Press, 2008.

———. *Woodrow Wilson: A Biography*. New York: Random House, 2009.

Creel, George. *Measuring Up Equal Suffrage*. New York: Men's League for Woman Suffrage, ca. 1909.

———. *Wilson and the Issues*. New York: Century and Co., 1916.

———. *Rebel at Large: Recollections of Fifty Crowded Years*. New York: G.P. Putnam's Sons, 1947.

Delap, Lucy, ed., and Maria DiCenzo and Leila Ryan. *Feminism and the Periodical Press, 1900–1918*. Vols. 1–3. New York: Routledge, 2006.

Dewey, John, and Charlene Haddock Seigfried, ed. *Feminist Interpretations of John Dewey.* State College: Penn State Press, 2002.

Downey, Kirstin. *The Woman behind the New Deal: The Life and Legacy of Frances Perkins— Social Security, Unemployment Insurance, and the Minimum Wage.* New York: Anchor Books, 2009.

Dubois, Ellen Carol. *Harriot Stanton Blatch and the Winning of Woman Suffrage.* New Haven, CT: Yale University Press, 1997.

Eastman, Max. *Journalism versus Art.* New York: Alfred A. Knopf, 1916.

———. *Venture.* New York: Albert and Charles Boni, 1927.

———. *Heroes I Have Known: Twelve Who Lived Great Lives.* New York: Simon and Schuster, 1942.

———. *Enjoyment of Living.* New York: Harper and Bros., 1948.

———. *Great Companions: Critical Memoirs of Some Famous Friends.* New York: Farrar, Straus and Cudahy, 1959.

Esmay, Lynn. *Lady of Yaddo: The Gilded Age Memoir of Katrina Trask.* Diamond Point, NY: French Mountain Press, 2013.

Flexner, Eleanor, and Ellen Fitzpatrick. Cambridge: Harvard Belknap Press, 1959, 1975.

Flexner, J.T. *An American Saga: The Story of Helen Thomas and Simon Flexner.* Boston: Little, Brown, 1984.

Formanek-Brunell, Miriam. *The Story of Rose O'Neill: An Autobiography.* Columbia: University of Missouri Press, 1997.

Franklin, Margaret Ladd, ed. *The Case for Woman Suffrage: A Bibliography.* New York: National College Equal Suffrage League (via NAWSA), 1913.

Franzen, Trisha. *Anna Howard Shaw: The Work of Woman Suffrage.* Urbana, IL: University of Illinois Press, 2014.

Friedl, Bettina, ed. *On to Victory: Propaganda Plays of the Woman Suffrage Movement.* Boston: Northeastern University Press, 1987.

Harper, Ida Husted, ed. *The History of the Woman Suffrage Movement.* Vols. V and VI. New York: NAWSA, 1922.

Havel, Hippolyte. "What's Anarchism?" Issued by the International Anarchist Relation Committee of America. Chicago: Free Society Group of Chicago; Detroit: International Group of Detroit, 1932. Paul Avrich Collection, Rare Book/Special Collections, Library of Congress.

Howe, Frederic C. *Confessions of a Reformer.* New York: Charles Scribner's Sons, 1925.

Humes, D.J. *Oswald Garrison Villard: Liberal of the 1920s.* Syracuse, NY: Syracuse University Press, 1960.

Hutchinson, George. *The Harlem Renaissance in Black and White.* Cambridge, MA: Harvard University Belknap Press, 1995.

Irwin, Will. *Propaganda and the News or What Makes You Think So!* Westport, CT: Greenwood Press, 1936.

———. *The Making of a Reporter.* New York: G.P. Putnam's Sons, 1942.

John, Angela, and Claire Eustance. *The Men's Share? Masculinities, Male Support and Women's Suffrage in Britain, 1890–1920.* New York: Routledge, 1997, 2014.

Johnson, Willis Fletcher. *George Harvey: A Passionate Patriot*. New York: Houghton Mifflin, 1929.

Kennedy, Ross A., ed. *A Companion to Woodrow Wilson*. West Sussex, UK: Wiley-Blackwell, 2013, especially, Barbara J. Steinson, chapter 18, "Wilson and Woman Suffrage," pp. 343–363.

Kerney, James. *The Political Education of Woodrow Wilson*. New York: The Century Company, 1926.

Kimmel, Michael S. *The History of Men: Essays in the History of American and British Masculinities*. Albany: State University of New York Press, 2005.

———. *Manhood in America: A Cultural History*. New York: Oxford University Press, 2012, 2006, 1998.

———, and Thomas E. Mosmiller. *Against the Tide: Pro-Feminist Men in the United States 1776–1990, A Documentary History*. Boston: Beacon Press, 1992.

Kuehl, W.F. *A Bibliography of the Writings of Hamilton Holt*. Winter Park, FL: Rollins College, 1959.

———. *Hamilton Holt: Journalist, Internationalist, Educator*. Gainesville: University of Florida Press, 1960.

Laidlaw, James Lees. *James Lees Laidlaw*. Privately published, 1932.

Larsen, Charles. *The Good Fight: The Remarkable Life and Times of Judge Ben Lindsey, the Colorful American Reformer Who Helped to Start the Juvenile Court System, Advocated a Sexual Revolution and Battled the Establishment in the Early 20th Century*. Chicago: Quadrangle Books, 1972.

Larson, Bruce L. *Lindbergh of Minnesota: A Political Biography*. New York: Harcourt, Brace, Jovanovich, 1971, 1973.

Lawrence, David. *The True Story of Woodrow Wilson*. New York: George H. Doran, 1924.

Lewis, David Levering. *W.E.B. Du Bois: Biography of a Race, 1868–1919*. New York: MacMillan, 1994.

Lumsden, Linda J. *Inez: The Life and Times of Inez Milholland*. Bloomington: Indiana University Press, 2004.

Lunardini, Christine. *From Equal Suffrage to Equal Rights: Alice Paul and the National Woman's Party, 1910–1928*. New York: New York University Press, 1986.

Martin, G.W. *CCB: The Life and Century of Charles C. Burlingham, New York's First Citizen, 1858–1959*. New York: Hill and Wang, 2005.

Menand, Louis. *The Metaphysical Club*. New York: Farrar, Straus, and Giroux, 2001.

Middleton, George. *Possession*. New York: Henry Holt, 1915.

———. *These Things Are Mine: The Autobiography of a Journeyman Playwright*. New York: MacMillan, 1947.

Miller, Kenneth E. *From Progressive to New Dealer: Frederic C. Howe and American Liberalism*. University Park: Pennsylvania State University Press, 2010.

Munhall, Patricia L., Ed Madden, and Virginia Fitzsimmons. *The Emergence of Man into the 21st Century*. Sudbury, MA: Jones and Bartlett, 2002.

Nathan, M., C.C. Catt, and National American Woman Suffrage Association Collection (Library of Congress). *Once Upon a Time and Today*. New York, London: G.P. Putnam's Sons, 1933.

O'Neill, W.L. *The Last Romantic: A Life of Max Eastman*. New York: Oxford University Press, 1978.

———. *Feminism in America: A History*. New Brunswick, NJ: Transaction, 1989.

Park, Maud Wood. *Front Door Lobby*. Minneapolis, MN: Filiquarian Publishing; Boston: Beacon Press, mss. 1960, 2009.

Paxton, Naomi. *Suffrage Plays*. London: Methuen Drama, Bloomsbury, 2013.

Petrash, Antonia. *Long Island and the Woman Suffrage Movement*. Charleston: History Press, 2013.

Phelps, Edith M. *Selected Articles on Woman Suffrage*. Minneapolis, MN: H.W. Wilson, 1910.

———. *Selected Articles on Woman Suffrage*. Minneapolis, MN: H.W. Wilson, 1912.

———. *Selected Articles on Woman Suffrage*. White Plains, NY: H.W. Wilson Company, 1916.

Pietrusza, David. *1920: The Year of the Six Presidents*. New York: Basic Books, 2007.

Pleck, Elizabeth H., and Joseph H. Pleck. *The American Man*. Englewood Cliffs, NJ: Prentice Hall, 1980.

Polier, Justine Wise, and James Waterman Wise. *The Personal Letters of Stephen Wise*. Boston: Beacon Press, 1956.

Ross, Ishbel. *Power with Grace: The Life of Mrs. Woodrow Wilson*. New York: G.P. Putnam's Sons, 1956.

Scott, Anne F., and Andrew MacKay Scott. *One Half the People: The Fight for Woman Suffrage*. Philadelphia: Lippincott, 1975.

Scott, William B., and Peter M. Ruckoff. *New York Modern: The Arts and The City*. Baltimore: Johns Hopkins University Press, 1999.

Shaw, Anna Howard. *The Story of a Pioneer*. Eugene, OR: Wipf and Stock, 1916.

Smith, Page. *America Enters the World*. New York: Penguin Books, 1985.

Stanton, E.C., S.B. Anthony, M.J. Gage, and I.H. Harper, eds. *History of Woman Suffrage*. Vol. I. New York: Arno Press, 1969.

———. *History of Woman Suffrage*. Salem, NH: Ayer Co., 1985.

Stevens, Doris, ed. Carol O'Hare. *Jailed for Freedom: American Women Win the Vote*. New York: Boni and Liveright, 1920.

Tarrant, S. *Men and Feminism*. Berkeley, CA: Seal Press, 2009.

Teel, Leonard Ray. *The Public Press 1900–1945: The History of American Journalism*. Westport, CT: Praeger, 2006.

Tuchman, Gaye. *Making News: A Study in the Construction of Reality*. New York: Free Press, 1978.

Urofsky, Melvin I. *A Voice That Spoke for Justice: The Life and Times of Stephen S. Wise*. Albany: State University of New York Press, 1982.

Van Vorris, Jacqueline. *Carrie Chapman Catt: A Public Life*. New York: Feminist Press, 1987.

Vaughn, Stephen L. *Holding Fast the Inner Lines: Democracy, Nationalism and the Committee on Public Information*. Chapel Hill: University of North Carolina Press, 1980.

Villard, Oswald Garrison. *Fighting Years: An Autobiography*. New York: Harcourt, Brace and Co., 1939.

————, C.C. Catt, and National American Woman Suffrage Association Collection (Library of Congress). *Women in the New York Municipal Campaign of 1901.* Boston, MA: J. Youngjohn, 1902.

Voss, Carl Hermann. *Stephen S. Wise: Servant of the People.* Philadelphia: Jewish Publication Society of America, 1969.

Ware, L. *George Foster Peabody: Banker, Philanthropist, Publicist.* Athens: University of Georgia Press, 1951.

White, William Allen. *Woodrow Wilson: The Man, His Times and His Task.* Boston: Houghton Mifflin, 1924.

Whitehouse, Vira B. *A Year as a Government Agent.* New York: Harper and Brothers, 1920.

Williams, Jesse Lynch. *And So They Were Married.* New York: Charles Scribner's Sons, 1914.

Wise, Stephen S. *Challenging Years: The Autobiography of Stephen Wise.* New York: G.P. Putnam's Sons, 1949.

Young, Art. *Art Young: His Life and Times.* New York: Sheridan House, 1939.

Zahniser, J.D., and Amelia R. Fry. *Alice Paul: Claiming Power.* New York: Oxford University Press, 2014.

## Unpublished Works

Behn, Beth. "Woodrow Wilson's Conversion Experience: The President and the Federal Woman Suffrage Amendment." Dissertation, University of Massachusetts, 2012.

Grossfeld, Gina Adrianne. "Constructing Cultures of Resistance: The American and British Suffrage Movements." Dissertation, State University of New York at Stony Brook, 1993.

Schmidt, Cynthia Ann Bolger. "Socialist-Feminism: Max Eastman, Floyd Dell and Crystal Eastman." Dissertation, Marquette University, 1983.

Sochen, June. "Now Let Us Begin: Feminism in Greenwich Village: 1910–1920." Dissertation, Northwestern University, 1967.

# Index

Brooke Kroeger is a professor of journalism at the Arthur L. Carter Journalism Institute of New York University and director of its graduate unit, Global and Joint Program Studies. She is a longtime journalist and the author of four previous books: *Nellie Bly: Daredevil, Reporter, Feminist*; *Fannie: The Talent for Success of Writer Fannie Hurst*; *Passing: When People Can't Be Who They Are*; and *Undercover Reporting: The Truth about Deception*. She divides her time between New York City and East Hampton, Long Island.